W9-CAZ-340

**Better Homes and Gardens**®

# Baking
## *Step by Step*

**Everything you need to know to start baking now!**

Houghton Mifflin Harcourt
Boston • New York • 2015

Copyright © 2015 by Meredith Corporation, Des Moines, Iowa.

All rights reserved.

For information about permission to reproduce selections from this book, write to Permissions, Houghton Mifflin Harcourt Publishing Company, 215 Park Avenue South, New York, New York 10003

www.hmhco.com

Library of Congress Cataloging-in-Publication Data is available.

ISBN 978-0-544-45617-4 (hbk)

ISBN 978-0-544-45618-1 (ebk)

Book design by Waterbury Publications, Inc., Des Moines, Iowa.

C&C 10 9 8 7 6 5 4 3 2 1

Printed in China

**Meredith Corporation**

Editors: Jan Miller and Tricia Laning, Waterbury Publications, Inc.

Contributing Editors: Ellen Boeke; Linda Henry; Lisa Kingsley, Mary Williams, Waterbury Publications, Inc.

Recipe Development and Testing: Better Homes and Gardens· Test Kitchen

Photographers: Pete Krumhardt, Scott Little, Kritsada Panichgul, Jay Wilde

Food Stylists: Nicole Faber, Greg Luna, Jill Lust, Janet Pittman, Charles Worthington

Prop Stylist: Sue Mitchell


**Houghton Mifflin Harcourt**

Publisher: Natalie Chapman

Editorial Director: Cindy Kitchel

Executive Editor: Anne Ficklen

Senior Editor: Adam Kowit

Editorial Associate: Molly Aronica

Production Director: Tom Hyland

Cover Designer: Ken Carlson, Waterbury Publications, Inc.


Cover photo: Strawberry Shortcakes, page 199

**Test Kitchen**

## A word about the Better Homes and Gardens® Test Kitchen

Our seal assures you that every recipe in *Baking Step by Step* has been tested in the Better Homes and Gardens® Test Kitchen. This means that each recipe is practical and reliable, and meets our high standards of taste appeal. We guarantee your satisfaction with this book for as long as you own it.

## How do I cut perfect bars and brownies?

## How do I get a tender, flaky piecrust every time?

## How do I work with puff pastry to make a really great baked Brie?

# What's in this book?

**7**   Intro to Baking

**73**   Oven-Fresh Cookies

**107**   Beyond Square Bars & Brownies

**133**   Irresistible Cakes

**161**   Everyday Snack Cakes & Cupcakes

**183**   Luscious Cheesecakes & Shortcakes

**203**   Anytime Desserts

**225**   Perfect Pies & Tarts

**263**   Pastry Shop Specialties

**289**   Quick-As-Can-Be Muffins & Breads

**317**   Scrumptious Scones & Biscuits

**337**   Your Daily Breads

**363**   Index

# Something new—for you.

There is something undeniably appealing and nurturing about baking. Especially in the high-tech world we live in—where we're inundated with cell phone calls and text messages, computer blips, and every kind of "virtual" thing imaginable—baking is all about simple, tactile, low-tech fun.

Baking a birthday cake for someone special or biting into a warm slice of buttered bread you made with your own hands is incredibly satisfying. It offers a break from the stressful world of business—not to mention that anything you bake from scratch tastes so much better than anything you buy in a box.

**Whatever your mood or the occasion, there's a yummy something in this book you'll want to bake—everything from a simple buttery shortbread that can be left plain or dressed up to the spectacular Chocolate-Peppermint Fantasy Cake.**

Given all of that, we—food editors, recipe developers, and cookbook writers—realize that the world has changed dramatically since some of us stood on a kitchen stool and dusted the kitchen with flour as we "helped" Mom bake cookies. Maybe you've already conquered cookie baking and want to move on to something more challenging—like cream puffs or crispy meringues. Or maybe you've never so much as beaten an egg. *Baking Step by Step* is designed with both kinds of bakers in mind—those who aspire to bake and those who are a little farther along on the learning curve. You can start with simple brownies or apple crisp and move up to soufflés.

It's also been created in a format that reflects our highly visual modern world. More than 300 recipes and nearly 1,000 photos show you—step-by-step—how to bake. As much as we live online, a trusted cookbook you can just pull off your shelf—and in which you can find just the recipe you're looking for—is still the best way to ensure your success.

*Baking Step by Step* is published by the same people who have been producing the best-selling cookbook in the country for more than 75 years. All of the recipes in this book have been tested and retested, if necessary, so we know they work—and that they'll work for you. Grab your oven mitts and start to stir things up!

## The Editors

*Better Homes and Gardens® Baking Step by Step*

# intro to
# BAKING

Here's everything you need to know about buying bakeware, whipping cream, and cracking eggs—a chapter you'll return to again and again.

## BAKING INGREDIENTS

Baking powder . . . . . . . . . . . . . . . . . . . . . . . . . . . . . . . . . . . . . . . . 30
Baking soda . . . . . . . . . . . . . . . . . . . . . . . . . . . . . . . . . . . . . . . . . . 30
Chocolate . . . . . . . . . . . . . . . . . . . . . . . . . . . . . . . . . . . . . . . 32–33
Dairy Products . . . . . . . . . . . . . . . . . . . . . . . . . . . . . . . . . . . 24–25
Eggs . . . . . . . . . . . . . . . . . . . . . . . . . . . . . . . . . . . . . . . . . . . 26–27
Fats & Oils . . . . . . . . . . . . . . . . . . . . . . . . . . . . . . . . . . . . . . . . . . 28
Flour . . . . . . . . . . . . . . . . . . . . . . . . . . . . . . . . . . . . . . . . . . . . . . . 3I
Nuts . . . . . . . . . . . . . . . . . . . . . . . . . . . . . . . . . . . . . . . . . . . 34–35
Spices . . . . . . . . . . . . . . . . . . . . . . . . . . . . . . . . . . . . . . . . . 36–37
Sugar . . . . . . . . . . . . . . . . . . . . . . . . . . . . . . . . . . . . . . . . . . . . . . 29
Yeast . . . . . . . . . . . . . . . . . . . . . . . . . . . . . . . . . . . . . . . . . . . . . . 63

## BAKING TECHNIQUES

Beating mixtures . . . . . . . . . . . . . . . . . . . . . . . . . . . . . . . . . . . . . . 57
Berries, washing . . . . . . . . . . . . . . . . . . . . . . . . . . . . . . . . . . . . . . 42
Bread dough, kneading . . . . . . . . . . . . . . . . . . . . . . . . . . . . . . . . 62
Bread dough, proofing . . . . . . . . . . . . . . . . . . . . . . . . . . . . . . . . 63
Bread dough, punching down . . . . . . . . . . . . . . . . . . . . . . . . . . 63
Butter, cutting in . . . . . . . . . . . . . . . . . . . . . . . . . . . . . . . . . . . . . 56
Butter, softening . . . . . . . . . . . . . . . . . . . . . . . . . . . . . . . . . . . . . 28
Chocolate, chopping . . . . . . . . . . . . . . . . . . . . . . . . . . . . . . . . . . 33
Chocolate, grating . . . . . . . . . . . . . . . . . . . . . . . . . . . . . . . . . . . . 33
Chocolate, melting in microwave . . . . . . . . . . . . . . . . . . . . . . . . 33
Coconut, toasting . . . . . . . . . . . . . . . . . . . . . . . . . . . . . . . . . . . . 40
Combining wet and dry ingredients . . . . . . . . . . . . . . . . . . . . . . 56
Cream cheese, softening . . . . . . . . . . . . . . . . . . . . . . . . . . . . . . 57
Dough, dropping from a teaspoon . . . . . . . . . . . . . . . . . . . . . . . 65
Dried fruit, plumping/rehydrating . . . . . . . . . . . . . . . . . . . . . . . . 4I
Eggs, beating egg whites . . . . . . . . . . . . . . . . . . . . . . . . . . . . . . 26
Eggs, beating egg yolks . . . . . . . . . . . . . . . . . . . . . . . . . . . . . . . 27
Folding in ingredients . . . . . . . . . . . . . . . . . . . . . . . . . . . . . . . . . 65
Herbs, snipping fresh herbs . . . . . . . . . . . . . . . . . . . . . . . . . . . . 49
Hot peppers, working with . . . . . . . . . . . . . . . . . . . . . . . . . . . . . 52
Measuring . . . . . . . . . . . . . . . . . . . . . . . . . . . . . . . . . . . . . . 54–55
Nutmeg, grating . . . . . . . . . . . . . . . . . . . . . . . . . . . . . . . . . . . . . 37
Nuts, toasting . . . . . . . . . . . . . . . . . . . . . . . . . . . . . . . . . . . . . . . 34
Pans, greasing and flouring . . . . . . . . . . . . . . . . . . . . . . . . . 59, 60
Pans, lining with foil/waxed paper . . . . . . . . . . . . . . . . . . . . . . . 58
Peaches & nectarines, peeling . . . . . . . . . . . . . . . . . . . . . . . . . . 43
Quick breads, removing from pan . . . . . . . . . . . . . . . . . . . . . . . . 60
Rolling pin, using . . . . . . . . . . . . . . . . . . . . . . . . . . . . . . . . . . . . . 6I
Sieve, using . . . . . . . . . . . . . . . . . . . . . . . . . . . . . . . . . . . . . . . . . 65
Spices, grinding . . . . . . . . . . . . . . . . . . . . . . . . . . . . . . . . . . . . . 37
Yeast, dissolving . . . . . . . . . . . . . . . . . . . . . . . . . . . . . . . . . . . . . 62

## COOKING TERMS

Beat . . . . . . . . . . . . . . . . . . . . . . . . . . . . . . . . . . . . . . . . . . . . . . . 69
Caramelize . . . . . . . . . . . . . . . . . . . . . . . . . . . . . . . . . . . . . . . . . 69
Crimp . . . . . . . . . . . . . . . . . . . . . . . . . . . . . . . . . . . . . . . . . . . . . . 69
Dash . . . . . . . . . . . . . . . . . . . . . . . . . . . . . . . . . . . . . . . . . . . . . . . 69
Dot . . . . . . . . . . . . . . . . . . . . . . . . . . . . . . . . . . . . . . . . . . . . . . . . 69
Flute . . . . . . . . . . . . . . . . . . . . . . . . . . . . . . . . . . . . . . . . . . . . . . . 69

Glaze . . . . . . . . . . . . . . . . . . . . . . . . . . . . . . . . . . . . . . . . . . . . . . 69
Scald . . . . . . . . . . . . . . . . . . . . . . . . . . . . . . . . . . . . . . . . . . . . . . 69
Sift . . . . . . . . . . . . . . . . . . . . . . . . . . . . . . . . . . . . . . . . . . . . . . . . 69
Steep . . . . . . . . . . . . . . . . . . . . . . . . . . . . . . . . . . . . . . . . . . . . . . 69
Weeping . . . . . . . . . . . . . . . . . . . . . . . . . . . . . . . . . . . . . . . . . . . 69
Zest . . . . . . . . . . . . . . . . . . . . . . . . . . . . . . . . . . . . . . . . . . . . . . . 69

**Emergency Substitutions** . . . . . . . . . . . . . . . . . . . . . . . . . . . . . . 7I

## EQUIPMENT

Baking dishes . . . . . . . . . . . . . . . . . . . . . . . . . . . . . . . . . . . . . . . I9
Baking pans . . . . . . . . . . . . . . . . . . . . . . . . . . . . . . . . . . . . . . I6–I7
Bakeware, purchasing . . . . . . . . . . . . . . . . . . . . . . . . . . . . . . . . . I8
Gadgets/tools . . . . . . . . . . . . . . . . . . . . . . . . . . . . IO, II, I3, I5, 2I
Knives . . . . . . . . . . . . . . . . . . . . . . . . . . . . . . . . . . . . . . . . . . . . . I4
Measuring cups and spoons . . . . . . . . . . . . . . . . . . . . . . . . . . . . I2
Mixing bowls . . . . . . . . . . . . . . . . . . . . . . . . . . . . . . . . . . . . . . . . I2
Saucepans and skillets . . . . . . . . . . . . . . . . . . . . . . . . . . . . . . . . 22
Small appliances . . . . . . . . . . . . . . . . . . . . . . . . . . . . . . . . . . . . 20

## FRUITS & VEGETABLES (BUYING, STORING, CUTTING INFORMATION)

Apples . . . . . . . . . . . . . . . . . . . . . . . . . . . . . . . . . . . . . . . . . 38–39
Bananas . . . . . . . . . . . . . . . . . . . . . . . . . . . . . . . . . . . . . . . . . . . 40
Berries . . . . . . . . . . . . . . . . . . . . . . . . . . . . . . . . . . . . . . . . . . . . . 42
Carrots . . . . . . . . . . . . . . . . . . . . . . . . . . . . . . . . . . . . . . . . . . . . . 48
Coconut . . . . . . . . . . . . . . . . . . . . . . . . . . . . . . . . . . . . . . . . . . . . 40
Cranberries . . . . . . . . . . . . . . . . . . . . . . . . . . . . . . . . . . . . . . . . . 43
Dried Fruit . . . . . . . . . . . . . . . . . . . . . . . . . . . . . . . . . . . . . . . . . . 4I
Garlic . . . . . . . . . . . . . . . . . . . . . . . . . . . . . . . . . . . . . . . . . . . . . . 48
Ginger . . . . . . . . . . . . . . . . . . . . . . . . . . . . . . . . . . . . . . . . . . . . . 48
Herbs . . . . . . . . . . . . . . . . . . . . . . . . . . . . . . . . . . . . . . . . . . . . . . 49
Leeks . . . . . . . . . . . . . . . . . . . . . . . . . . . . . . . . . . . . . . . . . . . . . . 50
Lemons . . . . . . . . . . . . . . . . . . . . . . . . . . . . . . . . . . . . . . . . . 44–45
Limes . . . . . . . . . . . . . . . . . . . . . . . . . . . . . . . . . . . . . . . . . . . 44–45
Peaches & Nectarines . . . . . . . . . . . . . . . . . . . . . . . . . . . . . . . . 43
Pears . . . . . . . . . . . . . . . . . . . . . . . . . . . . . . . . . . . . . . . . . . . 46–47
Peppers . . . . . . . . . . . . . . . . . . . . . . . . . . . . . . . . . . . . . . . . . . . . 52
Onions & Green Onions . . . . . . . . . . . . . . . . . . . . . . . . . . . . . . . 5I
Oranges . . . . . . . . . . . . . . . . . . . . . . . . . . . . . . . . . . . . . . . . . 44–45
Rhubarb . . . . . . . . . . . . . . . . . . . . . . . . . . . . . . . . . . . . . . . . . . . . 49
Zucchini & Yellow Squash . . . . . . . . . . . . . . . . . . . . . . . . . . . . . 50

**High-Altitude Baking** . . . . . . . . . . . . . . . . . . . . . . . . . . . . . . . . . . 70

**Kitchen Safety** . . . . . . . . . . . . . . . . . . . . . . . . . . . . . . . . . . . . . . . 72

## RECIPES

Caramel Sauce . . . . . . . . . . . . . . . . . . . . . . . . . . . . . . . . . . . . . . 64
Raspberry Sauce . . . . . . . . . . . . . . . . . . . . . . . . . . . . . . . . . . . . . 60
Sour Milk . . . . . . . . . . . . . . . . . . . . . . . . . . . . . . . . . . . . . . . . . . . 24
Sweetened Whipped Cream . . . . . . . . . . . . . . . . . . . . . . . . . . . . 25

**Storing Baked Goods** . . . . . . . . . . . . . . . . . . . . . . . . . . . . . . . . . 68

**Tricks from the Pros** . . . . . . . . . . . . . . . . . . . . . . . . . . . . . . . 66–67

# How to use this book

**When you walk by a bakery, does the smell pull you in? Do you ooh and ahh at the wares in the window? Baking is one of the most soul-satisfying skills you can have. Ready to learn how? Start here.**

### Why learn to bake?

There's nothing as homey and welcoming as the smell of bread baking in the oven—or as yummy as a soft, still-warm chocolate chip cookie. And there's the satisfaction you feel when you bake your first apple pie (it's called "pie pride"). It can't compare to anything else—not to mention that baking is just a whole lot of fun. Think you're all thumbs in the baking department? Don't know the difference between a torte and a tart? Never beaten butter or whipped cream? Don't worry about it. (And that's all about to change.) You're in good hands. Everything you need to know to get started baking—and to grow as a baker—is right here in this book.

### Designed with you in mind

Every recipe in this book is delicious and easy to make. Check the top of each for a Skill Level icon. Skill Level 1 means you'll be successful even if you've never heard of a spatula. As you work up to Levels 2 and 3, you'll still find these recipes simple, but you'll build on the skills you've already acquired.

**1** Skill Level
**2** Skill Level
**3** Skill Level

The first section of this book includes information you need to bone up on your baking vocabulary, ingredient knowledge, and skills. These pages will walk you through your kitchen arsenal and describe the gear you need and the extra stuff you might want as you discover how and what you like to bake. Next you'll learn about the building blocks

of baking—flour, spices, nuts, and so on—as well as how to prepare fresh produce. Once you're familiar with the tools and ingredients, you'll see step-by-step examples of basic baking techniques you need to know—and a few fancy tricks from the pros.

But here's the best part: At the bottom of every recipe page there's an "Ask Mom" feature that covers questions you might have. So even if you've never touched a measuring spoon or don't know what "zesting" means, you won't be stuck for long. Find your question, flip to the page number that follows, and you'll find the answer. (You may be telling *your own* mom a thing or two before long.)

**Ask Mom** How do I measure butter? pages 58, 5... 42 / How do I cut in butter? page 63 / What is the best... How do I separate an egg yolk? page 62 / How do I me...

## Ask Mom

At the bottom of each recipe page, you'll find an "Ask Mom" feature that covers questions you might have about that particular recipe. The question directs you to the page where you'll find the answer. It's that comprehensive. It's that easy. It's time to get baking.

# Baker's Toolbox

Whether you've promised the crew at the office a batch of homemade brownies or you're ready to tackle a four-layer birthday cake, you'll need the right gear. Here are the essentials—and a few extras too.

**A. Rasp grater/zester:** This is the ultimate tool for finely grating citrus peel, ginger, and fresh nutmeg. You can also use it to grate chocolate over a frosted cake as a garnish (or on top of your morning cappuccino).

**B. Fine-mesh sieve:** Use a sieve to drain wet ingredients, sift together dry ingredients, and to give a pan of brownies a dusting of powdered sugar. Sifting dry ingredients breaks up any lumps and aerates the ingredients so cakes and pastries turn out lighter.

**C. Ruler:** Use a standard ruler to measure the thickness of rolled cookie dough or the diameter of a piecrust, or as a straightedge to cut even strips of dough for a lattice-topped pie.

**D. Wooden spoon:** The classic cook's and baker's tools, wooden spoons are great for all kinds of stirring. They're sturdy enough to move through even the heaviest doughs. Hand wash them to avoid cracking.

**E. Rubber scraper:** Use these to get the last bits of anything from a bowl, jar, or pan. They're also great for folding together wet and dry ingredients. Silicone scrapers stand up to high heat better than those made of rubber.

**F. Offset spatula/spreader:** The beauty of an offset spatula lies in the bend in its blade. It allows you to frost a pan of brownies or spread cake batter evenly in a baking pan without dragging your knuckles across the surface you're trying to make smooth.

**G. Metal turner/spatula:** Use this to transfer cutout cookies from the counter to the pan and from the pan to a cooling rack after baking. An especially thin metal blade is handy. It's flexible enough to easily get under whatever it is you're moving without squishing the dough or breaking up the cookie or piece of cake.

**H. Pastry brush:** This softly bristled tool has many baking applications. Use it to grease a pan, slather layers of phyllo with melted butter, "paint" milk on top of a piecrust, and to apply an egg wash to the crust of a bread to make it glossy and attractive after it's baked.

**I. Whisk:** A wire whisk is a must for beating eggs, but it has lots of other uses too. It's perfect for stirring homemade custards and terrific for thoroughly mixing dry ingredients.

**J. Pastry blender:** If you like to bake pies or biscuits, this is a helpful tool for cutting cold butter or shortening into flour. You can use two butter knives—moved in a crisscross motion—but it's much easier and more efficient with a pastry blender.

**K. Pastry wheel:** This tool makes smooth sailing of cutting pastry dough. Unlike a knife, it doesn't pull the pastry dough (or crush the delicate layers of puff pastry), which can tear and/or toughen it. Pastry wheels can be flat or fluted. A fluted, crinkle-cut wheel creates a slightly scalloped edge on the pastry.

**L. Rolling pin:** There are two basic types of rolling pins. The one shown at right is the classic roller style. The other is the French-style rolling pin—an elongated rod with tapered ends. Rolling pins come in a variety of materials including wood, ceramic, metal, silicone, and marble. Use them to roll out piecrust, cookie dough, and puff pastry.

**M. Kitchen scissors:** Keep a pair strictly for kitchen use: snipping fresh herbs in a small bowl, opening packages, or cutting parchment paper before fitting it into a pan.

A  Rasp grater/zester

B  Fine-mesh sieve

C  Ruler

D  Wooden spoon

F  Offset spatula/spreader

G  Metal turner/spatula

E  Rubber scraper

H  Pastry brush

I  Whisk

J  Pastry blender

K  Pastry wheel

L  Rolling pin

M  Kitchen scissors

# Measure & Mix

Unless you have a good sense of proportion, you need measuring tools—and something in which to mix.

## Measuring Tools

Baking is science and art in equal measure. The art part pertains to the flavors and textures that are combined in a cookie, the shape your pastry takes, or how you decorate a cake. The science part is the crucial balance that has to be struck among flour, leavening, fats, and liquids. If they're not in perfect balance, your soufflé won't puff, your piecrust may crumble, or your quick bread may more closely resemble a doorstop than something you want to have with tea. That's not to scare you—just to emphasize the importance of not guessing when it comes to measuring ingredients. Having the right tools is the first step to baking success.

Use dry measuring cups only for dry goods such as flour, sugar, and oatmeal. Most sets have 1 cup, ½ cup, ⅓ cup, and ¼ cup.

Most sets of measuring spoons have a tablespoon, teaspoon, ½ teaspoon, and ¼ teaspoon. (You'll have to guess at a dash.)

A 1½-, 3-, and 5-quart set of mixing bowls will carry you through almost any kind of baking. If you plan on baking double batches of yeast breads, add a 7- or 8-quart bowl to the mix.

You'll be pulling out the glass measuring cups just about every time you bake. A 1-cup, 2-cup, and 4-cup are essential for measuring liquids.

### Nice to Have

Although you rarely have to measure out 8 cups of any one ingredient, an 8-cup measuring cup makes a great batter bowl. The lip makes pouring easy.

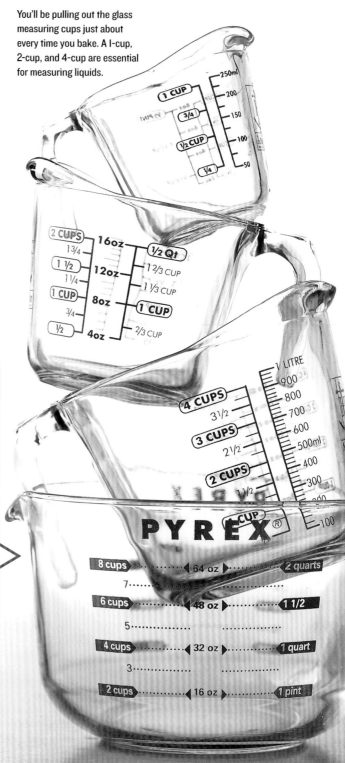

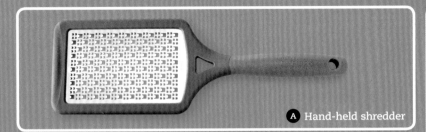

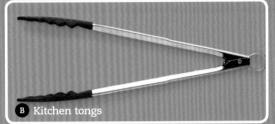

A Hand-held shredder

B Kitchen tongs

C Vegetable peeler

D Spatula/spreader

E Slotted spoon

F Custard cups

## Nice to Have

A kitchen scale ensures that your measurements are absolutely accurate. If a recipe calls for 5 ounces of chocolate and you have an 8-ounce bar, you can avoid guessing and measure exactly 5 ounces. Scales come in three types: spring, balance, and digital. The ingredients for some recipes are measured in grams—easily read on a digital scale.

**A. Hand-held shredder:** This coarse shredder is designed for shredding soft cheeses, raw vegetables such as carrots and zucchini—even fresh coconut, if you are ambitious.

**B. Kitchen tongs:** These function like a second set of hands—heatproof hands—that can pick up a hot muffin or turn over apple wedges in a hot skillet.

**C. Vegetable peeler:** Its obvious function is peeling potatoes, apples, or carrots, but a vegetable peeler also makes large, attractive strips of lemon or orange peel for cooking and garnishing, and strips of chocolate for garnishing.

**D. Spatula/spreader:** Use this handy dual-function tool to loosen cheesecakes or bars from a baking pan—or to easily spread frosting on cookies, cupcakes, and cakes.

**E. Slotted spoon:** This can be used to stir, of course, but is also great for straining. Use a slotted spoon to scoop a vanilla bean from custard or a cinnamon stick from a sauce or to smash ripe bananas for banana bread.

**F. Custard cups:** These small heatproof bowls serve as cooking and serving vessels for individual custards or puddings or as small prep bowls to hold premeasured ingredients.

**B** This is the big kahuna—the all-purpose knife for slicing and dicing. Chef's knives come in blade lengths ranging from 6 to 12 inches.

**C** This knife's serrated blade easily cuts through the crusts of breads—particularly European-style breads—without squashing the loaf.

**E** Keep a pair strictly for kitchen use: snipping fresh herbs in a small bowl, opening packages, or cutting baking parchment before fitting it into a pan.

**A** This smallest knife, with a 3- to 4-inch blade, is ideal for peeling and coring foods such as apples.

**D** Perfect for cleanly slicing juicy, ripe tomatoes, this serrated utility knife is also great for cutting all fruits and vegetables.

**E** Kitchen scissors

**A** Paring knife

**B** Chef's knife

**D** Tomato knife

Serrated knife

# Cutting Edge
## A set of good knives and knowing how to use them correctly—and safely—are crucial in the kitchen.

Good knives are expensive. You can skimp on the dinner plates, but kitchen knives are all about function. Invest in the very best ones you can afford—then hand wash and dry them and keep them professionally sharpened. Look for those that have high-carbon stainless-steel blades. The good news: High-quality knives, well cared for, will last for years.

# Baker's Toolbox continued ...

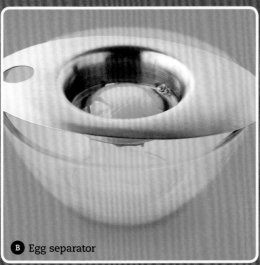

**A** Large colander

**B** Egg separator

## Nice to Have

Use a dough scraper with a broad blade to lift and turn sticky doughs—and to scrape them up from the counter for easy cleanup.

**C** Oven thermometer

**D** Citrus juicer

**A. Large colander:** Colanders can be made of fine-wire mesh or of stainless steel—like the one above—or enamel-coated steel. The stainless types are usually dotted with small holes. Use a colander to hold raw fruits or vegetables under running water as you wash them.

**B. Egg separator:** This gadget makes quick work of separating the yolk from the white. Handles suspend it over a cup that catches the white while the separator cradles the yolk.

**C. Oven Thermometer:** Individual ovens can vary quite widely in the accuracy of their thermostats. You can check the actual temperature of your oven with an oven thermometer. Adjust the temperature accordingly—or, if it's a major adjustment, get your oven thermostat fixed.

**D. Citrus juicer:** This sculpted tool makes extracting the juice from lemons, limes, and oranges a cinch. The sieve strains pulp and seeds; the spout makes pouring easy.

# Baker's Dozen

## Baking requires precision. Having the right bakeware will help you get impressive results.

Bakeware comes in several materials, including aluminum, nonstick coated aluminum or steel, silicone, and glass. Aluminum—nonstick or not—is a good choice. It is lightweight and conducts heat well, which ensures even baking and browning. Know this: You should wash and dry aluminum bakeware by hand.

**A. Rectangular baking pan:** A standard 13×9×2-inch pan is indispensable for baking nonlayer cakes.

**B. Round cake pan:** All birthday-cake bakers should have two of these. Pans are generally 8 or 9 inches across. Most layer-cake recipes work with either size.

**C. Tart pan:** A 9-inch tart pan with a removable bottom enables you to make authentic fruit and nut tarts—and to easily get them out of the pan and onto a plate.

**D. Loaf pan:** You'll need at least one of these to make most quick breads—two if you get into

Ⓐ Rectangular baking pan

Ⓑ Round cake pan

Ⓒ Tart pan

Ⓓ Loaf pan

Ⓔ Springform pan

Ⓕ Pie plate

Ⓖ Square baking pan

Ⓗ Wire rack

baking yeast breads. The most common size is 8×4×2 inches, though it's a good idea to have the larger 9×5×3-inch size too.

E. **Springform pan:** This pan has a latch that opens so you can remove the sides; it's crucial for cheesecake and deep-dish pizza. The most common sizes are 9 and 10 inches across.

F. **Pie plate:** Whether it's aluminum or glass, a 9-inch pie plate is a must-have.

G. **Square baking pan:** You'll need one of these for bar cookies, cakes, and corn bread. Choose either 9×9×2 inches or 8×8×2 inches.

H. **Wire rack:** You'll wind up with soggy cakes and cookies if you don't have a couple of these. They allow air to circulate around baked goods as they cool.

I. **Muffin pan:** The standard muffin pan has 12 cups. Many muffin and cupcake recipes make more than 12, so you can bake in stages or buy more than one.

J. **Cookie sheet:** This flat pan allows heat to circulate around the cookies and makes it easy to transfer them to a wire rack. Buy two.

K. **Fluted tube pan:** This 10-inch sculpted pan makes beautiful tube cakes (also called Bundt cakes), pound cakes, and coffee cakes.

L. **Pizza pan:** The most common size is 12 inches in diameter, but it doesn't hurt to have 10- and 14-inch pans too. The shallow, round pan is good for making cookie pizzas or for baking regular cookies in a pinch.

M. **Jelly-roll pan:** Even if you never make a jelly roll, you'll use this 15×10×1-inch pan to toast nuts and roast veggies.

**I** Muffin pan

**K** Fluted tube pan

**J** Cookie sheet

**M** Jelly-roll pan

**L** Pizza pan

# Purchasing Bakeware

## When it comes to bakeware, materials matter. What your pans are made of has an effect on your results.

Bakeware comes in a range of materials: aluminum, tin, stainless steel, glass, and pottery. The material and the finish affect the final product. Shiny bakeware reflects heat, slowing the browning process. Dark- and dull-finish bakeware absorbs more heat, increasing browning.

Cake, loaf, and muffin pans: Use sturdy, single-wall aluminum pans. Shiny pans reflect heat, which will give you thin, golden crusts. Dark or dull-finish pans absorb more heat, which means the crusts of your cakes and breads will be darker and crustier.

Pie plates: Because glass and dull-finish metal pie plates absorb and retain heat evenly, they're the best choices for baking beautifully browned piecrusts. Ceramic and pottery pie plates also have these qualities but often aren't standard size (standard-size pie plates hold about 3¾ cups of liquid). Disposable foil pans are usually smaller than standard pie plates, although deep-dish foil pie pans are closer to standard size.

Cookie sheets: Make sure the cookie sheets you select fit in your oven, allowing at least 1 to 2 inches of space all around. Cookies bake more evenly on light- to medium-color sheets, whether shiny or nonstick; dark cookie sheets may cause cookie bottoms to overbrown. Look for sturdy, heavyweight cookie sheets that won't warp and/or bend in the oven's heat. Choose one- or two-sided cookie sheets that allow heat to circulate around the cookies.

Insulated cookie sheets slow baking and tend to yield pale cookies with soft centers. And if you bake the cookies on an insulated sheet long enough to brown the bottoms, the rest of the cookie will be dry. However, if your oven runs a bit hot or browns cookies rapidly, insulated cookie sheets may improve results.

Use jelly-roll pans (15×10×1-inch baking pans) only for bar cookies. Other types of cookies won't bake evenly in a pan with sides.

Silicone bakeware: Becoming increasingly popular, silicone bakeware is the newest member of the bakeware family. It withstands high oven temperatures, bakes evenly, and immediately stops the baked goods from cooking any further after being removed from the oven. Unmolding is simply a matter of twisting the pan. However, silicone bakeware can be a little difficult to handle—you have to place it on a baking sheet to get it in and out of the oven.

# Baking Dishes
## Bread puddings, cobblers, and crisps are often made in a dish, not a pan. Here's the scoop on dishes.

Baking dishes and casseroles (here it's the name of the type of dish and not just the food you make in it) function for baking and serving. In the realm of baking, this usually means some kind of dessert. These dishes are often made of glass, ceramic, stoneware, or enamel-coated cast iron. Most of the glass varieties are oven-, microwave-, and freezer-safe; check the brand to be sure. Baking dishes can be round, oval, square, or rectangular and range in capacity from about 1 quart to more than 6 quarts. Although you may occasionally use a round dish for baking, you will most often reach for the ones with four corners.

**A. Square baking dish:** These small dishes (usually 2-quart) are perfect for baking and serving fruit crisps and cobblers. If you have a 2-quart gratin dish (see photo, below), you can substitute that with great results.

**B. Rectangular baking dish:** A 3-quart rectangular dish is the right size when making dessert for a crowd.

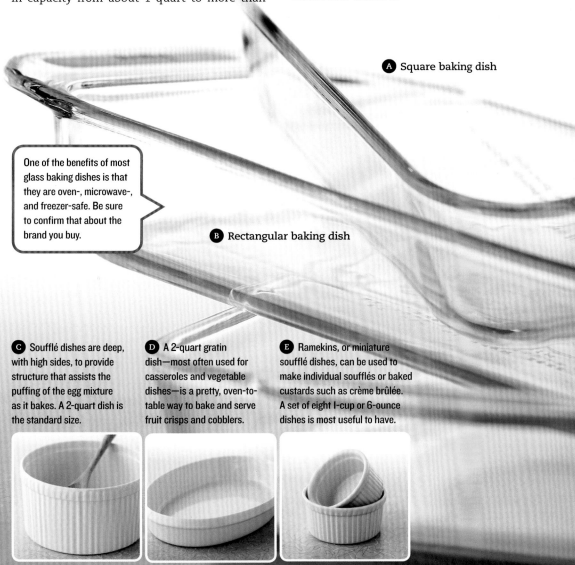

**A** Square baking dish

One of the benefits of most glass baking dishes is that they are oven-, microwave-, and freezer-safe. Be sure to confirm that about the brand you buy.

**B** Rectangular baking dish

**C** Soufflé dishes are deep, with high sides, to provide structure that assists the puffing of the egg mixture as it bakes. A 2-quart dish is the standard size.

**D** A 2-quart gratin dish—most often used for casseroles and vegetable dishes—is a pretty, oven-to-table way to bake and serve fruit crisps and cobblers.

**E** Ramekins, or miniature soufflé dishes, can be used to make individual soufflés or baked custards such as crème brûlée. A set of eight 1-cup or 6-ounce dishes is most useful to have.

# Mixing It Up

## Most baking prep can be done with a knife, whisk, and spoon, but electricity makes things much easier.

**A. Food processor:** This chopping, mincing, pureeing machine is arguably a cook's and baker's best friend. Most food processors have settings for both continuous running and pulsing—intermittent hits of power, which comes in handy if you plan use it for piecrust.

**B. Blender:** You can puree ingredients in a food processor, but the best tool for that task is a blender. Use it to puree berries, peaches, and other soft fruits for making sauces. (And if you have a good crepe recipe, it's great for blending the ingredients and beating in the eggs—then you can just pour the batter into the pan.)

**C. Hand mixer:** This small appliance is indispensable for baking. The most useful type has at least five speeds and enough power (at least 220 watts) to mix stiff cookie dough.

**B** Blender

**A** Food processor

**C** Hand mixer

An 8- to 10-cup bowl is a perfectly adequate size—unless you plan to make yeast bread dough in your food processor. Then you might consider one with a 14-cup capacity.

# Baker's Toolbox continued ...

A. Box grater A grater is used for shredding and grating cheeses, fruits, and vegetables. Most have fine and coarse sides; some may have a knuckle guard.

B. Garlic press This handy gadget makes quick work of mincing garlic. You simply peel the cloves, drop them in the perforated cup, then squeeze the hinged handles together. A flat foot crushes the clove, forcing it through the holes in the cup. It's neat and tidy, and your hands stay smelling sweet.

C. Parchment/baking mats Parchment paper and/or silicone baking mats make baking so much easier. They prevent baked goods from sticking—and make cleanup a breeze.

D. Rolling pin cover/pastry cloth Using a rolling pin cover and pastry cloth to roll out pie dough helps make tender crust. The cotton surfaces keep the dough from sticking, which prevents the addition of too much flour—which toughens the dough. They also absorb excess flour. These cloths do not require cleaning with every use. Simply shake out the flour, place in a resealable plastic bag, and store in the freezer.

E. Cookie cutters A standard cookie cutter is 2½ inches, but they come in ½-inch minis and 8- and 10-inch cutters too. Metal cutters—tin or copper—make the cleanest cut.

A Box grater

## Nice to Have

A spring-loaded food chopper is great for neatly and easily chopping nuts, fruits, and vegetables from coarse to finely chopped.

B Garlic press

## Nice to Have

With a pastry bag, a few decorating tips, a coupler, and a little practice, you can make professional-looking pastries in no time.

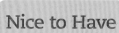

C Parchment/ baking mats

D Rolling pin cover/ pastry cloth

E Cookie cutters

# Cookware

## Yes, you actually do need a stovetop pot or pan (or two) in baking—not many, just a few crucial pieces.

Except for the simplest brownies, bars, and cookies, most baked goods are built with some flour-based baked element—such as a cake, pastry, or bread—and a series of embellishments such as sauces, fillings, toppings, and frostings. That's where the cookware comes in. The most important consideration in choosing cookware that you'll be using in baking is its heft. Because fats and sugars burn easily, your cookware needs to be heavy-duty to provide even, gentle heat—with no hot spots.

**A. Saucepans:** You need these to melt choco-late; make caramel, chocolate, and fruit sauces; and make custard. A 1-quart and a 2-quart saucepan will easily handle most of these jobs.

**B. Skillets:** A small skillet—such as a 6- or 8-inch—is good for toasting spices or those nuts that are best toasted on the stovetop rather than in the oven (such as pine nuts) and sesame seeds. A larger skillet—a good, basic, 10-inch skillet—serves the task of melt-ing sugar for the crunchy caramel topping on Crème Brûlée (see page 218) or cooking vege-tables for such things as savory tarts or pizzas.

Ⓐ Saucepans (1- and 2-quart)

Ⓑ 10-inch skillet

Copper and aluminum are the best conductors of heat. Copper is gorgeous but expensive—and aluminum reacts with many foods. Your best bet is pans that have an aluminum core and a stainless-steel exterior.

# Baking Ingredients

To bake, you need building blocks. This section is all about the foodstuffs required—from the basics of flour and butter to the embellishments of spices.

You wouldn't build a house without quality materials and an understanding of how they work together—how the basic structure is framed up and then how and with what the house is trimmed out. The same goes for baking. It's an endeavor that requires a certain degree of accuracy. The combination of ingredients, the proportion of ingredients one to another, even their temperature or size or shape—all have an effect on the final outcome. In these pages, you'll learn everything you need to know about how to identify, choose, and prepare ingredients for the best possible results.

### How do I do that?

You may have read about the "Ask Mom" feature on page 9. It works like this: If, for example,

## Nice to Know

Quality of ingredients matters. You have to be mindful of what you can afford, but consider how an ingredient will be used before picking and choosing what to splurge on and what to save on. If you're making a shortbread where the only flavor is butter, buy the best butter you can afford. If you're using a few tablespoons in a fruit crisp, save on the butter and splurge on gorgeous fruit.

you're making the Dessert Oven Pancake on page 211 and you need to know how to peel, core, and thinly slice pears, an "Ask Mom" question on that page will direct you to pages 46–47 in this section, where you'll see—step-by-step—exactly how to do it.

### Growing as a baker

The more you become familiar with basic ingredients, the more you'll be able to concentrate on creative ways to use them. You may only have to read once about how to zest a lemon or lime (see page 45) before you're figuring out all of the things you can stir it into, such as custards, frostings, and cheesecake batter.

## Mix It Up

The tools you use have an effect on how ingredients react—whether you use a whisk or an electric mixer to beat eggs or whether you use a fork or a potato masher to mash bananas for banana bread.

# Dairy Products

Much of the liquid used in baking—in all of its forms—is contributed by our bovine friends. Here's how to separate the cream from the milk.

**Buttermilk:** Buttermilk is a low-fat or fat-free milk to which a bacterial culture has been added. It is thick and creamy with a mildly acidic taste. Sour milk, made from milk and lemon juice or vinegar, can be substituted for buttermilk in baking recipes (see tip, below).

**Evaporated milk:** Evaporated milk is canned whole milk with about half of its water removed. It is sold in cans and can be stored at room temperature until opened. Evaporated milk, also available in low-fat and fat-free versions, is unsweetened, so it is not interchangeable with sweetened condensed milk.

**Half-and-half and light cream:** Half-and-half and light cream are interchangeable in most recipes. Light cream contains 18 to 30 percent milk fat; half-and-half is a mixture of milk and cream. Neither one contains enough fat to be whipped.

**Sweetened condensed milk:** Sweetened condensed milk is whole milk that has had water removed and sugar added. Like evaporated milk, it is sold in cans and can be stored at room temperature until opened. When baking

with sweetened condensed milk, use a can opener to remove the entire end of the can and give the milk a quick stir. Sweetened condensed milk is also available in low-fat and fat-free versions. It is not a suitable substitute for evaporated milk or fresh milk.

**Whipping cream:** Whipping cream contains at least 30 percent milk fat and can be beaten into whipped cream.

**Whole, low-fat, reduced-fat, and skim milk:** These milk types may be used interchangeably in recipes because they differ only in the amount of fat they contain, but this will directly affect the richness of flavor they give to foods. Recipes in this cookbook were tested using reduced-fat (2 percent) milk.

**Making sour milk:** If you find yourself without buttermilk, make some sour milk to use instead. Combine 1 tablespoon lemon juice or vinegar with enough milk to make 1 cup total liquid; stir. Let stand for 5 minutes before using.

Choose a bowl that's deep enough to allow the cream to double in volume (1 cup of cream gives you about 2 cups whipped). Put the bowl and the beaters of an electric mixer into the freezer for about 10 minutes before you begin to whip. (Cream whips better if it's very cold, and having the bowl and beaters cold will help too.) You can actually use a wire whisk and a cold bowl too—it will just take a little longer than if you use an electric mixer.

**1** In a chilled mixing bowl combine I cup whipping cream, 2 tablespoons sugar, and ½ teaspoon vanilla. Beat with an electric mixer on medium speed until soft peaks form (tips curl). **2** If desired, add with the vanilla: 2 tablespoons unsweetened cocoa powder plus I tablespoon sugar; 2 tablespoons amaretto, coffee, or hazelnut liqueur; or ¼ teaspoon ground cinnamon, nutmeg, or ginger. Or fold in ½ teaspoon finely shredded citrus peel after whipping.

### Easy Does It

Beat the cream on medium speed to avoid overbeating it. You'll know if you overdo it—you'll end up with butter in your bowl instead of cream!

# Eggs

Eggs are the "glue" that binds the other ingredients. They also help give rise, literally, to every kind of baked good. Here's how to get the best out of them.

**Selecting:** The recipes in this book were developed and tested using large eggs—they're your best bet for consistent results. When buying eggs, check for broken shells. Be sure the shells are clean and check the packing date (a number from 1 to 365, with 1 representing January 1 and 365 representing December 31) on the carton.

**Storing:** Refrigerate eggs in the coldest part of the refrigerator with the large ends up in their cartons. Eggs can be refrigerated for up to 5 weeks after the packing date.

**Room-temperature eggs:** Because eggs give baked goods more volume if they're not refrigerator-cold, many recipes call for room-temperature eggs—and it's crucial when using just the whites (see photos, below). Let eggs sit on the counter 30 minutes before using them.

**Consuming raw eggs:** Although it's tempting to nibble the chocolate chip cookie dough, it's not advisable. Uncooked eggs can carry salmonella, which can make you seriously ill.

## How do I beat egg whites?

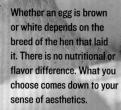

**1** To crack an egg, tap it firmly on the edge of a bowl or on a flat countertop. Pull the shell open with your thumbs.

**2** Use an egg separator to separate the yolk from the white. This prevents bacteria on the shell from contaminating the egg.

**3** Beat egg whites in a clean glass or metal bowl. Even a speck of fat (including the yolk) can prevent proper whipping.

**4** For soft peaks, beat with a mixer on medium speed until the egg whites form peaks with tips that curl when beaters are lifted.

Whether an egg is brown or white depends on the breed of the hen that laid it. There is no nutritional or flavor difference. What you choose comes down to your sense of aesthetics.

**5** For stiff peaks, beat on high speed until egg whites form peaks with tips that stand straight when the beaters are lifted.

**6** Oops! This is what happens when you overbeat egg whites—they get lumpy and won't blend in with other ingredients.

**1** In a mixing bowl beat the egg yolks with an electric mixer on high speed about 5 minutes or until they are thick and lemon color.

**2** After 2 to 3 minutes, they'll be the right color but probably not thick enough.

**3** When they're ready, they will hold a ribbon when the beaters are lifted from the bowl.

WHAT DOES LIGHTLY BEATEN MEAN? To lightly beat a whole egg, place the egg in a small bowl; beat with a fork until the egg is pale yellow with no streaks of white or yolk.

## Eggs vs. Egg Substitutes

Questions arise about using an egg substitute in a recipe that calls for whole eggs. The good news is you can use egg substitutes in many cases. When baking with an egg substitute, use ¼ cup of either refrigerated or frozen egg product, thawed, for each whole egg called for in the recipe for most cookies, cakes, and muffins. Do not, however, use an egg substitute when the recipe you are making relies on air being whipped into eggs for leavening, such as a sponge cake.

# Fats & Oils

Too much fat in your diet isn't good, but you need a little in your pastry. It adds rich taste and delicate texture to baked goods. Here's the skinny on fats.

**Butter is best:** Nothing is better than the flavor and richness that butter adds to cakes, cookies, and breads, which is why all the recipes in this book call for it. However, margarine can be substituted for butter if it contains enough fat. Buy only stick margarine that contains at least 80 percent vegetable oil. If you can't determine the oil content from the front of the package, check the nutrition label; the margarine should have at least 100 calories per tablespoon. Do not use products labeled vegetable oil spreads, light or reduced-fat margarine, or diet spreads. Always use butter in crumb toppings or crusts, pound cakes, shortbread, and sugar cookies.

**Storing butter:** Refrigerate butter in its original packaging for up to 1 month; to freeze, overwrap with moisture- and vaporproof wrap and freeze for up to 6 months.

**Softening butter:** If a recipe calls for softened butter and you've forgotten to set it out for 30 to 60 minutes, put it in a microwave-safe dish; microwave on 30 percent power (defrost) for 15 seconds. Check and repeat, if necessary.

**A word on oils:** Vegetable oils are made from corn, soybeans, sunflower seeds, or peanuts. Nut oils, such as walnut oil, have a pronounced nutty flavor. Olive oil is used mostly in recipes for focaccia, pizza dough, breads, and the occasional cake. Store cooking oil at room temperature for up to 6 months. Refrigerate nut oils; store olive oil in a cool, dark place for up to 6 months.

**1** Cold butter is firm and slices easily. Use it when the recipe just calls for "butter" in the ingredients list. **2** Softened butter has been allowed to come to room temperature. It is spreadable and blends easily into recipes. **3** Melted butter is sometimes used instead of cooking oil in a recipe.

**Cooking Oil:** Cooking oil is mildly flavored oil that is liquid at room temperature. It's made from vegetables, nuts, or seeds. For baking, cooking oils cannot be used interchangeably with solid fats because they are unable to hold air when beaten.

**Margarine:** Margarine, made from vegetable oil or animal fat, was developed as a substitute for butter. Butter is the recommendation for all recipes in this book.

**Shortening:** Shortening is a solid fat that has been made from vegetable oils. It is now available packaged in sticks marked conveniently with tablespoon and cup measurements. Plain and butter-flavor types can be used interchangeably. Once opened, use shortening within 6 months; discard if it has an odor or appears discolored.

**Butter:** Butter is available salted and unsalted and the two can be used interchangeably. If you use unsalted butter, however, you may want to slightly increase the amount of salt in a recipe.

**Butter Math: 1 pound = 4 sticks
1 stick = ½ cup = 8 tablespoons
½ stick = ¼ cup = 4 tablespoons**

# Sugar

A cookie without sugar would be a bit like a cracker—not at all what you want with a cup of coffee. Here's what you need to know about the sweet stuff.

**Storing:** If you store sugars in rustproof, airtight containers in a cool, dry place, all sugars will keep indefinitely. If brown sugar becomes hard, you can soften it by adding a piece of soft bread to the container; the sugar will absorb moisture from the bread and soften in a day or two. After the sugar has softened, remove the bread and keep the container tightly closed.

**Sugar substitutes:** The Better Homes and Gardens® Test Kitchen has done extensive testing with sugar substitutes and has found they work best in recipes where sugar is only needed for sweetening, such as in a custard sauce, rather than in baked recipes that require sugar for structure and browning. In some cases, sugar-substitute blends produced acceptable cakes, cookies, and quick breads, but often with an aftertaste. In general, when you bake with sugar substitutes, cake volumes tend to be lower, cookies more compact, and all baked products lighter in color because sugar is not present to caramelize and brown.

**Powdered sugar: As** the name suggests, powdered sugar is made by grinding granulated sugar into a fine powder and then adding a small amount of cornstarch to prevent lumping. Powdered sugar is also known as confectioner's sugar.

**Coarse sugar: Sparkly** coarse sugar, sometimes called decorating sugar, has much larger grains than granulated sugar. It's often used to decorate cookies and other baked goods; look for it where cake-decorating supplies are sold. Turbinado sugar (sometimes labeled as raw sugar) is a coarse sugar with a subtle molasses flavor.

**Granulated sugar: Also** referred to as white sugar, granulated sugar is the most commonly used sugar in baking. When a recipe calls for "sugar," this is the one to use. White sugar most commonly is available in a fine granulation, though superfine (also called ultrafine or castor sugar), a finer grind, is also available. Because superfine sugar dissolves so easily, it is ideal for frostings and meringues.

**Brown sugar: Brown** sugar is a mix of granulated sugar and molasses. Brown sugar is available in both light and dark varieties; dark brown sugar has more molasses and a stronger flavor. Unless otherwise specified, recipes in this cookbook were tested using light brown sugar.

Powdered sugar

Dark brown sugar

Turbinado sugar

Granulated sugar

Light brown sugar

Coarse sugar

Superfine sugar

Store all-purpose flour in an airtight container in a cool, dry place for up to 8 months. You can store other flours for up to 5 months. For longer storage refrigerate or freeze the flour in a moisture- and vaporproof container. Bring chilled flour to room temperature before using.

### What's the difference between baking soda and baking powder?

Both are leavening agents that produce carbon dioxide, which makes baked goods rise. Double-acting baking powder produces gases in two stages—first, when liquids are added, and second, during baking. Baking soda creates carbon dioxide bubbles instantly when it's mixed with acidic ingredients, such as buttermilk, sour cream, brown sugar, or lemon juice. Because the soda and acid begin to react as soon as a liquid is added, any recipe using baking soda should be baked immediately, before all of those bubbles deflate. Because recipes often call for small amounts of baking powder and baking soda, you may think these ingredients are not essential. They are! And because the chemical properties of the two are different, one cannot be substituted for the other. Store baking powder and baking soda in airtight containers in a cool, dry place. For best results, replace every 6 months or check the "use by" date on the containers.

## Sifting

Flour does not need to be sifted before using. Dry ingredients are often sifted together for even distribution and to eliminate any lumps. Place ingredients in a fine-mesh sieve and sift onto waxed paper or into a bowl.

# Flour

## Flour is the foundation of nearly every kind of baked good. It provides the structure for the sugar, fats, liquids, and flavorings that make the cake, literally.

**All-purpose flour:** This flour is made from a blend of soft and hard wheat flours and is a multipurpose flour for use in a range of baked goods. All-purpose flour comes bleached—chemically made whiter—and unbleached. Bleached flour makes cakes and breads as white as possible, but the two can be used interchangeably.

**Bread flour:** Bread flour contains more gluten than all-purpose flour, making it ideal for baking breads. It feels more granular than all-purpose flour. If you use a bread machine, use bread flour instead of all-purpose flour for the best results.

**Cake flour:** Cake flour is made from soft wheat and produces a tender, delicate crumb. It's too delicate for general baking but is often recommended for angel food and chiffon cakes. To substitute it for all-purpose flour, sift it before measuring and use 1 cup plus 2 tablespoons of cake flour for every 1 cup of all-purpose flour.

**Self-rising flour:** This flour is all-purpose flour with salt, baking powder, and baking soda added. It's not used for making baked goods containing yeast. Use it as a substitute for all-purpose flour in quick bread recipes, but omit the salt, baking powder, and baking soda.

**Whole wheat flour:** Whole wheat flour is a coarse-textured flour that is good in breads and some cookies but is generally not used in pastries and other delicate baked goods.

**Semolina flour:** This granular, starchy flour is what's left over from the processed wheat after the finer flour has been extracted. It's primarily used in cooked cereals and some pastas. It's also incorporated into some yeast breads to give them an earthy crunch.

**Specialty grain flours:** In baking, other grain flours such as graham, rye, oat, and buckwheat are always combined with all-purpose flour.

# Chocolate

Before you start baking with chocolate, it's helpful to understand how it's made. Here's a primer.

All chocolate starts with the fermented, dried, roasted, and cracked beans of the cacao tree. This process produces cocoa butter and an intensely flavored brown paste called chocolate liquor, or pure chocolate (cacao). Cocoa butter and cacao are combined with ingredients such as sugar, dry milk solids, lecithin, and vanilla. The percentage of pure chocolate helps determine the flavor of the chocolate and how it is used. The higher the percentage of cacao, the less sweet and more complex the chocolate.

Storing chocolate: Keep chocolate in a tightly covered container or sealed plastic bag in a cool, dry place. If stored at higher than 70°F, chocolate may "bloom," or develop a harmless gray film. Keep cocoa powder in a tightly covered container in that same cool, dry place. Bars and cocoa powder keep for up to one year.

Melting chocolate: Place chopped chocolate or chocolate pieces in a small heavy saucepan over low heat. Stir constantly until chocolate just begins to melt. Remove saucepan from heat and continue stirring until smooth. If necessary, return pan to the heat for a few more seconds. You can melt chocolate in a double boiler, but doing so increases the chance of getting a drop of water in the chocolate, which will cause it to seize up (stiffen).

### White chocolate

This isn't really chocolate at all because it contains no pure chocolate. It's called white chocolate because it contains cocoa butter. It has a milky, sweet flavor. In baking use only products with cocoa butter on the label.

### Unsweetened chocolate

Also called baking chocolate, this is pure chocolate and cocoa butter with no added sugar. Use it only for baking.

### Semisweet, bittersweet, and milk chocolate

Semisweet and bittersweet chocolate range between 35 percent and 70 percent pure chocolate with added cocoa butter and sugar. You can use them interchangeably. Creamy and mild milk chocolate is made with 10 percent to 35 percent pure chocolate.

### Candy coating

This chocolatelike product has most of the cocoa butter moved and replaced with vegetable fat. It's sometimes called confectioner's coating, almond bark, or summer coating. You can find it in assorted colors and flavors. It's used primarily in candymaking.

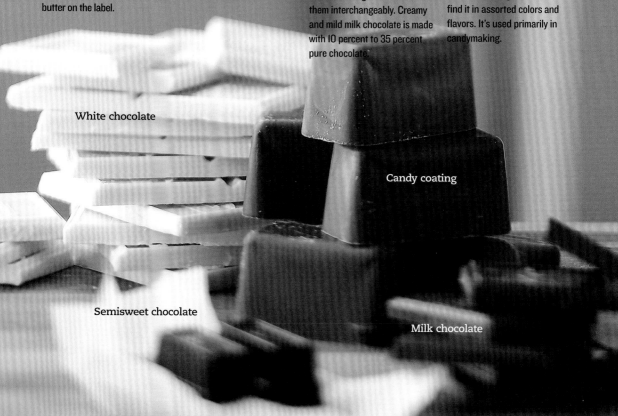

White chocolate

Candy coating

Semisweet chocolate

Milk chocolate

**Coarsely grated**
Rub a cool, firm square of chocolate across the large section of a handheld grater.

**Finely grated**
Rub a cool, firm square of chocolate across the fine section of a handheld grater. Clean the grater often to prevent clogging.

**Chocolate curls**
For large curls draw a vegetable peeler across the broad surface of a bar of room-temperature chocolate (milk chocolate works best). For smaller curls use the narrow side of the chocolate bar.

**Chopping**
Place chocolate block on a cutting board. With the widest part of a chef's knife, press down on the chocolate to break it into big chunks. To chop into smaller pieces, hold the tip of the knife in one place and make small chops with the back of the knife, moving side to side.

To melt chocolate in your microwave, place 1 cup chocolate pieces or 6 ounces chopped chocolate in a microwave-safe bowl. Microwave, uncovered, on 70 percent power (medium high) for 1 minute; stir. Microwave on 70 percent power for 1½ to 3 minutes more, stirring after every 15 seconds until the chocolate is melted and smooth.

# Nuts

In need of some nut knowledge? Here are the essentials of incorporating nature's rich and crunchy treats into your baking.

**Availability:** Shelled nuts are sold year-round in many forms: whole, chopped (labeled as pieces), oil- and dry-roasted, salted and unsalted, sugared, and spiced. Nuts in the shell are plentiful during the holidays, but many are not readily available the rest of the year.

**Selecting:** Shelled nuts should be plump and somewhat uniform in size and color. They should be firm, not limp or rubbery. When buying nuts in the shell, look for clean, unbroken shells without any splits, cracks, stains, and holes.

**Storing:** Because nuts contain high amounts of oil, they can turn rancid fairly quickly. For this reason, it's best to store nuts in resealable plastic freezer bags or containers for up to 8 months. Always taste nuts (frozen or not) before baking with them. Rancid nuts have a harsh taste and will ruin the flavor of anything they're in.

**Toasting nuts:** To toast whole nuts or large pieces, spread them out in a single layer in a shallow baking pan. Bake in a 350°F oven for 5 to 10 minutes or until the pieces are golden brown, stirring or shaking the pan once or twice. Check the nuts often to make sure they aren't getting too brown. If they start to overbrown, they can burn quickly and generally can't be salvaged.

Toast hazelnuts as directed above. To remove the papery skins, place a handful of warm nuts at a time in a clean, dry dish towel and rub vigorously until the skins come loose. If you like, put them in a fine-mesh sieve to shake out the little pieces of skin that can look like dirt.

**Grinding:** When grinding nuts, don't overdo it, or you'll end up with nut butter. If you're using a food processor, add 1 tablespoon of the sugar or flour from the recipe for each cup of nuts to help absorb some of the nut oil. Use a quick on/off motion, grind nuts in small batches, and let them cool after toasting and before grinding.

**Coarsely chopped:** These are large, irregular pieces that are more than ¼ inch in size.

**Chopped:** These are medium, irregular pieces that are just about ¼ inch in size.

**Finely chopped:** These are small, irregular pieces that are about ⅛ inch in size.

## Walnuts

English walnuts have a mild flavor, while black walnuts are rich and oily with an intense flavor.

## Peanuts

Oval, ivory-color peanuts have a rich, buttery flavor. Spanish peanuts are slightly smaller and covered with a reddish-brown skin; they are used primarily in candies. Cocktail peanuts are roasted in oil, while dry-roasted peanuts are roasted by a dry-heat method; both are available salted and unsalted. When a recipe calls for peanuts, cocktail or dry-roasted may be used.

## Pistachio nuts

The small pistachio has a pale green meat covered with a paper-thin, brown skin. The thin, smooth shells, which are split at one end, are often dyed red or green. The nuts have a mild, sweet flavor similar to almonds.

## Almonds

Almonds are flat, oval-shape nuts with reddish brown skin that can be removed by blanching. The smooth, light-color meat has a mild yet rich flavor. Almonds are available whole, sliced (with skin and shaved lengthwise down through the nut), slivered (skinless, narrow, quarter-moon-shape slices), and chopped.

## Cashews

Crescent-shape cashews have a rich, buttery flavor. You can buy them raw or roasted, salted or plain. Choose roasted cashews for baking unless specified otherwise.

## Macadamia nuts

These small, round tropical nuts taste rich, sweet, and buttery.

## Hazelnuts

Hazelnuts, also called filberts, are small, round nuts with a mild, sweet flavor. The nut meat is covered with a thin, brown skin that needs to be removed before you use them (see page 34).

## Pine nuts

Pine nuts are the small, creamy white seeds from a variety of pine tree. Their flavor ranges from mild and sweet to pungent. Pine nuts can be slender and pellet-shape or more triangular.

## Pecans

Pecans are rich and buttery. Pecans and walnuts are often used interchangeably.

A world without spices would be bland indeed. They add sweetness, savoriness, and warmth to all kinds of baked goods. Here's how to make them sing.

## Spice Tips

- Ground spices release their flavors quickly, so they can be used in recipes with short cooking times or can be added near the end of cooking in longer-cooking recipes.
- Whole spices need more time than ground to release their flavors. They work well in long-cooking recipes like soups and stews.
- If doubling a recipe, increase spices by 1½. Taste, then add more if necessary.
- Toasting whole spices, such as fennel or cumin seeds, intensifies their flavor. To toast, place them in a dry skillet and heat over medium heat until aromatic.
- Use a dry spoon when measuring spices to avoid introducing moisture into the container, which could cause the spice to deteriorate.

## Spice Types

Although this isn't a complete rundown of every spice in the world, it does include the ones you'll most commonly find in this book and in other baking recipes.

**Allspice:** Allspice is not actually a blend of "all spices" but is a spice unto itself. It is the dried unripened berry from a small evergreen tree. It has a dark reddish brown color, and its flavor is reminiscent of cloves, cinnamon, and nutmeg. Used in jerk and curry seasonings, sauces, baked goods, and teas, it is popular in Caribbean, Indian, English, and North American cooking.

**Apple pie spice:** Apple pie spice is a blend of cinnamon, nutmeg, and allspice, all flavors typical in apple pie.

### Nice to Know

Out of apple pie spice? Substitute ½ teaspoon ground cinnamon, ¼ teaspoon ground nutmeg, ⅛ teaspoon ground allspice, and a dash of ground cloves for 1 teaspoon spice blend. For every 1 teaspoon of pumpkin pie spice, you can substitute ½ teaspoon ground cinnamon, ¼ teaspoon ground ginger, ¼ teaspoon ground allspice, and ⅛ teaspoon ground nutmeg.

**Black pepper:** Black pepper is a small berry that grows on a vine. The berries are picked while still green and allowed to ferment. Then they are sun-dried until they shrivel and turn brownish black. They have a hot, biting flavor with hints of pine.

**Cardamom:** Cardamom comes from the fruit pods of a perennial flower. Cardamom is available in pods and seeds but is most commonly ground. Its flavor is aromatic and sweet with grapefruitlike and floral tones. It is used in pastries and in spice blends, such as Indian garam masala and curry powder.

**Cinnamon:** Cinnamon is the dried inner bark of various evergreen trees. Its flavor is sweet and pungent with a woody, warming flavor. Ground cinnamon is used often in baked goods and in spice blends.

**Cloves:** Cloves are the dried flower buds from a particular evergreen. They are reddish brown with a strong aroma and flavor. Their flavor is pungent and almost hot. Cloves are used often in Indian spice blends. In the U.S., cloves are used with meats, salad dressings, and desserts.

**Fennel:** Fennel is the dried ripe fruit of a tall, hardy plant with feathery foliage and yellow flowers. The oval seeds are harvested after the flowers have dried and they have hardened. They are used throughout the Mediterranean, China, and Scandinavia. Fennel's flavor is sweet and aromatic with a slight hint of licorice.

**Garlic powder:** Garlic powder is made from garlic cloves that have been dried and ground into granules. It is useful in baked goods to easily impart a garlic flavor that can be evenly distributed through the baked item.

**Ginger:** Ginger comes from a dried knobby root. Ground ginger is used in Indian, Asian, and European spice blends. Its flavor is pungent and warming with a lemon/citrus tone. Crystallized ginger is made by chopping fresh ginger and cooking it in syrup before drying it

Nutmeg: Nutmeg is the seed of a fruit that grows on a particular tree. The seed is light brown. (A netlike membrane, called mace, enwraps the seed when the fruit splits open. Its flavor is similar to nutmeg but is more delicate.) When ground or grated, it is most commonly used in sweet foods and baked goods. Its high oil content makes it strongly aromatic with citrus and pine flavors.

Pumpkin pie spice: Pumpkin pie spice is a blend of cinnamon, ginger, nutmeg, and all-spice, which are classic flavors of pumpkin pie.

**Great grating:** A rasp grater is the perfect tool for grating fresh nutmeg. Just run it back and forth along the serrated surface. (And, incidentally, preground nutmeg just can't compare to the awesome flavor and aroma of fresh ground.) Sprinkle it on your holiday eggnog or on your morning cappuccino.

**Daily grind:** For the freshest flavor, some recipes call for grinding whole spices. Use an inexpensive coffee grinder to easily grind whole spices. (Make sure to mark it for spices only, or your coffee may get spiced up too.)

**Storage:** Most spices have a "best by" or expiration date. In general, ground spices will last for 2 to 3 years if properly stored. Spice blends last for 1 to 2 years. Store spices tightly covered in a cool, dry place out of direct sunlight. Don't store them over the stove, near the dishwasher or sink, or near a window. To check for freshness, make sure the color of the spice is still vibrant and the aroma is still pungent. If the color and aroma have faded, the flavor probably has too.

Whole spices, such as nutmeg, will stay fresh for up to 4 years if they're properly stored—in an airtight container in a cool, dry place out of direct sunlight.

## Nice to Know

For the prettiest, most even slices of apple to use in a pie, use a melon baller to scoop the core out of each apple half. Place each half, cut side down, on a cutting board, and cut into ¼- to ⅛-inch-thick slices.

**Peeling:** To peel, use a vegetable peeler or paring knife; start at the stem end and circle around to the blossom end.

Apple Math: 1 pound apples = 4 small, 3 medium, 2 large = 2¾ cups sliced = 2 cups chopped

# Apples

**An apple isn't just an apple. Flavors range from sweet to tart, textures from crisp to tender. Certain varieties are better for baking (see below).**

**Availability:** Some apple varieties are available year-round and some are only available at specific times of the year. For most apples, peak season is September through November.

**Selecting:** Choose apples that are brightly colored and firm with smooth, shiny skin; avoid apples with bruises or soft spots. Handle apples gently to avoid bruising.

**Storing:** Store apples in a plastic bag for up to 6 weeks in the refrigerator crisper so they maintain their crispness and flavor; at room temperature, they get mushy and mealy.

Coring: **To remove the core, cut the apple into four pieces through the stem and blossom ends. Cut away the core and the stem and blossom ends.**

**Place the apple quarters on a cutting board and cut into slices of desired thickness.**

Chopping: **For bite-size pieces, slice wedges crosswise with the knife.**

**When you want your apples whole—for baked apples, for example—an apple corer makes quick work of removing the core without having to cut the apple into wedges.**

Jonagold

Golden Delicious

Braeburn

Granny Smith

Cortland

Jonathan

Availability: Bananas are available year-round.

Selecting: Choose plump, evenly colored yellow bananas flecked with tiny brown specks; avoid bananas with blemishes. Avoid brown bananas, which are overripe.

Storing: Store green or unripe bananas, uncovered, at room temperature until ripe. Ripe bananas can be refrigerated for several days; the peel will turn black, but the pulp will remain unchanged.

Kitchen tip: Ripe bananas can be mashed and then frozen. Place in a freezer container and freeze for up to 2 months. Thaw and use in cakes, breads, and muffins.

**Banana Math:**
1 pound = 3 or 4 medium
= 2 cups sliced =
1 cup mashed

### Potato masher
Bananas can be mashed with a potato masher—press down on them repeatedly until they're the right consistency.

### Plastic bag
You can also use your hands to mash bananas in a plastic bag. Snip the corner of the bag and squeeze mashed bananas out.

### Fork
A dinner fork works well too. Press the tines down onto the bananas repeatedly until they're the right consistency.

# Coconut

## This fluffy white stuff infuses anything it touches with a taste of the tropics.

Storing: Store unopened cans or packages of coconut at room temperature for 6 months; refrigerate both after opening.

Toasting coconut: To toast coconut, spread it in a single layer in a shallow baking pan. Bake in a 350°F oven for 5 to 10 minutes or until golden brown; stir once or twice during baking to prevent overbrowning.

What's the difference between coconut milk and cream of coconut? Coconut milk is the liquid extracted from pressed coconut meat that is mixed with water. It has the consistency of cow's milk. Cream of coconut is almost all sugar and is most often used in desserts and mixed drinks (look for it wherever liquor is sold). Cream of coconut looks a lot like sweetened condensed milk. Don't substitute one for the other.

Shredded and flaked coconut is available, sweetened or unsweetened, in plastic bags or cans. It can sometimes be found toasted. Cans of coconut milk and cream of coconut are also available (see left).

# Dried Fruit

Drying fruit intensifies its natural flavor and sweetness. Dried fruits add chewy texture and richness to all kinds of cakes, cookies, and breads.

**Availability:** Dried fruits are available year-round in supermarkets, online, and from catalogs; a wider selection of candied fruits is available during the holidays.

**Storing:** Unopened packages can be stored in a cool, dry place for up to 1 year. Once opened, wrap securely in a plastic bag and refrigerate.

**Cutting up:** Larger dried fruits such as apricots often need to be cut up before being used in a recipe. Use kitchen scissors to snip the fruit into smaller pieces. To prevent sticking, dip the blades frequently in hot water or spray them with nonstick cooking spray.

**Plumping/rehydrating:** To plump or partially rehydrate dried fruit for use as an ingredient, put it in a small saucepan and cover it with water. Bring to a boil, then cover and remove from heat. Let it stand for 5 minutes; drain.

Currants

Golden raisins

Dried cherries

Dried apples

Raisins

Dried bananas

Dried blueberries

Dried cranberries

Dried figs (Calimyrna)

Dried pineapple

Dried figs (Black Mission)

Dried plums (prunes)

Dried pears

Dates

Dried apricots

Candied fruit (red and green cherries, pineapple, citron, and citrus peels)

Dried papaya

Tropical-blend dried fruit bits (mango, papaya, pineapple)

# Berries
## You'll be greatly rewarded if you give these delicate summer fruits the gentle treatment they require.

**Availability:** Fresh berries really are best when the weather is warm. Blackberries are available June through August; blueberries are available late May through October; raspberries are available year-round, with peak season from May through September; and strawberries are available year-round, with peak season from June through September.

**Storing:** Refrigerate berries, loosely covered, in a single layer; heaping them on top of one another can crush the fruit. Store blackberries and raspberries for up to 3 days; store strawberries and blueberries for up to 5 days. Berries can be frozen by arranging washed berries on a baking sheet. Freeze until solid; transfer to freezer containers or bags for up to 1 year.

**Washing:** Put strawberries in a colander and gently rinse under cool water before removing the stems. If stems are removed first, the water can affect the texture and flavor of the strawberries.

**Stemming:** To remove the stem, use a paring knife to cut out the stem and hull. Or you can use a tweezerlike strawberry huller: Insert the ends of the huller into the strawberry, deep enough to get hold of the stem and core. Squeeze the end of the huller and pull the stem and core out.

**Slicing:** Place a whole strawberry on a cutting board, stem side down. Start cutting slices from one side of the strawberry and continue cutting slices into desired thickness.

## How do I wash fresh berries?

Berries of all kinds—including strawberries—are very delicate. Never wash any berries until right before you plan to use them, or they start to break down and get mushy. Blackberries, raspberries, and blueberries require special care. To rinse them, put them in a colander and dip them into a bowl of cold water (rinsing under running water can crush these fragile berries). Gently swish in the water and allow the berries to drain. Carefully spread out the washed berries in a single layer on a paper towel; pat dry with another paper towel.

# Peaches & Nectarines

**Availability:** Peaches and nectarines are available May through September; peak season is July and August.

**Selecting:** Choose peaches/nectarines that are fragrant and give slightly to pressure; avoid fruit with blemishes or bruises. Watch out for greenish fruit; it won't ripen.

**Storing:** Store unripe fruit at room temperature; store ripe fruit in the refrigerator for 3 to 5 days.

Nectarines can be used interchangeably with peaches. They are slightly smaller and are more reddish in color than peaches. You don't need to peel smooth-skinned nectarines.

**Peach/Nectarine Math:**
1 pound = 3 medium = 3 cups sliced = 2½ cups chopped

**1** To skin peaches or nectarines, bring a saucepan of water to boiling. Immerse peaches in boiling water for 30 seconds, making sure peaches are covered.

**2** Remove fruit with a slotted spoon and submerge in it a bowl of ice water. Let it stand in water for 30 seconds.

**3** Use your fingers or a small knife to peel away the skin from cooled fruit.

# Cranberries

## This very American fruit adds a mouth-puckering shot of freshness to quick breads and desserts.

**Availability:** Bags of fresh cranberries are in stores for the holiday season, from mid-September through December. Some stores sell frozen berries year-round.

**Selecting:** Look for bags that contain plump, bright berries. The scarlet color will vary from light to dark but doesn't affect the quality. When ready to use, sort out and discard any shriveled, soft, or crushed berries; rinse under running water.

**Storing:** Store bags of cranberries in the refrigerator for up to 1 month. To freeze, place bags in resealable freezer bags; freeze for up to 1 year. For best results when using frozen cranberries in recipes, do not thaw.

Chopping cranberries by hand can be tedious, so try chopping them—a few cups at a time—by pulsing them in your food processor.

**Cranberry Math:** One 12-ounce bag = about 3 cups chopped

# Citrus

Lemons, limes, and oranges are rare exceptions to the rule that summer fruit is best. They're in season during the winter and give all kinds of baked goods a burst of sunny, refreshing flavor.

At most supermarkets, a lemon is a lemon and a lime is a lime—but you will see several types of oranges. The two most common ones are juicy Valencia oranges and easy-to-peel navel oranges. Valencias are small to medium in size and have a smooth, thin peel. Navel oranges generally are larger and have a pebbly, thicker peel and a button shape at the end opposite the stem; they're seedless and easy to section. Look for well-formed citrus fruits that are heavy for their size—which means they're full of juice—and have a colorful skin. Bruised and wrinkled fruit is past its prime. A slight greenish tinge found on the surface of some oranges doesn't affect the eating quality.

Store citrus fruit in the refrigerator crisper for 2 to 3 weeks for the best flavor. Be sure to rinse the fruit thoroughly, scrub with a clean produce brush, and dry with paper towels before cutting it up or shredding the peel.

Orange: Look for fruit with shiny skin free of blemishes, wrinkles, soft spots, and mold.

Persian lime: This is the formal name of the common lime. Look for limes that are bright green and shiny.

Blood orange: The flesh of these juicy oranges is tinged with pink or red.

Lemon: Look for firm, plump lemons with glossy, bright yellow color and no tinge of green.

Tangerine: Part of the family of mandarin oranges, this sweet citrus fruit has thick, rough skin.

## Nice to Know

It's difficult to extract much juice from a lemon, lime, or orange without a citrus juicer (see page 45), but if you don't have one, pierce the cut surface of the fruit all over with a fork before squeezing it over a bowl. You can also microwave the unsqueezed fruit on high for 10 seconds and roll it on the counter to release the juice from the pulp.

**Citrus Math:**

1 medium lemon = 2 teaspoons finely shredded peel = 3 tablespoons juice

1 medium lime = 1½ teaspoons finely shredded peel = 2 tablespoons juice

1 medium orange = 1 tablespoon finely shredded peel = ⅓ cup juice = ⅓ cup sections

**Juicing:** The best way to juice citrus fruit is with a hand juicer—a ridged cone set on a dish to catch the juices. Place half of a lemon, lime, or orange on the hand juicer; press down and twist. You can also use a handheld wooden reamer.

**Using a zester:** When you want thin, attractive strips of citrus peel, use a zester. Pull it across the skin to remove fine strips from the surface of the fruit.

**Using a rasp grater:** Lightweight and easy to use, this tool is ideal for making the finest pieces of peel. Remove just the colored part of the peel (the zest). Avoid the white stuff (pith). It's bitter.

**Using a box grater:** This tool has sides with both fine and coarse holes, giving you options for the size of the shredded peel.

## Nice to Know

Sometimes you want your pear halves to stay intact—if you're making a simple baked pear dessert, for instance—but you still want to get the core out. You can use a melon baller to scoop out the seeds, then use a paring knife to cut away the stem.

If you're cutting up the pear, cut the peeled (or unpeeled) pear in half, then cut each half in half again and cut away the center core with a paring knife.

Slicing: To slice or chop the pear, place cored, peeled or unpeeled quarters side by side and thinly slice, then chop if desired.

To peel a pear, first rinse it thoroughly under cool running water, then pat dry. Use a vegetable peeler to remove the pear skin. One technique is to start cutting at the blossom end and cut toward the stem end.

# How do I buy and prepare pears?

The juiciest, finest-textured pears are available in the fall, when the fruit is at its peak—the perfect time to make a bubbly pear cobbler or a batch of muffins.

**Availability:** Bartlett pears are available from July through December; Bosc pears can be found from August through May.

**Selecting:** Look for firm, fragrant, unblemished pears. Handle pears with care because they bruise easily.

**Storing:** Most of the pears you buy at the supermarket are not quite ripe. Store them at room temperature until they ripen, then refrigerate for up to 5 days. Refrigeration slows ripening. To test for ripeness for all varieties of pears, gently press near the stem end. If it yields, it's ready to eat.

**Bosc:** This slender-necked, ruddy yellow pear has a sweet-tart flavor and holds its shape well when cooked.

**Pear Math:** 1 medium pear = 1 cup chopped or sliced

**Red Bartlett:** These are ripe and ready when their skin is a brilliant red.

**Green Bartlett:** You'll know these are ripe and ready when their skin is bright yellow.

# Carrots

The natural sweetness of carrots makes them versatile in all kinds of baked goods, both sweet and savory. They're as at home in Winter Vegetable Tarts with Bacon and Goat Cheese (page 256) as they are in Pineapple-Carrot Loaves (page 168). Choose smooth, straight, rigid, bright orange carrots that aren't cracked and dried out. Carrots are generally sold with-out tops; however, if you buy them with tops attached, be sure the tops look fresh and are not wilted or slimy. Carrots with tops are generally a little fresher and sweeter than those without. Also the more slender they are, the sweeter they are. Store carrots (without tops) in a plastic bag in the refrigerator for up to 2 weeks.

**Carrot Math:**

**1 medium carrot = ½ cup finely shredded**

**1** Rinse carrots under cool tap water and scrub with a clean produce brush. Peeling is optional; use a vegetable peeler to remove peel. Trim off tip and stem.

**2** To slice carrots, use a small chef's knife. If carrots are small, you might be able to line up several side by side on a cutting surface, then cut into ¼-inch slices.

**3** To shred carrots, hold one at a 45-degree angle and rub it across a handheld or box grater. Use the fine grates or large grates, depending on the recipe.

# Garlic

Garlic bulbs yield 12 to 16 small cloves. Choose firm, plump bulbs that still have their dry, papery skin. There should be no sprouting or soft spots. To peel a clove, press on the unpeeled clove using the heel of your hand placed on the flat side of a broad-bladed knife. This loosens the skin. Peel the skin with your fingers and trim the root end with a knife.

Garlic Math: 1 clove garlic = ½ teaspoon minced

# Ginger

Look for fresh ginger (sometimes called gingerroot) that is firm and has smooth, slightly shiny, fresh-looking skin that isn't shriveled. Store unpeeled ginger wrapped in a paper towel in the refrigerator for 2 to 3 weeks. To peel, rinse ginger under cool tap water. Cut off one end of the root and use a vegetable peeler to remove the thin brown peel.

Ginger Math: 1 teaspoon grated fresh ginger = ¼ teaspoon ground ginger

# Rhubarb

## The appearance of tart, rosy-hued rhubarb in the market means spring has arrived.

First a caveat: Eat only the stalks of rhubarb. The leaves are poisonous! Now here's the rest of what you need to know:

**Availability:** The peak season for homegrown rhubarb is April through June; hothouse rhubarb is available year-round.

**Selecting:** Look for moderately thin, crisp stalks free of disease or insect damage; avoid any wilted or pithy stalks.

**Storing:** Cut off and discard leaves, if present. Store unwashed stalks in sealed plastic bags in the refrigerator for up to 1 week. It's best to store fresh rhubarb as whole stalks because cut pieces will dry out more quickly. Rhubarb can also be cut into ½- to 1-inch pieces and frozen in freezer bags for up to 6 months.

**Rhubarb Math:** 1 pound stalks = 3 to 5 stalks = 3 cups chopped

# Herbs

Fresh herbs add spark to food. Choose herbs that have fresh-looking leaves without brown spots. Fresh herbs are highly perishable, so buy as you need them—or, better yet, grow them in your garden or in a pot on your windowsill.

Herbs come in two categories—those with delicate stems, such as cilantro, parsley, basil, and mint—and those with woody stems, such as thyme, oregano, and rosemary. Woody herbs need to be stripped from their stems before using. To do this, hold the stem in one hand and—starting at the top of the stem—strip off the leaves by running the fingers of your other hand firmly down the stem.

**Snipping:** Herbs with delicate stems can be snipped—stems and all—in a glass measure with kitchen scissors. Snip only the leaves of woody-stemmed herbs, such as rosemary.

**Chiffonade:** A chiffonade is a bunch of thin strips or shreds. To create a chiffonade of herbs, roll up larger leaves, such as basil, and cut across the roll.

**Storing:** To store fresh herbs, cut ½ inch from the stems. Stand stem ends in a small jar with some water. Loosely cover leaves with a plastic bag and store in the refrigerator. (Don't refrigerate basil—it may blacken.)

# Zucchini & Yellow Squash

Julienne: To make julienne sticks, trim ends and cut squash into 2- to 3-inch chunks. Cut into ¼-inch planks. Stack planks and cut into sticks.

Choose summer squash that are firm, heavy for their size, and free of cuts and soft spots. Don't panic over a few blemishes: Since they are so tender skinned, sometimes the exteriors aren't perfect. Smaller squash have a more delicate flavor than larger ones. Avoid summer squash that are shriveled.

Store wrapped summer squash in the refrigerator for up to 5 days.

In baking, summer squash are often shredded, using the same method as for carrots (see page 48).

Slicing: To slice, place halved squash, flat side down, on a cutting surface and make crosswise slices that are about ¼ inch thick. Or, for smaller squash, don't halve; just cut across into rounds.

# How do I work with leeks?

## Their distinctive, mild, oniony flavor is worth the little bit of fussing you have to do to prepare them.

Leeks look like giant green onions but have a more assertive flavor. The leaves of leeks should be crisp and healthy looking. Leeks that are 1½ inches or smaller in diameter are more tender than larger leeks, so the smaller the better. Wrap unwashed leeks in paper towels before refrigerating, tightly wrapped in a plastic bag, for up to 5 days. Wash them well right before using—their accordion leaves are filled with grit and dirt (see below.)

**1** Using a chef's knife and a cutting surface, cut a thin slice from the root end of the leek. Cut off the dark green leaves and remove any wilted outer leaves. Continue cutting into slices.

**2** To wash, rinse leek slices in a colander under cool running water. Drain leeks on paper towels.

**3** Or, to cut a leek lengthwise, cut all the way through the root end.

**4** To wash, hold the leek halves under the faucet with the root ends up. Rinse leek under cool running water, separating and lifting the leaves with your fingers to make sure that all the dirt is flushed out and removed.

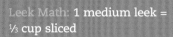

Leek Math: **1 medium leek = ⅓ cup sliced**

# Onions & Green Onions

When heat in any form is applied to onions—by sauteing, grilling, or baking—their natural sugars caramelize and turn yummy. Before they get cooked, though, here's what you need to know.

There are three basic types of dry onions—and then there are green onions. Dry varieties include yellow onions, which have a full flavor and are most often used in cooking and baking. White onions have a sharper flavor than yellow onions. Red onions are sharp but sweet. Availability: All three types are available all year, although the special sweet onion varieties—such as Vidalia, Walla Walla, and Maui—are available only March through August.

Selecting: Look for onions that are firm and heavy for their size and have papery outer skins and short necks. Avoid onions that are sprouting or have soft spots. Storing: Don't refrigerate onions. Store in a cool, dry, ventilated place for several weeks.

Buy green onions that have fresh-looking green tops and clean white ends. Store, unwashed and wrapped in paper towels in a plastic bag, in the refrigerator for up to 5 days.

## How do I chop an onion?

**1** Rinse the onion thoroughly under cool tap water. To chop, use a chef's knife to slice off the stem and root ends on a cutting surface.

**2** Remove the papery outer skins. Cut the onion in half from top end to root end.

**3** Place each onion half, flat side down, on the cutting surface and make side-by-side vertical slices from stem end to root end. Holding the slices together, cut across the slices, making tiny pieces.

## How do I slice green onions?

**1** Rinse onions under cool tap water and remove wilted tops or slimy skins on the white parts. Trim off root ends and 2 inches from green tops. Lay several onions on a cutting surface and cut across into slices.

**2** For larger pieces, line up the trimmed onions and cut into I-inch or longer pieces.

Onion & Green Onion Math:
1 medium onion
    = ½ cup chopped
1 large onion
    = 1 cup chopped
1 medium green onion
    = 2 tablespoons sliced

# Peppers

**Peppers are bold in many ways. Mild-tasting sweet peppers come in eye-popping shades of green, orange, yellow, and red. And hot peppers—with their wide range of heat levels—add a touch of fire to food.**

All peppers—whether they're sweet or hot (also called chile peppers)—are botanically in the *Capsicum* family. So when you're buying either type, you want to look for the same things. Pick peppers that are glossy, have bright color, and are a good shape for the variety. Steer clear of peppers that are shriveled or bruised or have soft spots.

Refrigerate sweet peppers, covered, for up to 5 days.

Store most chile peppers in the refrigerator, unwashed and wrapped in paper towels in a plastic bag, for up to 10 days. (There is an exception. Serrano chiles shouldn't be stored in plastic but instead kept in the vegetable crisper.) Wash sweet or hot peppers right before you use them. Rinse them thoroughly and scrub with a clean produce brush, then prep as needed. Chile peppers take a bit of extra precaution (see "Hot Stuff," below).

Pepper Math: **1 medium sweet pepper = 1 cup strips = ¾ cup chopped**

**1** To remove the stem and seeds from a sweet pepper, hold it upright on a cutting surface. Use a sharp knife to slice each of the sides from the pepper. You should have 4 large flat pieces that are free of seeds and stem. The stem, seeds, and ribs should all be in one unit that can easily be discarded.

**2** To chop sweet peppers, cut the large flat pepper pieces lengthwise into strips. Line up the strips and cut across the strips into the size you want.

## Hot Stuff

When working with fresh chile peppers, wear disposable plastic or rubber gloves. Chiles contain volatile oils that can burn your skin and eyes; avoid contact with them as much as possible. If your bare hands do touch the chiles, wash your hands and nails well with soap and hot water. If you get some of the oils in your eyes, flush them with cool water. Cut the chiles in half; remove seeds and membrane; then cut up. The seeds and membrane are the hottest parts of the pepper; some people choose to leave them in because they like the heat.

# Baking Techniques & Tricks

**Every discipline has its fundamentals. This section covers all of the basic skills you need to know to start baking—and to keep baking better and better.**

You've heard the phrase: You have to walk before you can run. The same concept can be applied to baking. Before you decide to dive in and bake a cake or make a soufflé, you might want to know the best way to measure flour or crack an egg—or how to know when your cakes, cookies, and yeast breads are ready to come out of the oven. Those techniques—plus a lot more—are spelled out, step-by-step, in this section.

## Just Ask

More often than not—because recipe writers want recipes to be as short and streamlined as possible—not absolutely every detail is explained. Often they make a few assumptions about how some things are done, trimming language from a recipe to keep it from becoming gargantuan. A recipe may, for example, call for "½ cup almonds, toasted." But that may leave you wondering: "How do I toast almonds?" (See page 34.) Or it may call for topping something off with Sweetened Whipped Cream. "How do I make that?" (See page 25.)

You can also learn all about the magic of yeast-bread baking (see pages 62–63) or find a couple of recipes for simple, last-minute dessert sauces to serve over cake, cheesecake or ice cream (see Raspberry Sauce on page 60 and Caramel Sauce on page 64).

If you have a question on a technique, this section will answer it.

## Safety Concerns

The kitchen is a happy place, but it's also a place that bears some caution. As with any kind of cooking, fire, hot ovens and pans, hot liquids, and sharp objects are a part of baking. Read through the information on kitchen safety (see page 72) to keep your baking experience injury-free—and then just dig in and have fun.

# How do I measure ingredients?

Although it's important to measure ingredients accurately in any kind of cooking, baking requires measurement precision to ensure optimum results.

The first step to proper measuring is having the right tools. Check out page 12 for the specifics, but here's the most fundamental thing to know: Use dry measuring cups for dry ingredients and liquid measuring cups for liquids. It's especially important when measuring flour to fluff it a little by gently stirring it with a spoon before spooning it into the cup (see below). If you don't, too much flour can get packed into the measuring cup, and you can wind up with dry cakes or dense, dry breads.

The other important thing to remember is to avoid measuring over the bowl in which you're mixing. It's tempting to avoid a mess on the counter, but you run the risk of spilling too much salt, baking soda, etc., into the bowl.

**Flour:** Before measuring flour, stir the flour in the canister to aerate and loosen it. Lightly spoon flour into a dry measuring cup or measuring spoon; level it off with a knife. If you skip the aeration step or shake the cup to level it rather than use a knife, you can add too much flour.

**Baking Powder:** Before measuring baking powder, stir it to loosen it. Scoop up a heaping spoonful. Level it off by dragging it across the edge of the metal lip inside the can—the lip is designed just for that purpose.

**Measuring Math:**

3 teaspoons = 1 tablespoon
1 tablespoon = $\frac{1}{2}$ fluid ounce
4 tablespoons = $\frac{1}{4}$ cup
$5\frac{1}{3}$ tablespoons = $\frac{1}{3}$ cup
8 tablespoons = $\frac{1}{2}$ cup
$10\frac{2}{3}$ tablespoons = $\frac{2}{3}$ cup
12 tablespoons = $\frac{3}{4}$ cup
16 tablespoons = 1 cup
1 cup = $\frac{1}{2}$ pint = 8 fluid ounces

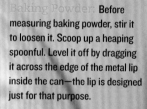

**Sugar/Brown Sugar:** Spoon granulated or powdered sugar into a dry measuring cup and level it off. Pack brown sugar, on the other hand, firmly into the measuring cup until it is level. Brown sugar should hold the shape of the measuring cup when it is turned out.

**Shortening/Peanut Butter:** Spoon shortening or peanut butter into a dry measuring cup. Pack it firmly into the cup and level off the top. Run a rubber spatula around the inside of the cup to push out the shortening or peanut butter.

**Butter/Stick Shortening:** Sticks of butter and shortening have tablespoon markings on the wrapper—8 per stick. Just cut off what you need with a sharp knife.

**Liquids:** Pour liquids into a measuring cup. Get at eye level with the cup and fill just to the measuring line. Before measuring sticky ingredients—such as honey—lightly coat the measuring cup (or spoon) with nonstick cooking spray.

# How do I combine wet and dry ingredients?

When you're making quick breads and muffins, you want the result to be tender and fine grained. The best way to ensure this is to not overmix your batter, which produces a tough texture. The more you mix, the more gluten builds up in the flour. This is desirable in yeast breads and pizza doughs—which is why you knead them—but not so desirable in quick breads and muffins. Follow the method below—and don't be afraid of a few lumps!

1. Use a spatula or wooden spoon to gently push the dry ingredients (flour, leavening, salt, spices) against the sides of the bowl to make a well.

2. When the wet ingredients are combined, pour them into the well. Use a rubber scraper to mix. Run the scraper around the edge of the bowl and reach to the bottom of the bowl, pulling dry ingredients over and into the wet ingredients.

3. Stop mixing while the batter is still lumpy. If you stir out all the lumps, your finished product may have peaks on top and tough texture.

# How do I cut in butter?

Every kind of pastry—whether it's a pie or tart crust or commercially made puff pastry—relies on little bits of butter mixed into the flour to create crisp, flaky layers upon baking. You make the little bits from bigger bits of butter using a pastry blender. If you don't have this tool, use two table knives. Move the blades next to each other, pulling in opposite directions through the butter.

1. First cut the cold butter into ½- to 1-inch chunks, then add it to the dry ingredients.

2. Using a pastry blender, gently press and cut butter into smaller and smaller pieces until mixture looks like coarse crumbs. Use a rubber scraper to scrape butter buildup off of the blender.

# How do I soften cream cheese?

Cold cream cheese is quite firm—it won't blend very easily into that cheesecake you're making (that you hope will be silky and creamy, of course). If you've forgotten to leave the block on the counter a couple of hours ahead of time, you can speed up softening by cutting it into 1-inch cubes and letting it stand at room temperature for about 1 hour. If you're really in a hurry, use the microwave method (see below).

**Speed Softening:**
Unwrap the cream cheese and place it in a microwave-safe bowl. Microwave 3 ounces on 100 percent power (high) for 10 to 20 seconds or 8 ounces for 30 to 60 seconds. Let stand for 5 minutes.

# How do I beat mixtures?

In baking, an electric mixer serves two very important functions: It blends ingredients together—butter and sugar, eggs and sugar, wet and dry ingredients—and it incorporates air. As you beat eggs, for instance, tiny air bubbles are created in the eggs, which expand when they are exposed to the hot air in the oven. This helps to create height and add lightness to the texture of all kinds of baked goods. But you can't be brazen and go full bore with the mixer. Ingredients such as butter are beaten to different consistencies, stages, and textures for various recipes. See the photos below for the basic method for creaming (blending) fat and sugar. You'll use this method for almost any kind of cake you bake.

**Creaming:** Many recipes begin by beating the fat (shortening or butter) with an electric mixer for 30 seconds on high speed until it is very creamy.

**Light and Fluffy:** The next step is to add the sugar and beat until the mixture is light and fluffy (this usually takes about 5 minutes). Thorough beating is important to dissolve the sugar crystals.

**Scraping:** While you're mixing, some of the batter will climb the sides of the mixing bowl. For thorough mixing, stop your mixer occasionally and use a rubber spatula to scrape down the batter.

# How do I keep baked goods from sticking to the pan?

There's nothing much worse than having a homemade cake stuck in the pan. Here's how to ensure yours pop out, beautifully intact, every time.

There are three ways to get baked goods to release easily from a pan. The first one is to grease the pan with solid shortening, butter, or nonstick cooking spray and then line it with waxed paper—a method used mostly for cakes. The second, used most often for brownies, bar cookies, and fudge, is to line the pan with foil, leaving some hanging over the edge. The additional advantage of this method is that it allows you to easily lift the bars out of the pan before cutting them. The third method, also used mostly for cakes, is to grease or butter and then flour the pan. Follow the recipe directions for preparing the pan.

## How to line a pan with waxed paper

**1** Grease the bottom and sides of the pan with shortening. Set the pan on a piece of waxed paper and trace around the pan with a pencil.

**2** With a clean pair of kitchen scissors, cut just inside the traced line on the paper.

**3** Fit the cut piece of waxed paper in the pan, pressing it into the corners and smoothing out any wrinkles or bubbles.

## How to line a pan with foil

**1** Tear a piece of foil that is larger than the pan. Shape the foil over the outside of the pan bottom. Cut slits at the corners to make it fit neatly.

**2** Gently lift the shaped foil off of the pan.

**3** Turn the pan over and fit the shaped foil into it. Leave an inch or two of overhang to use as "handles" to lift the baked good out of the pan.

# How to grease and flour a pan

**1** With a pastry brush or paper towel, brush shortening evenly over the bottom of the pan, taking care not to leave any uncoated shiny spots.

**2** When greasing the sides and corners of the pan, turn the pan on that end so you can better see what you're doing. You don't have to go all the way to the top of the pan.

**3** When the pan is completely greased, sprinkle a couple of spoonfuls of all-purpose flour in the bottom of it.

**4** To distribute the flour over the pan, hold it on one edge and tap the other with your free hand. The flour will "skate" over the greased surface and stick to it. When the pan bottom is coated, tilt the pan, tapping it to move the flour over the sides. Tap out any extra flour into the sink.

# What does it mean to lightly flour a surface?

Recipes for piecrust and yeast bread often call for working with dough "on a lightly floured surface." This simply means to sprinkle a tablespoon or two of flour on your work surface—just a dusting over a fairly wide area.

# How do I make a basic Raspberry Sauce?

Thaw 3 cups of frozen unsweetened raspberries. Do not drain. Place half of the berries in a blender. Cover and blend until berries are smooth. Press berries through a fine-mesh sieve over a bowl. Repeat with remaining berries. In a small saucepan combine $\frac{1}{3}$ cup sugar and 1 teaspoon cornstarch. Add raspberry puree. Cook and stir over medium heat until thickened and bubbly. Cook and stir 2 minutes more. Transfer to a bowl. Cool slightly. Cover; chill leftovers for up to 1 week.

A raspberry sauce recipe is a good thing to have in your back pocket. It's delicious drizzled on a simple wedge of chocolate cake or cheesecake, or over a crisp, snowy-white meringue.

# How do I remove cakes and quick breads from the pan?

If you've properly greased and/or floured your pan (and each recipe will tell you exactly how to do that), your cakes and quick breads should easily slip from the pan if you follow the method below. Just remember: Before you cut, slice, or frost anything, it should be completely cool.

**1** Take the pan out of the oven and let it sit on a cooling rack for 5 to I0 minutes. Run a paring knife around the perimeter of the pan to loosen the bread from the sides.

**2** Once the loaf has been loosened, turn it out into a clean kitchen towel (it's still hot!) and place it, right side up, on a cooling rack to cool completely.

# How do I use a rolling pin?

## This simple tool performs an important function—turning that lump of dough into thin, delicate pastry.

**1** Start by placing a flattened ball of dough on a lightly floured surface. Start in the center and roll into an oval.

**2** For the most even pastry, it's important to continue rolling from the center in all directions. If you see any thicker spots, work on those in particular.

**3** As you continue to roll from the center in all directions, you will create a circle of dough (or close to it) that will fit easily into a pie or tart pan.

**4** If your dough starts to stick—either to the rolling pin or to your work surface—gently lift up one section of it and sprinkle a little flour underneath before you continue rolling.

# How do I work with bread dough?

Although it's all perfectly explained by science, there's something slightly magical about making yeast bread. Here's how you make the magic work.

There are two main events that take place in yeast bread baking—one of them more than once—that give yeast breads their characteristic chewy-tender, spongy, tuggy texture. One is proofing, and the other is kneading. The technique of properly proofing the yeast relies on getting the temperature of the water just right (see Step 1, below). The same goes for prop-erly proofing (raising) the dough after you've kneaded it (see Step 4, page 63). The other event, of course, is the kneading of the dough. The texture and lightness of your yeast bread depends on the effectiveness of your technique (see Steps 2 and 3, below) and how long you knead the dough. It may seem awkward at first, but the more you do it, the easier it will get.

**1** When you're dissolving the yeast, check the temperature of the heated mixture with an instant-read thermometer. If the mixture is too hot, the yeast will die and the bread won't rise. If it's too cold, the yeast won't activate and the bread won't rise. Follow the temperature guidelines in each recipe.

**2** To knead dough, fold it and push down with the heel of your hand.

**3** Turn the dough, fold, and push down again. Repeat this process until dough is smooth and elastic.

Before you cover your dough and set it aside to rise, take a good look at it so you'll know when it's doubled in size. This visual test is the first one you do before you do the finger test (see Step 5, page 63).

Kneading builds up a protein structure called gluten, which gives body to the finished bread. The longer you knead, the more gluten builds up. That doesn't mean you should knead until your arms hurt. (Kneading dough, incidentally, is one of the most satisfying aspects of baking bread. It's excellent for working out your frustrations, and it's great exercise for your arms.) It just means you shouldn't knead for less than the time the recipe specifies. If you cut out early, you run the risk of baking a doorstop instead of a loaf of bread. Knead vigorously for the time the recipe says—and then give it the finger-push test. Dough is ready to be set aside to proof if, when you gently poke a finger in it, the dough bounces back and the hole (for the most part) fills in. This is what is meant by an "elastic" dough. Incidentally, this test is just the opposite of when the dough has already proofed once and is ready to be punched down (see Step 6, below). Some doughs are ready to be shaped after one rising; others require a second, shorter rising. You want to stop short of doubling the dough the second time so that it has more "oven spring"—a final, dramatic rise spurred by exposure to the heat of the oven.

**6** To punch dough down, push your fist into the center. Use your fingers to pull dough edges into the center.

**4** Proofing (rising) a yeast bread correctly can mean the difference between success and failure. Let yeast breads rise in a draft-free location that has a temperature between 80°F and 85°F. A perfect spot is your oven. To use your unheated oven for rising, place the bowl of dough (covered with plastic wrap) on the center rack and a bowl of warm water on the lower rack.

**5** To see if dough has doubled in size and is ready to be shaped, press two fingers ½ inch into the center. Remove your fingers. If the indentation remains, the dough is ready to be punched down.

## What is yeast?

Active dry yeast is a tiny, dehydrated granule that feeds on sugar in dough and creates carbon dioxide gas that makes dough rise. Quick-rising dry active yeast (also called instant yeast) is more active than regular yeast and can substantially cut down on rising time. Recipes in this book were tested using active dry yeast. To use quick-rising yeast, omit the first rising time (just let the bread rest for 10 minutes). The dough should rise in about two-thirds the time given for the second rising. Once it's opened, store yeast in the refrigerator.

# How do I make Caramel Sauce?

## Almost everything you need to make this scrumptious sauce is a pantry item or staple.

In a heavy medium saucepan combine ½ cup whipping cream, ½ cup butter, ¾ cup packed brown sugar, and 2 tablespoons light-color corn syrup. Bring to boiling over medium-high heat (about 5 to 6 minutes), whisking occasionally. Reduce heat to medium. Boil gently for 3 minutes more. Remove from heat. Stir in 1 teaspoon vanilla. Let sauce cool 15 minutes before serving over pound cake, apple crisp, or ice cream. Cover and chill any leftovers for up to 2 weeks (let stand at room temperature for 1 hour before serving).

As the cream, butter, sugar, and corn syrup cook, be very careful when you're whisking—sugar and fat get hot very fast and tend to splatter a bit.

After the sauce has bubbled for 8 or 9 minutes, it's done. The 15-minute cooling time allows the sauce to thicken slightly before you serve it.

# How do I use a sieve?

A fine-mesh sieve has multiple uses in baking. The tapping technique accomplishes lots of tasks.

Use a fine-mesh sieve like this one (shown at right) to sift flour, dust baked goods with powdered sugar, and tidy up chopped nuts or chunks of crushed hard candy, candy bars, or cookies. See the recipe for Peppermint Fudge Pie on pages 250–251 and the recipe for Chocolate Cake on page 139 for examples. You can also use it to strain solids from liquids, such as separating the pulp from the juice in fruit purees.

You don't want to dump candy dust on your fabulous frozen fudge pie—just the pretty pieces. Place the crushed candy in the sieve, then tap the edge to separate the dust from the chunks.

## What does it mean to drop from a rounded teaspoon?

Most drop cookie recipes call for the dough to be dropped from a rounded teaspoon. All this means is that you scoop a ball of dough with a teaspoon from your flatware set and slide it onto the cookie sheet with another.

## What does it mean to fold in ingredients?

Folding is a method of gently mixing ingredients—dry and wet ingredients or delicate ingredients like beaten egg whites—that can't withstand stirring. Use a rubber spatula to cut down through the mixture, move across the bottom of the bowl, and come back up, folding the mixture from the bottom over the top.

# Top 10 tricks only the pros know

Professional bakers and pastry chefs pick up lots of cool tricks along the way that help make their jobs easier. This collection of insider secrets gives your baking the benefits of their experience.

## Trick #3

Cake a little dry? Brush it with a little flavored syrup (like the kind you put in your latte) or flavored liqueur, such as Grand Marnier or amaretto.

## Trick #4

If you're using a plastic bag as a pastry bag to pipe a sauce or icing onto a baked good (you simply snip a tiny hole in one corner of it), it can be a little floppy to fill. Set it in a measuring cup, fold the top of the bag over the edge of the cup, and pour the sauce or icing in.

## Trick #7

How clever is this? To make a diamond pattern on a cake or pan of brownies with a dusting of powdered sugar, set the cake or brownies under two cooling racks that are stacked crosswise to each other. Dust over the top with powdered sugar, then gently remove the racks.

## Trick #8

Trim a perfect pie. Cut pastry scraps with a decorative cookie cutter, then place them on top of the pie. To get them to stick, brush the backs of the cutouts with a little water before positioning them.

## Trick #1

Make a pretty plate. This is the way they do it in restaurants. Fill a squeeze bottle full of chocolate, caramel, or raspberry sauce, then squeeze it onto the plate in a decorative fashion. Set a piece of cake, cheesecake, tart, or meringue on top and serve.

## Trick #2

Patch your piecrust. As you roll your dough out, if a piece breaks off or if it starts to get oddly shaped, you can reshape it. Cut off an irregular piece of dough with a pastry or pizza wheel, then set it in a spot that will make your pastry more symmetrical. Roll over it with the rolling pin to seal the seam.

## Trick #5

Always have fresh cookies at the ready. You can freeze dough in a log so you can just cut off a few slices and return the log to the freezer, or you can scoop the dough into balls with a small ice cream scoop. Freeze the balls on a baking sheet, transfer to a resealable freezer bag, and then bake as desired. Thaw them for 10 to 15 minutes on a baking sheet before popping them into the oven.

## Trick #6

To quickly cut circles of waxed or parchment paper for lining pans, fold a large circle of paper into eighths. Place the point in the center of the pan and cut a semicircle along the perimeter of the pan. Unfold and flatten the paper—and you have a right-size circle of paper ready to go.

## Trick #9

Make a quick faux trifle. Save leftover unfrosted cake pieces. Wrap them well and freeze. When you need a quick dessert, thaw the cake and cut it into pieces. Serve it topped with fruit, Raspberry Sauce (page 60), pudding, ice cream, Sweetened Whipped Cream (page 25), or a combination of those.

## Trick #10

Make dessert croutons. Brush pastry scraps with melted butter, sprinkle with cinnamon and sugar, cut into thin strips, and bake at 375°F for 10 to 12 minutes or until brown and crisp. Use to top ice cream, custard pies, and any dessert that could use a little crunch.

# Storing Baked Goods

You don't want to go through the effort—as much fun as it might be—to bake something wonderful, just to have its freshness and flavor compromised because it wasn't properly stored. Here's how to wrap it.

1. Yeast breads Place cooled yeast breads and rolls in airtight containers or bags and store at room temperature for 2 to 3 days; they become stale more quickly if chilled.

2. Quick breads Wrap completely cooled quick breads in plastic wrap or foil and place in resealable plastic bags. Store at room temperature for up to 3 days.

3. Cakes Most cakes can be covered and stored at room temperature for up to 3 days. If you don't have a cake cover, put a large bowl over it. (Or stick a few toothpicks in the cake and cover with plastic wrap.) If the filling or frosting contains whipped cream, cream cheese, or eggs, store it, covered, in the refrigerator.

4. Cheesecakes Cover cheesecakes with plastic wrap and refrigerate for up to 3 days.

5. Cookies/bars Arrange cooled cookies in an airtight container in single layers separated by sheets of waxed paper; store at room temperature for up to 3 days. (Do not mix soft and crisp cookies in the same container because the crisp cookies will soften.) Store bars in a tightly covered container or store them in the baking pan, tightly covered with plastic wrap or foil. Any cookies with a cream cheese or yogurt frosting or filling must be stored in the refrigerator.

Pies Fruit pies may stand at room temperature for 24 hours; cover and refrigerate for longer storage. Cover custard and cream pies with plastic wrap and refrigerate for up to 2 days.

## Nice to Know

To pack and ship cookies, wrap them in plastic wrap, singly or in back-to-back pairs. Place in a foil-lined box in alternate layers with filler such as bubble wrap, foam packing pieces, or crumpled tissue paper, ending with a layer of the filler. Tape the box and mark it "perishable."

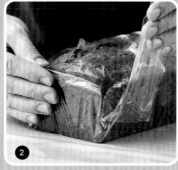

# Odds and Ends

## Stumped on an ingredient you've never heard of—or on a technique you've read about in a recipe? Here are a few terms you may need to know.

Almond paste A creamy mixture made of ground blanched almonds and sugar. For the best results, use an almond paste without syrup or liquid glucose. Almond paste is used as a filling in pastries, cakes, and candies.

Beat To make a mixture smooth by briskly whipping or stirring it with a spoon, fork, wire whisk, rotary beater, or electric mixer.

Blend To combine two or more ingredients until smooth and uniform in texture, flavor, and color; done by hand or with an electric blender or mixer.

Caramelize To heat and stir sugar until it melts and browns. Caramelized, or burnt, sugar is used in recipes such as flan, crème brûlée, and candy-coated nuts.

Crème fraîche A dairy product made from whipping cream and a bacteria culture. It has a sharp, tangy flavor similar to sour cream, but softer and milder. Look for it in the specialty dairy case at your supermarket.

Crimp To pinch or press pastry dough together using your fingers, a fork, or another utensil. A piecrust edge is often crimped.

Cut in To work a solid fat, such as butter, into dry ingredients, usually with a pastry blender.

Dash A measure equal to $1/16$ teaspoon. Can be measured by filling a $1/4$-teaspoon measure one-fourth full.

Dot To place small pieces of an ingredient (usually bits of butter) on top of a dish. Recipes for fruit pies often direct you to "dot" the filling with butter before positioning the top crust so that the butter will melt evenly over the fruit.

Extract and oil Products based on the aromatic essential oils of plant materials that are distilled by various means. In extracts, the highly concentrated oils are suspended in some kind of alcohol to make them easier to combine with other foods. Almond, anise, lemon, mint, orange, peppermint, and vanilla are among the extracts sold.

Flavoring An imitation extract made of chemical compounds. Unlike an extract or oil, a flavoring often does not contain any of the original food it resembles. Common imitation flavorings include banana, black walnut, brandy, cherry, chocolate, coconut, maple, pineapple, raspberry, rum, strawberry, and vanilla.

Flute To make a scalloped, decorative pattern or impression in food, usually a piecrust.

Glaze A thin, glossy coating on a food. There are lots of kinds of glazes. A mixture of powdered sugar and milk, for example, can be drizzled on cookies, cakes, and breads as a glaze.

Leavening Agents that make baked goods rise when mixed with liquids. The most commonly used leavenings are baking soda, baking powder, and yeast.

Mascarpone cheese A very rich cream cheese made primarily of cream, most often used in Italian desserts.

Parchment paper A grease- and heat-resistant paper used to line baking pans, to wrap foods in packets for baking, or to make disposable pastry bags.

Scald To heat a liquid, often milk, to a temperature below the boiling point; tiny bubbles begin to appear on the edge of the liquid when it reaches the proper temperature.

Sift To put one or more dry ingredients, especially flour or powdered sugar, through a sifter or sieve to remove lumps and incorporate air.

Steep To allow a dry ingredient—such as a vanilla bean—to soak in and flavor a liquid, such as cream, that is usually hot.

Vanilla bean The pod of an orchid plant that is dried and cured. During curing, the pod turns dark brown and shrivels to the size of a pencil.

Weeping When liquid separates out of a solid, such as jelly, custard, and meringue.

Zest The colored outer portion of citrus fruit such as lemons, limes, and oranges. Zest is rich in fruit oils and is often used as a seasoning.

# Baking in Thin Air

**If you live at a high altitude, it's helpful to understand how that affects the baking process—and to get familiar with common recipe adjustments.**

## General High-Altitude Issues

At altitudes higher than 3,000 feet above sea level, water boils at lower temperatures, causing moisture to evaporate more quickly than at sea level. This can cause foods to dry out during cooking and baking. Because of the lower boiling point, foods that are steamed or boiled take longer to cook. Also lower air pressure may cause baked goods that use yeast, baking powder, baking soda, egg whites, or steam to rise excessively, then fall.

## Suggestions for Baking

These estimates are based on an altitude of 3,000 feet above sea level; at higher altitudes you may need to alter these measures proportionately. Make just one change at a time and see how each affects the results. For cakes:
● Increase the baking temperature by 15°F to 25°F to help set the batter.
● For cakes leavened by air, such as angel food, beat the egg whites only to soft peaks; otherwise the batter may expand too much.
● For cakes made with shortening, you may want to try any one of the following:
● Decrease the baking powder by 1/8 teaspoon per 1 teaspoon called for;
● Decrease the sugar by up to 1 tablespoon for each 1 cup called for;
● Increase the liquid by 1 to 2 tablespoons for each 1 cup called for.
● For cakes that contain 1 cup or more of fat or chocolate, reduce the shortening by 1 to 2 tablespoons per 1 cup and add an egg to prevent the cake from falling.
● Cookies generally yield good results at high altitudes, but if not, try slightly increasing baking temperature; slightly decreasing baking powder or soda, fat, and/or sugar; and/or slightly increasing liquids and flour.

## Convection Ovens

In a convection oven air is circulated by a fan, as opposed to the static heat in a standard oven. This results in a faster, more even distribution of heat. Most recipes can be converted for convection. Follow the instructions from your oven manufacturer, keeping these things in mind:
● Always preheat completely. Position the oven racks before you turn on the oven because they will heat up quickly.
● So that hot air circulates around the food, place it in the center of the oven; leave space between pans and oven walls. Open the oven door as little as possible.
● When converting recipes for convection baking, use the temperature and time from the original recipe but check for doneness after three-quarters of the baking time has elapsed. Or reduce the original temperature by 25°F.
● Use the doneness test given in the original recipe; even when food appears golden brown, it may not be done.

● Muffins, biscuits, and muffinlike quick breads generally need little adjustment, but if they develop a bitter or alkaline flavor, decrease baking soda or powder slightly. Because cakelike quick breads are more delicate, you may need to follow adjustment guidelines for cakes.
● Yeast breads will rise more quickly at high altitudes. Allow unshaped dough to rise only until double in size, then punch it down. Repeat this rising step once more before shaping dough. Flour tends to be drier at high altitudes and sometimes absorbs more liquid. If your yeast dough seems dry, add more liquid and reduce the amount of flour next time.
● Piecrusts usually don't need adjustment, though slightly more liquid may be needed.

## For More Information

For more information on cooking at high altitudes, check out the website of the Colorado State University Department of Food Science and Human Nutrition Cooperative Extension at http://www.ext.colostate.edu/pubs/foodnut/p41.pdf

# Emergency Subs

Coming up empty-handed on an ingredient doesn't mean your baking excursion has come to a halt. Here are some substitutions for common ingredients.

| If you don't have ... | Substitute ... |
| --- | --- |
| Apple pie spice, I teaspoon | ½ teaspoon ground cinnamon plus ¼ teaspoon ground nutmeg, ⅛ ground allspice, and dash ground cloves or ginger |
| Baking powder, I teaspoon | ½ teaspoon cream of tartar plus ¼ teaspoon baking soda |
| Buttermilk, I cup | I tablespoon lemon juice or vinegar plus enough milk to make I cup (let stand for 5 minutes before using), or I cup plain yogurt |
| Chocolate, semisweet, I ounce | 3 tablespoons semisweet chocolate pieces, or I ounce unsweetened chocolate plus I tablespoon granulated sugar |
| Chocolate, sweet baking, 4 ounces | ¼ cup unsweetened cocoa powder plus ⅓ cup granulated sugar and 3 tablespoons shortening |
| Chocolate, unsweetened, I ounce | 3 tablespoons unsweetened cocoa powder plus I tablespoon cooking oil or shortening |
| Egg, I whole | 2 egg whites or 2 egg yolks, or ¼ cup refrigerated or frozen egg product, thawed |
| Ginger, grated fresh, I teaspoon | ¼ teaspoon ground ginger |
| Half-and-half or light cream, I cup | I tablespoon melted butter or margarine plus enough whole milk to make I cup |
| Pumpkin pie spice, I teaspoon | ½ teaspoon ground cinnamon plus ¼ teaspoon ground ginger, ¼ teaspoon ground allspice, and ⅛ teaspoon ground nutmeg |
| Sour cream, I cup | I cup plain yogurt |
| Yeast, active dry, I package | about 2 ¼ teaspoons active dry yeast |

## Nice to Know

If you can't come up with a substitution for an ingredient, see if a trusted friend or neighbor can spot you some of whatever you need. Just be sure to pay it back. It's a nice way to be neighborly.

# Kitchen Safety

The kitchen may be the heart of the home, but it's also a danger zone with heat, fire, sharp objects, and potentially slippery floors. Be safety smart and everyone will wind up full, whole, and happy.

### The Hottest Spot in the House

According to the National Fire Protection Association, three out of every 10 house fires start in the kitchen. Most are preventable if you observe a few commonsense rules:

● Never leave the stovetop unattended when you're frying, grilling, broiling, or boiling. If you have to walk away for even a minute, turn off the stove.

● If you're simmering or baking something over a long period of time, check on it regularly to be sure it's not boiling over or burning. Stay in the house and, if you have to, use a timer to remind you that the stove or oven is on.

● Don't wear loose clothing or dangling sleeves while cooking. That's just a wick waiting to be lit!

● Keep a fire extinguisher in the kitchen just in case you do have a grease fire. Never, ever throw water on a grease fire; it causes a violent spattering reaction and can spread the flammable grease—and the fire—everywhere.

### Nice to Know

There are two kinds of kitchen exhaust systems—updraft and downdraft. An updraft system is usually contained in a hood over the stove. It sucks hot air, grease, and smoke up and vents it out of the house. A downdraft system is usually built into the cooktop and pulls hot air, grease, and smoke down and out of the kitchen. Find out which type your kitchen has—and use it!

● Never use a kitchen towel as a pot holder; it can drag down onto the burner or touch an oven element and catch on fire—and never leave a pot holder sitting on top of a pot lid.

### Beyond Smoke and Fire

Fire isn't the only hazard in the kitchen. When you're cooking, there are always opportunities for getting burned by hot liquid or a hot utensil. To prevent burns:

● Always turn a pot handle toward the back of the stove so you don't bump into it—or so that a child doesn't grab it.

● Never leave a spoon—wooden, metal, or otherwise—sitting in a pan as it simmers. It can get hot and you can get burned when you go to grab it, or it can flip out of the pan and spatter hot soup or sauce or oatmeal everywhere.

### On Other Safety Fronts

● Always store knives in a knife block or on a magnetic wall-mounted strip—never in a kitchen drawer.

● Wipe up spills of any kind immediately. When you're moving fast and are distracted by your kitchen tasks, it's far too easy to slip and fall.

## In Case of Fire

Keep a fire extinguisher in the kitchen in case of a grease fire. You can smother a small fire with baking soda, salt, or flour, but never throw water on a grease fire—it can spread the fire elsewhere.

# oven-fresh
## COOKIES

Pour yourself a glass of milk—then take your pick of these finger-food sweets, from classic chocolate chip to fruit-filled shortbread fancy enough for a party or a homemade gift.

2

**Chocolate Chip Cookie Bars** ① ................................. 75

**Chocolate Chip Cookie Pizzas** ① ............................... 75

**Cookie-Baking Basics**.................................76–77

## CUTOUT COOKIES
Chocolate-Cherry Pockets ③ ........................... 102

Chocolate-Orange Shortbread ② ....................... 100

Gingerbread Cutouts ③ .............................. 106

Gingerbread People Cutouts ③ ......................... 106

Lemon-Poppy Seed Shortbread ② ...................... 100

Lime Zingers ② ..................................... 104

Shortbread ② ...................................... 101

Shortbread Rounds ② ............................... 101

Shortbread Strips ② ................................ 101

Spiced Shortbread ② ................................ 100

Sugar Cookie Cutouts ② ............................. 99

## DROP COOKIES
Big Chocolate Chip Cookies ① .......................... 75

Big Oatmeal Cookies ① .............................. 79

Candy Bar Cookies ① ................................ 80

Carrot Cookies ① ................................... 80

Chocolate Chip Cookies ① ............................ 75

Chocolate-Peanut Cookies ① ...........................81

Chocolate-Raisin Cookies ① ...........................81

Cinnamon-Apple Cookies ① ........................... 80

Coconut-Cherry Cookies ① ............................ 80

Cranberry-Hazelnut Cookies ① ..........................81

Everything Good Cookies ① ........................... 78

Frosted Walnut Cookies ② ............................ 83

Macadamia Nut and White Chocolate Chip Cookies ① ...... 75

Oatmeal Chippers ① ..................................81

Oatmeal Cookies ① .................................. 79

Orange-Date Cookies ① .............................. 80

Peppermint Cookies ① ................................81

Raisin-Walnut Cookies ① ............................. 80

Toffee-Pecan Cookies ① ...............................81

Ultimate Chocolate-Dipped Cookies ② .................. 82

## FILLED COOKIES
Chocolate-Cherry Pockets ③ ........................... 102

Chocolaty Caramel Thumbprints ③ ...................... 96

Cranberry-Fig Tassies ③ .............................. 98

Eggnog Nut Thumbprints ③ ........................... 94

Pecan Shortbread Logs ② .............................. 97

## FROSTINGS
Butter Frosting ① ..................................... 83

Chocolate Ganache ① ................................. 82

Lemon Frosting ① .................................... 106

Powdered Sugar Icing ① ............................... 99

## SHAPED COOKIES
Cherry-Walnut Balls ② ................................ 92

Milk Chocolate Chunk Peanut Butter Cookies ② .......... 93

Peanut Butter Blossoms ② ............................. 93

Praline Snickerdoodles ② ..............................91

Snickerdoodles ② .....................................91

## SLICED COOKIES
Almond Biscotti ② .................................... 89

Brown Sugar Icebox Cookies ② ......................... 84

Buttery Mint Slices ③ ................................. 88

Cashew-Chocolate Biscotti ② .......................... 89

Hazelnut Biscotti ② .................................. 89

Pistachio Biscotti ② .................................. 89

Sugar-and-Spice Coffee Slices ② ....................... 87

Two-Tone Peanut Butter Slices ③ ...................... 86

**Sugar Cookie Squares** ② .......................................99

**1** Skill Level

**Flavor Changes**
Change up your chips! Semisweet chocolate may be the classic candy in America's favorite cookie, but have a little fun with milk chocolate pieces, butterscotch-flavor pieces, or candy-coated semisweet chocolate pieces.

# Chocolate Chip Cookies

¾ cup butter, softened (photo 1, page 76)

¼ cup shortening

1 cup packed brown sugar

½ cup granulated sugar

¾ teaspoon baking soda

½ teaspoon salt

2 eggs

1 teaspoon vanilla

2½ cups all-purpose flour

1 12-ounce package (2 cups) semisweet chocolate pieces

1½ cups chopped walnuts, pecans, or hazelnuts (filberts), toasted if desired (optional)

**1** Preheat oven to 375°F. In a large mixing bowl beat butter and shortening with an electric mixer on medium to high speed for 30 seconds (photo 2, page 76). Add the brown sugar, granulated sugar, baking soda, and salt. Beat until combined, scraping sides of bowl occasionally (photo 3, page 76). Beat in eggs and vanilla until combined (photo 4, page 76). Beat in as much of the flour as you can with the mixer (photo 5, page 76). Using a sturdy rubber scraper or wooden spoon, stir in any remaining flour, the chocolate pieces, and, if desired, nuts (photo 6, page 76).

**2** Drop dough by rounded teaspoons 2 inches apart onto an ungreased cookie sheet (photo 1, page 79). Bake in the preheated oven for 8 to 9 minutes or until edges are light brown. Transfer to a wire rack and let cool. Makes about 60 cookies.

Per cookie: 92 cal., 5 g total fat (3 g sat. fat), 13 mg chol., 55 mg sodium, 12 g carbo., 1 g fiber, 1 g pro.

Big Chocolate Chip Cookies: Prepare as above, except use a ¼-cup measure or scoop to drop mounds of dough about 4 inches apart onto an ungreased cookie sheet (photo 2, page 79). If desired, flatten dough mounds to circles about ¾ inch thick. Bake in the preheated oven for 10 to 12 minutes or until edges are light brown. Let stand for 1 minute on cookie sheet. Transfer to a wire rack and let cool. Makes about 18 cookies.

Chocolate Chip Cookie Bars: Prepare as above, except press the dough into an ungreased 15×10×1-inch baking pan. Bake in the preheated oven for 15 to 20 minutes or until golden. Cool in pan on a wire rack. Cut into bars. Makes 48 bars.

Chocolate Chip Cookie Pizzas: Prepare as above, except do not stir chocolate pieces and nuts into the dough. Press half of the dough into an ungreased 12-inch pizza pan, leaving a ½-inch border around the edge. Sprinkle half of the chocolate pieces and nuts over the top, pressing in lightly. Repeat with a second ungreased 12-inch pizza pan and the remaining dough and toppings. Bake in the preheated oven about 15 minutes or until tops are evenly brown. Cool on a wire rack. Frost as desired. Cut each pizza into 16 wedges. Makes 32 wedges total.

Macadamia Nut and White Chocolate Chip Cookies: Prepare as above, except substitute white baking pieces for the semisweet chocolate pieces. Stir in one 3.5-ounce jar macadamia nuts, chopped, with the baking pieces.

**Ask Mom** How do I drop dough from a teaspoon? p. 65, 79 / How do I measure butter? p. 55 / How do I measure flour? p. 54 / How do I measure shortening? p. 55 / How do I measure sugar? p. 55 / How do I soften butter? p. 28, 76 / How do I store cookies? p. 68, 87 / What are chopped nuts? p. 34 / What is baking soda? p. 30, 319 / What is semisweet/bittersweet chocolate? p. 32 / What is vanilla? p. 128 / What's that nut? p. 34–35

# Cookie-Baking Basics

## Cookies are often the gateway to baking for newbies. They're so simple and satisfying to make. Success is almost assured, if you follow a few crucial pointers.

Be sure to combine the ingredients in the order specified in the recipe (most follow the method below) to ensure smooth, lump-free dough.

Then follow the instructions for using an ungreased or greased cookie sheet. Chocolate Chip Cookies (page 75), for instance, won't stick to an ungreased sheet. In fact, if you put them on a greased baking sheet, they'll spread out too much during baking. You also need to place the cookies far enough apart on the cookie sheet. If they're too close together, the hot air in the oven can't easily circulate around them and they'll bake unevenly—and run together. Let baked cookies stand on the cookie sheet for a minute to avoid squishing them before moving them to a wire rack to cool.

**1** Butter and shortening need to be room-temperature soft so they blend completely with the sugar and other ingredients. To speed up the softening of butter, cut the cold stick into pieces and break the pieces apart.

**2** Beat butter or shortening with an electric mixer until it is smooth. This ensures that the butter is adequately softened and eliminates lumps.

**3** Beat in the sugar and other dry ingredients, except flour. This process is called creaming. Creaming incorporates air into the dough, helping to ensure light cookies. Scrape the sides of the bowl as needed to get a uniform mixture.

**4** Beat in the eggs and any other liquid ingredients, such as vanilla, until uniformly combined. There should be no streaks of egg in the mixture.

**5** Beat in as much flour as you can with the electric mixer. Some hand mixers bog down if dough gets too stiff (you'll hear the motor slowing and working harder). Don't burn out the mixer.

**6** Work in any remaining flour and dry ingredients, such as nuts, chocolate pieces, or oats, with a heavy-duty scraper or a wooden spoon. Stir just until all the flour is incorporated.

## What's the best way to mix in the flour?

The easiest way to beat the butter, sugar, and eggs together for most cookie recipes is with a handheld electric mixer. However, as the flour is added and the dough gets stiffer, most models don't have enough power to get through the dough without straining the motor. You'll need to stir in the flour with a sturdy spoon if you're using a handheld mixer to combine the other ingredients. If you have a stand mixer (right), use it. Most stand mixers have the power to incorporate all of the flour—even into the stiffest doughs.

**7** Stir the flour into the cookie dough a little at a time. It keeps the flour from jumping out of the bowl and making a mess—and prevents pockets of flour in the finished cookies.

## DON'T BREAK YOUR STRIDE—OR YOUR SCRAPER.
If you don't have a really sturdy rubber or silicone scraper, the best way to stir stiff cookie dough is with a good old-fashioned wooden spoon.

# Everything Good Cookies

½ cup butter, softened
  (photo I, page 76)

½ cup shortening

I cup granulated sugar

I cup packed brown sugar

I teaspoon baking powder

I teaspoon baking soda

2 eggs

2 tablespoons milk

2 teaspoons vanilla

2 cups whole wheat flour

2 cups regular or quick-cooking rolled oats

I cup chopped toasted nuts

I cup raisins or other snipped dried fruit

¼ cup toasted wheat germ

**1** Preheat oven to 375°F. In a very large mixing bowl beat butter and shortening with an electric mixer on medium to high speed for 30 seconds (photo 2, page 76). Add the granulated sugar, brown sugar, baking powder, and baking soda. Beat until combined, scraping sides of bowl occasionally (photo 3, page 76). Beat in eggs, milk, and vanilla until combined (photo 4, page 76). Beat in as much of the flour as you can with the mixer (photo 5, page 76). Using a sturdy rubber scraper or wooden spoon, stir in any remaining flour, the oats, nuts, raisins, and wheat germ (photo 6, page 76).

**2** Drop dough by rounded teaspoons 2 inches apart onto an ungreased cookie sheet (photo 1, page 79). Bake in the preheated oven about 8 minutes or until light brown. Transfer to a wire rack and let cool. Makes about 72 cookies.

Per cookie: 83 cal., 4 g total fat (I g sat. fat), 9 mg chol., 34 mg sodium, I2 g carbo., I g fiber, I g pro.

MEASURE FIRST THEN MIX **Baking is a precise business—it matters how accurately you measure your ingredients. Be the model of baking efficiency: Have everything measured and organized before you start mixing. It'll save time and help avoid mistakes.**

**Ask Mom** How do I drop dough from a teaspoon? p. 65, 79 / How do I measure butter? p. 55 / How do I measure flour? p. 54 / How do I measure shortening? p. 55 / How do I measure sugar? p. 55 / How do I soften butter? p. 28, 76 / How do I store cookies? p. 68, 87 / How do I toast nuts? p. 34 / What are chopped nuts? p. 34 / What is baking powder? p. 30, 3I9 / What is baking soda? p. 30, 3I9 / What is vanilla? p. I28 / What's that flour? p. 3I

# Oatmeal Cookies

¾ cup butter, softened (photo I, page 76)

I cup packed brown sugar

½ cup granulated sugar

I teaspoon baking powder

¼ teaspoon baking soda

¼ teaspoon salt

½ teaspoon ground cinnamon (optional)

¼ teaspoon ground cloves (optional)

2 eggs

I teaspoon vanilla

I½ cups all-purpose flour

2 cups regular rolled oats

**1** Preheat oven to 375°F. In a large mixing bowl beat butter with an electric mixer on medium to high speed for 30 seconds (photo 2, page 76). Add the brown sugar, granulated sugar, baking powder, baking soda, salt, and, if desired, cinnamon and cloves. Beat until combined, scraping sides of bowl occasionally (photo 3, page 76). Beat in eggs and vanilla until combined (photo 4, page 76). Beat in as much of the flour as you can with the mixer (photo 5, page 76). Using a sturdy rubber scraper, stir in any remaining flour and the rolled oats (photo 6, page 76).

**2** Drop dough by rounded teaspoons 2 inches apart onto an ungreased cookie sheet (below). Bake in the preheated oven for 8 to 10 minutes or until edges are light brown. Let stand for 1 minute on cookie sheet. Transfer to a wire rack and let cool. Makes about 48 cookies.

Per cookie: 84 cal., 3 g total fat (2 g sat. fat), I6 mg chol., 49 mg sodium, I2 g carbo., I g fiber, I g pro.

Big Oatmeal Cookies: Prepare as above, except use a ¼-cup measure to drop dough 4 inches apart onto cookie sheet (below). Press into 3-inch circles. Bake for 8 to 10 minutes or until edges are golden. Let stand for 1 minute on cookie sheet. Makes about 10 cookies.

**Flavor Changes** Crisp and chewy as it is, this is one flexible cookie. Turn the page for great stir-in ideas that transform this homey cookie a dozen different ways.

**1** Using a flatware teaspoon, "drop," or push, a scoop of dough onto cookie sheet with a second spoon.

**2** For big cookies, scoop dough into a ¼-cup measure, then transfer to cookie sheet. Press dough mounds into 3-inch circles before baking.

**Ask Mom** Can I use quick-cooking oats instead of regular rolled oats? p. 35I / How do I drop dough from a teaspoon? p. 65, 79 / How do I measure butter? p. 55 / How do I measure flour? p. 54 / How do I measure sugar? p. 55 / How do I soften butter? p. 28, 76 / How do I store cookies? p. 68, 87 / What are cloves? p. 36 / What is baking powder? p. 30, 3I9 / What is

## Candy Bar Cookies

1 ½ cups miniature candy-coated chocolate pieces

Prepare Oatmeal Cookies (page 79) as directed, except after stirring in oats, stir in candy-coated chocolate pieces.

## Carrot Cookies

1 ½ cups shredded carrot

Prepare Oatmeal Cookies (page 79) as directed, except after stirring in oats, stir in carrot.

## Raisin-Walnut Cookies

1 cup raisins
½ cup chopped walnuts

Prepare Oatmeal Cookies (page 79) as directed, except after stirring in oats, stir in the raisins and walnuts.

## Cinnamon-Apple Cookies

¾ cup chopped dried apple
¾ cup cinnamon-flavor pieces

Prepare Oatmeal Cookies (page 79) as directed, except after stirring in oats, stir in apple and cinnamon-flavor pieces.

## Coconut-Cherry Cookies

¾ cup snipped dried cherries
¾ cup flaked coconut

Prepare Oatmeal Cookies (page 79) as directed, except after stirring in oats, stir in dried cherries and coconut.

## Orange-Date Cookies

1 ½ teaspoons finely shredded orange peel
1 ½ cups chopped dates

Prepare Oatmeal Cookies (page 79) as directed, except beat in orange peel with the butter and after stirring in oats, stir in dates.

## Toffee-Pecan Cookies

¾ cup shredded carrot
½ cup chopped pecans or almonds, toasted

Prepare Oatmeal Cookies (page 79) as directed, except after stirring in oats, stir in the toffee pieces and pecans.

## Cranberry-Hazelnut Cookies

1 cup dried cranberries
½ cup chopped hazelnuts, toasted

Prepare Oatmeal Cookies (page 79) as directed, except after stirring in oats, stir in the cranberries and hazelnuts.

## Chocolate-Raisin Cookies

1 ½ cups chocolate-covered raisins

Prepare Oatmeal Cookies (page 79) as directed, except after stirring in oats, stir in chocolate-covered raisins.

## Peppermint Cookies

1 cup white baking pieces
½ cup finely crushed hard peppermint candies

Prepare Oatmeal Cookies (page 79) as directed, except after stirring in oats, stir in white baking pieces and peppermint candies. Line cookie sheet with parchment paper or foil before dropping dough as directed. Let cookies stand for 2 minutes on cookie sheet before transferring to wire rack to cool.

## Oatmeal Chippers

1 ½ cups semisweet chocolate, butterscotch-flavor, or peanut-butter flavor pieces

Prepare Oatmeal Cookies (page 79) as directed, except after stirring in oats, stir in desired-flavor baking pieces.

## Chocolate-Peanut Cookies

1 cup semisweet chocolate pieces
½ cup dry-roasted peanuts

Prepare Oatmeal Cookies (page 79) as directed, except after stirring in oats, stir in chocolate pieces and peanuts.

# Ultimate Chocolate-
## Dipped Cookies

1½ cups all-purpose flour

½ cup unsweetened cocoa powder

1 teaspoon baking powder

1 teaspoon salt

1 12-ounce package (2 cups) semisweet or bittersweet chocolate pieces

¾ cup butter, softened (photo 1, page 76)

1½ cups packed brown sugar

3 eggs

1 teaspoon vanilla

1 cup white baking pieces or semisweet chocolate pieces

1 recipe Chocolate Ganache

**1** Preheat oven to 350°F. In a medium bowl stir together the flour, cocoa powder, baking powder, and salt. Set aside. In a medium heavy saucepan combine the 2 cups chocolate pieces and 2 tablespoons of the butter. Heat and stir over low heat until smooth. Set aside to cool slightly.

**2** In a large mixing bowl beat remaining butter with an electric mixer on medium to high speed for 30 seconds (photo 2, page 76). Add the brown sugar. Beat until combined, scraping sides of bowl occasionally (photo 3, page 76). Beat in eggs, one at a time, scraping sides of bowl after each addition. Beat in melted chocolate mixture and the vanilla (below). Add the flour mixture; beat on low speed until combined. Stir in the white baking pieces (below). Drop dough by rounded teaspoons 2 inches apart onto an ungreased cookie sheet (photo 1, page 79).

**3** Bake in the preheated oven for 8 to 10 minutes or until edges are firm. Transfer to a wire rack and let cool. Dip cookies into Chocolate Ganache (below). Makes about 72 cookies.

**Chocolate Ganache:** Place 1 cup semisweet chocolate pieces in a medium bowl; set aside. In a small heavy saucepan combine ½ cup whipping cream, 1 tablespoon butter, and 1 tablespoon granulated sugar. Bring just to boiling, stirring to dissolve sugar. Pour hot cream mixture over chocolate; let stand for 5 minutes. Stir until smooth. Let cool to room temperature before using.

Per cookie: 102 cal., 6 g total fat (3 g sat. fat), 17 mg chol., 57 mg sodium, 13 g carbo., 1 g fiber, 1 g pro.

**1** Spoon the melted chocolate mixture into the beaten egg mixture.

**2** Beat the melted chocolate mixture into the egg mixture until there are no streaks of either mixture.

**3** After the flour is beaten in, use a sturdy scraper or wooden spoon to stir in the white baking pieces.

**4** Dip cooled cookies one-third to halfway into ganache. Place dipped cookies on a wire rack until ganache is set.

**Ask Mom** How do I drop dough from a teaspoon? p. 65, 79 / How do I measure butter? p. 55 / How do I measure flour? p. 54 / How do I measure sugar? p. 55 / How do I soften butter? p. 28, 76 / How do I store cookies? p. 68, 87 / What is baking powder? p. 30, 319 / What is cocoa powder? p. 170 / What is semisweet/bittersweet chocolate? p. 32 / What is vanilla? p. 128 / What is white

# Frosted Walnut Cookies

½ cup shortening
1½ cups packed brown sugar
1 teaspoon baking soda
½ teaspoon baking powder
½ teaspoon salt
2 eggs
1 teaspoon vanilla
2½ cups all-purpose flour
1 8-ounce carton dairy sour cream
⅔ cup chopped walnuts
1 recipe Butter Frosting
Chopped walnuts or walnut halves (optional)

**1** Preheat oven to 375°F. Grease a cookie sheet; set aside.

**2** In a large mixing bowl beat shortening with an electric mixer on medium to high speed for 30 seconds (photo 2, page 76). Add brown sugar, baking soda, baking powder, and salt. Beat until well mixed, scraping sides of bowl occasionally. Beat in eggs and vanilla until combined. (photo 4, page 76). Add flour and sour cream alternately to sugar mixture, beating until combined after each addition. Stir in the ⅔ cup nuts.

**3** Drop dough by rounded teaspoons 2 inches apart onto the prepared cookie sheet (photo 1, page 79). Bake in the preheated oven for 10 to 12 minutes or until edges are light brown. Transfer to a wire rack and let cool.

**4** Spread Butter Frosting on cooled cookies. If desired, top with additional chopped walnuts. Makes about 60 cookies.

Butter Frosting: In a medium mixing bowl beat ⅓ cup butter, softened, with 2 cups powdered sugar. Beat in ¼ cup milk and 1½ teaspoons vanilla until smooth. Gradually beat in 2 cups additional powdered sugar. If necessary, beat in additional milk to make spreading consistency.

Per cookie: 115 cal., 5 g total fat (2 g sat. fat), 12 mg chol., 57 mg sodium, 18 g carbo., 0 g fiber, 1 g pro.

**Which Walnut?** There are two kinds of walnuts: English walnuts and black walnuts. English walnuts are more common and probably more familiar to you. Black walnuts have a strong, almost smoky flavor. If you like them, you'll love them in these cookies.

**Ask Mom** How do I drop dough? p. 65, 79 / How do I grease a baking pan? p. 59 / How do I measure butter? p. 55 / How do I measure flour? p. 54 / How do I measure shortening? p. 55 / How do I measure sugar? p. 55 / How do I soften butter? p. 28, 76 / How do I store cookies? p. 68, 87 / What are chopped nuts? p. 34 / What is baking powder? p. 30, 319 / What is baking soda? p. 30, 319 / What is powdered sugar? p. 29 / What is vanilla? p. 128 / What's that flour? p. 31 / What's that nut? p. 34–35

# Brown Sugar Icebox Cookies

½ cup shortening

½ cup butter, softened
(photo I, page 76)

1¼ cups packed brown sugar

½ teaspoon baking soda

¼ teaspoon salt

I egg

I teaspoon vanilla

2½ cups all-purpose flour

¾ cup ground toasted hazelnuts (filberts) or pecans

⅔ cup finely chopped toasted hazelnuts (filberts) or pecans (optional)

I to I½ cups semisweet or milk chocolate pieces (optional)

I tablespoon shortening (optional)

**1** In a large mixing bowl beat the ½ cup shortening and the butter with an electric mixer on medium to high speed for 30 seconds (photo 2, page 76). Add the brown sugar, baking soda, and salt. Beat until combined, scraping sides of bowl occasionally (photo 3, page 76). Beat in egg and vanilla until combined (photo 4, page 76). Beat in as much of the flour as you can with the mixer (photo 5, page 76). Using a sturdy rubber scraper or wooden spoon, stir in any remaining flour and the ¾ cup ground nuts (photo 6, page 76). Divide dough in half.

**2** On waxed paper, shape each portion of dough into a 10-inch-long log. Lift and smooth the waxed paper to help shape the logs (below). If desired, roll logs in the ⅔ cup finely chopped nuts (below). Wrap each log in plastic wrap. Chill about 4 hours or until firm enough to slice.

**3** Preheat oven to 375°F. Cut logs into ¼-inch-thick slices (below). Place slices 1 inch apart on an ungreased cookie sheet. Bake in the preheated oven for 10 to 12 minutes or until edges are firm. Transfer to a wire rack and let cool.

**4** If desired, in a small heavy saucepan combine chocolate pieces and the 1 tablespoon shortening. Heat and stir over low heat until smooth. Cool slightly. Transfer chocolate mixture to a small resealable plastic bag; seal bag. Snip off a tiny piece of one corner of the bag. Drizzle melted chocolate over cookies. Let stand until set. Makes about 72 cookies.

Per cookie: 65 cal., 4 g total fat (I g sat. fat), 7 mg chol., 33 mg sodium, 7 g carbo., 0 g fiber, I g pro.

**1** Place dough on a sheet of waxed paper. Use the waxed paper to lift and shape dough into a log.

**2** Spread chopped nuts on waxed paper and roll log in nuts to coat. Gently press nuts into dough as you roll.

**3** Place wrapped rolls in tall glasses and lay them on their sides in the refrigerator. This helps keep their shape.

**4** Using a sharp knife, cut rolls into slices. Rotate rolls while cutting them to prevent flattening one side.

**Ask Mom** How do I measure butter? p. 55 / How do I measure flour? p. 54 / How do I measure shortening? p. 55 / How do I measure sugar? p. 55 / How do I soften butter? p. 28, 76 / How do I store cookies? p. 68, 87 / How do I toast nuts? p. 34 / What are chopped nuts? p. 34 / What does drizzle mean? p. 69, 85 / What is baking powder? p. 30, 319 / What is baking soda? p. 30, 319 / What is semisweet/bittersweet chocolate? p. 32 / What is vanilla? p. 128 / What's that flour? p. 31 / What's that nut? p. 34–35

**MINIMIZE MESS.** Make cleanup a breeze by placing the cookies on a wire rack over a sheet of waxed paper or parchment paper to catch inevitable drips of melted chocolate. (The same trick works for icing too.) Then just wad it up and toss it.

Make sure you use a heavy plastic bag for drizzling the warm chocolate mixture. Lightweight sandwich bags may be weakened by the heat and break at the seams.

# Two-Tone Peanut Butter Slices

¾ cup creamy peanut butter
½ cup butter, softened
   (photo I, page 76)
½ cup granulated sugar
½ cup packed brown sugar
½ teaspoon baking powder

½ teaspoon baking soda
I egg
I teaspoon vanilla
1½ cups all-purpose flour
1½ ounces unsweetened chocolate, melted and slightly cooled

**1** In a large mixing bowl beat peanut butter and butter with an electric mixer on medium to high speed for 30 seconds (photo 2, page 76). Add the granulated sugar, brown sugar, baking powder, and baking soda. Beat until combined, scraping sides of bowl occasionally (photo 3, page 76). Beat in egg and vanilla until combined (photo 4, page 76). Beat in as much of the flour as you can with the mixer (photo 5, page 76). Using a sturdy rubber scraper or wooden spoon, stir in any remaining flour (photo 6, page 76).

**2** Divide dough in half. Stir melted chocolate into one portion of dough (below). Divide each dough portion in half. On a lightly floured surface, roll each portion of dough into a 10-inch-long log. Wrap logs in plastic wrap; chill for 1 to 2 hours or until firm.

**3** Cut logs in half lengthwise (below). Place the cut side of one peanut butter log and the cut side of one chocolate log together; press to seal (below). Roll the log lightly to smooth seams. Repeat with remaining log halves. Wrap and chill logs for 1 to 2 hours or until firm.

**4** Preheat oven to 375°F. Cut two-tone logs into ¼-inch-thick slices (photo 4, page 84). Place slices 1 inch apart on an ungreased cookie sheet. Bake in the preheated oven about 8 minutes or until edges are light brown and slightly firm. Transfer to a wire rack and let cool. Makes about 120 cookies.

Per cookie: 3I cal., 2 g total fat (I g sat. fat), 4 mg chol., 2I mg sodium, 3 g carbo., 0 g fiber, I g pro.

**1** Place half of the dough in a bowl and add the melted chocolate. Stir until dough is a uniform color.

**2** Using a long sharp knife, cut dough logs in half the long way. You should have eight log halves.

**3** Place the cut sides of a peanut butter log and a chocolate log together. Press edges to seal and roll to smooth out the logs.

**Ask Mom** How do I measure butter? p. 55 / How do I measure flour? p. 54 / How do I measure peanut butter? p. 55 / How do I measure sugar? p. 55 / How do I soften butter? p. 28, 76 / How do I store cookies? p. 68, 87 / What is baking powder? p. 30, 3I9 / What is baking soda? p. 30, 3I9 / What is unsweetened chocolate? p. 32 / What is vanilla? p. 128 / What's that flour? p. 3I

# Sugar-and-Spice Coffee Slices

½ cup butter, softened
  (photo I, page 76)
¼ cup shortening
I cup granulated sugar
½ cup packed brown sugar
I teaspoon baking powder
I teaspoon ground cinnamon

¼ teaspoon salt
2 tablespoons instant espresso powder
I tablespoon hot water
I egg
2 cups all-purpose flour
I recipe Coffee Topping
  Coffee beans (optional)

**1** In a large mixing bowl beat butter and shortening with an electric mixer on medium to high speed for 30 seconds (photo 2, page 76). Add granulated sugar, brown sugar, baking powder, cinnamon, and salt. Beat until combined, scraping sides of bowl occasionally (photo 3, page 76). In a small bowl stir together the espresso powder and hot water until dissolved. Add to sugar mixture along with the egg; beat until combined (photo 4, page 76). Beat in as much of the flour as you can with the mixer (photo 5, page 76). Using a sturdy rubber scraper or wooden spoon, stir in any remaining flour (photo 6, page 76).

**2** Divide dough into thirds. Shape each portion into a 7×2×1-inch loaf. Wrap each loaf in plastic wrap; chill dough about 2 hours or until firm.*

**3** Preheat oven to 375°F. Cut loaves into ⅜-inch-thick slices. Place slices about 2 inches apart on an ungreased cookie sheet. Sprinkle slices with Coffee Topping. If desired, gently press a few coffee beans onto each slice.

**4** Bake in the preheated oven for 9 to 10 minutes or until edges are light brown. Let stand for 1 minute on cookie sheet. Transfer to a wire rack and let cool. Makes about 48 cookies.

**Coffee Topping:** In a small bowl stir together ¼ cup granulated sugar and 1 teaspoon instant espresso powder.

***Note:** You can refrigerate loaves for up to 3 days or freeze them for up to 1 week before baking.

Per cookie: 77 cal., 3 g total fat (2 g sat. fat), 9 mg chol., 37 mg sodium, 12 g carbo., 0 g fiber, 0 g pro.

HOW DO I STORE COOKIES? For most cookies, layer cooled cookies between sheets of waxed paper in an airtight container. They'll stay fresh at room temperature for 3 days. Or freeze them for up to 3 months.

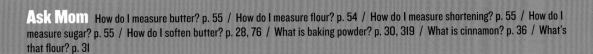

**Ask Mom** How do I measure butter? p. 55 / How do I measure flour? p. 54 / How do I measure shortening? p. 55 / How do I measure sugar? p. 55 / How do I soften butter? p. 28, 76 / What is baking powder? p. 30, 319 / What is cinnamon? p. 36 / What's that flour? p. 31

# Buttery Mint Slices

½ cup butter, softened
  (photo I, page 76)

⅔ cup sugar

I teaspoon baking powder

½ teaspoon salt

I egg

I tablespoon milk

I teaspoon vanilla

2 cups all-purpose flour

⅓ cup green mint or chocolate-mint baking
  pieces, melted and slightly cooled

⅓ cup white baking pieces,
  melted and slightly cooled

**1** In a large mixing bowl beat butter with an electric mixer on medium to high speed for 30 seconds (photo 2, page 76). Add the sugar, baking powder, and salt. Beat until combined, scraping sides of bowl occasionally (photo 3, page 76). Beat in egg, milk, and vanilla until combined (photo 4, page 76). Beat in as much of the flour as you can with the mixer (photo 5, page 76). Using a sturdy rubber scraper or wooden spoon, stir in any remaining flour (photo 6, page 76).

**2** Divide dough in half. Stir melted mint baking pieces into half of the dough (below). Divide mint dough into thirds. Stir melted white baking pieces into remaining dough. Divide white dough in half.

**3** Line an 8×4×2-inch loaf pan with plastic wrap. Press one portion of the mint dough into pan (below). Press half of the white dough on top of mint layer. Repeat the layers, finishing with mint dough on top. Cover with plastic wrap. Chill for at least 2 hours or until firm.

**4** Preheat oven to 350°F. Remove dough brick from pan and unwrap; place on cutting board. Cut brick crosswise into ¼-inch-thick slices. Cut each slice in half crosswise (below). Place slices 2 inches apart on an ungreased cookie sheet.

**5** Bake in the preheated oven about 10 minutes or until edges are set. Transfer to a wire rack and let cool. Makes about 72 cookies.

Per cookie: 4I cal., 2 g total fat (I g sat. fat), 6 mg chol., 3I mg sodium, 5 g carbo., 0 g fiber, 0 g pro.

**1** Place half the dough in a bowl. Add melted mint pieces; stir until well mixed.

**2** Alternately, you could knead the melted mint pieces into the dough.

**3** Use waxed paper to press the two doughs in even layers in the lined loaf pan.

**4** Using a sharp knife, cut dough brick into thin slices. Cut slices in half crosswise.

**Ask Mom** How do I measure butter? p. 55 / How do I measure flour? p. 54 / How do I measure sugar? p. 55 / How do I melt chocolate? p. 32, 33 / How do I soften butter? p. 28, 76 / What is baking powder? p. 30, 3I9 / What is vanilla? p. I28 / What's that flour? p. 3I

# Pistachio Biscotti

2¾ cups all-purpose flour
1½ cups sugar
1½ teaspoons baking powder
1 teaspoon salt
2 eggs

2 egg yolks
6 tablespoons butter, melted
1½ teaspoons finely shredded lemon peel (optional)
1 cup coarsely chopped pistachio nuts

**1** Preheat oven to 325°F. Lightly grease one large or two smaller cookie sheets; set aside. In a large bowl stir together the flour, sugar, baking powder, and salt. Make a well in the center of the flour mixture. Place eggs and yolks in the well; stir into the flour mixture. Add butter and, if desired, lemon peel. Stir until dough starts to form a ball. Stir in pistachios.

**2** Turn the dough out onto a lightly floured surface; divide dough into thirds. Shape each portion into a 14-inch-long log. Place logs about 3 inches apart on the prepared cookie sheet(s); flatten logs slightly until about 1½ inches wide (below).

**3** Bake in the preheated oven for 25 to 30 minutes or until firm and light brown. Remove from oven and place cookie sheet(s) on a wire rack; let cool for 15 minutes.

**4** Transfer logs to a cutting board. Using a serrated knife, cut logs diagonally into ½-inch-thick slices (below). Place slices, cut sides down, on cookie sheets. Bake in the preheated oven for 10 minutes. Turn cookies over (below); bake for 10 to 15 minutes more or until crisp and golden brown. Transfer to a wire rack and let cool. Makes about 84 cookies.

**Almond or Hazelnut Biscotti:** Prepare as above, except substitute orange peel for the lemon peel and chopped almonds or hazelnuts (filberts) for the pistachios.

**Cashew-Chocolate Biscotti:** Prepare as above, except omit the peel and substitute ½ cup chopped cashews and ½ cup finely chopped bittersweet chocolate for the pistachios.

Per cookie: 47 cal., 2 g total fat (1 g sat. fat), 12 mg chol., 40 mg sodium, 7 g carbo., 0 g fiber, 1 g pro.

**1** Place logs on a lightly greased baking sheet. Flatten them with your hands until about 1½ inches wide.

**2** Using a serrated knife, cut baked logs at an angle into slices.

**3** Using a spatula, turn biscotti over halfway through the second baking period.

**Ask Mom** How do I measure butter? p. 55 / How do I measure flour? p. 54 / How do I measure sugar? p. 55 / How do I shred lemon/lime/orange peel? p. 45, 105 / How do I work with eggs? p. 26–27 / What are chopped nuts? p. 34 / What is a serrated knife? p. 14 / What is baking powder? p. 30, 319 / What is semisweet/bittersweet chocolate? p. 32 / What's that flour? p. 31 / What's that nut? p. 34–35

**WHAT ARE TOFFEE PIECES?** Toffee is a caramelly, crunchy candy made by boiling sugar or molasses, butter, and milk. It's sold in bits for baking, usually alongside chocolate chips. Stir it into cookies, sprinkle it on a cake, or use it as an ice cream topping.

These Praline Snickerdoodles are a variation on the classic cinnamon-sugar-coated recipe. They simply have toffee bits and chopped pecans added to the dough.

# Snickerdoodles

| | |
|---|---|
| 3 cups all-purpose flour | 1½ cups sugar |
| 1 teaspoon cream of tartar | 2 eggs |
| 1 teaspoon baking soda | 1 teaspoon vanilla |
| ¼ teaspoon salt | ¼ cup sugar |
| 1 cup butter, softened (photo 1, page 76) | 2 teaspoons ground cinnamon |

**1** In a medium bowl stir together the flour, cream of tartar, baking soda, and salt. Set aside. In a large mixing bowl beat butter with an electric mixer on medium to high speed for 30 seconds (photo 2, page 76). Add the 1½ cups sugar. Beat until combined, scraping sides of bowl occasionally (photo 3, page 76). Beat in eggs and vanilla until combined (photo 4, page 76). Beat in as much of the flour mixture as you can with the mixer (photo 5, page 76). Using a sturdy rubber scraper or wooden spoon, stir in any remaining flour mixture (photo 6, page 76). Cover and chill dough about 1 hour or until easy to handle.

**2** Preheat oven to 375°F. In a small bowl stir together the ¼ cup sugar and the cinnamon. Shape dough into 1½-inch balls (photos 1–3, page 92). Roll balls in sugar-cinnamon mixture. Place balls 2 inches apart on an ungreased cookie sheet.

**3** Bake in the preheated oven for 10 to 12 minutes or until edges are golden brown. Transfer to a wire rack and let cool. Makes about 48 cookies.

**Per cookie:** 94 cal., 4 g total fat (3 g sat. fat), 19 mg chol., 69 mg sodium, 13 g carbo., 0 g fiber, 0 g pro.

**Praline Snickerdoodles:** Prepare as above, except stir in 1 cup toffee pieces and ½ cup chopped pecans after the flour mixture.

**Good to Know** When you make the effort to bake homemade cookies, you want them to stay as fresh as possible for as long as possible. For short-term storage, arrange cookies in an airtight container in single layers separated by sheets of waxed paper. Store at room temperature for up to 3 days. (If they're frosted with cream cheese frosting, you'll need to refrigerate them.) For long-term storage, let them cool, then package in freezer bags or containers and freeze for up to 3 months. Before serving, thaw them in the container about 15 minutes.

**②** Skill Level

**Good to Know** Be sure to drain the cherries really well and dab them almost dry with a paper towel. If a lot of cherry liquid gets into the dough, the cookies will be too soft in texture—and probably some shade of pink. That's good for cotton candy, maybe, but not for these cookies.

# Cherry-Walnut Balls

¼ cup coarsely chopped maraschino cherries

I cup butter, softened (photo I, page 76)

½ cup powdered sugar

½ teaspoon almond extract

½ teaspoon vanilla

2 cups all-purpose flour

¾ cup chopped walnuts, toasted

Powdered sugar

**1** Preheat oven to 325°F. Drain maraschino cherries on paper towels; pat dry to remove any excess liquid. Set cherries aside.

**2** In a large mixing bowl beat butter with an electric mixer on medium to high speed for 30 seconds (photo 2, page 76). Add the ½ cup powdered sugar, the almond extract, and vanilla. Beat until combined, scraping sides of bowl occasionally (photo 3, page 76). Beat in as much of the flour as you can with the mixer (photo 5, page 76). Using a wooden spoon, stir in any remaining flour, the nuts, and cherries (photo 6, page 76). Shape dough into 1-inch balls (below). Place balls 2 inches apart on an ungreased cookie sheet.

**3** Bake in the preheated oven for 18 to 20 minutes or until bottoms are light brown. Let stand for 5 minutes on cookie sheet. Roll warm cookies in powdered sugar to coat. Transfer to a wire rack and let cool. If desired, roll cooled cookies in additional powdered sugar before serving. Makes about 48 cookies.

Per cookie: 74 cal., 5 g total fat (3 g sat. fat), 10 mg chol., 27 mg sodium, 6 g carbo., 0 g fiber, 0 g pro.

**①** To make even-size balls, pat the dough into an 8×6-inch rectangle on a sheet of waxed paper.

**②** Using a sharp knife, cut the rectangle lengthwise and crosswise at I-inch intervals to make 48 pieces.

**③** Roll the pieces of dough into equal-size balls with your hands.

**④** While the cookies are still warm, roll them in powdered sugar to coat.

**Ask Mom** How do I measure butter? p. 55 / How do I measure flour? p. 54 / How do I soften butter? p. 28, 76 / What are chopped nuts? p. 34 / What is a maraschino cherry? p. 185 / What is powdered sugar? p. 29 / What is vanilla? p. 128 / What's that flour? p. 31 / What's that nut? p. 34–35

# Peanut Butter Blossoms

½ cup shortening
½ cup peanut butter
½ cup granulated sugar
½ cup packed brown sugar
1 teaspoon baking powder
⅛ teaspoon baking soda
1 egg
2 tablespoons milk
1 teaspoon vanilla
1¾ cups all-purpose flour
¼ cup granulated sugar
   Milk chocolate kisses or stars, unwrapped

**1** Preheat oven to 350°F. In a large mixing bowl beat shortening and peanut butter with an electric mixer on medium to high speed for 30 seconds (photo 2, page 76). Add the ½ cup granulated sugar, the brown sugar, baking powder, and baking soda. Beat until combined, scraping sides of bowl occasionally (photo 3, page 76). Beat in egg, milk, and vanilla until combined (photo 4, page 76). Beat in as much of the flour as you can with the mixer (photo 5, page 76). Using a sturdy rubber scraper or wooden spoon, stir in any remaining flour (photo 6, page 76).

**2** Shape dough into 1-inch balls (photos 1–3, page 92). Roll balls in the ¼ cup granulated sugar. Place balls 2 inches apart on an ungreased cookie sheet.

**3** Bake in the preheated oven for 10 to 12 minutes or until edges are firm and bottoms are light brown. Immediately press a chocolate kiss into the center of each cookie. Transfer to a wire rack and let cool. Makes about 60 cookies.

**Per cookie:** 91 cal., 5 g total fat (2 g sat. fat), 5 mg chol., 25 mg sodium, 11 g carbo., 0 g fiber, 1 g pro.

Milk Chocolate Chunk Peanut Butter Cookies: Prepare as above, except stir 1½ cups chopped milk chocolate (about 8 ounces) in with the flour. Shape and bake as directed. Omit milk chocolate kisses or stars.

WANT A QUICK KISS? Unless you have lots of time on your hands (or a very patient assistant), unwrapping 60 chocolate kisses—the number needed for this recipe—is a little bit fussy. Look for "unwrapped" kisses in the baking aisle.

**Ask Mom** How do I chop chocolate? p. 33 / How do I measure flour? p. 54 / How do I measure peanut butter? p. 55 / How do I measure shortening? p. 55 / How do I measure sugar? p. 55 / What is baking powder? p. 30, 319 / What is baking soda? p. 30, 319 / What is vanilla? p. 128 / What's that flour? p. 31

# Eggnog Nut Thumbprints

¾ cup butter, softened
  (photo 1, page 76)
½ cup sugar
⅛ teaspoon ground nutmeg
 2 egg yolks
 1 teaspoon vanilla

1½ cups all-purpose flour
 2 egg whites, lightly beaten
1½ cups finely chopped walnuts
 1 recipe Rum Filling
   Grated fresh nutmeg or ground nutmeg (optional)

**1** In a large mixing bowl beat butter with an electric mixer on medium to high speed for 30 seconds (photo 2, page 76). Add the sugar and the ⅛ teaspoon nutmeg. Beat until combined, scraping sides of bowl occasionally (photo 3, page 76). Beat in egg yolks and vanilla until combined (photo 4, page 76). Beat in as much of the flour as you can with the mixer (photo 5, page 76). Using a sturdy rubber scraper or wooden spoon, stir in any remaining flour (photo 6, page 76). If necessary, cover and chill dough about 1 hour or until easy to handle.

**2** Preheat oven to 375°F. Grease a cookie sheet; set aside. Shape dough into 1-inch balls (photos 1–3, page 92). Dip balls in beaten egg whites, then roll in chopped walnuts to coat (below). Place balls about 1 inch apart on the prepared cookie sheet. Press thumb into the center of each ball (below).

**3** Bake in the preheated oven for 12 to 15 minutes or until edges are light brown. Transfer to a wire rack and let cool. Just before serving, pipe about ½ teaspoon Rum Filling into the center of each cookie (below). If desired, sprinkle with additional nutmeg. Makes about 40 cookies.

Rum Filling: In a medium mixing bowl beat ¼ cup butter, softened, with an electric mixer on medium to high speed for 30 seconds. Add 1 cup powdered sugar. Beat until fluffy, scraping sides of bowl occasionally. Beat in 1 teaspoon rum or ¼ teaspoon rum extract and enough milk (1 to 2 teaspoons) to make filling of spreading consistency.

Per cookie: 96 cal., 6 g total fat (3 g sat. fat), 22 mg chol., 46 mg sodium, 9 g carbo., 0 g fiber, 1 g pro.

**1** Dip dough balls in egg whites to coat. Use a fork to remove balls from the whites, letting any excess drip off.

**2** Transfer coated balls to a bowl with the chopped nuts. Roll to coat with nuts and place on the baking sheet.

**3** Using your thumb, press an indentation in the centers of the dough balls.

**4** Spoon Rum Filling into a resealable bag. Snip off one corner of the bag; squeeze filling into cooled cookies.

**Ask Mom** How do I grease a baking pan/dish? p. 59 / How do I measure butter? p. 55 / How do I measure flour? p. 54 / How do I measure sugar? p. 55 / How do I soften butter? p. 28, 76 / How do I work with eggs? p. 26–27 / What are chopped nuts? p. 34 / What is nutmeg? p. 37 / What is powdered sugar? p. 29 / What is vanilla? p. 128 / What's that flour? p. 31 / What's that nut? p. 34–35

**HOW DO I GET THE FILLING IN THE COOKIES?** You can spoon it in, but the tidiest way to do it is by piping it in. You can use a small resealable plastic bag with the corner snipped off—or a disposable decorating bag meant for tips, with the pointed end snipped off.

Originally for woodworking, rasps have come onto the kitchen scene for all kinds of grating jobs—cheeses, citrus zest, and hard spices. This narrow spice grater makes quick work of whole nutmeg.

**Ingredient Info** Nutmeg is sold both ground and whole. Ground nutmeg is certainly convenient—it can simply be measured and used, but its flavor quickly fades in storage. And as with other spices, there really is nothing quite like the flavor and aroma of freshly grated nutmeg. Keep whole nutmeg in a cool, dry place and it will last almost indefinitely. You'll just need to make a small investment in a rasp grater like the one shown here. If you don't want to do that, you can certainly use ground nutmeg. Just buy it in small quantities and replace it after 6 months to a year.

# Chocolaty Caramel Thumbprints

| | |
|---|---|
| 1 egg | 2 tablespoons milk |
| 1 cup all-purpose flour | 1 teaspoon vanilla |
| ⅓ cup unsweetened cocoa powder | 16 vanilla caramels, unwrapped |
| ¼ teaspoon salt | 3 tablespoons whipping cream |
| ½ cup butter, softened (photo 1, page 76) | 1¼ cups finely chopped pecans |
| ⅔ cup sugar | ½ cup (3 ounces) semisweet chocolate pieces |
| | 1 teaspoon shortening |

**1** Separate egg; place yolk and white in separate bowls. Cover and chill egg white until needed. In a medium bowl stir together the flour, cocoa powder, and salt. Set aside. In a large mixing bowl beat butter with an electric mixer on medium to high speed for 30 seconds (photo 2, page 76). Add the sugar. Beat until combined, scraping sides of bowl occasionally (photo 3, page 76). Beat in egg yolk, milk, and vanilla until combined (photo 4, page 76). Beat in as much of the flour mixture as you can with the mixer (photo 5, page 76). Using a sturdy rubber scraper or wooden spoon, stir in any remaining flour mixture (photo 6, page 76). Wrap dough in plastic wrap; chill about 1 hour or until easy to handle.

**2** Preheat oven to 350°F. Grease a cookie sheet; set aside. In a small heavy saucepan heat and stir caramels and cream over low heat until smooth; set aside. Lightly beat reserved egg white. Shape dough into 1-inch balls (photos 1–3, page 92). Dip balls in beaten egg white, then roll in chopped pecans to coat (photos 1–2, page 94). Place balls about 1 inch apart on the prepared cookie sheet. Press thumb into the center of each ball.

**3** Bake in the preheated oven about 10 minutes or until edges are firm. Remove from oven. If cookie centers puff during baking, re-press with the bowl of a spoon. Spoon about ½ teaspoon melted caramel mixture into the center of each cookie. (If necessary, reheat caramel mixture to keep it spoonable.) Transfer to a wire rack set over waxed paper and let cool.

**4** In another small heavy saucepan heat and stir chocolate pieces and shortening over low heat until smooth. Let cool slightly. Drizzle melted chocolate over cookies. Let stand until set. Makes about 36 cookies.

Per cookie: 114 cal., 7 g total fat (3 g sat. fat), 15 mg chol., 49 mg sodium, 12 g carbo., 1 g fiber, 1 g pro.

**Ask Mom** How do I grease a baking pan? p. 59 / How do I measure butter? p. 55 / How do I measure flour? p. 54 / How do I measure sugar? p. 55 / How do I melt chocolate? p. 32, 33 / How do I soften butter? p. 28, 76 / How do I work with eggs? p. 26–27 / What are chopped nuts? p. 34 / What does drizzle mean? p. 69, 85 / What is cocoa powder? p. 170 / What is semisweet/bittersweet chocolate? p. 32 / What is vanilla? p. 128 / What is whipping cream? p. 24 / What's that flour? p. 31 / What's that nut? p. 34–35

(2) Skill Level

# Pecan Shortbread Logs

1¼ cups all-purpose flour

3 tablespoons packed brown sugar

½ cup cold butter

¼ cup pecans, finely chopped

4 teaspoons seedless raspberry jam or apricot preserves

½ cup powdered sugar

1 tablespoon rum, brandy, or milk

**Good to Know** When you're slicing biscotti-style cookies after they're baked (like these shortbreads), be sure to use a serrated knife and a gentle sawing motion to cut the slices. Don't press too hard or your cookies will crumble!

**1** Preheat oven to 325°F. In a large bowl stir together the flour and brown sugar. Using a pastry blender, cut in butter until mixture resembles fine crumbs and starts to cling. Stir in the pecans. Using your hands, shape the mixture into a ball and knead until smooth (photo 1, page 101). Divide dough in half.

**2** On a lightly floured surface, roll each portion of dough into a 7-inch-long log (below). Place logs 4 inches apart on an ungreased cookie sheet. Make a ¼-inch-deep groove lengthwise down the center of each log, leaving a ½-inch edge on the ends (below). Stir jam until nearly smooth (snip any large pieces of fruit if using apricot preserves). Spoon jam into grooves in logs (below).

**3** Bake in the preheated oven about 30 minutes or until logs are light brown. Cool completely on cookie sheet on a wire rack. Transfer cooled logs to a cutting board. Using a serrated knife, cut logs into 1-inch-thick slices (below). In a small bowl stir together powdered sugar and rum until smooth. Drizzle over cookies. Makes about 14 cookies.

Per cookie: 148 cal., 8 g total fat (4 g sat. fat), 17 mg chol., 48 mg sodium, 17 g carbo., 1 g fiber, 1 g pro.

**1** Roll dough portions into round logs that are 7 inches long. Use a clean ruler to check the length.

**2** Use your finger to make a shallow groove down the length of each log. Be careful not to flatten the logs.

**3** Stir the jam so it is easily spoonable, then spoon it evenly into the grooves in each log.

**4** After the logs are cooled, use a serrated knife and a gentle sawing motion to cut the logs into slices.

# Cranberry-Fig Tassies

½ cup butter, softened (photo I, page 76)

I 3-ounce package cream cheese, softened

I cup all-purpose flour

¼ cup finely chopped pecans

I teaspoon finely shredded orange peel

½ cup orange juice

⅓ cup finely chopped dried Calimyrna figs*

I egg

¾ cup packed brown sugar

½ teaspoon vanilla

Dash salt

¼ cup finely chopped cranberries

I recipe Sweetened Whipped Cream (page 25) or powdered sugar (optional)

**1** In a large mixing bowl beat butter and cream cheese with an electric mixer on medium to high speed for 30 seconds (photo 2, page 76). Using a wooden spoon, stir in flour and pecans. Wrap dough in plastic wrap; chill about 1 hour or until easy to handle.

**2** Preheat oven to 325°F. Shape dough into 24 balls (photos 1–3, page 92); place each ball in an ungreased 1¾-inch muffin cup. Press dough evenly against bottom and up sides of each muffin cup (below).

**3** In a small saucepan combine orange juice and figs. Bring just to boiling; remove from heat. Let stand for 10 minutes to soften figs. Drain off any excess juice and discard. Set figs aside. In a medium bowl beat egg with a fork. Stir in orange peel, sugar, vanilla, and salt. Stir in figs and cranberries. Spoon about 2 teaspoons of fig mixture into each dough-lined muffin cup (below).

**4** Bake in the preheated oven for 30 to 35 minutes or until edges are golden. Let stand for 5 minutes in muffin cups. Remove tassies from muffin cups by running a knife around edges to loosen (below). Transfer to a wire rack and let cool. If desired, garnish cooled tassies with Sweetened Whipped Cream or dust with powdered sugar before serving. Makes 24 tassies.

*****Note:** Before chopping the figs, be sure to remove and discard the tough stem ends.

Per tassie: II4 cal., 6 g total fat (3 g sat. fat), 23 mg chol., 50 mg sodium, I4 g carbo., I g fiber, I g pro.

**1** Using your fingers, press dough evenly over bottoms and all the way up the sides of muffin cups.

**2** Use a measuring teaspoon to spoon fig mixture into dough cups. Don't overfill or filling will stick to pan

**3** After tassies are baked, loosen the hot tassies from muffin cups with a knife. Use knife to lift tassies from cups.

2 Skill Level

**Good to Know** If you don't have time to ice your cookies but still want them to look nice, sprinkle some colored sugar on before baking. Standard colored sugar is available at most grocery stores. You can find fancier decorative sugars at specialty food shops and crafts stores.

# Sugar Cookie Cutouts

⅔ cup butter, softened
   (photo 1, page 76)

¾ cup granulated sugar

1 teaspoon baking powder

¼ teaspoon salt

1 egg

1 tablespoon milk

1 teaspoon vanilla

2 cups all-purpose flour

1 recipe Powdered Sugar Icing (optional)

**1** Preheat oven to 375°F. In a large mixing bowl beat butter with an electric mixer on medium to high speed for 30 seconds (photo 2, page 76). Add the granulated sugar, baking powder, and salt. Beat until combined, scraping sides of bowl occasionally (photo 3, page 76). Beat in egg, milk, and vanilla until combined (photo 4, page 76). Beat in as much of the flour as you can with the mixer (photo 5, page 76). Using a sturdy rubber scraper, stir in any remaining flour (photo 6, page 76). Divide dough in half. Wrap in plastic wrap; chill about 30 minutes or until easy to handle.

**2** On a lightly floured surface, roll half the dough at a time until ⅛ inch thick (below). To roll, start from the center and push dough out toward the edges until it is a uniform thickness. Using a 2½-inch cookie cutter, cut out desired shapes. Place cutouts 1 inch apart on an ungreased cookie sheet (below).

**3** Bake in the preheated oven for 7 to 8 minutes or until edges are firm and bottoms are very light brown. Transfer to a wire rack and let cool. If desired, frost with Powdered Sugar Icing. Makes about 36 cookies.

Per cookie: 73 cal., 4 g total fat (2 g sat. fat), 16 mg chol., 66 mg sodium, 9 g carbo., 0 g fiber, 1 g pro.

**Sugar Cookie Squares:** Prepare dough as above, except increase milk to 2 tablespoons. Pat dough into an ungreased 15×10×1-inch baking pan (chilling dough is not necessary). Bake for 10 to 12 minutes or until edges are firm but not brown. Cool in pan on a wire rack. Spread ¼ recipe Cream Cheese Frosting (page 121) over bars. Cut into squares. Makes 40 squares.

**Powdered Sugar Icing:** In a bowl stir together 1 cup powdered sugar, 1 tablespoon milk, and ¼ teaspoon vanilla. Stir in additional milk, 1 teaspoon at a time, until drizzling consistency.

**1** Lightly sprinkle work surface with flour. Too much flour toughens the dough.

**2** To prevent sticking, dip the cookie cutter in flour each time you use it.

**3** Using a wide metal spatula, transfer cutouts to a cookie sheet.

**Ask Mom** How do I measure butter? p. 55 / How do I measure flour? p. 54 / How do I measure sugar? p. 55 / How do I soften butter? p. 28, 76 / How do I use a rolling pin? p. 61, 228 / What is a lightly floured surface? p. 60 / What is baking powder? p. 30, 319 / What is powdered sugar? p. 29 / What is vanilla? p. 128 / What's that flour? p. 31

**WHAT'S SHORTBREAD?** It doesn't get much simpler than this classic English cookie—just three ingredients in the basic recipe. That's why quality counts. Don't be tempted to use anything but pure real butter. (And always serve it with a cup of tea.)

1. **Chocolate-Orange Shortbread:** Prepare as on page IOI, except add 1½ teaspoons finely shredded orange peel with the butter. After cutting in the butter, stir in ⅓ cup miniature semisweet chocolate pieces.

2. **Lemon-Poppy Seed Shortbread:** Prepare as on page IOI, except stir I tablespoon poppy seeds into flour mixture and add I teaspoon finely shredded lemon peel with the butter.

3. **Spiced Shortbread:** Prepare as on page IOI, except substitute brown sugar for the granulated sugar and stir ½ teaspoon ground cinnamon, ¼ teaspoon ground ginger, and ⅛ teaspoon ground cloves into the flour mixture.

Skill Level

**Good to Know**
Although you want the dough to be smooth, not crumbly, before you pat or roll it out, be sure not to overwork it. Do the least amount of kneading needed for the most tender shortbread.

# Shortbread

1¼ cups all-purpose flour
3 tablespoons granulated sugar
½ cup cold butter

**1** Preheat oven to 325°F. In a medium bowl stir together flour and sugar. Using a pastry blender, cut in butter until mixture resembles fine crumbs and starts to cling. Using your hands, shape the mixture into a ball and knead until smooth (below).

**2** To make shortbread wedges, on an ungreased cookie sheet, pat or roll the dough into an 8-inch circle (below). Make a scalloped edge (below). Cut circle into 16 wedges (below). Leave wedges in the circle.

**3** Bake in the preheated oven for 25 to 30 minutes or until bottom just starts to brown and center is set. Cut circle into wedges again while warm. Let stand for 5 minutes on cookie sheet. Transfer to a wire rack and let cool. Makes 16 wedges.

Per wedge: 98 cal., 6 g total fat (4 g sat. fat), 16 mg chol., 62 mg sodium, 10 g carbo., 0 g fiber, 1 g pro.

**Shortbread Rounds:** Prepare dough as above. On a lightly floured surface, roll dough until ½ inch thick. Using a 1½-inch round cutter, cut dough into circles, rerolling scraps as necessary. Place circles 1 inch apart on an ungreased cookie sheet. Bake in the preheated oven for 20 to 25 minutes.

**Shortbread Strips:** Prepare dough as above. On a lightly floured surface, roll dough into a 8×4-inch rectangle about ½ inch thick. Using a utility knife, cut rectangle in half lengthwise, then crosswise into 16 pieces. Bake as for rounds.

**1** Gently knead the dough by squeezing it and pressing it against the sides of the bowl until smooth. Don't overwork the dough.

**2** Using your fingers, pat the dough into an 8-inch circle. It should be about ½ inch thick.

**3** Crimp the edges of the shortbread circle by pressing your fingers and thumb toward each other.

**4** Using a sharp knife, cut the shortbread circle into equal wedges before it is baked.

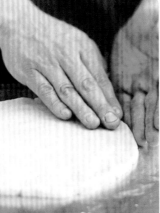

**Ask Mom** How do I cut in butter/shortening? p. 56 / How do I measure butter? p. 55 / How do I measure flour? p. 54 / How do I measure sugar? p. 55 / How do I shred lemon/lime/orange peel? p. 45, 105 / How do I soften butter? p. 28, 76 / How do I use a rolling pin? p. 61, 228 / What are cloves? p. 36 / What is a pastry blender? p. 10, 11 / What is cinnamon? p. 36 / What is ginger? p. 36 / What is semisweet/bittersweet chocolate? p. 32 / What's that flour? p. 31

# Chocolate-Cherry Pockets

½ cup butter, softened (photo 1, page 76)
1 3-ounce package cream cheese, softened
1½ cups powdered sugar
⅓ cup unsweetened cocoa powder
½ teaspoon baking powder
¼ teaspoon baking soda
¼ teaspoon salt
1 egg

½ teaspoon vanilla
1¾ cups all-purpose flour
½ cup cherry preserves
2 tablespoons snipped dried cherries
1 teaspoon brandy (optional)
4 ounces bittersweet or semisweet chocolate, chopped
2 teaspoons shortening
Sliced almonds, toasted

1 In a large mixing bowl beat butter and cream cheese with an electric mixer on medium to high speed for 30 seconds (photo 2, page 76). Add the powdered sugar, cocoa powder, baking powder, baking soda, and salt. Beat until combined, scraping sides of bowl occasionally (photo 3, page 76). Beat in egg and vanilla until combined (photo 4, page 76). Beat in as much of the flour as you can with the mixer (photo 5, page 76). Using a sturdy rubber scraper or wooden spoon, stir in any remaining flour (photo 6, page 76). Divide dough in half. Wrap each half in plastic wrap; chill dough about 2 hours or until easy to handle.

2 Meanwhile, for cherry filling, in a small bowl stir together the cherry preserves (snip any large pieces), dried cherries, and, if desired, brandy.

3 Preheat oven to 375°F. Line two cookie sheets with foil; set aside. On a lightly floured surface, roll half the dough at a time until ⅛ inch thick (photo 1, page 99). To roll, start from the center and push dough out toward the edges until it is a uniform thickness. Using a 3-inch scalloped or plain round cutter, cut out dough. Spoon a scant teaspoon of the cherry filling onto the center of each cutout (photo 1, page 103). Brush edges of the cutouts with water (photo 2, page 103). Fold each cutout in half over filling. Using your finger, gently press edges to seal (photo 3, page 103). Place filled cookies 1 inch apart on the prepared cookie sheets.

4 Bake in the preheated oven for 8 to 9 minutes or until edges are firm. Transfer to a wire rack set over waxed paper or parchment paper and let cool.

5 In a small heavy saucepan combine chocolate and shortening. Heat and stir over low heat until smooth. Use a spoon to drizzle chocolate over cookies (photo 4, page 103). Sprinkle with almonds. If desired, drizzle cookies again with chocolate. Let stand until set. Makes about 30 cookies.

**Per cookie:** 134 cal., 7 g total fat (4 g sat. fat), 18 mg chol., 71 mg sodium, 18 g carbo., 1 g fiber, 1 g pro.

**Good to Know** Fruit preserves generally have some chunkiness to them. If your cherry preserves has large pieces of fruit in it that may inhibit filling your cookies neatly, simply snip them in smaller pieces with a pair of clean kitchen scissors.

**Ask Mom** How do I chop chocolate? p. 33 / How do I measure butter? p. 55 / How do I measure flour? p. 54 / How do I snip dried fruit? p. 41, 102 / How do I soften butter/cream cheese? p. 28, 76, 57 / How do I toast nuts? p. 34 / What is a lightly floured surface? p. 60 / What is baking powder/baking soda? p. 30, 319 / What is cocoa powder? p. 170 / What is powdered sugar? p. 29 / What is bittersweet chocolate? p. 32 / What is vanilla? p. 128 / What's that dried fruit? p. 41 / What's that flour? p. 31

**ARE THERE OTHER FILLING OPTIONS?** Chocolate is wonderful paired with certain fruits. Classic combinations include chocolate with cherry, orange, or apricot. For apricot filling, use 2 tablespoons snipped dried apricots and ½ cup apricot preserves.

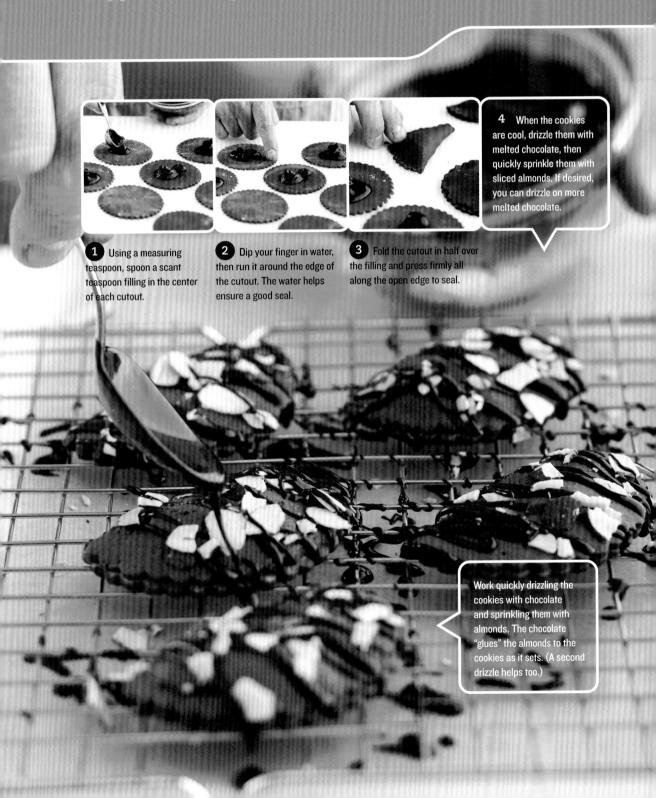

**4** When the cookies are cool, drizzle them with melted chocolate, then quickly sprinkle them with sliced almonds. If desired, you can drizzle on more melted chocolate.

**1** Using a measuring teaspoon, spoon a scant teaspoon filling in the center of each cutout.

**2** Dip your finger in water, then run it around the edge of the cutout. The water helps ensure a good seal.

**3** Fold the cutout in half over the filling and press firmly all along the open edge to seal.

Work quickly drizzling the cookies with chocolate and sprinkling them with almonds. The chocolate "glues" the almonds to the cookies as it sets. (A second drizzle helps too.)

# Lime Zingers

| | |
|---|---|
| 1 cup butter, softened (photo 1, page 76) | ¾ cup finely chopped Brazil nuts or hazelnuts (filberts) |
| ½ cup granulated sugar | ½ of an 8-ounce package cream cheese, softened |
| 2 teaspoons finely shredded lime peel | 1 cup powdered sugar |
| ¼ cup lime juice | 1 tablespoon lime juice |
| 1 teaspoon vanilla | 1 teaspoon vanilla |
| 2¼ cups all-purpose flour | Finely shredded lime peel (optional) |

**1** Preheat oven to 350°F. In a large mixing bowl beat butter with an electric mixer on medium to high speed for 30 seconds (photo 2, page 76). Add the granulated sugar. Beat until combined, scraping sides of bowl occasionally (photo 3, page 76). Beat in the 2 teaspoons lime peel, ¼ cup lime juice, and 1 teaspoon vanilla until combined. Beat in as much of the flour as you can with the mixer (photo 5, page 76). Using a wooden spoon, stir in any remaining flour and the nuts (photo 6, page 76). Divide dough in half.

**2** On a lightly floured surface, roll half of the dough at a time until ¼ inch thick (photo 1, page 99). To roll, start from the center and push dough out toward the edges until it is a uniform thickness. Using a 2-inch scalloped or plain round cutter, cut out dough. Place cutouts 1 inch apart on ungreased cookie sheet (photo 3, page 99).

**3** Bake in the preheated oven for 8 to 10 minutes or until edges are light brown. Transfer to a wire rack and let cool.

**4** For frosting, in a medium mixing bowl combine cream cheese, powdered sugar, the 1 tablespoon lime juice, and 1 teaspoon vanilla. Beat with an electric mixer on medium speed until smooth. Spread frosting on cooled cookies. If desired, sprinkle with additional lime peel. Makes about 42 cookies.

Per cookie: 110 cal., 7 g total fat (4 g sat. fat), 15 mg chol., 39 mg sodium, 11 g carbo., 0 g fiber, 1 g pro.

**1** Using a spatula or table knife, spread frosting on tops of cooled cookies.

**2** Place the frosted cookies on a wire rack set over paper before sprinkling with lime peel.

**Ingredient Info**
Buttery-tasting Brazil nuts are actually the giant seeds of a tree that grows in South America's Amazon jungle. They're big, rich, and very high in fat—which is why they taste so good. Look for the raw (not roasted), unsalted variety for this recipe.

**Ask Mom** How do I juice a lemon/lime? p. 44, 45 / How do I measure butter? p. 55 / How do I measure flour? p. 54 / How do I measure sugar? p. 55 / How do I shred lemon/lime/orange peel? p. 45, 105 / How do I soften butter? p. 28, 76 / How do I soften cream cheese? p. 57 / How do I use a rolling pin? p. 61, 228 / What are chopped nuts? p. 34 / What is a lightly floured surface? p. 60 / What is powdered sugar? p. 29 / What is vanilla? p. 128 / What's that flour? p. 31 / What's that nut? p. 34–35

**FOR THE PRETTIEST PEEL:** Before you begin grating the lime peel, make sure it's washed well and thoroughly dried. If there's any moisture left on the surface of the lime, the lacy pieces of peel will clump up—and that's not pretty.

The best way to evenly sprinkle the fresh lime peel on the iced cookies is to shred it directly over them using a rasp grater. Just be sure to get only the green peel, not the bitter white pith.

# Gingerbread Cutouts

½ cup shortening
½ cup granulated sugar
1 teaspoon baking powder
1 teaspoon ground ginger
½ teaspoon baking soda
½ teaspoon ground cinnamon
½ teaspoon ground cloves

½ cup molasses
1 egg
1 tablespoon white vinegar
2½ cups all-purpose flour
1 recipe Lemon Frosting or 2 recipes Powdered Sugar Icing (page 99)
Decorative candies, colored sugar, coconut, and/or decorating gel (optional)

**1** In a large mixing bowl beat shortening with an electric mixer on medium to high speed for 30 seconds (photo 2, page 76). Add the granulated sugar, baking powder, ginger, baking soda, cinnamon, and cloves. Beat until combined, scraping sides of bowl occasionally (photo 3, page 76). Beat in molasses, egg, and vinegar until combined (photo 4, page 76). Beat in as much of the flour as you can with the mixer (photo 5, page 76). Using a sturdy rubber scraper or wooden spoon, stir in any remaining flour (photo 6, page 76). Divide dough in half. Wrap each half in plastic wrap; chill dough about 3 hours or until easy to handle.

**2** Preheat oven to 375°F. Grease a cookie sheet; set aside. On a lightly floured surface, roll half the dough at a time until ⅛ inch thick (photo 1, page 99). To roll, start from the center and push dough out toward the edges until it is a uniform thickness. Using a 2½-inch cookie cutter, cut out desired shapes. Place cutouts 1 inch apart on prepared cookie sheet (photo 3, page 99).

**3** Bake in the preheated oven for 5 to 6 minutes or until edges are light brown. Let stand for 1 minute on cookie sheet. Transfer to a wire rack and let cool. Decorate cookies with Lemon Frosting and, if desired, decorative candies. Makes 36 cookies.

Per cookie: 125 cal., 5 g total fat (2 g sat. fat), 11 mg chol., 42 mg sodium, 20 g carbo., 0 g fiber, 0 g pro.

**Gingerbread People Cutouts:** Prepare as above, except roll dough until ¼ inch thick. Cut with 4½- to 6-inch people-shape cookie cutters. Bake in the preheated oven for 7 to 9 minutes or until edges are light brown. Makes about 12 cookies.

**Lemon Frosting:** In a medium mixing bowl beat 6 tablespoons butter, softened, with an electric mixer on medium to high speed for 30 seconds. Gradually add 1 cup powdered sugar, mixing well. Beat in 1 tablespoon lemon juice. Gradually beat in an additional 1 cup powdered sugar. If necessary, stir in milk or lemon juice, 1 teaspoon at a time, to make a frosting of spreading or piping consistency.

**Ask Mom** How do I grease a baking pan? p. 59 / How do I juice a lemon? p. 44, 45 / How do I measure butter? p. 55 / How do I measure flour? p. 54 / How do I measure shortening? p. 55 / How do I measure sugar? p. 55 / How do I soften butter? p. 28, 76 / How do I use a rolling pin? p. 61, 228 / What are cloves? p. 36 / What is baking powder? p. 30, 319 / What is baking soda? p. 30, 319 / What is cinnamon? p. 36 / What is ginger? p. 36 / What is powdered sugar? p. 29 / What's that flour? p. 31

# beyond square
## BARS &
## BROWNIES

The beauty of bar cookies and brownies:
There's so much payoff for so little effort.
All you need is one pan and a (simple) plan.

## BARS

Banana-Chocolate Chip Bars ① . . . . . . . . . . . . . . . . . . . . 109
Coconut-Date Bars ② . . . . . . . . . . . . . . . . . . . . . . . . . . . . .122
Cranberry Pear Bars ② . . . . . . . . . . . . . . . . . . . . . . . . . . . 116
Holiday Layer Bars ① . . . . . . . . . . . . . . . . . . . . . . . . . . . 114
Lemon Curd Bars ② . . . . . . . . . . . . . . . . . . . . . . . . . . . . 119
Northwest Pecan Treats ② . . . . . . . . . . . . . . . . . . . . . . . 115
Oatmeal-Caramel Bars ② . . . . . . . . . . . . . . . . . . . . . . . . 120
Peanut Butter Blondie Bars ① . . . . . . . . . . . . . . . . . . . . 110
Pumpkin Bars ① . . . . . . . . . . . . . . . . . . . . . . . . . . . . . . . 121
Rhubarb Bars ② . . . . . . . . . . . . . . . . . . . . . . . . . . . . . . . 117
Toffee Fingers ② . . . . . . . . . . . . . . . . . . . . . . . . . . . . . . . .111
Ultimate Bar Cookies ② . . . . . . . . . . . . . . . . . . . . . . . . . 112

## BROWNIES

Candy Bar Brownies ③ . . . . . . . . . . . . . . . . . . . . . . . . . . 129
Cappuccino Brownies ③ . . . . . . . . . . . . . . . . . . . . . . . . . 130
Chocolate-Cherry Brownies ② . . . . . . . . . . . . . . . . . . . . 126
Chunky Path Brownies ② . . . . . . . . . . . . . . . . . . . . . . . . 128
Cream Cheese Brownies ③ . . . . . . . . . . . . . . . . . . . . . . . 131
Espresso Brownies ② . . . . . . . . . . . . . . . . . . . . . . . . . . . 127
Extra-Chocolate Brownies ② . . . . . . . . . . . . . . . . . . . . . 126
Fudgy Brownies ② . . . . . . . . . . . . . . . . . . . . . . . . . . . . . 124

Macaroon Brownies ② . . . . . . . . . . . . . . . . . . . . . . . . . . 127
Malted Milk Brownies ② . . . . . . . . . . . . . . . . . . . . . . . . . 127
Mint Brownies ② . . . . . . . . . . . . . . . . . . . . . . . . . . . . . . 126
Orange-Nut Brownies ② . . . . . . . . . . . . . . . . . . . . . . . . . 126
Peanut Butter Brownies ② . . . . . . . . . . . . . . . . . . . . . . . 126
Peppermint-Fudge Brownie Bites ① . . . . . . . . . . . . . . . . 123
Raspberry and White Chocolate Brownies ① . . . . . . . . . 132
Raspberry Brownies ② . . . . . . . . . . . . . . . . . . . . . . . . . . 127
S'more Brownies ② . . . . . . . . . . . . . . . . . . . . . . . . . . . . . 127
Strawberry-Banana Brownies ② . . . . . . . . . . . . . . . . . . . 126
Turtle Brownies ② . . . . . . . . . . . . . . . . . . . . . . . . . . . . . 127

## FROSTINGS

Chocolate-Cream Cheese Frosting ② . . . . . . . . . . . . . . . .124
Chocolate Frosting ① . . . . . . . . . . . . . . . . . . . . . . . . . . . 130
Chocolate Glaze ① . . . . . . . . . . . . . . . . . . . . . . . . . . . . . 131
Chocolate-Peanut Topper ① . . . . . . . . . . . . . . . . . . . . . . 128
Chocolate Topper ① . . . . . . . . . . . . . . . . . . . . . . . . . . . . 128
Coconut Frosting ① . . . . . . . . . . . . . . . . . . . . . . . . . . . . .122
Cream Cheese Frosting ① . . . . . . . . . . . . . . . . . . . . . . . . 121
Peanut Butter Frosting ① . . . . . . . . . . . . . . . . . . . . 110, 129

**What's a saucepan brownie?** . . . . . . . . . . . . . . . . . . . . . 125

① Skill Level

**Flavor Changes**
Please all frosting fans—and make it look pretty too—by using half a can each of chocolate and vanilla frostings, swirling them together on the bars (below).

# Banana-Chocolate Chip Bars

- 1  16.5-ounce roll refrigerated peanut butter cookie dough*
- 1  cup regular rolled oats
- ½  cup mashed ripe banana
- ½  cup miniature semisweet chocolate pieces
- ½  cup chopped dry-roasted peanuts
- 1  16-ounce can chocolate or vanilla frosting

**1** Preheat oven to 350°F. If desired, line a 13×9×2-inch baking pan with foil, leaving about 1 inch extending over the ends of pan. Lightly grease foil or pan; set pan aside. In a large bowl combine the cookie dough, oats, banana, chocolate pieces, and peanuts; mix well. Spread mixture evenly into the bottom of the prepared pan (below).

**2** Bake in the preheated oven about 25 minutes or until golden brown. Cool in pan on a wire rack. Spread frosting over cooled bars (below). If using foil, remove bars from pan, using the overlapping foil to lift bars (photo 2, page 111); place on cutting board. Cut into bars. Makes 36 bars.

**\*Note:** If desired, substitute one 16.5-ounce roll refrigerated chocolate chip and peanut butter cookie dough for plain peanut butter cookie dough. Omit chocolate pieces.

**Per bar:** 158 cal., 8 g total fat (2 g sat. fat), 4 mg chol., 75 mg sodium, 21 g carbo., 1 g fiber, 3 g pro.

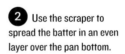 ① Using a sturdy rubber scraper, transfer batter to the prepared pan.

② Use the scraper to spread the batter in an even layer over the pan bottom.

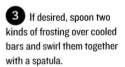 ③ If desired, spoon two kinds of frosting over cooled bars and swirl them together with a spatula.

**Ask Mom** Can I use quick-cooking oats instead of regular rolled oats? p. 351 / How do I cut bars/brownies? p. 113 / How do I grease a baking pan/dish? p. 59 / How do I line a pan with foil? p. 58 / How do I mash bananas? p. 40 / What are chopped nuts? p. 34 / What is semisweet/bittersweet chocolate? p. 32

**1** Skill Level

**Good to Know** When you use a purchased cookie dough, you're good to go on a quick dessert. These bars are customized and "crunchified" with the addition of graham cracker crumbs to a refrigerated peanut butter cookie dough.

# Peanut Butter
## Blondie Bars

- 1  32-ounce package (or two 16.5-ounce packages) refrigerated peanut butter cookie dough
- 1⅓ cups graham cracker crumbs (about 19 graham crackers)
- 1  recipe Peanut Butter Frosting
- ⅔  cup candy-coated peanut butter-flavor pieces
- ½  cup chopped dry-roasted peanuts
- ½  cup miniature semisweet chocolate pieces

**1** Preheat oven to 350°F. If desired, line a 13×9×2-inch baking pan with foil, leaving about 1 inch of foil extending over the ends of the pan; set aside.

**2** In a large bowl knead together the cookie dough and graham cracker crumbs until combined (dough will be stiff). Press the dough evenly into the bottom of the prepared pan. Bake in the preheated oven about 20 minutes or until evenly puffed and light brown across the top. Cool in pan on a wire rack (bars will fall slightly during cooling).

**3** Spread Peanut Butter Frosting over cooled bars. Immediately sprinkle with peanut butter-flavor pieces, peanuts, and chocolate pieces. If using foil, remove bars from pan, using the overlapping foil to lift bars (photo 2, page 111); place on cutting board. Cut into bars. Makes 36 bars.

**Peanut Butter Frosting:** In a medium saucepan heat and stir ¼ cup peanut butter and ¼ cup butter, softened, just until smooth. Stir in 2 cups powdered sugar and 1 teaspoon vanilla. Stir in about 2 tablespoons milk to make frosting of spreading consistency.

Per bar: 225 cal., 12 g total fat (4 g sat. fat), 10 mg chol., 154 mg sodium, 27 g carbo., 1 g fiber, 4 g pro.

**Ask Mom** How do I cut bars/brownies? p. 113 / How do I line a pan with foil? p. 58 / How do I make cracker/cookie crumbs? p. 129 / How do I measure butter? p. 55 / How do I measure peanut butter? p. 55 / How do I soften butter? p. 28, 76 / What are chopped nuts? p. 34 / What is powdered sugar? p. 29 / What is semisweet/bittersweet chocolate? p. 32 / What is vanilla? p. 128

**2** Skill Level

# Toffee Fingers

1¼ cups all-purpose flour
¾ teaspoon baking powder
¼ teaspoon salt
½ cup butter, softened (photo 1, page 76)
¼ cup powdered sugar

2 tablespoons packed brown sugar
½ cup toffee pieces
½ cup semisweet chocolate pieces
1 teaspoon shortening
¼ cup toffee pieces

**1** Preheat oven to 325°F. If desired, line an 8×8×2-inch square baking pan with foil, leaving about 1 inch of foil extending over the ends of the pan; set aside.

**2** In a small bowl stir together the flour, baking powder, and salt; set aside. In a large mixing bowl beat butter with an electric mixer on medium to high speed for 30 seconds (photo 2, page 76). Add powdered sugar and brown sugar. Beat until combined, scraping sides of bowl occasionally (photo 3, page 76). Beat in flour mixture (combined mixture seems dry but comes together as you beat). Stir in the ½ cup toffee pieces. Press mixture evenly into the bottom of the prepared pan (photo 1, page 119); prick dough with fork every ½ inch (below).

**3** Bake in the preheated oven about 20 minutes or until light brown. Cool slightly in pan on a wire rack.

**4** If using foil, remove warm bars from pan, using the overlapping foil to lift bars (below); place on cutting board. Cut into eight 1-inch strips (below). Cut each strip crosswise into three pieces, making 24 bars. Transfer bars to a wire rack placed over waxed paper; cool completely.

**5** In a small heavy saucepan heat and stir chocolate pieces and shortening over low heat until smooth. Cool slightly. Drizzle bars with melted chocolate. Immediately sprinkle bars with the ¼ cup toffee pieces (below). Let bars stand until chocolate is set. Makes 24 bars.

**Per bar:** 121 cal., 7 g total fat (4 g sat. fat), 11 mg chol., 80 mg sodium, 14 g carbo., 0 g fiber, 0 g pro.

**1** Using the tines of a flatware fork, prick holes in the dough. This will prevent air bubbles from forming.

**2** Use the overlapping foil to lift the warm bars from the pan and transfer them to a cutting board.

**3** Using a long sharp knife, cut the bars into eight 1-inch strips. Cut the strips crosswise into thirds.

**4** After drizzling bars with chocolate, quickly sprinkle toffee bits on bars before chocolate sets.

**Ask Mom** How do I cut bars/brownies? p. 113 / How do I line a pan with foil? p. 58 / How do I measure butter? p. 55 / How do I measure flour? p. 54 / How do I measure sugar? p. 55 / How do I melt chocolate? p. 32, 33 / How do I soften butter? p. 28, 76 / What are toffee pieces? p. 90 / What does drizzle mean? p. 69, 85 / What is baking powder? p. 30, 319 / What is powdered sugar?

(2) Skill Level

**Good to Know** What makes these bar cookies the "ultimate"? There is not another good thing to add to them—they have it all: two kinds of nuts (including decadent macadamias), white and milk chocolate, and caramel.

# Ultimate Bar Cookies

  2  cups all-purpose flour
½  cup packed brown sugar
½  cup butter, softened (photo 1, page 76)
  1  cup coarsely chopped walnuts
  1  3-ounce jar macadamia nuts, coarsely chopped (⅔ cup)
  6  ounces white chocolate baking bars, chopped (1 cup)
  1  cup milk chocolate pieces
¾  cup butter
½  cup packed brown sugar

**1** Preheat oven to 350°F. If desired, line a 13×9×2-inch baking pan with foil, leaving about 1 inch of foil extending over the ends of pan; set aside. In a medium mixing bowl beat flour, ½ cup brown sugar, and the ½ cup butter with an electric mixer on medium speed until mixture resembles fine crumbs. Press mixture evenly into the bottom of the prepared pan (photo 1, page 119).

**2** Bake in the preheated oven about 15 minutes or until light brown. Remove from oven. Sprinkle nuts, baking bars, and milk chocolate pieces over hot crust.

**3** In a small saucepan cook and stir the ¾ cup butter and ½ cup brown sugar over medium heat until bubbly. Cook and stir for 1 minute more. Pour sugar mixture evenly over bars. Bake about 15 minutes more or until just bubbly around edges. Cool in pan on a wire rack. If using foil, remove bars from pan, using the overlapping foil to lift bars (photo 2, page 111); place on cutting board. Cut into bars. Makes 36 bars.

**Per bar:** 204 cal., 14 g total fat (7 g sat. fat), 19 mg chol., 62 mg sodium, 19 g carbo., 1 g fiber, 2 g pro.

**Ask Mom**  How do I chop chocolate? p. 33 / How do I line a pan with foil? p. 58 / How do I measure butter? p. 55 / How do I measure flour? p. 54 / How do I measure sugar? p. 55 / How do I soften butter? p. 28, 76 / What are chopped nuts? p. 34 / What is white chocolate? p. 32 / What's that flour? p. 31 / What's that nut? p. 34-35

**DO BAR COOKIES HAVE TO BE SQUARE?** Not at all. With just a few easy cuts, bar cookies can be any one of a number of shapes. Squares are simple and kid-friendly, triangles are a little bit fancy, and diamonds are the fanciest of all. (See below for how to cut them.)

These bars are easier to cut when out of the pan. Line the pan with foil and use the foil to lift the bars out (photo 2, page III). Then use a long sharp knife to cut the bars into the desired shapes.

1  Using a long knife, cut the bars lengthwise into even strips. For square bars, cut the strips crosswise into the desired size.

2  For diamond-shape bars, cut the strips at an angle into the desired size.

3  For small triangles, cut the bars into squares, then cut the squares in half from corner to corner.

**Good to Know**
Be sure to use crispy gingersnaps, not chewy ones, in this no-mix recipe. Crispy gingersnaps crush easily and create a light, delicate crust. Chewy ones would make it dense and hard.

# Layer Bars

½ cup butter

1½ cups finely crushed gingersnaps (about 25 cookies)

6 ounces white chocolate baking bars, chopped, or white baking pieces (1 cup)

⅔ cup dried cranberries or tart red cherries, snipped

⅓ cup diced candied orange peel*

1 cup pistachio nuts, chopped

1 14-ounce can (1¼ cups) sweetened condensed milk

1⅓ cups flaked coconut

**1** Preheat oven to 350°F. If desired, line a 13×9×2-inch baking pan with foil, leaving about 1 inch of foil extending over the ends of pan. Place butter in the prepared pan. Place pan in the preheated oven until the butter melts. Remove pan from oven. Tilt pan to coat bottom of pan with butter. Sprinkle cookie crumbs evenly over the bottom of the pan.

**2** Layer the white chocolate, cranberries, candied orange peel, and pistachio nuts on top of cookie crumbs. Pour sweetened condensed milk evenly over fruit and nut layers. Sprinkle with coconut.

**3** Bake in the preheated oven about 25 minutes or until coconut is light gold. Cool in pan on a wire rack. If using foil, remove bars from pan, using the overlapping foil to lift bars (photo 2, page 111); place on cutting board. Cut into bars. Makes 42 bars.

*Note: Candied orange peel can usually be found near the dried fruit in your supermarket's baking aisle.

Per bar: 134 cal., 7 g total fat (4 g sat. fat), 10 mg chol., 68 mg sodium, 16 g carbo., 1 g fiber, 2 g pro.

**Ask Mom** How do I cut bars/brownies? p. 113 / How do I line a pan with foil? p. 58 / How do I make cracker/cookie crumbs? p. 129 / How do I measure butter? p. 55 / How do I snip dried fruit or preserves? p. 41, 102 / What are chopped nuts? p. 34 / What is sweetened condensed milk? p. 24 / What is white chocolate? p. 32 / What's that dried fruit? p. 41 / What's that nut? p. 34–35

(2) Skill Level

**Flavor Changes** If "treat" is synonymous with "chocolate," you can substitute ⅓ cup miniature semisweet chocolate pieces for the dried cherries or cranberries.

# Northwest Pecan Treats

3 cups all-purpose flour
½ cup sugar
½ teaspoon salt
1 cup cold butter
2½ cups chopped pecans
⅓ cup dried cherries or cranberries, snipped

4 eggs, lightly beaten
1¼ cups dark-color corn syrup
1¼ cups sugar
3 tablespoons butter, melted
2 teaspoons vanilla

**1** Preheat oven to 350°F. If desired, line a 15×10×1-inch baking pan with foil, leaving about 1 inch of foil extending over the ends of the pan. Grease foil or pan; set pan aside.

**2** In a large bowl stir together the flour, the ½ cup sugar, and the salt. Using a pastry blender, cut in the cold butter until mixture resembles coarse crumbs. Press flour mixture evenly into the bottom of the prepared pan (photo 1, page 119). Bake in the preheated oven for 20 minutes. (Crust will appear cracked.) Remove pan from oven.

**3** Sprinkle pecans and dried cherries over hot crust (below). In a large glass measure or bowl whisk eggs, corn syrup, the 1¼ cups sugar, the melted butter, and vanilla until combined (below). Slowly pour egg mixture over all (below).

**4** Bake for 25 to 30 minutes more or until set. Cool completely in pan on a wire rack. If using foil, remove bars from pan, using the overlapping foil to lift bars (photo 2, page 111); place on cutting board. Cut into bars. Makes 48 bars.

**Per bar:** 170 cal., 9 g total fat (3 g sat. fat), 30 mg chol., 76 mg sodium, 21 g carbo., 1 g fiber, 1 g pro.

**1** Sprinkle the pecans and cherries evenly over the hot baked crust.

**2** In a large glass measuring cup, whisk together egg, syrup, sugar, melted butter, and vanilla.

**3** Carefully pour the egg mixture evenly all over the pecans and cherries.

**Ask Mom** How do I cut bars/brownies? p. 113 / How do I cut in butter? p. 56 / How do I line a pan with foil? p. 58 / How do I measure butter? p. 55 / How do I measure flour? p. 54 / How do I measure liquids? p. 55 / How do I measure sugar? p. 55 / How do I snip dried fruit or preserves? p. 41, 102 / How do I work with eggs? p. 26–27 / What are chopped nuts? p. 34 / What is a pastry blender? p. 10, 11 / What is vanilla? p. 128 / What's that dried fruit? p. 41 / What's that flour? p. 31 / What's that nut? p. 34–35

# Cranberry Pear Bars

2 cups all-purpose flour
½ cup packed brown sugar
¾ cup cold butter
1 cup regular rolled oats

⅔ cup pear nectar or apple juice
⅔ cup packed brown sugar
2 cups fresh cranberries
⅛ teaspoon ground nutmeg

**1** Preheat oven to 350°F. If desired, line a 13×9×2-inch baking pan with foil, leaving about 1 inch of foil extending over the ends of pan. Set aside.

**2** In a medium bowl stir together the flour and the ½ cup brown sugar. Using a pastry blender, cut in butter until mixture resembles fine crumbs. Stir in the oats. Reserve 1 cup oats mixture. Press remaining oats mixture evenly into the bottom of the prepared pan (photo 1, page 119). Bake in the preheated oven about 15 minutes or until light brown.

**3** Meanwhile, in a medium saucepan stir together the pear nectar and the ⅔ cup brown sugar. Bring to boiling, stirring to dissolve sugar. Add cranberries. Return to boiling; reduce heat. Simmer, uncovered, about 10 minutes or until slightly thickened, stirring occasionally. Remove from heat; stir in nutmeg.

**4** Spread cranberry mixture evenly over baked crust (below). Sprinkle with reserved oats mixture (below). Bake about 25 minutes more or until top is light brown. Cool in pan on a wire rack. If using foil, remove bars from pan, using the overlapping foil to lift bars (photo 2, page 111); place on cutting board. Cut into bars. Makes 32 bars.

**Per bar:** 122 cal., 5 g total fat (3 g sat. fat), 11 mg chol., 34 mg sodium, 19 g carbo., 1 g fiber, 1 g pro.

**①** Spoon the cranberry mixture all over the hot baked crust.

**②** Use the back of the spoon to spread cranberry mixture in an even layer over the crust.

**③** Sprinkle the reserved oats mixture evenly over the cranberry layer.

**Ask Mom** Can I use quick-cooking oats instead of regular rolled oats? p. 351 / How do I cut bars/brownies? p. 113 / How do I cut in butter/shortening? p. 56 / How do I line a pan with foil? p. 58 / How do I measure butter? p. 55 / How do I measure flour? p. 54 / How do I measure liquids? p. 55 / How do I measure sugar? p. 55 / What is a pastry blender? p. 10, 11 / What is nutmeg? p. 37 / What's that flour? p. 31

**Good to Know** If it isn't rhubarb season and you're craving the tart taste of this harbinger of spring, frozen rhubarb works perfectly fine. You don't have to thaw it before using it either: it cooks into a saucelike mixture whether it's fresh or frozen.

 Skill Level

# Rhubarb Bars

3 cups fresh or frozen unsweetened, sliced rhubarb
1 cup granulated sugar
¼ cup water
½ cup granulated sugar
2 tablespoons all-purpose flour
1 teaspoon vanilla
1½ cups all-purpose flour
1½ cups quick-cooking rolled oats
1 cup packed brown sugar
¼ teaspoon baking soda
1 cup shortening
½ cup chopped pecans or walnuts
Chopped pecans or walnuts (optional)

**1** Preheat oven to 375°F. If desired, line a 13×9×2-inch baking pan with foil, leaving about 1 inch of foil extending over the ends of pan. Grease foil or pan; set pan aside.

**2** In a medium saucepan stir together the rhubarb, the 1 cup granulated sugar, and the water. Bring to boiling; reduce heat. Cover and simmer for 5 minutes. Meanwhile, in a small bowl stir together the ½ cup granulated sugar and the 2 tablespoons flour. Stir sugar mixture into rhubarb mixture. Cook and stir about 1 minute more or until thick. Remove from heat; stir in vanilla. Set aside.

**3** In a medium bowl stir together the 1½ cups flour, the oats, brown sugar, and baking soda. Using a pastry blender, cut in shortening until mixture resembles coarse crumbs. Stir in the ½ cup pecans. Reserve 1 cup of the crumb mixture.

**4** Press the remaining crumb mixture evenly into the bottom of the prepared pan. Spread rhubarb mixture over top. Sprinkle with the reserved crumb mixture and, if desired, additional chopped nuts. Bake in the preheated oven for 30 to 35 minutes or until the top is golden. Cool in pan on a wire rack. If using foil, remove bars from pan, using the overlapping foil to lift bars (photo 2, page 111); place on cutting board. Cut into bars. Store bars, covered, in an airtight container in the refrigerator for up to 3 days. Makes 45 bars.

**Per bar:** 122 cal., 5 g total fat (1 g sat. fat), 0 mg chol., 10 mg sodium, 17 g carbo., 1 g fiber, 1 g pro.

CAN I USE A 13×9 GLASS BAKING DISH? It's not ideal. Metal pans are better for getting an evenly brown top on baked goods—but if glass is what you happen to have, just be sure to reduce the baking temperature by 25°F.

**Ask Mom** How do I cut bars? p. 113 / How do I cut in shortening? p. 56 / How do I grease a baking pan? p. 59 / How do I line a pan with foil? p. 58 / How do I measure flour? p. 54 / How do I measure liquids? p. 55 / How do I measure shortening? p. 55 / How do I measure sugar? p. 55 / How do I prepare rhubarb? p. 49, 117 / What are chopped nuts? p. 34 / What is a pastry blender? p. 10, 11 / What is baking soda? p. 30, 319 / What is vanilla? p. 128 / What's that flour? p. 31 / What's that nut? p. 34–35

## WHEN DO I START CHECKING FOR DONENESS?
Ovens can vary greatly in how they bake, so it's best to start checking your bars and brownies (and anything, really) at the low end of the time range so you don't burn your beautiful baked goods.

Classic lemon bars get a tropical twist with a topping of coconut and almonds. You can use rich, buttery pecans in place of the almonds, if you like.

② Skill Level

**Ingredient Info**
Lemon curd is a
creamy, sweet-tart
concoction made from
cooking lemon juice,
sugar, butter, and egg
yolks until the mixture
thickens. When cool,
it's spreadable. It's
most commonly used
as a topping and tart
filling. Look for it at
gourmet markets—and
some supermarkets.

# Lemon **Curd Bars**

  1 cup butter, softened (photo 1, page 76)
  1 cup sugar
  2 cups all-purpose flour
½ teaspoon baking powder
  1 10- to 12-ounce jar lemon curd
⅔ cup flaked coconut
½ cup slivered or sliced almonds or coarsely chopped pecans, toasted

**1** Preheat oven to 375°F. If desired, line a 13×9×2-inch baking pan with foil, leaving about 1 inch of foil extending over the ends of pan. Grease foil or pan; set pan aside.

**2** In a large mixing bowl beat butter with an electric mixer on medium to high speed for 30 seconds (photo 2, page 76). Add the sugar. Beat until combined, scraping sides of bowl occasionally (photo 3, page 76). Add flour and baking powder; beat until just combined and mixture resembles coarse crumbs. Reserve ⅔ cup of the crumb mixture; set aside. Press the remaining crumb mixture evenly into the bottom of the prepared pan (below).

**3** Bake in the preheated oven for 5 to 8 minutes or until top is golden. Remove from oven. Spread lemon curd over hot crust to within ½ inch of the edges of the pan (below). In a medium bowl stir together reserved crumb mixture, the coconut, and almonds. Sprinkle crumb mixture over lemon curd (below).

**4** Bake for 18 to 20 minutes more or until edges are golden and topping is brown. Cool in pan on a wire rack. If using foil, remove bars from pan, using the overlapping foil to lift bars (photo 2, page 111); place on cutting board. Cut into bars. Makes 32 bars.

**Per bar:** 156 cal., 9 g total fat (5 g sat. fat), 23 mg chol., 18 mg sodium, 20 g carbo., 1 g fiber, 1 g pro.

**①** Spoon the crumb mixture over the bottom of the pan, then use your hand to press into an even layer.

**②** Spread lemon curd evenly over hot crust, leaving a ½-inch border all around the edges.

**③** Sprinkle crumb mixture in an even layer all over the lemon curd.

**Ask Mom** How do I cut bars? p. 113 / How do I grease a baking pan/dish? p. 59 / How do I line a pan with foil? p. 58 / How do I measure butter? p. 55 / How do I measure flour? p. 54 / How do I measure sugar? p. 55 / How do I soften butter? p. 28, 76 / How do

② Skill Level

**Good to Know** This recipe may make a whopping 60 bars, but they're admittedly petite in size. With an ingredient list that includes 1 cup of butter, 2 whole cups of brown sugar, chocolate, nuts, and caramel, they're super-rich. (Bet you can't eat just one.)

# Oatmeal-Caramel Bars

1 cup butter, softened
   (photo 1, page 76)
2 cups packed brown sugar
2 eggs
2 teaspoons vanilla
1 teaspoon baking soda
2½ cups all-purpose flour

3 cups quick-cooking rolled oats
1 cup miniature semisweet chocolate pieces
½ cup chopped walnuts or pecans
30 vanilla caramels (9 ounces), unwrapped (below)
3 tablespoons milk

**1** Preheat oven to 350°F. If desired, line a 15×10×1-inch baking pan with foil, leaving about 1 inch of foil extending over the ends of the pan; set aside.

**2** In a large mixing bowl beat butter with an electric mixer on medium to high speed for 30 seconds (photo 2, page 76). Add the brown sugar. Beat until combined, scraping sides of bowl occasionally (photo 3, page 76). Beat in eggs, vanilla, and baking soda until combined (photo 4, page 76). Beat in as much of the flour as you can with the mixer (photo 5, page 76). Using a sturdy rubber scraper or wooden spoon, stir in any remaining flour and the oats (photo 6, page 76). Press two-thirds of the oats mixture (about 3⅓ cups) evenly into the bottom of the prepared pan (photo 1, page 111). Sprinkle with chocolate pieces and nuts.

**3** In a medium saucepan heat and stir the caramels and milk over low heat until smooth (below). Drizzle caramel mixture over chocolate and nuts (below). Drop the remaining oats mixture over the caramel (below).

**4** Bake in the preheated oven for 22 to 25 minutes or until top is light brown. Cool in pan on a wire rack. If using foil, remove bars from pan, using the overlapping foil to lift bars (photo 2, page 111); place on cutting board. Cut into bars. Makes 60 bars.

Per bar: 140 cal., 6 g total fat (3 g sat. fat), 16 mg chol., 61 mg sodium, 21 g carbo., 1 g fiber, 2 g pro.

① Unwrap the caramels and place them in a medium saucepan.

② Using a heat-resistant silicone scraper, heat and stir caramels and milk over low heat until melted and smooth.

③ Drizzle the caramel mixture all over the chocolate and nuts on the crust.

④ Drop the remaining oat mixture in teaspoon-size chunks evenly over the caramel layer.

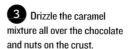
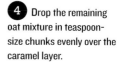

**Ask Mom** How do I cut bars/brownies? p. 113 / How do I line a pan with foil? p. 58 / How do I measure butter? p. 55 / How do I measure flour? p. 54 / How do I measure sugar? p. 55 / How do I soften butter? p. 28, 76 / What are chopped nuts? p. 34 / What does drizzle mean? p. 69, 85 / What is baking soda? p. 30, 319 / What is semisweet/bittersweet chocolate? p. 32 / What is vanilla?

**Good to Know** When you're looking for a quick-fix dessert, this simple stir-together recipe is great to have in your back pocket. It's moist and well spiced and really hits the spot with a cup of coffee—especially in the fall.

# Pumpkin Bars

2 cups all-purpose flour
2 teaspoons baking powder
2 teaspoons ground cinnamon
1 teaspoon baking soda
¼ teaspoon salt
4 eggs, lightly beaten

1 15-ounce can pumpkin
1⅔ cups sugar
1 cup cooking oil
¾ cup chopped pecans (optional)
1 recipe Cream Cheese Frosting
Pecan halves (optional)

**1** Preheat oven to 350°F. If desired, line a 15×10×1-inch baking pan with foil, leaving about 1 inch of foil extending over the ends of the pan; set aside. In a medium bowl stir together the flour, baking powder, cinnamon, baking soda, and salt; set aside.

**2** In a large bowl stir together eggs, pumpkin, sugar, and oil until combined (below). Stir in the flour mixture until combined (below). If desired, stir in chopped pecans (below). Spread batter evenly in the prepared pan.

**3** Bake in the preheated oven for 25 to 30 minutes or until a wooden toothpick inserted in the center comes out clean (below). Cool in pan on a wire rack. Spread Cream Cheese Frosting over cooled bars. If desired, top with pecan halves. If using foil, remove bars from pan, using the overlapping foil to lift bars (photo 2, page 111); place on cutting board. Cut into bars. Makes 24 bars.

Cream Cheese Frosting: In a medium mixing bowl beat two 3-ounce packages cream cheese, softened; ½ cup butter, softened; and 2 teaspoons vanilla with an electric mixer on medium speed until fluffy. Gradually add 4 cups powdered sugar, beating until smooth.

Per bar: 315 cal., 17 g total fat (6 g sat. fat), 54 mg chol., 184 mg sodium, 40 g carbo., 1 g fiber, 3 g pro.

**1** Place the eggs, pumpkin, sugar, and oil in a large bowl. Stir together until well mixed.

**2** Add the flour mixture to pumpkin mixture. Gently stir together just until all the flour is moistened. Do not overmix.

**3** Gently stir the chopped pecans into the batter until they are evenly distributed in batter.

**4** To test doneness, stick a toothpick in the center of the bars. The toothpick should come out with no unbaked batter on it.

**Ask Mom** How do I cut bars? p. 113 / How do I line a pan with foil? p. 58 / How do I measure butter/sugar/liquids? p. 55 / How do I measure flour? p. 54 / How do I soften butter? p. 28, 76 / How do I soften cream cheese? p. 57 / How do I work with eggs? p. 26–27 / What are chopped nuts? p. 34 / What is baking powder/soda? p. 30, 319 / What is canned pumpkin? p. 302 / What is cinnamon? p. 36 / What is cooking oil? p. 28 / What is powdered sugar? p. 29 / What is vanilla? p. 128 / What's that flour? p. 31

# Coconut-Date Bars

2 cups all-purpose flour
1 ½ cups sugar
2 teaspoons baking powder
¼ teaspoon salt
1 cup butter
¾ cup canned unsweetened coconut milk

2 eggs
1 teaspoon vanilla
1 cup flaked coconut, toasted
1 8-ounce package (1 ⅓ cups) chopped dates
1 recipe Coconut Frosting
½ cup flaked coconut, toasted

**1** Preheat oven to 350°F. If desired, line a 15×10×1-inch baking pan with foil, leaving about 1 inch of foil extending over the ends of the pan. Grease foil or pan; set aside. In a large mixing bowl stir together the flour, sugar, baking powder, and salt; set aside.

**2** In a small saucepan combine butter and coconut milk. Bring just to boiling, stirring occasionally. Add butter mixture to flour mixture; beat with an electric mixer on medium speed until combined. Add eggs and vanilla; beat for 1 minute. Fold in the 1 cup coconut and the dates. Spread batter evenly in the prepared pan.

**3** Bake in the preheated oven about 30 minutes or until a wooden toothpick inserted in the center comes out clean (photo 4, page 121). Cool in pan on a wire rack. Spread Coconut Frosting over cooled bars. Sprinkle with the ½ cup coconut. If using foil, remove bars from pan, using the overlapping foil to lift bars (photo 2, page 111); place on cutting board. Cut into bars. Makes 36 bars.

Coconut Frosting: In a medium mixing bowl beat one 3-ounce package cream cheese, softened, and 2 tablespoons butter, softened, with an electric mixer on medium to high speed until combined. Beat in 2 tablespoons canned unsweetened coconut milk and ½ teaspoon vanilla. Gradually add 4 cups powdered sugar, beating until smooth.

Per bar: 228 cal., 10 g total fat (7 g sat. fat), 30 mg chol., 103 mg sodium, 34 g carbo., 1 g fiber, 1 g pro.

**Ask Mom** How do I cut bars? p. 113 / How do I grease a baking pan? p. 59 / How do I line a pan with foil? p. 58 / How do I measure butter/sugar/liquids? p. 55 / How do I measure flour? p. 54 / How do I soften butter? p. 28, 76 / How do I soften cream cheese? p. 57 / How do I toast coconut? p. 40 / What is baking powder? p. 30, 319 / What is coconut milk? p. 40 / What is powdered sugar? p. 29 / What is vanilla? p. 128 / What's that dried fruit? p. 41 / What's that flour? p. 31

**Good to Know** The best way to crush the candies is to put them in a resealable plastic bag and lightly pound with a rolling pin. Be careful not to get overzealous—you'll end up with powder. To get perfect pieces, put the crushed candy in a fine-mesh sieve to shake out the dust (page 65).

# Peppermint-Fudge Brownie Bites

I   16- to 18-ounce package refrigerated triple-chocolate cookie dough
I   cup tiny marshmallows
⅓   cup miniature semisweet chocolate pieces
¼   cup crushed striped round peppermint candies or candy canes
⅓   cup miniature semisweet chocolate pieces
I   teaspoon shortening

**1** Preheat oven to 350°F. If desired, line an 8×8×2-inch baking pan with foil, leaving about 1 inch of foil extending over the ends of the pan. Break up cookie dough and place in the prepared pan. Press dough evenly into the bottom of the prepared pan.

**2** Bake in the preheated oven for 18 minutes. Immediately sprinkle the marshmallows and ⅓ cup chocolate pieces over top. Bake for 3 to 4 minutes more or until marshmallows are puffed but not brown (below). Sprinkle with crushed peppermint candies. Cool completely.

**3** If using foil, remove brownies from pan, using the overlapping foil to lift brownies (photo 2, page 111); place on cutting board. Using a long, sharp knife, cut into squares (below). In a small saucepan heat and stir ⅓ cup chocolate pieces and the shortening over low heat until smooth. Drizzle brownies with melted chocolate. Let stand until chocolate is set. Makes 25 brownies.

Per brownie: 125 cal., 5 g total fat (2 g sat. fat), 3 mg chol., 60 mg sodium, 19 g carbo., 0 g fiber, 1 g pro.

**1** Bake bars until the marshmallows are puffed up but not toasted or brown. Sprinkle with peppermints.

**2** Using foil, lift brownies from pan and place on a cutting board. Cut into squares using a sharp knife.

**3** A hot knife cuts through marshmallows more easily. Between cuts, run the knife under hot water and pat dry.

**Ask Mom** How do I line a pan with foil? p. 58 / How do I melt chocolate? p. 32, 33 / What does drizzle mean? p. 69, 85 / What is semisweet/bittersweet chocolate? p. 32

# Fudgy Brownies

**Good to Know** These brownies are yummy au naturel—or simply with a sprinkle of powdered sugar. If you go with the Chocolate-Cream Cheese Frosting, be sure to store the frosted brownies in the refrigerator.

½ cup butter

3 ounces unsweetened chocolate, coarsely chopped (photo 1, page 125)

1 cup sugar

2 eggs

1 teaspoon vanilla

⅔ cup all-purpose flour

¼ teaspoon baking soda

½ cup chopped nuts (optional)

1 recipe Chocolate-Cream Cheese Frosting (optional)

**1** In a medium saucepan heat and stir butter and unsweetened chocolate over low heat until smooth (photo 2, page 125); set aside to cool. Preheat oven to 350°F. If desired, line an 8×8×2-inch baking pan with foil, leaving about 1 inch of the foil extending over the ends of pan. Grease foil or pan; set pan aside.

**2** Stir the sugar into the cooled chocolate mixture (photo 3, page 125). Add the eggs, one at a time, beating with a wooden spoon just until combined (photo 4, page 125). Stir in vanilla. In a small bowl stir together the flour and baking soda. Add flour mixture to chocolate mixture; stir just until combined (photos 5–6, page 125). If desired, stir in nuts. Spread the batter evenly in the prepared pan.

**3** Bake in the preheated oven for 30 minutes. Cool in pan on a wire rack. If desired, spread Chocolate-Cream Cheese Frosting over cooled brownies. If using foil, remove brownies from pan, using the overlapping foil to lift brownies (photo 2, page 111); place on cutting board. Cut into squares. Makes 16 brownies.

Per brownie: 155 cal., 9 g total fat (6 g sat. fat), 42 mg chol., 71 mg sodium, 18 g carbo., 1 g fiber, 2 g pro.

Chocolate-Cream Cheese Frosting: In a small heavy saucepan heat and stir 1 cup semisweet chocolate pieces over low heat until smooth. Remove from heat; let cool. In a medium bowl stir together two 3-ounce packages softened cream cheese and ½ cup powdered sugar. Stir in melted chocolate until smooth.

**Flavor Changes** If you're a brownie purist, this is your nirvana. If you like a little extrapolation, turn to page 126 for a dozen fabulous stir-in ideas .

**Ask Mom** How do I cut brownies? p. 113 / How do I grease a baking pan? p. 59 / How do I line a pan with foil? p. 58 / How do I measure butter? p. 55 / How do I measure flour? p. 54 / How do I measure sugar? p. 55 / How do I soften cream cheese? p. 57 / What are chopped nuts? p. 34 / What is baking soda? p. 30, 319 / What is powdered sugar? p. 29 / What is semisweet chocolate? p. 32 / What is unsweetened chocolate? p. 32 / What is vanilla? p. 128 / What's that flour? p. 31 / What's that nut? p. 34–35

**WHAT'S A SAUCEPAN BROWNIE?** As the name implies, they're mixed completely in a saucepan—no mixing bowl needed. That makes them simple to make and even easier to clean up. Use the suggested pan size to avoid slopping or scorching ingredients.

**1** Using a chef's knife, coarsely chop chocolate bars or pieces on a cutting board.

**2** Heat and stir the butter and chocolate over low heat until smooth and melted.

**3** After the chocolate mixture has cooled, stir in the sugar until dissolved.

**4** Add the eggs one at a time. Stir vigorously after each addition until the eggs are incorporated.

**5** Combine the flour and baking soda in a bowl, then add the flour mixture all at once to the chocolate mixture.

**6** Gently stir just until all of the flour mixture is moistened. If desired, stir in the nuts.

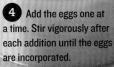

## Mint Brownies

½ teaspoon peppermint extract
1 cup chopped layered chocolate-mint candies

Prepare Fudgy Brownies (page 124) as directed, except stir in peppermint extract with the vanilla. Use the frosting option. After frosting the brownies, sprinkle chopped candies over the top.

## Chocolate-Cherry Brownies

½ cup snipped dried cherries
2 tablespoons rum or orange juice
½ cup coarsely chopped bittersweet chocolate

Prepare Fudgy Brownies (page 124) as directed, except first soak cherries in rum for 30 minutes; drain and discard rum. Fold cherries and chopped chocolate into the batter.

## Peanut Butter Brownies

1 ¼ cups chopped bite-size chocolate-covered peanut butter cups

Prepare Fudgy Brownies (page 124) as directed, except stir ¾ cup of the chopped peanut butter cups into the batter. Use the frosting option. After frosting the brownies, sprinkle the remaining ½ cup chopped peanut butter cups over top.

## Orange-Nut Brownies

2 teaspoons finely shredded orange peel
Whole hazelnuts (filberts)
Candied orange peel

Prepare Fudgy Brownies (page 124) as directed, except stir orange peel into the batter and use hazelnuts as the nuts. Use the frosting option. Garnish each brownie with candied orange peel and a whole hazelnut.

## Strawberry-Banana Brownies

⅓ cup sliced fresh strawberries
⅓ cup sliced fresh banana
¼ cup chopped peanuts
Sweetened Whipped Cream (page 25)

Prepare Fudgy Brownies (page 124) as directed; use frosting option. In a bowl toss together berries and banana. Sprinkle fruit mixture and the peanuts over frosting. Top each brownie with Sweetened Whipped Cream.

## Extra-Chocolate Brownies

¾ cup white baking pieces
Shaved bittersweet chocolate

Prepare Fudgy Brownies (page 124) as directed, except stir white baking pieces into the batter. Use the frosting option. After frosting the brownies, sprinkle shaved chocolate over the top.

## S'more Brownies

¾ cup tiny marshmallows
½ cup honey graham cereal

Prepare Fudgy Brownies (page 124) as directed, except before baking, sprinkle marshmallows and cereal over top of the batter. Bake as directed until marshmallows are puffed. Do not use frosting option.

## Malted Milk Brownies

¼ cup malted milk powder
½ cup coarsely chopped malted milk balls

Prepare Fudgy Brownies (page 124) as directed, except stir in the malted milk powder with the flour. Use the frosting option. After frosting the brownies, sprinkle chopped malted milk balls over the top.

## Espresso Brownies

1½ teaspoons instant espresso powder
2 teaspoons hot water
½ teaspoon ground cinnamon

Prepare Fudgy Brownies (page 124) as directed, except dissolve 1 teaspoon of the espresso powder in the hot water. Add espresso mixture and cinnamon with the eggs. Use the frosting option, except stir the remaining ½ teaspoon espresso powder into the melted chocolate.

## Macaroon Brownies

½ cup chopped soft macaroon cookies

Prepare Fudgy Brownies (page 124) as directed, using almonds as the nuts. Use the frosting option. After frosting the brownies, sprinkle chopped macaroon cookies over the top.

## Turtle Brownies

¾ cup vanilla caramels (16 to 18)
1 tablespoon milk

Prepare Fudgy Brownies (page 124) as directed, using pecans as the nuts. Before baking, in a microwave-safe bowl combine caramels and milk; microwave on high (100 percent power) about 1 minute or until melted, stirring once. Drizzle melted caramel over top of the batter. Bake as directed.

## Raspberry Brownies

⅔ cup raspberry preserves
Fresh raspberries

Prepare Fudgy Brownies (page 124) as directed. After baking, spread preserves over warm brownies. Let cool. Use the frosting option. Garnish each brownie with fresh raspberries.

# Chunky Path **Brownies**

| | |
|---|---|
| 2 cups all-purpose flour | ⅓ cup unsweetened cocoa powder |
| 2 cups sugar | 2 eggs |
| 1 teaspoon baking soda | ½ cup buttermilk or sour milk |
| ¼ teaspoon salt | 1½ teaspoons vanilla |
| 1 cup butter | 3 cups tiny marshmallows |
| 1 cup water | 1 recipe Chocolate Topper or Chocolate-Peanut Topper |

**1** Preheat oven to 350°F. If desired, line a 15×10×1-inch baking pan with foil, leaving about 1 inch of foil extending over the ends of the pan. Grease foil or pan; set pan aside. In a large mixing bowl stir together the flour, sugar, baking soda, and salt; set aside.

**2** In a medium saucepan combine butter, water, and cocoa powder. Bring to boiling, stirring constantly. Add the chocolate mixture to the flour mixture; beat with an electric mixer on medium speed until combined. Add eggs, buttermilk, and vanilla; beat for 1 minute (batter will be thin). Pour batter into the prepared pan.

**3** Bake in the preheated oven about 25 minutes or until a wooden toothpick inserted in the center comes out clean (photo 4, page 121). Sprinkle marshmallows over hot brownies. Top with Chocolate Topper or Chocolate-Peanut Topper. Cool in pan on a wire rack. If using foil, remove brownies from pan, using the overlapping foil to lift brownies (photo 2, page 111); place on cutting board. Using a hot knife, cut into bars (photo 3, page 123). Makes 48 brownies.

**Per brownie:** 155 cal., 8 g total fat (5 g sat. fat), 25 mg chol., 84 mg sodium, 20 g carbo., 1 g fiber, 1 g pro.

**Chocolate Topper:** In a medium saucepan combine one 12-ounce package (2 cups) semisweet chocolate pieces, ½ cup whipping cream, and ¼ cup butter. Heat and stir over medium-low heat until smooth. Drizzle over brownies.

**Chocolate-Peanut Topper:** In a medium saucepan combine 1⅓ cups semisweet chocolate pieces, 1 cup creamy peanut butter, and 3 tablespoons butter. Heat and stir over medium-low heat until smooth. Drizzle over brownies. Sprinkle with 1 cup chopped dry-roasted peanuts.

**THE RIGHT STUFF.** Real vanilla extract is made by soaking vanilla beans in alcohol and aging it. Imitation vanilla is made entirely of artificial flavorings. If your budget allows, buy extract. Imitation vanilla is no match for the flavor and aroma of the real deal.

**Ask Mom** How do I cut brownies? p. 113 / How do I grease a baking pan? p. 59 / How do I line a pan with foil? p. 58 / How do I make sour milk? p. 24 / How do I measure butter? p. 55 / How do I measure flour? p. 54 / How do I measure liquids? p. 55 / How do I measure peanut butter? p. 55 / How do I measure sugar? p. 55 / What is baking soda? p. 30, 319 / What is buttermilk? p. 24 / What is cocoa powder? p. 170 / What is semisweet chocolate? p. 32 / What is whipping cream? p. 24 / What's that flour? p. 31

# Candy Bar Brownies

1¼ cups finely crushed graham crackers (about 18 graham cracker squares) (below)

¼ cup sugar

¼ cup finely chopped dry-roasted peanuts

½ cup butter, melted

½ cup butter

2 ounces unsweetened chocolate, chopped

1 cup sugar

2 eggs, lightly beaten

1 teaspoon vanilla

⅔ cup all-purpose flour

½ cup peanut butter-flavor pieces

1 recipe Peanut Butter Frosting

¼ cup dry-roasted peanut halves

**1** Preheat oven to 350°F. If desired, line an 11×7×1½-inch or a 9×9×2-inch baking pan with foil, leaving about 1 inch of foil extending over the ends of pan; set aside. In a medium bowl stir together the graham crackers, the ¼ cup sugar, and the ¼ cup chopped peanuts. Stir in the melted butter. Press graham cracker mixture evenly into the bottom of the prepared pan. Bake in the preheated oven about 5 minutes or until crust appears set. Remove from oven.

**2** In a medium heavy saucepan heat and stir the ½ cup butter and the chocolate over low heat until smooth (photo 2, page 125). Remove from heat. Stir in the 1 cup sugar, the eggs, and vanilla just until combined. Stir in flour and peanut butter-flavor pieces. Spread chocolate mixture evenly over baked crust (below).

**3** Bake about 20 minutes more or until center appears set. Cool in pan on a wire rack. Spread Peanut Butter Frosting over cooled brownie (below). If using foil, remove brownies from pan, using the overlapping foil to lift brownies (photo 2, page 111); place on cutting board. Cut into 1-inch squares. Place a peanut half on each square. Makes 70 bite-size brownies.

**Peanut Butter Frosting:** In a medium mixing bowl beat ¼ cup butter, softened, and 2 tablespoons peanut butter with an electric mixer on low speed for 30 seconds. Gradually beat in 1 cup powdered sugar. Beat in 1 tablespoon milk and ½ teaspoon vanilla. Gradually beat in 1 cup additional powdered sugar and enough milk to make frosting of spreading consistency.

Per brownie: 89 cal., 5 g total fat (3 g sat. fat), 15 mg chol., 45 mg sodium, 11 g carbo., 0 g fiber, 1 g pro.

**1** Finely grind graham crackers in a food processor with a blade attachment.

**2** Alternately, place crackers in a sealed plastic bag; crush with a rolling pin.

**3** Using an offset spatula, spread the chocolate mixture over the warm baked crust.

**4** When brownies are cool, spread frosting evenly over top.

**Ask Mom** How do I chop chocolate? p. 33 / How do I cut bars/brownies? p. 113 / How do I line a pan with foil? p. 58 / How do I measure butter? p. 55 / How do I measure flour? p. 54 / How do I measure sugar? p. 55 / How do I melt chocolate? p. 32, 33 / How do I soften butter? p. 28, 76 / How do I work with eggs? p. 26–27 / What are chopped nuts? p. 34 / What is powdered sugar? p. 29 / What is unsweetened chocolate? p. 32 / What is vanilla? p. 128 / What's that flour? p. 31 / What's that nut? p. 34–35

# Cappuccino Brownies

⅔ cup all-purpose flour

¼ teaspoon baking soda

½ cup butter

3 ounces unsweetened chocolate, chopped
(photo 1, page 125)

1 cup granulated sugar

2 eggs

1 teaspoon vanilla

1 teaspoon instant coffee crystals

1 tablespoon whipping cream

1 cup powdered sugar

2 tablespoons butter, softened

1 recipe Chocolate Frosting

**1** Preheat oven to 350°F. Combine flour and soda; set aside. If desired, line an 8×8×2-inch baking pan with foil, leaving 1 inch of foil extending over ends of pan. Grease foil or pan; set aside.

**2** In a medium saucepan heat and stir the ½ cup butter and the unsweetened chocolate over low heat until smooth (photo 2, page 125). Remove from heat; cool slightly. Stir in granulated sugar (photo 3, page 125). Add eggs, one at a time, beating with a wooden spoon just until combined (photo 4, page 125). Stir in vanilla. Add flour mixture to chocolate mixture; stir just until combined (photos 5-6, page 125). Spread batter evenly in the prepared pan.

**3** Bake in the preheated oven for 30 minutes. Transfer pan to a wire rack. In a bowl stir together coffee crystals and cream until crystals dissolve. Stir in powdered sugar and the 2 tablespoons butter until creamy. If necessary, add a little additional cream until mixture is of spreading consistency. Spread coffee mixture over the warm brownies (below). Cool completely.

**4** Spread Chocolate Frosting over cooled brownies (below). Chill about 1 hour or until frosting is set. If using foil, remove brownies from pan, using the overlapping foil to lift brownies (photo 2, page 111); place on cutting board. Cut into squares. Makes 16 brownies.

**Chocolate Frosting:** In a small saucepan combine 1 cup semisweet chocolate pieces and ⅓ cup whipping cream. Heat and stir over low heat until smooth and mixture begins to thicken.

Per brownie: 264 cal., 16 g total fat (10 g sat. fat), 54 mg chol., 84 mg sodium, 32 g carbo., 2 g fiber, 2 g pro.

**1** Using an offset spatula, spread coffee mixture evenly over the warm brownies.

**2** Spread hot Chocolate Frosting evenly over cooled brownies. Chill until set.

**Ingredient Info**

You may not want to make coffee with them (unless you're on a camping trip), but instant coffee crystals make great mocha flavor in these brownies. Look for them in the same aisle as regular coffee.

**Ask Mom** How do I chop chocolate? p. 33 / How do I cut bars/brownies? p. 113 / How do I grease a baking pan/dish? p. 59 / How do I measure butter? p. 55 / How do I measure flour? p. 54 / How do I measure sugar? p. 55 / How do I soften butter? p. 28, 76 / What is baking soda? p. 30, 319 / What is powdered sugar? p. 29 / What is semisweet/bittersweet chocolate? p. 32 / What is unsweetened chocolate? p. 32 / What is vanilla? p. 128 / What is whipping cream? p. 24 / What's that flour? p. 31

# Cream Cheese Brownies

8 ounces semisweet chocolate, chopped

3 tablespoons butter

4 eggs

1¼ cups sugar

2 teaspoons vanilla

1 cup all-purpose flour

1 teaspoon baking powder

¾ cup chopped toasted macadamia nuts, pecans, or walnuts

1 8-ounce package cream cheese, softened

⅔ cup sugar

2 tablespoons all-purpose flour

1 tablespoon lemon juice

1 recipe Chocolate Glaze

**1** If desired, line a 13×9×2-inch baking pan with foil, leaving about 1 inch of foil extending over the ends of pan. Grease foil or pan; set aside. In a large heavy saucepan heat and stir chocolate and butter over low heat until smooth (photo 2, page 125); set aside to cool.

**2** Preheat oven to 350°F. In a bowl beat 2 eggs until foamy (below). Add 1¼ cups sugar, ⅓ cup *water*, and 1 teaspoon of the vanilla; beat on medium speed 6 minutes or until slightly thickened. Beat in chocolate mixture. Stir in the 1 cup flour, the baking powder, and ¼ teaspoon *salt*; stir in nuts. Spread half of the batter in the prepared pan; set pan and remaining batter aside.

**3** In a medium mixing bowl beat cream cheese, the ⅔ cup sugar, the remaining 2 eggs, the 2 tablespoons flour, the lemon juice, and the remaining 1 teaspoon vanilla with an electric mixer on medium speed until smooth. Spread cream cheese mixture evenly over batter in pan (below). Spoon remaining batter in small spoonfuls evenly over the cream cheese mixture (below). Using a knife, swirl batter and cream cheese mixture to marble (below). Bake in the preheated oven for 45 minutes. Cool in pan on wire rack. Spread Chocolate Glaze over brownies. Chill about 1 hour or until glaze is set. If using foil, remove brownies from pan, using the overlapping foil to lift brownies (photo 2, page 111); place on cutting board. Cut into bars. Makes 32 brownies.

Chocolate Glaze: In a small saucepan heat and stir ⅓ cup whipping cream and 6 ounces finely chopped semisweet chocolate over low heat until smooth.

**1** Beat eggs on medium speed of an electric mixer until foamy but not thickened.

**2** Using an offset spatula, evenly spread the cream cheese mixture over chocolate batter.

**3** Spoon the chocolate batter evenly all over the cream cheese layer.

**4** Using a table knife tip, swirl the spooned batter and cream cheese layers together.

**Ask Mom** How do I chop chocolate? p. 33 / How do I cut brownies? p. 113 / How do I juice a lemon? p. 44, 45 / How do I line a pan with foil? p. 58 / How do I measure butter/sugar/liquids? p. 55 / How do I measure flour? p. 54 / How do I melt chocolate? p. 32, 33 / How do I soften cream cheese? p. 57 / How do I toast nuts? p. 34 / What are chopped nuts? p. 34 / What is baking soda? p. 30, 319 / What is semisweet chocolate? p. 32 / What is vanilla? p. 128 / What is whipping cream? p. 24 / What's that flour? p. 31

# Raspberry and White
## Chocolate Brownies

½ cup butter

2 ounces white baking chocolate, chopped
(photo I, page 125)

2 eggs

⅔ cup sugar

I teaspoon vanilla

I cup all-purpose flour

½ cup chopped toasted almonds

½ teaspoon baking powder

Dash salt

I cup fresh raspberries

2 ounces white baking chocolate, melted

**1** Preheat oven to 350°F. If desired, line an 8×8×2-inch baking pan with foil, leaving about 1 inch of foil extending over the ends of pan. Grease foil or pan; set pan aside.

**2** In a medium saucepan heat and stir butter and the chopped white chocolate over low heat until smooth (photo 2, page 125). Remove from heat. Add eggs, sugar, and vanilla. Beat lightly with a wooden spoon just until combined. Stir in the flour, almonds, baking powder, and salt. Spread batter evenly in the prepared pan. Sprinkle with raspberries.

**3** Bake in the preheated oven for 30 to 35 minutes or until golden. Cool in pan on a wire rack. If using foil, remove brownies from pan, using the overlapping foil to lift brownies (photo 2, page 111); place on cutting board. Cut into bars. Drizzle bars with the melted white chocolate. Serve brownies the same day they are prepared. Makes 20 brownies.

Per brownie: I46 cal., 8 g total fat (4 g sat. fat), 34 mg chol., 62 mg sodium, I6 g carbo., I g fiber, 2 g pro.

For a fun presentation, use a round cutter to cut out brownies before drizzling with melted white chocolate. Garnish with fresh berries.

**Ask Mom** How do I chop chocolate? p. 33 / How do I cut brownies? p. II3 / How do I grease a baking pan? p. 59 / How do I line a pan with foil? p. 58 / How do I measure butter/sugar? p. 55 / How do I measure flour? p. 54 / How do I melt chocolate? p. 32, 33 / How do I toast nuts? p. 34 / How do I wash fresh berries? p. 42 / What does drizzle mean? p. 69, 85 / What is baking powder? p. 30, 3I9 / What is vanilla? p. I28 / What is white chocolate? p. 32 / What's that flour? p. 3I / What's that nut? p. 34–35

# irresistible
# CAKES

Nothing says "special occasion" like a homemade cake—whether it's single layer, triple layer, rolled and filled, white, yellow, or rich dark chocolate.

4

Angel Cake, Tinted ① ..............................................150

BUTTER AND SHORTENING CAKES
Citrus Yellow Cake ② ....................................135
Coconut White Cake ② ...............................138
White Cake ② ........................................138
Yellow Cake ② ......................................135

Cake-Baking Basics..........................................136–137

CAKE ROLLS
Pumpkin Cake Roll ② ...................................148
Strawberry Cake Roll ② ..............................149

Cherry Compote ③ ...........................................159

CHOCOLATE CAKES
Chocolate Cake ② .....................................139
Chocolate-Peppermint Fantasy Cake ③ ..................140
German Chocolate Cake ② ...........................142
White Chocolate Snowdrift Cake ② .....................143

FILLINGS, FROSTINGS, AND ICINGS
Almond Butter Frosting ① ..............................145
Butter Frosting ① ....................................145
Chocolate Butter Frosting ① ...........................145
Chocolate Sour Cream Frosting ② .....................144
Citrus Butter Frosting ① ..............................145
Coconut-Pecan Frosting ② ...........................142
Coffee Butter Frosting ① .............................145
Cream Cheese Filling ① ...............................148
Cream Cheese Frosting ① .............................144
Creamy White Frosting ① .............................144
Mocha Cream ② ....................................160
No-Cook Fudge Frosting ① ...........................144
Penuche Frosting ② ..................................145
Peppermint Butter Frosting ① .........................145
Sour Cream Frosting ① ..............................146
Tangerine Glaze ①....................................151

MINIATURE CAKES
Malibu Rum Baby Cakes ② ..............................152
Molten Chocolate Cakes with Cherry Compote ② .........159

TORTES
Lemon-Berry Ribbon Torte ② ..........................146
Walnut-Cappuccino Torte ② ...........................160

TUBE CAKES
Lime-Infused Coconut Cake ② ..........................154
Sour Cream-Walnut Date Cake with Tangerine Glaze ② .....151

UPSIDE-DOWN CAKES
Polenta and Plum Cake ① ...............................157
Upside-Down One Bowl Apple Cake ② ...................156
Upside-Down Peach Caramel Crunch Cake ① ............155

(2) Skill Level

# Yellow Cake

¾ cup butter

3 eggs

2½ cups all-purpose flour

2½ teaspoons baking powder

½ teaspoon salt

1¾ cups sugar

1½ teaspoons vanilla

1¼ cups milk

1 recipe Chocolate Butter Frosting (page 145) or Penuche Frosting (page 145)

**Good to Know** If there is one cake in your repertoire, make it this basic but beautifully flexible butter cake. You can fill it with frosting, fruit preserves, or lemon curd. Or serve single layers cut into wedges and topped with fresh fruit and a spoonful of whipped cream.

**1** Let butter and eggs stand at room temperature for 30 minutes. Grease, lightly flour, and line bottoms of two 9×1½-inch or 8×1½-inch round cake pans with waxed paper (photo 1, page 136) or grease one 13×9×2-inch baking pan; set the pan(s) aside. In a medium bowl stir together flour, baking powder, and salt (photo 2, page 136); set aside.

**2** Preheat oven to 375°F. In a large mixing bowl beat butter with an electric mixer on medium to high speed for 30 seconds (photo 3, page 136). Gradually add sugar, about ¼ cup at time, beating on medium speed and scraping sides of bowl until well combined (photo 4, 136). Beat on medium speed for 2 minutes more (photo 5, page 136). Add eggs, one at a time, beating until combined after each addition (photo 6, page 136). Beat in vanilla. Alternately add flour mixture and milk to butter mixture, beating on low speed after each addition just until combined (photo 7, page 137).

**3** Spread batter evenly into the prepared pan(s) (photo 8, page 137). Bake in the preheated oven for 20 to 25 minutes for 9-inch pans, 30 to 35 minutes for 8-inch pans, 25 to 30 minutes for 13×9×2-inch pan, or until a wooden toothpick inserted near the center(s) comes out clean (photo 9, page 137). Cool cake layers in pans on wire racks for 10 minutes. Remove cake layers from pans (photos 10–11, page 137); remove waxed paper (photo 12, page 137) and cool thoroughly on racks. Or place 13×9×2-inch cake in pan on a wire rack; cool thoroughly. Frost with Chocolate Butter Frosting or Penuche Frosting (photos 13–14, page 137). Makes 12 to 16 servings.

**Citrus Yellow Cake:** Prepare as above, except stir 2 teaspoons finely shredded orange or lemon peel into batter. Frost with Citrus Butter Frosting (page 145).

Per serving: 413 cal., 16 g total fat (9 g sat. fat), 94 mg chol., 349 mg sodium, 63 g carbo., 1 g fiber, 5 g pro.

**Ask Mom** How do I grease and flour a pan? p. 59 / How do I measure butter? p. 55 / How do I measure flour? p. 54 / How do I measure liquids? p. 55 / How do I measure sugar? p. 55 / How do I shred lemon/lime/orange peel? p. 45, 105 / How do I store a frosted cake? p. 137 / What is baking powder? p. 30, 319 / What is vanilla? p. 128 / What's that flour? p. 31

# Cake-Baking Basics

## Few desserts rise to a special occasion like a homemade cake. Here's how to make any cake you bake turn out gorgeous and great-tasting.

The first step in making almost any butter-based cake is simply a little waiting time. Most cakes benefit greatly from butter and eggs that have been set on the counter about 30 minutes to allow them to come to room temperature. The butter will blend more easily with other ingredients if it's slightly softened, and the eggs will give your cake more volume.

When baking your cake, be sure to bake at the recommended temperature. If the oven temperature is too hot, your cake may develop tunnels and cracks; if it's too low, the cake can have a coarse texture. When you check for doneness, check at the minimum baking time—but don't open the oven door any earlier than that, to prevent your cake from falling.

**4** Add the sugar in small amounts, about ¼ cup at a time. The small additions of sugar make it easier to incorporate more air into the mixture.

**1** Cut waxed paper to fit the bottom of the pan(s). Grease and lightly flour the pan(s), then place waxed paper in the pan(s).

**2** Stir together the dry ingredients—flour, baking powder and/or soda, salt, and sometimes cocoa powder and/or spices.

**3** Use an electric mixer on medium speed to beat softened butter or shortening.

**5** Beat the butter and sugar until the mixture has a light, fluffy texture. Scrape the bowl occasionally while beating.

**6** Break each egg into a custard cup and add one at a time to the butter-sugar mixture. Beat well after each addition.

**7** Alternately add the flour mixture and liquid, beating on low after each addition. Begin and end with the flour mixture.

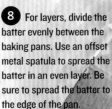

**8** For layers, divide the batter evenly between the baking pans. Use an offset metal spatula to spread the batter in an even layer. Be sure to spread the batter to the edge of the pan.

**9** Check for doneness after minimum baking time. Insert a wooden toothpick near the center. If it comes out clean, the cake is done.

**10** Let cake(s) cool in pan(s) for 10 minutes. Place a wire rack over the top of the cake and flip the cake and pan.

**11** Lift the pan off the cake, being careful not to tear the edges of the cake.

**12** Gently peel the waxed paper off the cake. Cool layers completely before frosting. Allow about 1 hour for the cake to cool.

**13** To frost layer cakes, place a layer on a cake plate. Spread about ½ cup of the frosting over the first layer.

**14** Top with the second layer. Spread a thin coating of frosting on the sides to seal in crumbs. Finish frosting the sides and top.

**HOW DO I STORE A FROSTED CAKE?** After frosting a cake, let it stand an hour or two before covering it loosely with foil, plastic wrap, or a cake cover. If the frosting contains cream cheese, whipped cream, or sour cream, store the cake in the refrigerator.

# White Cake

½ cup butter or shortening

4 egg whites

2 cups all-purpose flour

1 teaspoon baking powder

½ teaspoon baking soda

½ teaspoon salt

1¾ cups sugar

1 teaspoon vanilla

1⅓ cups buttermilk or sour milk

1 recipe Creamy White Frosting (page 144) or Almond Butter Frosting (page 145)

**1** Let butter and egg whites stand at room temperature for 30 minutes. Grease, lightly flour, and line bottoms of two 9×1½-inch or 8×1½-inch round cake pans with waxed paper (photo 1, page 136) or grease one 13×9×2-inch baking pan; set the pan(s) aside. In a medium bowl stir together flour, baking powder, baking soda, and salt (photo 2, page 136); set aside.

**2** Preheat oven to 350°F. In a large mixing bowl beat butter with an electric mixer on medium to high speed for 30 seconds (photo 3, page 136). Gradually add sugar, about ¼ cup at a time, beating on medium speed and scraping sides of bowl until well combined (photo 4, page 136). Beat in vanilla. Add egg whites, one at a time, beating until combined after each addition (photo 6, page 136). Alternately add flour mixture and buttermilk to butter mixture, beating on low speed after each addition just until combined (photo 7, page 137).

**3** Spread batter evenly into the prepared pan(s) (photo 8, page 137). Bake in the preheated oven for 20 to 25 minutes for 9-inch pans, 30 to 35 minutes for 8-inch pans or 13×9-inch pan, or until a wooden toothpick inserted near the center(s) comes out clean (photo 9, page 137). Cool cake layers in pans on wire racks for 10 minutes. Remove cake layers from pans (photos 10–11, page 137). Cool thoroughly on racks. Or place 13×9×2-inch cake in pan on a wire rack; cool thoroughly. Frost with Creamy White Frosting or Almond Butter Frosting (photos 13–14, page 137). Makes 12 to 16 servings.

**Per serving:** 344 cal., 11 g total fat (5 g sat. fat), 29 mg chol., 290 mg sodium, 58 g carbo., 1 g fiber, 4 g pro.

Coconut White Cake: Prepare as above, except stir ¾ cup toasted flaked coconut into batter. Spread ½ cup peach preserves (cut up large pieces) between layers. Frost with Butter Frosting (page 145). Sprinkle with flaked coconut.

**Ask Mom** How do I grease and flour a pan? p. 59 / How do I make sour milk? p. 24 / How do I measure butter? p. 55 / How do I measure flour? p. 54 / How do I measure shortening? p. 55 / How do I measure sugar? p. 55 / How do I snip preserves? p. 41, 102 / How do I store a frosted cake? p. 137 / How do I toast coconut? p. 40 / How do I work with eggs? p. 26–27 / What is baking powder? p. 30, 319 / What is baking soda? p. 30, 319 / What is buttermilk? p. 24 / What is vanilla? p. 128 / What's that flour? p. 31

(2) Skill Level

**Good to Know** Dress up a simple frosted cake with coarsely chopped cookies or candy bars, or with whole individual candies, such as chocolate stars or kisses, gumdrops, or nonpareils.

# Chocolate Cake

¾ cup butter

3 eggs

2 cups all-purpose flour

¾ cup unsweetened cocoa powder

1 teaspoon baking soda

¾ teaspoon baking powder

½ teaspoon salt

2 cups sugar

2 teaspoons vanilla

1½ cups milk

1 recipe Creamy White Frosting (page 144) or Chocolate Sour Cream Frosting (page 144)

Chopped chocolate sandwich cookies with white filling or chocolate candy (optional)

**1** Let butter and eggs stand at room temperature for 30 minutes. Grease bottoms of two 9×1½-inch round cake pans. Line pans with waxed paper (photo 1, page 136). Grease and flour bottoms and sides of pans. Or grease one 13×9×2-inch baking pan. Set pan(s) aside. In a medium bowl stir together flour, cocoa powder, baking soda, baking powder, and salt (photo 2, page 136); set aside.

**2** Preheat oven to 350°F. In a large mixing bowl beat butter with an electric mixer on medium to high speed for 30 seconds (photo 3, page 136). Gradually add sugar, ¼ cup at a time, beating on medium speed and scraping sides of bowl until well combined (photo 4, page 136). Beat on medium speed for 2 minutes (photo 5, page 136). Add eggs, one at a time, beating after each addition (photo 6, page 136). Beat in vanilla. Alternately add flour mixture and milk to butter mixture, beating on low speed after each addition just until combined (photo 7, page 137). Beat on medium to high speed for 20 seconds more.

**3** Spread batter evenly into prepared pan(s) (photo 8, page 137). Bake in the preheated oven for 30 to 35 minutes for 9-inch pans, 35 to 40 minutes for 13×9×2-inch pan, or until a wooden toothpick inserted near the center(s) comes out clean (photo 9, page 137). Cool cake layers in pans on wire racks for 10 minutes. Remove from pans (photos 10–11, page 137); peel off waxed paper (photo 12, page 137). Cool thoroughly on racks. Or place 13×9×2-inch cake in pan on a wire rack; cool thoroughly. Frost with Creamy White Frosting or Chocolate Sour Cream Frosting (photos 13–14, page 137). If desired, sprinkle with chopped cookies. Makes 12 to 16 servings.

**Per serving:** 661 cal., 32 g total fat (11 g sat. fat), 88 mg chol., 337 mg sodium, 89 g carbo., 1 g fiber, 6 g pro.

**Ask Mom** How do I grease and flour a pan? p. 59 / How do I measure butter? p. 55 / How do I measure flour? p. 54 / How do I measure liquids? p. 55 / How do I measure sugar? p. 55 / How do I store a frosted cake? p. 137 / What is baking powder? p. 30, 319 / What is baking soda? p. 30, 319 / What is cocoa powder? p. 170 / What is vanilla? p. 128 / What's that flour? p. 31

# Chocolate-Peppermint Fantasy Cake

1 recipe Chocolate Cake (page 139)
1 cup whipping cream
¼ cup butter
1 pound chopped bittersweet chocolate
1 tablespoon peppermint schnapps or
   ½ teaspoon peppermint extract
2 cups whipping cream

½ cup coarsely chopped peppermint sticks, candy canes, and/or other hard peppermint candies (3 ounces)
Chocolate curls (below) (optional)
Coarsely chopped peppermint sticks, candy canes, and/or other hard peppermint candies (optional)

**1** Prepare Chocolate Cake as directed using two 9×1½-inch round cake pans. Bake and cool cake layers as directed.

**2** In a medium saucepan heat and stir the 1 cup whipping cream and the butter over medium heat until butter melts. Remove from heat. Add chopped chocolate (below); let stand, uncovered, for 5 minutes. Stir mixture until smooth (below).

**3** For the peppermint fudge filling, transfer 1¼ cups of the chocolate mixture to a small bowl. Stir peppermint schnapps into chocolate mixture in bowl. Cover and chill for 1 to 2 hours, stirring occasionally, or until mixture is cold. Let remaining chocolate mixture in saucepan cool to room temperature.

**4** To assemble, place a cake layer on a serving plate. Stir the ½ cup finely chopped peppermint For the chocolate whipped cream frosting, in a large chilled mixing bowl beat the 2 cups whipping cream with an electric mixer on medium speed until soft peaks form. Fold in the remaining room-temperature chocolate mixture, half at a time (below).

**5** To assemble, place a cake layer on a serving plate. Stir the ½ cup finely chopped peppermint sticks into the peppermint fudge filling. Spread the filling evenly over the cake. Top with the remaining cake layer. Spread chocolate whipped cream frosting over top and sides of cake. If desired, sprinkle chocolate curls and additional coarsely chopped peppermint sticks over top of cake. Cover and chill for up to 4 hours. Store any leftover cake in the refrigerator. Makes 12 to 16 servings.

Per serving: 860 cal., 57 g total fat (35 g sat. fat), 179 mg chol., 396 mg sodium, 90 g carbo., 6 g fiber, 8 g pro.

**1** Chop the chocolate to ensure that it melts evenly and smoothly. Stir the chocolate, in small batches, into the cream mixture.

**2** Let the mixture stand for 5 minutes. The chocolate will melt but retain its shape. Stir the mixture until smooth.

**3** For frosting, gently fold half of the cooled chocolate mixture into the whipped cream. Then fold in the remaining chocolate mixture.

**4** To make chocolate curls, use a vegetable peeler to shave thin slivers from a chunk of chocolate.

**Ask Mom** How do I chop chocolate? p. 33 / How do I crush hard candies? p. 123 / How do I measure butter? p. 55 / How do I store a frosted cake? p. 137 / How do I whip cream? p. 25 / What does fold mean? p. 65 / What is semisweet/bittersweet chocolate? p. 32 / What is whipping cream? p. 24

# CAN I USE ANY CHOCOLATE TO MAKE THE CURLS?

Both bittersweet and milk chocolates can be made into curls, but milk chocolate is easier to use because it's softer than bittersweet. Use the short side of the bar for narrow curls, the long side for wide ones.

For better control, use your dry hands to sprinkle the candy on top of the cake, but use a spoon to scatter the curls. If you handle the delicate curls, the heat from your hands will melt them.

# German Chocolate Cake

1 4-ounce package sweet baking
chocolate, chopped
1½ cups milk
2 cups all-purpose flour
1 teaspoon baking soda
¾ teaspoon baking powder
½ teaspoon salt
¾ cup butter, softened
1¾ cups sugar
3 eggs
2 teaspoons vanilla
1 recipe Coconut-Pecan Frosting

**1** In a small saucepan cook and stir chocolate and milk over low heat until chocolate is melted; cool. Grease bottoms of two 9×1½-inch round cake pans. Line pans with waxed paper (photo 1, page 136). Grease and flour bottoms and sides of pans. Set pans aside. Stir together flour, baking soda, baking powder, and salt (photo 2, page 136); set aside.

**2** Preheat oven to 350°F. Beat butter on medium to high speed for 30 seconds (photo 3, page 136). Gradually add sugar, beating on medium speed after each addition (about 3 minutes). Beat for 2 minutes more (photos 4–5, page 136). Add eggs, one at a time, beating after each addition (photo 6, page 136). Beat in vanilla. Alternately add flour and chocolate mixtures (photo 7, page 137). Beat on medium to high speed for 20 seconds. Spread batter into the prepared pans (photo 8, page 137). Bake for 30 to 35 minutes or until done (photo 9, page 137). Cool cake layers in pans on wire racks for 10 minutes. Remove cake layers from pans (photos 10–11, page 137); peel off waxed paper (photo 12, page 137). Cool thoroughly on racks. Spread Coconut-Pecan Frosting over the top of each layer (below). Store cake in the refrigerator. Makes 12 to 16 servings.

Coconut-Pecan Frosting: In a medium saucepan combine 2 eggs, two 5-ounce cans (1⅓ cups) evaporated milk, 1⅓ cups sugar, and ½ cup butter. Cook and stir over medium heat for 6 to 8 minutes or until thickened and bubbly. Remove saucepan from heat; stir in 2⅔ cups flaked coconut and 1 cup chopped pecans (below). Cover and cool thoroughly.

Per serving: 761 cal., 42 g total fat (25 g sat. fat), 150 mg chol., 496 mg sodium, 90 g carbo., 4 g fiber, 10 g pro.

**1** Once the egg mixture is thick and bubbly, use a wooden spoon to add the coconut and pecans.

**2** Stir the frosting to mix well. Let the frosting stand at room temperature until completely cooled.

**3** Use a fork to spread the frosting to the edge of the first cake layer. Top with remaining layer and spread with remaining frosting

**Ask Mom** How do I chop chocolate? p. 33 / How do I grease and flour a pan? p. 59 / How do I measure butter? p. 55 / How do I measure flour? p. 54 / How do I measure liquids? p. 55 / How do I measure sugar? p. 55 / How do I soften butter? p. 28, 76 / How do I store a frosted cake? p. 137 / What are chopped nuts? p. 34 / What is baking powder? p. 30, 319 / What is baking soda? p. 30, 319 / What is evaporated milk? p. 24 / What is vanilla? p. 128 / What's that flour? p. 31 / What's that nut? p. 34–35

# White Chocolate Snowdrift Cake

¾ cup whipping cream
8 ounces white baking chocolate, chopped
1 package 2-layer-size white cake mix

⅓ cup unsweetened cocoa powder
1 8-ounce package cream cheese, cut up and softened
1 cup powdered sugar

**1** For frosting, in a medium saucepan combine whipping cream and white baking chocolate. Cook, stirring occasionally, over low heat until chocolate is completely melted and smooth. Transfer to a large mixing bowl; cover and chill until completely cold, at least 2 hours.

**2** Preheat oven to 350°F. Lightly grease and flour two 9×1½-inch or 8×1½-inch round cake pans (photo 1, page 136); set aside. Prepare cake mix according to package directions using egg whites. Spoon about 1½ cups of batter into each cake pan. Sift cocoa powder over batter remaining in bowl; stir until blended (below). Spoon portions of chocolate batter onto cake batter in pans (below). Swirl gently to marble and spread batter evenly (below).

**3** Bake in the preheated oven according to package directions, except check cakes several minutes before minimum time indicated on package.* Cool cake layers in pans on wire racks for 10 minutes. Remove layers from pans; cool thoroughly on wire racks (photos 10-12, page 137).

**4** Add cream cheese to chilled white baking chocolate mixture; beat with an electric mixer on medium speed until smooth. Gradually add powdered sugar, beating until sugar is completely combined. (Mixture should hold soft peaks; do not overbeat.) Use immediately. Place one cake layer on a serving platter. Frost with about ¾ cup frosting (photo 13, page 137). Top with second cake layer. Frost top and sides of cake (photo 14, 137). Serve immediately or cover and chill until serving time (up to 4 hours). Makes 12 servings.

*Note: The added cocoa powder makes the cakes bake in less time.

Per serving: 458 cal., 25 g total fat (13 g sat. fat), 45 mg chol., 382 mg sodium, 55 g carbo., 0 g fiber, 7 g pro.

**1** Sift the cocoa powder into the remaining batter. Sifting prevents the cocoa from forming clumps and makes mixing easier.

**2** Drop the chocolate batter by spoonfuls over the cake batter in the pan.

**3** Use a table knife to gently swirl the chocolate batter through the white batter for a marbled effect.

**Ask Mom** How do I chop chocolate? p. 33 / How do I grease and flour a pan? p. 59 / How do I measure liquids? p. 55 / How do I soften cream cheese? p. 57 / How do I store a frosted cake? p. 137 / How do I work with eggs? p. 26-27 / What are soft peaks? p. 26 / What is cocoa powder? p. 170 / What is powdered sugar? p. 29 / What is whipping cream? p. 24 / What is white chocolate? p. 32

# How do I make basic frostings for my cakes?

Frosting serves two purposes. It adds flavor and richness, of course, but it also helps to keep the cake from drying out. With the basic repertoire of frostings on this page and the next, you're covered—no matter what kind of cake you've baked.

## Cream Cheese Frosting

In a large mixing bowl beat one 8-ounce package softened cream cheese, ½ cup softened butter, and 2 teaspoons vanilla with electric mixer on medium speed until fluffy. Gradually beat in 5½ cups powdered sugar. If necessary, beat in additional powdered sugar to reach spreading consistency. Recipe frosts tops and sides of two 8- or 9-inch layers. Store frosted cake in refrigerator. Makes 3¾ cups.

## No-Cook Fudge Frosting

In large mixing bowl combine 8 cups powdered sugar and 1 cup unsweetened cocoa powder. Add 1 cup softened butter, ⅔ cup boiling water, and 2 teaspoons vanilla. Beat with electric mixer on low speed until combined. Beat 1 minute on medium speed. If necessary, cool about 20 minutes or until mixture reaches spreading consistency. Or, if frosting is too thick, add additional boiling water, 1 tablespoon at a time, until mixture reaches spreading consistency. Makes 4 cups.

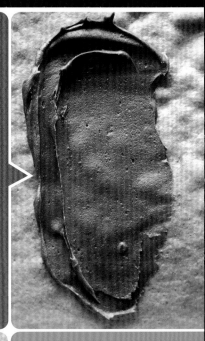

## Creamy White Frosting

In a large mixing bowl beat 1 cup shortening, 1½ teaspoons vanilla, and ½ teaspoon almond extract with an electric mixer on medium speed for 30 seconds. Slowly add 2 cups powdered sugar, beating well. Add 2 tablespoons milk. Gradually beat in an additional 2 cups powdered sugar and 1 to 2 tablespoons milk to reach spreading consistency. Recipe frosts tops and sides of two 8- or 9-inch cake layers. Makes 3 cups.

## Chocolate Sour Cream Frosting

In a large saucepan melt one 12-ounce package (2 cups) semisweet chocolate pieces and ½ cup butter over low heat, stirring frequently. Cool for 5 minutes. Stir in one 8-ounce carton sour cream. Gradually add 4½ cups powdered sugar, beating with an electric mixer on medium speed until smooth. Recipe frosts tops and sides of two 8- or 9-inch cake layers. Cover and store frosted cake in refrigerator. Makes 4 cups.

## Butter Frosting

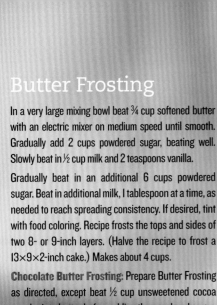

In a very large mixing bowl beat ¾ cup softened butter with an electric mixer on medium speed until smooth. Gradually add 2 cups powdered sugar, beating well. Slowly beat in ½ cup milk and 2 teaspoons vanilla.

Gradually beat in an additional 6 cups powdered sugar. Beat in additional milk, I tablespoon at a time, as needed to reach spreading consistency. If desired, tint with food coloring. Recipe frosts the tops and sides of two 8- or 9-inch layers. (Halve the recipe to frost a 13×9×2-inch cake.) Makes about 4 cups.

**Chocolate Butter Frosting:** Prepare Butter Frosting as directed, except beat ½ cup unsweetened cocoa powder into butter before adding the powdered sugar.

**Citrus Butter Frosting:** Prepare Butter Frosting as directed, except substitute ½ cup fresh lemon, orange, or lime juice for the ½ cup milk and add ½ teaspoon finely shredded lemon or lime peel or I teaspoon finely shredded orange peel with the juice.

**Coffee Butter Frosting:** Prepare Butter Frosting as directed, except omit vanilla and substitute ½ cup strong brewed coffee for the ½ cup milk.

**Almond Butter Frosting:** Prepare Butter Frosting as directed, except substitute ½ teaspoon almond extract for the vanilla.

**Peppermint Butter Frosting:** Prepare Butter Frosting as directed, except substitute I teaspoon peppermint extract for the vanilla. If desired, stir in ¼ cup crushed peppermint candies.

## Penuche Frosting

In a 2-quart saucepan melt ½ cup butter; stir in I cup packed brown sugar. Cook and stir over medium heat until bubbly (below). Remove from heat. Add ¼ cup milk and I teaspoon vanilla; stir with a wooden spoon until smooth. Stir in 3½ cups powdered sugar. Beat by hand about 3 minutes or until smooth and frosting reaches spreading consistency. Immediately use to frost tops of two 8- or 9-inch layers or top of one 13×9×2-inch cake. If frosting becomes too thick to spread, add hot water, a few drops at a time, until frosting returns to spreading consistency. Makes about 2 cups.

② Skill Level

**Flavor Changes**
Customize this lovely
cake by switching
up the types of fruit
curds and preserves
you use. Try orange
curd with peach or
apricot preserves, lime
curd with blackberry
preserves, or—for the
holidays—cranberry
curd with fig preserves
or orange marmalade.

# Lemon-Berry
# Ribbon Torte

  3 eggs
1½ cups all-purpose flour
1½ teaspoons baking powder
1½ cups granulated sugar
 ¾ cup milk
  3 tablespoons butter
   Powdered sugar
 ⅔ cup purchased lemon curd
 ⅔ cup raspberry preserves
  1 recipe Sour Cream Frosting
   Fresh raspberries (optional)

**1** Let eggs stand at room temperature for 30 minutes. Lightly grease the bottom of a 15×10×1-inch baking pan. Line the bottom of the pan with waxed paper (photo 1, page 136). Grease and lightly flour the waxed paper and sides of pan; set aside. In a small bowl stir together flour and baking powder (photo 2, page 136); set aside.

**2** Preheat oven to 350°F. In a large mixing bowl beat eggs with an electric mixer on high speed about 4 minutes or until thick and lemon colored. Gradually add granulated sugar, beating on medium speed for 4 to 5 minutes or until light and fluffy (photos 1–2, page 147). Add the flour mixture; beat on low to medium speed just until combined.

**3** In a small saucepan combine milk and butter; heat and stir until butter melts. Add milk mixture to batter, beating until combined.

**4** Spread batter evenly into the prepared pan. Bake in the preheated oven for 20 to 25 minutes or until cake springs back when lightly touched (photo 3, page 147). Immediately loosen edges of cake from pan; turn cake out onto a clean kitchen towel sprinkled with powdered sugar (photo 4, page 147). Carefully remove the waxed paper. Cool completely. Cut cake crosswise into thirds; set aside.

**5** To assemble torte, place one of the cake layers on a serving plate. Spread with lemon curd. Top with another cake layer; spread with raspberry preserves. Top with remaining cake layer. Frost top and sides of cake with Sour Cream Frosting. Cover and chill torte for 2 to 4 hours before serving. If desired, garnish cake with raspberries. Makes 12 servings.

**Sour Cream Frosting:** In a large mixing bowl combine one 8-ounce carton dairy sour cream, 1 cup whipping cream, ¾ cup powdered sugar, and 1 teaspoon vanilla. Beat with an electric mixer on medium speed until mixture thickens and holds stiff peaks.

Per serving: 458 cal., 17 g total fat (10 g sat. fat), 111 mg chol., 111 mg sodium, 74 g carbo., 2 g fiber, 3 g pro.

**Ask Mom** How do I grease, flour, and line a pan with waxed paper? p. 59, 58, 67 / How do I measure butter/liquids/sugar? p. 55 / How do I measure flour? p. 54 / How do I store a frosted cake? p. 137 / How do I wash berries? p. 42 / How do I work with eggs? p. 26–27 / What are stiff peaks? p. 26 / What is baking powder? p. 30, 319 / What is lemon curd? p. 119 / What is powdered sugar? p. 29 / What is vanilla? p. 128 / What is whipping cream? p. 24 / What's that flour? p. 31

**CHANNEL YOUR INNER PASTRY CHEF.** One of the coolest things about this dessert is that you can make an elegant, European-style torte simply by cutting and stacking a sheet cake. No special skills needed. (For a shortcut, you could start with a purchased cake.)

**1** Add the sugar a little at a time, beating after each addition until the sugar is incorporated into the eggs.

**2** Continue beating on medium speed until the mixture is light and fluffy. The mixture should flow from the beaters in a thick stream.

**3** The cake is done when it springs back when you lightly touch the surface with the tip of your finger.

**4** Loosen edges of hot cake from pan. Invert over a powdered-sugar-coated towel. The cake should slide from the pan. If it sticks, tap the pan gently on the counter and try again.

Spread the preserves and curd nearly to the edge of the cake layer but not all of the way to it. When you place a layer on top, the fillings spread out—and you don't want them to ooze into the frosting.

2 Skill Level

**Good to Know** Yes, you really do roll the kitchen towel up with the cake—that's why it's so important that it be clean and made of fuzz-free cotton. It keeps the cake from sticking to itself. You also need to roll the cake right after it comes out of the pan. If it cools too much, it will crack.

# Pumpkin Cake Roll

3 eggs
¾ cup all-purpose flour
2 teaspoons ground cinnamon
1 teaspoon baking powder
1 teaspoon ground ginger
½ teaspoon salt
½ teaspoon ground nutmeg

1 cup granulated sugar
⅔ cup canned pumpkin
1 teaspoon lemon juice
1 cup finely chopped walnuts
  Powdered sugar
1 recipe Cream Cheese Filling

**1** Let eggs stand at room temperature for 30 minutes. Grease a 15×10×1-inch baking pan. Line pan with waxed paper (photo 1, page 136). Grease paper; set pan aside. In a small bowl stir together flour, cinnamon, baking powder, ginger, salt, and nutmeg (photo 2, page 136); set aside.

**2** Preheat oven to 375°F. In a large mixing bowl beat eggs with an electric mixer on high speed for 5 minutes or until thick and lemon colored (photo 1, page 147). Gradually add granulated sugar, beating on medium speed until light and fluffy (photo 2, page 147). Stir in pumpkin and lemon juice. Add flour mixture; beat on low to medium speed just until combined.

**3** Spread batter evenly into prepared pan. Sprinkle with nuts. Bake about 15 minutes or until top springs back when touched (photo 3, page 147). Immediately loosen edges of cake from pan; turn out onto clean kitchen towel sprinkled with powdered sugar (photo 4, page 147). Remove waxed paper (photo 12, page 137). Starting with a narrow end, roll up cake and towel (below). Cool on a wire rack. Unroll cake. Spread with Cream Cheese Filling (below). Reroll cake (below). Trim ends of cake. Cover and chill for 2 to 48 hours. Makes 8 servings.

**Cream Cheese Filling:** Beat two 3-ounce packages softened cream cheese, ¼ cup softened butter, and ½ teaspoon vanilla until smooth. Beat in 1 cup powdered sugar until smooth.

Per serving: 455 cal., 25 g total fat (9 g sat. fat), 119 mg chol., 310 mg sodium, 52 g carbo., 2 g fiber, 8 g pro.

**1** Starting from a narrow end, roll up the warm cake with the towel into a spiral.

**2** Roll to the end of the towel. Place the rolled cake on a wire rack and cool completely, about 1 hour.

**3** Unroll the cooled cake, leaving the cake on the towel. Spread the filling over the cake to within 1 inch of edges.

**4** Reroll the cake using the towel to lift the cake and guide you to make an even roll.

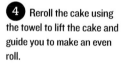

**Ask Mom** How do I grease a baking pan? p. 59 / How do I juice a lemon? p. 44, 45 / How do I line a pan with waxed paper? p. 58, 67 / How do I measure butter/sugar/flour? p. 54–55 / How do I soften butter/cream cheese? p. 28, 76, 57 / What are chopped nuts? p. 34 / What is baking powder? p. 30, 319 / What is canned pumpkin? p. 302 / What is cinnamon/ginger/nutmeg? p. 36–37 / What is powdered sugar? p. 29 / What is vanilla? p. 128 / What's that flour? p. 31 / What's that nut? p. 34–35

# Strawberry Cake Roll

3 eggs

1 cup all-purpose flour

1 teaspoon baking powder

¼ teaspoon salt

¾ cup finely chopped fresh strawberries

¼ cup frozen mixed berry juice concentrate, thawed

½ cup granulated sugar

¾ cup finely chopped pecans

Powdered sugar

3 cups strawberry ice cream

**1** Let eggs stand at room temperature for 30 minutes. Lightly grease a 15×10×1-inch baking pan. Line pan with waxed paper (photo 1, page 136); set pan aside. In a small bowl combine flour, baking powder, and salt (photo 2, page 136); set aside.

**2** Preheat oven to 375°F. In a small saucepan combine strawberries and juice concentrate. Bring mixture to boiling; reduce heat to low. Cook, stirring and mashing with a spoon, about 4 minutes or until slightly thickened. Remove from heat; cool to room temperature. Set aside.

**3** In a large mixing bowl beat eggs with an electric mixer on high speed about 5 minutes or until thick and lemon colored (photo 1, page 147). Gradually add strawberry mixture and granulated sugar, beating on medium speed until sugar is almost dissolved. Sprinkle flour mixture over egg mixture; fold in gently just until combined.

**4** Spread batter evenly into the prepared pan. Sprinkle with pecans. Bake in the preheated oven for 12 to 15 minutes or until top springs back when lightly touched (photo 3, page 147). Immediately loosen edges of cake from pan; turn cake out onto a clean kitchen towel sprinkled with powdered sugar (photo 4, page 147). Carefully remove waxed paper (photo 12, page 137). Starting with a narrow end, roll up warm cake and towel together (photos 1–2, page 148). Cool on a wire rack.

**5** Unroll cake. Stir ice cream to soften; carefully spread on cake to within 1 inch of edges. Reroll cake using the towel as a guide (photo 4, page 148). Trim ends of cake. Place on a baking sheet; cover and freeze for 4 to 24 hours. Slice to serve. Makes 10 servings.

Per serving: 233 cal., 10 g total fat (2 g sat. fat), 71 mg chol., 104 mg sodium, 33 g carbo., 2 g fiber, 5 g pro.

The best way to cut neat slices of a cake roll of any kind—especially one filled with ice cream—is to use a long serrated knife. Rinse the blade in warm water and briefly dry it between cuts.

**1** Skill Level

# Tinted Angel Cake

1 16-ounce package angel food cake mix

¾ teaspoon Kool-Aid tropical punch, pink lemonade, black cherry, or other flavor unsweetened soft drink mix

4 cups powdered sugar

3 tablespoons hot water

1 tablespoon grenadine syrup or maraschino cherry liquid or ¼ teaspoon Kool-Aid unsweetened soft drink mix

White baking chocolate curls or small multicolored decorative candies

**1** In a large mixing bowl combine angel food cake mix and ¾ teaspoon Kool-Aid mix. Prepare and bake cake according to package directions. Immediately invert cake; cool thoroughly in inverted pan (below). Loosen sides of cake from pan; remove cake from pan (below).

**2** In a medium bowl combine powdered sugar, hot water, and grenadine syrup. If necessary, add additional hot water, 1 teaspoon at a time, to make icing of drizzling consistency. Drizzle icing over cake. Top with white baking chocolate curls or decorative candies. Makes 12 servings.

Per serving: 293 cal., 0 g total fat (0 g sat. fat), 0 mg chol., 259 mg sodium, 71 g carbo., 0 g fiber, 3 g pro.

**1** Cool the cake upside down to set the structure. Invert the cake in pan over a bottle with a long-neck.

**3** Using a long knife or metal spatula, gently push the cake from the pan. Go around the center of the pan as well as the edge.

**4** Run the spatula under the bottom of the cake to loosen it from the pan. Gently lift the cake from the pan.

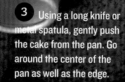

**2** If the tube pan has legs, you can simply turn the pan upside down on the counter. Be sure the cake is completely cool before you remove it from the pan.

# Sour Cream-Walnut Date Cake
## With Tangerine Glaze

⅓ cup all-purpose flour

3 tablespoons packed brown sugar

3 tablespoons butter

⅔ cup finely snipped pitted dates

½ cup finely chopped walnuts or pecans

1 package 2-layer-size yellow cake mix

1 8-ounce carton dairy sour cream

¾ cup water

3 eggs

½ cup cooking oil

¾ teaspoon ground cardamom or ground nutmeg

1 recipe Tangerine Glaze

**1** Grease and flour a 10-inch fluted tube pan (below); set aside. Mix flour and brown sugar. Using a pastry blender, cut in butter until crumbly. Stir in dates and nuts; set aside.

**2** Preheat oven to 350°F. In a large mixing bowl beat cake mix, sour cream, water, eggs, oil, and cardamom with an electric mixer on low speed until moistened. Beat for 2 minutes on medium speed. Pour half of the batter into prepared pan. Sprinkle date mixture over batter in pan (below). Pour remaining batter over date mixture, spreading evenly.

**3** Bake for 45 to 55 minutes or until a wooden toothpick inserted near the center of cake comes out clean (photo 9, page 137). Place cake in pan on a wire rack. Prick holes over the cake's surface with a fork. Slowly spoon about half of the Tangerine Glaze over hot cake. Let stand for 10 minutes, allowing the glaze to soak in. Loosen sides of cake. Invert onto a cake plate; remove the pan. Prick holes in the top of the cake with tines of fork (below). Slowly spoon the remaining Tangerine Glaze over cake (below). Cool thoroughly. Makes 12 servings.

**Tangerine Glaze:** In a small saucepan combine ½ cup granulated sugar, ½ cup tangerine or orange juice, and 2 tablespoons butter. Bring to boiling; reduce heat. Simmer, uncovered, for 3 minutes, stirring frequently. Remove from heat; set aside.

Per serving: 472 cal., 25 g total fat (9 g sat. fat), 74 mg chol., 344 mg sodium, 60 g carbo., 1 g fiber, 6 g pro.

**1** Use a pastry brush to brush shortening over the inside of a fluted tube pan. Be sure to coat the insides of the grooves.

**2** Sprinkle the date and nut filling over the cake batter in the pan. Use either your fingers or a spoon to evenly spread the filling.

**3** After placing the cake on a plate, use the fork to poke holes into the top of the cake.

**4** Slowly spoon the remaining Tangerine Glaze over the cake, allowing the glaze to soak into the cake.

**Ask Mom** How do I cut in butter/shortening? p. 56 / How do I grease and flour a pan? p. 59 / How do I measure butter? p. 55 / How do I measure flour? p. 54 / How do I measure liquids? p. 55 / How do I measure sugar? p. 55 / How do I snip dried fruit or preserves? p. 41, 102 / What are chopped nuts? p. 34 / What is a pastry blender? p. 10, 11 / What is cardamom? p. 36 / What is cooking oil? p. 28 / What is nutmeg? p. 37 / What's that dried fruit? p. 41 / What's that flour? p. 31 / What's that nut? p. 34–35

② Skill Level

**Ingredient Info**
Malibu rum is a coconut-flavored rum that's distilled in Barbados. It's widely available, but if you can't find it, you can use light rum.

# Malibu Rum Baby Cakes

1 8-ounce can pineapple slices (juice pack)
¼ cup dried apricots, quartered
¼ cup Malibu rum or light rum
3 tablespoons butter
½ cup packed brown sugar
    Nonstick cooking spray for baking
1⅓ cups all-purpose flour
¼ cup flaked coconut
2 teaspoons baking powder
¼ cup butter, softened
½ cup granulated sugar
1 egg
    Sweetened Whipped Cream (page 25) (optional)

**1** Drain pineapple well, reserving liquid (you should have about ⅓ cup juice). Set pineapple slices aside. In a small saucepan combine reserved pineapple juice, apricots, and rum. Bring the mixture just to boiling; remove from heat. Let stand for 15 minutes. Strain, reserving both the liquid and the apricots. In the same saucepan combine the 3 tablespoons butter, the brown sugar, and 1 tablespoon of the reserved liquid. Cook and stir over medium heat until butter is melted and sugar is dissolved.

**2** Lightly coat the insides of six 10-ounce ramekins or custard cups or 1-cup fluted tube pans with cooking spray. Spoon the brown sugar mixture evenly into the prepared ramekins. Cut each pineapple slice into 6 pieces. Arrange pineapple and apricots evenly on top of the sugar mixture. Set aside.

**3** Preheat oven to 350°F. In a small bowl stir together flour, coconut, and baking powder (photo 2, page 136); set aside. Measure the remaining juice mixture; add enough water to equal ⅔ cup; set aside.

**4** In a medium mixing bowl beat the ¼ cup butter with an electric mixer on medium to high speed for 30 seconds (photo 3, page 136). Add granulated sugar and beat until light and fluffy (photos 4–5, page 136). Add egg and beat until combined (photo 6, page 136). Alternately add the ⅔ cup liquid and the flour mixture, beating on low speed after each addition just until combined (photo 7, page 137).

**5** Carefully spoon batter over fruit in ramekins. Bake in the preheated oven about 25 minutes or until tops spring back when lightly touched (photo 3, page 147). Cool in ramekins on wire racks for 5 minutes. Using a metal spatula, loosen cakes from ramekins; invert cakes onto serving plates. Serve warm.* If desired, top with Sweetened Whipped Cream. Makes 6 servings.

*Note: To reheat cakes, wrap loosely in foil; bake in a 350°F oven about 10 minutes or until warm. Or microwave, uncovered, on 100 percent power (high) about 30 seconds or until warm.

Per serving: 446 cal., 16 g total fat (10 g sat. fat), 71 mg chol., 212 mg sodium, 67 g carbo., 2 g fiber, 2 g pro.

**Ask Mom** How do I measure butter? p. 55 / How do I measure flour? p. 54 / How do I measure sugar? p. 55 / How do I snip dried fruit or preserves? p. 41, 102 / How do I soften butter? p. 28, 76 / How do I use a sieve? p. 65 / What is a custard cup? p. 13 / What is a ramekin? p. 19 / What is baking powder? p. 30, 319 / What's that dried fruit? p. 41 / What's that flour? p. 31

**PICK YOUR CAKE SHAPE.** These baby cakes take on different forms depending on the type of vessel you use to bake them. Custard cups will give you shorter, wider cakes, while ramekins will give you taller, more slender cakes.

The yum factor of these little cakes depends in large part on serving them warm so the syrup is warm and gooey. You can make them a few hours ahead—just heat before serving (see page 152).

# Lime-Infused Coconut Cake

I cup butter
5 eggs
3 cups all-purpose flour
I teaspoon baking powder
½ cup shortening
2½ cups granulated sugar
½ cup cream of coconut
¼ cup lime juice

¼ cup water
I teaspoon vanilla
I cup flaked coconut, toasted
I cup powdered sugar
Milk
½ teaspoon finely shredded lime peel
¼ teaspoon coconut extract

**1** Let butter and eggs stand at room temperature for 30 minutes. Grease and lightly flour a 10-inch fluted tube pan (photo 1, page 151); set pan aside. In a medium bowl stir together flour and baking powder (photo 2, page 136); set aside.

**2** Preheat oven to 325°F. In a very large mixing bowl combine butter and shortening; beat with an electric mixer on medium to high speed until well mixed (photo 3, page 136). Gradually add granulated sugar, beating until light and fluffy (photos 4–5, page 136). Add eggs, one at a time, beating for 1 minute after each addition and scraping sides of bowl often (photo 6, page 136). In a small bowl combine cream of coconut, lime juice, water, and vanilla. Alternately add flour mixture and cream of coconut mixture to butter mixture, beating on low to medium speed after each addition just until combined (photo 7, page 137). Fold in the coconut.

**3** Spread batter evenly into the prepared pan. Bake in the preheated oven for 65 to 75 minutes or until a wooden toothpick inserted near the center of the cake comes out clean (photo 9, page 137). Cool in pan on wire rack for 10 minutes. Remove cake from pan (photos 10–11, page 137). Cool completely on a wire rack.

**4** For icing, in a small bowl combine powdered sugar, 1 tablespoon milk, lime peel, and coconut extract. Stir in enough additional milk, 1 teaspoon at a time, to make icing of drizzling consistency. Place cooled cake on cake plate; drizzle icing over cake. Makes 12 to 16 servings.

Per serving: 638 cal., 33 g total fat (19 g sat. fat), 129 mg chol., 187 mg sodium, 81 g carbo., 2 g fiber, 5 g pro.

**Ask Mom** How do I grease and flour a pan? p. 59 / How do I juice a lemon/lime? p. 44, 45 / How do I measure butter? p. 55 / How do I measure flour? p. 54 / How do I measure liquids? p. 55 / How do I measure shortening? p. 55 / How do I measure sugar? p. 55 / How do I shred lemon/lime/orange peel? p. 45, 105 / How do I toast coconut? p. 40 / What does drizzle mean? p. 69, 85 / What is coconut milk? p. 40 / What is powdered sugar? p. 29 / What is vanilla? p. 128 / What's that flour? p. 31

① Skill Level

**Good to Know**
Caramel ice cream topping tends to be a little stiff when it's cold or even room temperature. For easy drizzling, warm it just slightly in the microwave before using it.

# Upside-Down Peach Caramel Crunch Cake

1 15- to 16-ounce can peach slices in light syrup

½ cup peach schnapps or rum

½ cup packed brown sugar

1 cup chopped pecans

1 package 2-layer-size yellow cake mix

½ of a 12.25-ounce jar caramel ice cream topping

1 recipe Sweetened Whipped Cream (page 25) (optional)

**1** Line a 13×9×2-inch baking pan with foil; grease foil. Set aside. Drain peach slices, reserving peach juice in a 2-cup glass measure; add peach schnapps. Cut any thick peach slices in half (below); set aside. Sprinkle brown sugar evenly over bottom of the prepared pan. Sprinkle with pecans. Arrange peach slices over pecans (below); set aside.

**2** Preheat oven to 350°F. Prepare cake according to package directions, except substitute the peach juice mixture for water called for in cake mix directions (may need to add water to equal amount called for in cake mix or discard extra juice if more than the amount of water called for in cake mix).

**3** Carefully pour batter over peaches in pan, being careful not to disturb peaches and pecans (below). Bake in the preheated oven for 45 to 50 minutes or until a wooden toothpick inserted near the center comes out clean (photo 9, page 137). Remove the cake from the oven. Cool on a wire rack for 20 minutes. Invert onto a large serving platter. Carefully peel off foil. Drizzle caramel ice cream topping over each serving in a zigzag design or swirls. Serve warm. If desired, serve with Sweetened Whipped Cream. Makes 12 to 16 servings.

Per serving: 371 cal., 12 g total fat (1 g sat. fat), 1 mg chol., 344 mg sodium, 61 g carbo., 2 g fiber, 3 g pro.

**①** Cut any thick peach slices in half to make all of the slices about the same thickness.

**②** Place the peach slices on top of the brown sugar and pecans in the pan. Arrange the slices so each piece of cake will have at least 1 slice.

**③** Using a measuring cup, gently drizzle the cake batter over the peach slices.

**④** With a rubber scraper, spread the batter in an even layer to the edges of the pan. Take care not to disturb the peach slices.

**Ask Mom** How do I line a pan with foil? p. 58 / How do I measure sugar? p. 55 / What are chopped nuts? p. 34 / What does drizzle mean? p. 69, 85 / What's that nut? p. 34–35

# Upside-Down
## One-Bowl Apple Cake

⅓ cup butter, cut up

6 very small red cooking apples (1¼ to 1½ pounds)

⅓ cup packed brown sugar

1⅓ cups all-purpose flour

⅔ cup granulated sugar

2 teaspoons baking powder

1 teaspoon ground ginger

1 teaspoon ground cinnamon

⅔ cup milk

¼ cup butter, softened

1 egg

1 teaspoon vanilla

Cinnamon or vanilla ice cream (optional)

**1** Preheat oven to 350°F. Place the ⅓ cup butter in a 9×9×2-inch baking pan. Place in oven about 5 minutes or until butter is melted. Meanwhile, halve apples; remove stems. With a measuring teaspoon or melon baller, scoop out apple cores (below). Sprinkle brown sugar over melted butter in pan; stir to combine. Arrange 9 of the apple halves in the butter mixture, cut sides down (below). Return to oven; bake for 10 to 15 minutes or until bubbly.

**2** Meanwhile, coarsely shred the remaining 3 apple halves (below); set aside. In a medium mixing bowl combine flour, granulated sugar, baking powder, ginger, and cinnamon. Add the shredded apple, milk, the ¼ cup softened butter, the egg, and vanilla. Beat with an electric mixer on low speed until combined. Beat on medium speed for 1 minute.

**3** Carefully spoon batter over apples in pan, spreading evenly (some apple may be exposed). Bake in the preheated oven about 35 minutes or until a wooden toothpick inserted near the center of cake comes out clean (photo 9, page 137). Cool in pan on a wire rack for 5 minutes. Loosen edges and invert onto a cake plate. Spread any topping left in pan over cake (below). Cool for 20 minutes before serving. If desired, serve with ice cream. Makes 9 servings.

Per serving: 313 cal., 13 g total fat (8 g sat. fat), 56 mg chol., 157 mg sodium, 47 g carbo., 2 g fiber, 3 g pro.

**1** Use a measuring spoon or melon baller or spoon to scoop the core from each apple half. Be sure to remove all of the woody portions.

**2** Place the apple halves, cut sides down, in the brown sugar-butter mixture. Space the apple halves evenly apart in the pan.

**3** Rub the remaining apple halves along the large holes of a box grater to form coarse shreds.

**4** Invert the cake onto a plate and lift off the pan. Use a rubber scraper to remove any topping remaining in pan and spread over cake.

**Ask Mom** How do I measure butter? p. 55 / How do I measure flour? p. 54 / How do I measure liquids? p. 55 / How do I measure sugar? p. 55 / How do I soften butter? p. 28, 76 / What is a good baking/cooking apple? p. 39, 287 / What is baking powder? p. 30, 319 / What is cinnamon? p. 36 / What is ginger? p. 36 / What is vanilla? p. 128 / What's that flour? p. 31

**1** Skill Level

# Polenta and Plum Cake

- 1 cup butter
- 4 egg yolks
- 2 eggs
- 4 plums, pitted and cut into wedges
- ¼ cup packed brown sugar
- 1 cup all-purpose flour
- ½ cup yellow cornmeal
- 1½ teaspoons baking powder
- ⅛ teaspoon salt
- ¾ cup granulated sugar
- 1 teaspoon finely shredded lemon or orange peel
- 1 teaspoon vanilla
- 1 recipe Sweetened Whipped Cream (page 25) (optional)

**1** Let butter, egg yolks, and whole eggs stand at room temperature for 30 minutes. Lightly grease and flour bottom and sides of a 9-inch springform pan; line bottom with a 9-inch circle of parchment paper. Arrange plums on parchment in pan. Sprinkle brown sugar over the plums; set aside. In a small bowl combine flour, cornmeal, baking powder, and salt (photo 2, page 136); set aside.

**2** Preheat oven to 350°F. In a large mixing bowl beat the butter with an electric mixer on medium to high speed for 30 seconds (photo 3, page 136). Gradually add granulated sugar, beating on medium speed until light and fluffy (photos 4–5, page 136). Add egg yolks and eggs, one at a time, beating until combined after each addition (photo 6, page 136). Beat in lemon peel and vanilla; beat until combined. Add flour mixture, beating on low speed until combined.

**3** Carefully spoon batter over plums in pan, spreading evenly (photos 3–4, page 155). Bake in the preheated oven about 50 minutes or until a wooden toothpick inserted near the center of cake comes out clean (photo 9, page 137). Cool cake in pan on a wire rack for 20 minutes. Remove sides of pan; cool cake completely. Invert cake onto serving platter; carefully remove bottom of pan and parchment. If desired, serve with Sweetened Whipped Cream. Makes 10 servings.

Per serving: 356 cal., 21 g total fat (13 g sat. fat), 173 mg chol., 216 mg sodium, 37 g carbo., 1 g fiber, 4 g pro.

**CAN I MAKE THESE AHEAD?** You can—which makes them great for a dinner party. Prepare the recipe through Step 4, then cover and chill up to 4 hours. Bake as directed in Step 5 while you're eating dinner. They're ready when you're ready for dessert.

**1** Spoon enough batter into each ramekin until it is about 1 inch deep. Spread the batter evenly with the back of the spoon.

**2** Divide the filling into 8 evenly sized portions. On the work surface, use your fingers to form each portion into a ball.

**3** Gently place a ball of filling on top of the batter in the center of a ramekin. Let the filling sit on top of the batter; do not push it into the batter.

**4** Carefully spoon the batter over the filling. Gently spread the batter to cover the filling, making sure the filling does not touch the sides of the ramekin.

If you've ever had Black Forest torte, you know that chocolate and cherries are a fabulous combination. Here Cherry Compote mingles with warm, fudgy chocolate sauce in a most delightful way.

**Good to Know** Also known as "lava" cakes, "molten" cakes feature an ooey-gooey, melty chocolate ganache that bubbles out when they're baked and oozes out when they're cut into. Their effort vs. wow-factor ratio is happily disproportionate: They're not difficult to make, but they make a great impression.

# Molten Chocolate Cakes
# With Cherry Compote

Butter

1⅓ cups chopped semisweet chocolate or semisweet chocolate pieces (8 ounces)

1 tablespoon butter

½ cup whipping cream

4 ounces semisweet chocolate, coarsely chopped

½ cup butter

4 eggs

½ cup sugar

½ cup all-purpose flour

1 recipe Cherry Compote

Vanilla ice cream (optional)

**1** Generously butter eight 6-ounce ramekins. For filling, in a small saucepan combine chocolate pieces, the 1 tablespoon butter, and the whipping cream. Cook and stir over low heat until chocolate is melted and mixture is smooth. Cool at room temperature for 15 minutes. Cover and chill for 1 to 2 hours or until fudgelike in consistency.

**2** Preheat oven to 375°F. In a small saucepan combine chopped semisweet chocolate and the ½ cup butter. Cook and stir over low heat until chocolate is melted and mixture is smooth. Cool slightly.

**3** In a large mixing bowl combine eggs and sugar; beat with an electric mixer on medium to high speed for 5 minutes. Beat in flour and melted chocolate mixture. Spoon enough of the batter into each ramekin to measure 1 inch in depth (photo 1, page 158).

**4** Divide chilled filling into eight portions. Working quickly, use your hands to shape each portion into a ball (photo 2, page 158). Place a ball of filling on top of the batter in each ramekin; do not allow the filling to touch the sides of the ramekins (photo 3, page 158). Divide remaining batter among ramekins (photo 4, page 158). Place ramekins on a large baking sheet.

**5** Bake in the preheated oven for 15 to 18 minutes or until centers are puffed. Remove from oven; let stand at room temperature for 10 minutes. Using a knife, loosen sides; invert onto serving plates. Serve immediately with warm Cherry Compote. If desired, serve with small scoops of vanilla ice cream. Makes 8 servings.

Cherry Compote: In a small saucepan combine 1 cup orange juice and ½ teaspoon finely shredded orange peel. Bring just to boiling over medium heat. In a small bowl combine ¼ cup sugar and 1 tablespoon cornstarch. Stir sugar mixture into orange juice mixture. Return to boiling. Cook and stir for 2 minutes more. Remove from heat. Stir in 1½ cups pitted fresh or thawed frozen sweet cherries and, if desired, 2 tablespoons cherry brandy or brandy. Allow to cool slightly before serving.

Per serving: 547 cal., 34 g total fat (20 g sat. fat), 161 mg chol., 136 mg sodium, 60 g carbo., 4 g fiber, 6 g pro.

**Ask Mom** How do I chop chocolate? p. 33 / How do I measure butter? p. 55 / How do I measure flour? p. 54 / How do I measure liquids? p. 55 / How do I measure sugar? p. 55 / How do I shred lemon/lime/orange peel? p. 45, 105 / What is a ramekin? p. 19 / What is semisweet/bittersweet chocolate? p. 32 / What is whipping cream? p. 24 / What's that flour? p. 31

# Walnut-Cappuccino Torte

1 8-ounce package semisweet chocolate, cut up
1⅓ cups milk chocolate pieces (8 ounces)
1 cup whipping cream
2 tablespoons instant coffee crystals
5 eggs
¼ cup coffee liqueur or brewed coffee

1 teaspoon vanilla
½ cup all-purpose flour
¼ cup sugar
1 cup chopped toasted walnuts or pecans
1 recipe Mocha Cream

**1** In a heavy medium saucepan heat semisweet chocolate, milk chocolate, whipping cream, and coffee crystals over low heat until chocolate is melted, stirring constantly. Cool to room temperature. Let eggs stand at room temperature for 30 minutes. Grease and flour the bottom and sides of a 9-inch springform pan; set aside.

**2** Preheat oven to 325°F. In a large mixing bowl beat eggs, coffee liqueur, and vanilla with an electric mixer on low speed until combined. Gradually add flour and sugar, beating on medium to high speed for 8 minutes. (The batter should be light and slightly thickened.) Stir about one-fourth of the batter into the chocolate mixture (below). Stir chocolate mixture into the remaining egg mixture (below). Stir in nuts.

**3** Spread batter evenly into the prepared pan. Bake in the preheated oven for 40 to 45 minutes or until slightly puffed around the outer edges (center will be slightly soft) (below). Cool in pan on a wire rack for 20 minutes. Loosen and remove sides of pan. Cool completely. Cover and chill for 4 to 24 hours. To serve, let stand at room temperature for 30 minutes. Top with Mocha Cream. Makes 12 to 16 servings.

Mocha Cream: In a chilled small mixing bowl beat ½ cup whipping cream and 2 tablespoons coffee liqueur with an electric mixer on medium speed just until soft peaks form.

Per serving: 462 cal., 32 g total fat (12 g sat. fat), 134 mg chol., 56 mg sodium, 35 g carbo., 3 g fiber, 8 g pro.

**1** Stir about ¼ of the batter into the cooled chocolate mixture. This lightens the chocolate mixture.

**2** Stir the chocolate mixture into the batter in the bowl. Use a scraper to lightly stir until the two mixtures are combined with no streaks.

**3** When done, the outside edge will be slightly puffed and the center will be softly set. Cool for 20 minutes before removing sides of pan.

**Ask Mom** How do I chop chocolate? p. 33 / How do I grease and flour a pan? p. 59 / How do I measure flour? p. 54 / How do I measure sugar? p. 55 / How do I toast nuts? p. 34 / How do I wash fresh berries? p. 42 / What are chopped nuts? p. 34 / What is a springform pan? p. 16, 17 / What is milk chocolate? p. 32 / What is semisweet/bittersweet chocolate? p. 32 / What is vanilla? p. 128 / What is whipping cream? p. 24 / What's that flour? p. 31 / What's that nut? p. 34–35

# everyday
# SNACK CAKES
# & CUPCAKES

**Hungry for a little something sweet? These one-pan cakes are simple enough to have around for any day of the week.**

5

**Butter Cake, Gooey** ② ........................................... 175

## CHOCOLATE CAKES

Chocolate Candy-Graham Cake ② ....................... 163

Chocolate Chip-Oatmeal Cake ① ........................ 164

## CUPCAKES

Almond Cupcakes ① ................................... 179

Candy Cupcakes ① .................................... 179

Chocolate Chip Cupcakes ① ............................ 178

Cinnamon-Orange Cupcakes ① ......................... 179

Coconut Cupcakes ① .................................. 178

Cranberry-Pistachio Cupcakes ① ....................... 178

Espresso Cupcakes ① ................................. 178

Hawaiian Cupcakes ① ................................. 178

Lemon Cupcakes ① ................................... 179

Little Pumpkin Cakes ③ ............................... 180

Peanut Butter Cupcakes ② ............................ 182

Peppermint Cupcakes ① .............................. 179

Raspberry Cupcakes ① ............................... 178

Simple White Cupcakes with Creamy Frosting ① .......... 176

Toffee Cupcakes ① ................................... 179

## FROSTINGS AND TOPPINGS

Caramelized Hazelnut Brittle ③ ......................... 181

Creamy Frosting ① ................................... 176

## FRUIT AND VEGETABLE CAKES

Applesauce Cake ② .................................. 165

Banana Split Cake ③ ................................. 170

Pineapple-Carrot Loaves ② ........................... 168

Rhubarb and Spice Snacking Cake ② .................. 166

Triple-Nut Zucchini Cake ② ........................... 167

## POUND CAKES

Cranberry Pound Cake ② .............................. 174

Lemon-Poppy Seed Pound Cake ① ..................... 172

Orange-Rosemary Pound Cake ① ...................... 172

# Chocolate Candy-**Graham Cake**

Nonstick cooking spray

1¼ cups graham cracker crumbs

¼ cup sugar

⅓ cup butter

4 2.1-ounce bars chocolate-covered crisp peanut butter candy bars, chilled and crushed (below)

1 package 2-layer-size Swiss chocolate or devil's food cake mix

1¼ cups water

½ cup cooking oil

3 eggs

1 cup milk chocolate pieces

**1** Preheat oven to 350°F. Line a 13×9×2-inch baking pan with heavy foil; lightly coat foil with nonstick cooking spray (below). Set aside.

**2** In a medium bowl combine cracker crumbs and sugar. Using a pastry blender, cut in butter until mixture resembles coarse crumbs (below). Press crumb mixture into bottom of pan. Bake for 10 minutes. Remove from oven; sprinkle with half of the crushed candy.

**3** In a large mixing bowl combine cake mix, water, oil, and eggs. Beat with an electric mixer on low speed for 30 seconds, scraping sides of bowl. Beat on high speed for 2 minutes.

**4** Spread the batter over the crumb layer in pan (below). Bake in the preheated oven about 45 minutes or until a wooden toothpick inserted near the center of cake comes out clean (photo 9, page 137). Remove from oven; immediately sprinkle with the remaining crushed candy and the milk chocolate pieces. Cool cake completely in pan on a wire rack. To remove cake from pan, chill in the refrigerator about 10 minutes or until chocolate is firm. Use the foil to lift the cake from the pan. Carefully peel off foil; cut cake into squares. Makes 12 servings.

Per serving: 592 cal., 31 g total fat (12 g sat. fat), 72 mg chol., 500 mg sodium, 72 g carbo., 2 g fiber, 7 g pro.

**1** Fit the foil smoothly into the baking pan, pressing firmly into edges and corners the pan. Spray the foil with a light mist of nonstick spray.

**2** Cut the butter into pieces and add to the crumb mixture. Use an up-and-down motion with a pastry blender to cut in the butter.

**3** Chill the candy bars before crushing them. Place the candy bars in a resealable plastic bag. Smash them with the back of a wooden spoon.

**4** Pour the batter evenly over the crust and candy by moving the bowl over the pan as you pour and scraping the batter into the pan.

**Ask Mom** How do I cut in butter/shortening? p. 56 / How do I line a pan with foil? p. 58 / How do I make cracker/cookie crumbs? p. 129 / How do I measure butter? p. 55 / How do I measure liquids? p. 55 / How do I measure sugar? p. 55 / How do I remove a piece of cake from a pan? p. 165 / What is a pastry blender? p. 10, 11 / What is cooking oil? p. 28 / What is milk chocolate? p. 32

**1** Skill Level

# Chocolate Chip-Oatmeal Cake

- 1 cup quick-cooking rolled oats
- 1¾ cups boiling water
- 1 cup granulated sugar
- 1 cup packed brown sugar
- ½ cup butter, cut up and softened
- 2 eggs
- 1¾ cups all-purpose flour
- 1 tablespoon unsweetened cocoa powder
- 1 teaspoon baking soda
- 1 teaspoon salt
- 1 12-ounce package (2 cups) semisweet chocolate pieces
- ¾ cup chopped walnuts

**1** Place oats in a large bowl. Pour boiling water over the oats (below); let stand for 10 minutes. Grease and flour a 13×9×2-inch baking pan; set aside.

**2** Preheat oven to 350°F. Add granulated sugar, brown sugar, and butter to oats mixture (below); stir until butter is melted. Stir in eggs until combined. Stir in flour, cocoa powder, baking soda, and salt until combined. Stir in 1 cup of the chocolate pieces (below).

**3** Pour the batter into the prepared pan. Sprinkle with walnuts and the remaining chocolate pieces (below). Bake in the preheated oven about 40 minutes or until a wooden toothpick inserted near the center of cake comes out clean (photo 9, page 137). Cool completely in pan on a wire rack. Makes 20 servings.

Per serving: 297 cal., 13 g total fat (6 g sat. fat), 33 mg chol., 166 mg sodium, 38 g carbo., 3 g fiber, 2 g pro.

**1** Heat the water in a saucepan until boiling. Pour the boiling water over the oats. If necessary, stir to moisten all the oats.

**2** Add the sugars and the softened butter to the oat mixture. The butter should be at room temperature so it will blend into the batter.

**3** Gently stir 1 cup of the chocolate pieces into the batter with a rubber scraper just until distributed. Be careful not to overmix.

**4** Use your fingers to evenly sprinkle the remaining cup of chocolate pieces and the nuts over the batter.

**Ask Mom** How do I grease and flour a pan? p. 59 / How do I measure butter? p. 55 / How do I measure flour? p. 54 / How do I measure liquids? p. 55 / How do I measure sugar? p. 55 / How do I remove a piece of cake from a pan? p. 165 / How do I soften butter? p. 28, 76 / What are chopped nuts? p. 34 / What is baking soda? p. 30, 319 / What is cocoa powder? p. 170 / What is semisweet/bittersweet chocolate? p. 32 / What's that flour? p. 31 / What's that nut? p. 34–35

# Applesauce Cake

| | |
|---|---|
| ½ cup butter | ½ teaspoon ground cloves |
| 2 eggs | ¼ teaspoon baking soda |
| 2½ cups all-purpose flour | 2 cups sugar |
| 1½ teaspoons baking powder | 1½ cups applesauce |
| 1 teaspoon ground cinnamon | ½ cup raisins |
| ¾ teaspoon ground nutmeg | ½ cup chopped walnuts |
| ½ teaspoon salt | 1 recipe Penuche Frosting (page 145) |

**1** Let butter and eggs stand at room temperature for 30 minutes. Lightly grease a 13×9×2-inch baking pan; set aside. In a medium bowl stir together flour, baking powder, cinnamon, nutmeg, salt, cloves, and baking soda (photo 2, page 136). Set aside.

**2** Preheat oven to 350°F. In a large mixing bowl beat butter with an electric mixer on medium to high speed for 30 seconds (photo 3, page 136). Gradually add sugar, about ¼ cup at a time, beating on medium speed and scraping sides of bowl (photos 4–5, page 136). Add eggs, one at a time, beating until combined after each addition (photo 6, page 136). Alternately add flour mixture and applesauce, beating on low speed after each addition just until combined (photo 7, page 137). Stir in raisins and walnuts.

**3** Spread batter evenly into the prepared pan (photo 8, page 137). Bake in the preheated oven for 40 to 45 minutes or until a wooden toothpick inserted near the center of cake comes out clean (photo 9, page 137). Cool completely in pan on a wire rack. Frost with Penuche Frosting. Makes 12 servings.

**Make-ahead directions:** Bake cake, cool completely, and freeze (without frosting) for up to 1 month. Thaw and frost cake before serving.

Per serving: 548 cal., 20 g total fat (10 g sat. fat), 76 mg chol., 286 mg sodium, 116 g carbo., 2 g fiber, 3 g pro.

A small metal turner or spatula is perfect for getting pieces of cake out of the pan. The narrow, flexible blade can easily get into tight corners and under the cake without destroying it.

**Ask Mom** How do I grease a baking pan? p. 59 / How do I measure butter? p. 55 / How do I measure flour? p. 54 / How do I measure sugar? p. 55 / How do I remove a piece of cake from a pan? p. 165 / What are chopped nuts? p. 34 / What are cloves? p. 36 / What is baking powder? p. 30, 319 / What is baking soda? p. 30, 319 / What is cinnamon? p. 36 / What is nutmeg? p. 37 / What's that dried fruit? p. 41 / What's that flour? p. 31 / What's that nut? p. 34–35

# Rhubarb and Spice
# Snacking Cake

⅓ cup granulated sugar

⅓ cup chopped pecans

1 tablespoon butter, melted

1 teaspoon ground cinnamon

1 cup all-purpose flour

½ teaspoon baking soda

⅛ teaspoon ground nutmeg

¼ cup butter, softened

¾ cup packed brown sugar

1 egg

⅓ cup dairy sour cream

1 cup chopped fresh rhubarb or frozen unsweetened rhubarb, thawed, drained, and chopped

¼ cup golden raisins

1 teaspoon finely shredded lemon peel

**1** Grease and flour an 8×8×2-inch or a 9×9×2-inch baking pan; set aside. For topping, in a small bowl combine granulated sugar, pecans, the 1 tablespoon melted butter, and ½ teaspoon of the cinnamon until crumbly; set aside. In another small bowl stir together flour, baking soda, the remaining ½ teaspoon cinnamon, nutmeg, and ¼ teaspoon *salt* (photo 2, page 136); set aside.

**2** Preheat oven to 350°F. In a medium mixing bowl beat the ¼ cup butter with an electric mixer on medium to high speed for 30 seconds (photo 3, page 136). Beat in brown sugar until well combined (photos 4–5, page 136). Beat in egg (photo 6, page 136). Add flour mixture alternately with sour cream to butter mixture, beating until combined after each addition (batter will be thick). Stir in rhubarb, raisins, and lemon peel (below).

**3** Spread batter evenly in the prepared pan (below). Sprinkle with topping (below). Bake in pre-heated oven for 30 to 35 minutes for 8×8×2-inch pan or 25 to 30 minutes for 9×9×2-inch pan or until a toothpick inserted near the center of cake comes out clean (photo 9, page 137). Cool in pan on a wire rack for 30 minutes. Serve warm or cool. Makes 9 servings.

Per serving: 276 cal., 12 g total fat (6 g sat. fat), 45 mg chol., 223 mg sodium, 41 g carbo., 2 g fiber, 3 g pro.

**1** The batter will be very stiff. Use a sturdy rubber scraper or a wooden spoon to stir in the rhubarb, raisins, and lemon peel.

**2** Scrape the batter from the bowl into the pan. Use an offset metal spatula to evenly spread the batter to the edges of the pan.

**3** Crumble the topping with your fingers and sprinkle it evenly over the batter, completely covering the top.

**Ask Mom** How do I grease and flour a pan? p. 59 / How do I measure butter/sugar? p. 55 / How do I measure flour? p. 54 / How do I prepare rhubarb? p. 49, 117 / How do I remove a piece of cake from a pan? p. 165 / How do I shred lemon peel? p. 45, 105 / How do I soften butter? p. 28, 76 / What are chopped nuts? p. 34 / What is baking soda? p. 30, 319 / What is cinnamon? p. 36 / What is nutmeg? p. 37 / What's that dried fruit? p. 41 / What's that flour? p. 31 / What's that nut? p. 34–35

# Triple-Nut Zucchini Cake

¾ cup chopped walnuts
¾ cup chopped pecans
¾ cup slivered almonds, chopped
¾ cup rolled oats
2 cups all-purpose flour
2 cups granulated sugar
I teaspoon baking powder
I teaspoon salt

¼ teaspoon baking soda
3 cups shredded zucchini
I cup cooking oil
3 eggs, lightly beaten
I teaspoon vanilla
⅓ cup butter
3 tablespoons half-and-half, light cream, or milk
⅔ cup packed brown sugar

**1** Preheat oven to 350°F. Grease a 13×9×2-inch baking pan; set aside. In a 15×10×1-inch baking pan combine ½ cup of the walnuts, ½ cup of the pecans, ½ cup of the almonds, and the oats. Bake in preheated oven about 12 minutes or until toasted, stirring two to three times (below). Set aside on a wire rack.

**2** In a large mixing bowl stir together flour, granulated sugar, baking powder, salt, and baking soda. Stir in zucchini, oil, eggs, and vanilla until combined. Stir in toasted nut mixture.

**3** Spread batter evenly into the prepared pan. Bake in the preheated oven for 35 to 40 minutes or until a wooden toothpick inserted near the center comes out clean (photo 9, page 137). Cool in pan on a wire rack for 1 hour.

**4** In a small saucepan combine butter and half-and-half. Cook and stir until butter melts. Add brown sugar; stir until sugar dissolves. Remove from heat. Stir in the remaining nuts.

**5** Spread nut mixture over cake in pan (below). Broil 4 inches from the heat for 1½ to 2 minutes or until topping is bubbly and golden (below). Cool in pan for 1 hour on a wire rack before serving. Makes 20 servings.

Per serving: 386 cal., 24 g total fat (5 g sat. fat), 41 mg chol., 182 mg sodium, 42 g carbo., 2 g fiber, 4 g pro.

**1** Bake the nuts just until they turn light golden brown. Check often to make sure they aren't getting too brown. Nuts burn quickly.

**2** Spoon the hot nut topping over the warm cake. Use a wooden spoon or heat-resistant rubber scraper to remove all of the mixture.

**3** With an offset metal spatula, quickly spread the nut mixture over the warm cake. Spread gently to avoid tearing the cake.

**4** Place the cake under the broiler so that the top is about 4 inches from the heat element. Broil until the topping bubbles.

# Pineapple-Carrot Loaves

¾ cup butter

½ of an 8-ounce package cream cheese

4 eggs

2½ cups all-purpose flour

1 tablespoon baking powder

1 tablespoon finely shredded lemon peel

½ teaspoon salt

1 pound carrots, cut up

1 cup pecans, toasted

1½ cups sugar

1 8-ounce can crushed pineapple (juice pack), drained

½ of a recipe Cream Cheese Frosting (page 144)

Fresh or canned pineapple slices, drained and halved (optional)

**1** Let butter, cream cheese, and eggs stand at room temperature for 30 minutes. Grease the bottoms and 1 inch up the sides of two 8×4×2-inch loaf pans. Set pans aside. In a large bowl stir together flour, baking powder, lemon peel, and salt (photo 1, page 136); set aside.

**2** Preheat oven to 350°F. In a food processor bowl* process carrots with on-off turns until finely chopped (photo 1, page 169). Add pecans and ½ cup of the sugar; process until pecans are finely chopped (photo 2, page 169).

**3** In a very large mixing bowl beat butter and cream cheese with an electric mixer on medium to high speed for 30 seconds. Gradually beat in the remaining 1 cup sugar until well combined, scraping sides of bowl. Add eggs, one at a time, beating until combined after each addition. Stir in carrot mixture and drained crushed pineapple until combined (photo 3, page 169). Stir in the flour mixture.

**4** Divide batter evenly between the prepared pans. Bake in the preheated oven for 50 to 55 minutes or until a wooden toothpick inserted near centers of cakes comes out clean (photo 9, page 137). Cool cakes in pans on a wire rack for 10 minutes. Remove from pans (photo 4, page 169); cool completely.

**5** Frost with Cream Cheese Frosting. Serve immediately or cover and store in the refrigerator for up to 3 days. If desired, just before serving top with pineapple halves. Makes 2 loaves (16 servings).

*Note: If you do not have a food processor, finely shred the carrots and finely chop the pecans. Prepare as directed above, except add the sugar all at once, stir in the shredded carrot with the pineapple, and stir the pecans in with the flour mixture.

Per serving: 470 cal., 23 g total fat (11 g sat. fat), 99 mg chol., 340 mg sodium, 63 g carbo., 2 g fiber, 6 g pro.

**Good to Know** This loaf-shape carrot cake is a two-for-one deal. Because it makes two cakes, you can eat one now and freeze one for another day. Cool completely, then wrap it, unfrosted, in plastic wrap or aluminum foil. Freeze in a freezer bag or airtight container for up to 4 months. Thaw it at room temperature for several hours. Frost it with Cream Cheese Frosting and decorate it with the pineapple slices, if you want, right before serving.

**SAY YES TO FRESH.** If only fresh pineapple will do, you can have your cake and eat it too. Look in the produce section of your supermarket for whole pineapple that's been shelled and cored. Slice it thinly and lay it in overlapping slices on the cake.

**1** Cut the carrots into l-inch pieces. Process the carrots until they are finely chopped, stopping the processor frequently and scraping the bowl.

**2** Add the pecans and ½ cup of the sugar. Process until the pecans are in small pieces but are still large enough to be visible. Stop processing before the nuts turn to powder.

**3** Add the carrot-pecan mixture to the beaten egg mixture. Gently stir until the carrot-pecan mixture is well distributed through the egg mixture.

**4** Use a metal spatula to gently loosen the cake from the pan. Be careful not to tear the cake. Invert the pan and gently remove the cake. Turn the cake right side up and cool on a rack.

This carrot cake may be nontraditional (it's flavored with lemon peel instead of cinnamon and infused with crushed pineapple), but it's every bit as moist and delicious as the original.

# Banana Split Cake

| | |
|---|---|
| I cup butter | ½ cup dairy sour cream |
| 4 eggs | ½ cup milk |
| 3 cups all-purpose flour | I teaspoon vanilla |
| 2 teaspoons baking powder | ½ cup strawberry preserves |
| I teaspoon salt | Few drops red food coloring |
| ¼ teaspoon baking soda | ½ cup presweetened cocoa powder (not low-calorie) |
| I½ cups sugar | I cup chocolate fudge ice cream topping |
| ½ cup mashed ripe banana (I large) | Fresh strawberries (optional) |

**1** Let the butter and eggs stand at room temperature for 30 minutes. Grease and flour a 13×9×2-inch baking pan. In a medium bowl stir together flour, baking powder, salt, and baking soda (photo 2, page 136). Set aside.

**2** Preheat oven to 350°F. In a large bowl beat butter with an electric mixer on medium to high speed for 30 seconds (photo 3, page 136). Gradually add sugar, about ¼ cup at a time, beating until well combined and scraping sides of bowl (photos 4–5, page 136). Add eggs, one at a time, beating until combined after each addition (photo 6, page 136). In a small bowl combine banana, sour cream, milk, and vanilla. Alternately add flour mixture and banana mixture to butter mixture, beating on low speed after each addition just until combined (photo 7, page 137).

**3** In a small bowl stir together 1 cup of the batter, the strawberry preserves, and red food coloring (photo 1, page 171). In another small bowl stir together another 1 cup of the batter and the cocoa powder. Spoon the remaining plain batter into the prepared pan. Spoon chocolate and strawberry batters into small mounds randomly over the plain batter (photo 2, page 171). Use a narrow metal spatula to gently swirl the batters (photo 3, page 171); spread evenly.

**4** Bake in the preheated oven for 40 to 45 minutes or until a wooden toothpick inserted near the center of cake comes out clean (photo 9, page 137). Cool completely in pan on a wire rack.

**5** When ready to serve, in a small saucepan heat ice cream topping just until of drizzling consistency. Drizzle over each serving. If desired, top with strawberries. Makes 16 servings.

**Per serving:** 410 cal., 17 g total fat (11 g sat. fat), 87 mg chol., 359 mg sodium, 60 g carbo., 1 g fiber, 4 g pro.

**Ingredient Info** You'll need to do a little label reading to get the right cocoa for this recipe. Presweetened cocoa powder is a drink mix that contains cocoa powder, sugar, and flavorings—but no milk solids or powdered milk. It's usually mixed with milk to make hot cocoa. Look for it—not instant hot cocoa mix, which does contain milk solids—to use in this recipe. And be sure to get the stuff that contains real sugar—not a sugar substitute.

**Ask Mom** How do I grease and flour a pan? p. 59 / How do I mash bananas? p. 40 / How do I measure butter? p. 55 / How do I measure flour? p. 54 / How do I measure liquids? p. 55 / How do I measure sugar? p. 55 / What does drizzle mean? p. 69, 85 / What is baking powder? p. 30, 319 / What is baking soda? p. 30, 319 / What is vanilla? p. 128 / What's that flour? p. 31

**TELL THEM YOU WORK IN MARBLE.** The technique of swirling differently flavored and/or colored batters together is a simple thing to do—and it delivers impressive results. Just don't get overzealous. You'll end up with a cake of a *really* different color.

**1**

**2**

**3**

**1. Mix the strawberry batter:** Place 1 cup of the plain batter in a medium bowl. Add the strawberry preserves and gently fold the preserves into the batter. The red food coloring gives the batter a striking red color, so be sure to use it. Fold in 2 or 3 drops and check color. Add more coloring if needed.

**2. Add batter to pan:** Spread the plain batter in an even layer over the bottom of the pan, being sure to fill the corner. Drop spoonfuls of strawberry and chocolate batter over the plain batter. Alternate the mounds of strawberry and chocolate batters.

**3. Swirl to marble:** Use a narrow metal spatula to swirl the strawberry, chocolate, and plain batters together. Be sure to cut through to the bottom of the pan to scoop up some of the plain batter. Stop swirling when you have a reached a pleasing marble pattern. If you overdo it, the finished cake will have a muddy color instead of a colorful marbled appearance.

# Orange-Rosemary Pound Cake

- 1 16-ounce package pound cake mix
- ½ cup dairy sour cream
- 2 eggs
- ⅓ cup water
- 1½ teaspoons finely shredded orange peel
- 1 teaspoon snipped fresh rosemary
- Raspberries, blueberries, or blackberries (optional)
- Dairy sour cream (optional)

**1** Preheat oven to 350°F. Grease and lightly flour a 9×5×3-inch loaf pan. Set aside.

**2** In a large bowl combine cake mix, sour cream, eggs, and water. Beat with an electric mixer on low speed for 30 seconds. Beat on medium speed for 3 minutes. Stir in orange peel and snipped rosemary.

**3** Pour batter evenly into the prepared pan. Bake in the preheated oven for 45 to 55 minutes or until a wooden toothpick inserted near the center of cake comes out clean (photo 9, page 137). Cool cake in pan on a wire rack for 10 minutes. Remove cake from pan (photo 4, page 169); cool completely on wire rack. If desired, serve cake with berries and additional sour cream. Makes 12 to 14 servings.

**Per serving:** 190 cal., 7 g total fat (3 g sat. fat), 39 mg chol., 149 mg sodium, 30 g carbo., 0 g fiber, 3 g pro.

**Lemon-Poppy Seed Pound Cake:** Prepare as above, except substitute ½ cup lemon low-fat yogurt for the ½ cup sour cream and omit orange peel and rosemary. Stir 2 tablespoons poppy seeds, 1 teaspoon finely shredded lemon peel, and 2 tablespoons lemon juice into batter.

**Good to Know** Pound cake was originally made with one pound each of flour, butter, sugar, and eggs—hence, its name. (It was probably pretty dense.) Since then variations have evolved that include leavenings such as baking powder or baking soda (thank goodness!) and flavorings such as fruits, nuts, seeds, herbs, and citrus peel.

**Ask Mom** How do I grease and flour a pan? p. 59 / How do I juice a lemon/lime? p. 44, 45 / How do I measure liquids? p. 55 / How do I shred lemon/lime/orange peel? p. 45, 105 / How do I snip fresh herbs? p. 49 / How do I wash fresh berries? p. 42 / What are poppy seeds? p. 299

# A CAKE FOR ALL SEASONS.

Pound cake is the little black dress of the cake world—so versatile and always appropriate. Its fine crumb, rich texture, and buttery taste make it equally delicious plain or dressed up with fruit, dessert sauces, or whipped cream.

Pound cake lends itself to all kinds of uses. Slice it and cut in half diagonally, slice it thinly and stack it with fruit preserves between layers, or cube and skewer it for dipping in chocolate fondue.

174

Snack Cakes & Cupcakes

# Cranberry Pound Cake

¾ cup butter

3 eggs

⅔ cup dried cranberries, snipped dried cherries, dried blueberries, and/or currants

2½ cups all-purpose flour

1 teaspoon baking powder

½ teaspoon baking soda

½ teaspoon salt

1¼ cups granulated sugar

1 tablespoon finely shredded orange or lemon peel

1½ teaspoons vanilla

1 8-ounce carton dairy sour cream

**1** Let butter and eggs stand at room temperature 30 minutes. Grease and flour a 9×5×3-inch loaf pan; set aside. Pour boiling water over cranberries; let stand 10 minutes (below). Drain; set aside. Stir together flour, baking powder, baking soda, and salt (photo 2, page 136); set aside.

**2** Preheat oven to 325°F. In a large mixing bowl beat butter with a mixer on medium to high speed 30 seconds (photo 3, page 136). Add sugar, 3 tablespoons at a time, beating about 6 minutes or until very light and fluffy (below). Add peel and vanilla. Add eggs, one at a time, beating well on low to medium speed after each (below). Alternately add flour mixture and sour cream, beating on low speed after each addition until combined (below). Stir in cranberries.

**3** Spoon batter into prepared pan. Bake in preheated oven 70 minutes or until a wooden toothpick inserted near the center of cake comes out clean (photo 9, page 137). (Cake will be high in pan.) Cool on a wire rack for 10 minutes. Remove cake from pan (photo 4, page 169). Cool completely on wire rack. Makes 10 servings.

Per serving: 417 cal., 20 g total fat (12 g sat. fat), 110 mg chol., 336 mg sodium, 54 g carbo., 1 g fiber, 6 g pro.

**1** To plump cranberries, pour enough boiling water over them to cover and let stand. Drain well before adding to the batter.

**2** Add the sugar gradually, about 3 tablespoons at a time. Beat after each addition until the sugar is mixed into the butter.

**3** Add the eggs one at a time. Beat well after each egg for a total of about 6 minutes. Beat until the batter is very light and fluffy.

**4** Add about a third of the flour mixture; beat on low. Then beat in half the sour cream. Repeat, ending with the final third of flour mixture.

**Ask Mom** How do I grease and flour a pan? p. 59 / How do I measure butter? p. 55 / How do I measure flour? p. 54 / How do I measure sugar? p. 55 / How do I shred lemon/lime/orange peel? p. 45, 105 / How do I snip dried fruit or preserves? p. 41, 102 / What is baking soda? p. 30, 319 / What is vanilla? p. 128 / What's that dried fruit? p. 41 / What's that flour? p. 31

② Skill Level

# Gooey Butter Cake

1 cup all-purpose flour
3 tablespoons granulated sugar
⅓ cup cold butter
1¼ cups granulated sugar
¾ cup butter, softened
¼ cup light-colored corn syrup
1 egg
1 cup all-purpose flour
1 5-ounce can (⅔ cup) evaporated milk
Powdered sugar (optional)

**Flavor Changes** This simple, buttery cake is great paired with fresh berries. Just bake the cake as directed, then serve it with 4 cups of fresh berries of your choice—raspberries, blueberries, sliced strawberries, or blackberries. Top pieces of the cake with the berries or serve them on the side.

**1** Preheat oven to 350°F. For crust, in a bowl mix 1 cup flour and the 3 tablespoons granulated sugar. Using a pastry blender, cut in the ⅓ cup butter until mixture resembles fine crumbs (below). Pat into the bottom of a 9×9×2-inch baking pan (below); set aside.

**2** In a medium mixing bowl beat the 1¼ cups granulated sugar and the ¾ cup butter with an electric mixer on medium speed until combined. Beat in corn syrup and egg just until combined. Alternately add the remaining 1 cup flour and the evaporated milk, beating just until combined after each addition (batter will appear slightly curdled) (below).

**3** Pour batter into the crust-lined baking pan. Bake in the preheated oven about 35 minutes or until the cake is nearly firm when gently shaken. Cool in pan on a wire rack. If desired, sift powdered sugar over cake before serving (below). Makes 12 servings.

**Per serving:** 347 cal., 18 g total fat (11 g sat. fat), 5 mg chol., 142 mg sodium, 44 g carbo., 1 g fiber, 3 g pro.

**①** Cut the butter into the flour mixture until pieces are the size of coarse crumbs and the mixture starts to cling together.

**②** Transfer the crumb mixture to the baking pan and use your fingers to press it into an even layer.

**③** After adding the flour and the evaporated milk, the batter appears curdled. Don't try to beat the batter until it is smooth.

**④** To serve, cut the cake into squares. If you like, rub a spoon over powdered sugar in a fine-mesh sieve to lightly dust the cake squares.

# Simple White Cupcakes
## with Creamy Frosting

⅓ cup butter

2 eggs

1 cup all-purpose flour

1 teaspoon baking powder

¼ teaspoon baking soda

⅛ teaspoon salt

⅔ cup sugar

1 teaspoon vanilla

⅓ cup buttermilk or sour milk

1 recipe Creamy Frosting

**Good to Know**

Letting the butter and eggs stand at room temperature for 30 minutes before using them is an important first step. The butter will blend better with the other ingredients—and the eggs will make your cupcakes lighter and fluffier than if they were used cold.

**1** Let butter and eggs stand at room temperature for 30 minutes. Grease and flour twelve 2½-inch muffin cups (photos 2–3, page 177) or line with paper bake cups (photo 1, page 177); set aside. In a medium bowl stir together flour, baking powder, baking soda, and salt (photo 2, page 136); set aside.

**2** Preheat oven to 350°F. In a large mixing bowl beat butter with an electric mixer on medium to high speed for 30 seconds (photo 3, page 136). Add sugar and vanilla. Beat on medium to high speed about 2 minutes or until light and fluffy, scraping sides of bowl as necessary (photos 4–5, page 136). Add eggs, one at a time, beating until combined after each addition (photo 6, page 136). Alternately add flour mixture and buttermilk to butter mixture, beating on low speed after each addition just until combined (photo 7, page 137).

**3** Spoon batter into the prepared muffin cups, filling each about half full (photo 4, page 177). Bake for 18 to 20 minutes or until a wooden toothpick inserted in the centers comes out clean. Cool cupcakes in muffin cups on a wire rack for 5 minutes. Remove cupcakes from muffin cups and cool completely on wire rack. Generously spread Creamy Frosting over cupcakes. Makes 12 cupcakes.

Creamy Frosting: In a large mixing bowl beat together 4 ounces softened cream cheese and 2 tablespoons softened butter with an electric mixer on medium to high speed until smooth. Beat in 1 teaspoon vanilla. Gradually add 2½ cups powdered sugar, beating until smooth.

Make-ahead directions: Place frosted cupcakes in an airtight container and chill in the refrigerator for up to 24 hours. For longer storage, keep unfrosted cupcakes in an airtight container at room temperature for up to 2 days or in the freezer for up to 6 months. Thaw frozen cupcakes at room temperature for 1 hour before frosting. Store frosting in an airtight container in the refrigerator for up to 2 days.

Per cupcake: 411 cal., 18 g total fat (12 g sat. fat), 71 mg chol., 225 mg sodium, 58 g carbo., 1 g fiber, 3 g pro.

**FUN WITH FROSTING.** There are several ways to put the icing on these charming cakes. You can simply swirl it on with a knife. Or, if you want to get fancy, pipe it in concentric circles with a pastry bag fitted with a star or plain tip (which will give you dots).

Transform these little cakes into a dozen different desserts, from kid-friendly, candy-infused sweets to sophisticated treats for grown-ups. Turn to page 178 to see how.

**1** To line the muffin cups, simply place a paper bake cup in each muffin cup.

**2** To grease the muffin cups, dip a pastry brush in shortening and spread over the bottom and sides of each muffin cup.

**3** To flour, sprinkle a pinch of all-purpose flour in each cup. Tilt the pan in all directions to coat the sides. Turn the pan upside down and tap out any extra flour.

**4** Use two tablespoons to transfer the batter to the muffin cups. Fill the cups half full with batter to avoid the cupcakes' overflowing the cups.

## Coconut Cupcakes

1 cup flaked coconut, toasted

Prepare and frost Simple White Cupcakes with Creamy Frosting (page 176) as directed. Sprinkle frosted cupcakes with coconut.

## Raspberry Cupcakes

48 to 60 fresh raspberries

Prepare batter for Simple White Cupcakes (page 176) as directed. Place 3 to 4 raspberries on top of batter in each cup. Bake and cool as directed. After frosting with Creamy White Frosting, top each cupcake with a raspberry .

## Hawaiian Cupcakes

½ cup chopped macadamia nuts
½ cup tropical blend mixed dried fruit bits

Prepare and frost Simple White Cupcakes with Creamy Frosting (page 176) as directed. Sprinkle tops with macadamia nuts and dried fruit bits.

## Chocolate Chip Cupcakes

1½ teaspoons finely shredded orange peel
½ cup miniature semisweet chocolate pieces

Prepare Simple White Cupcakes (page 176) as directed, except add orange peel with the butter. Fold chocolate pieces into batter. Bake and frost as directed.

## Espresso Cupcakes

1½ teaspoons espresso powder
½ cup chopped chocolate-covered espresso beans

Prepare and bake Simple White Cupcakes (page 176) as directed. Prepare Creamy Frosting as directed, except add espresso powder to butter. Sprinkle frosted cupcakes with beans.

## Cranberry-Pistachio Cupcakes

½ cup chopped dried cranberries
½ cup shelled pistachio nuts

Prepare Simple White Cupcakes with Creamy Frosting (page 176) as directed. Sprinkle frosted cupcakes with dried cranberries and pistachio nuts.

## Cinnamon-Orange Cupcakes

  2  tablespoons orange marmalade

  ¼  teaspoon ground cinnamon

Bake Simple White Cupcakes (page 176) as directed. Prepare Creamy Frosting as directed, except stir marmalade and cinnamon into frosting. Frost cupcakes.

## Lemon Cupcakes

  1½  teaspoons finely shredded lemon peel

  ¼  cup purchased lemon curd

Prepare Simple White Cupcakes with Creamy Frosting (page 176) as directed, except add lemon peel to butter. Prepare frosting as directed; frost cupcakes. Top each with 1 teaspoon of lemon curd; swirl with frosting. If desired, sprinkle with additional lemon peel.

## Candy Cupcakes

  12  bite-size chocolate-covered peanut butter cups, unwrapped

  ½  crushed crunchy chocolate-covered peanut butter candy bar

Prepare Simple White Cupcakes (page 176) as directed, except top batter in each cup with 1 peanut butter cup. Bake and frost as directed. Sprinkle with crushed candy bar.

## Toffee Cupcakes

  ½  cup chopped cashews

  ½  cup toffee pieces

  ½  cup caramel ice cream topping

Prepare and frost Simple White Cupcakes with Creamy Frosting (page 176) as directed. Sprinkle with cashews and toffee bits. Drizzle with ice cream topping.

## Almond Cupcakes

  ¼  to ½ teaspoon almond extract

  ½  cup sliced almonds, toasted

  ¼  teaspoon almond extract

Prepare Simple White Cupcakes (page 176) as directed, except reduce vanilla to ½ teaspoon and add ¼ to ½ teaspoon almond extract. Prepare frosting as directed, except reduce vanilla to ½ teaspoon and add ¼ teaspoon almond extract. Sprinkle with almonds.

## Peppermint Cupcakes

    Grated white chocolate

    Coarsely crushed peppermint candies

Prepare and frost Simple White Cupcakes with Creamy Frosting (page 176) as directed. Sprinkle frosted cupcakes with grated white chocolate and peppermint candies.

# Little Pumpkin Cakes

| | |
|---|---|
| 1 cup all-purpose flour | ¾ cup sugar |
| ¾ teaspoon baking powder | ⅓ cup cooking oil |
| ¾ teaspoon pumpkin pie spice | ½ of a 15-ounce can pumpkin (¾ cup plus 2 tablespoons) |
| ½ teaspoon salt | 1 recipe Creamy Frosting (page 176) |
| ¼ teaspoon baking soda | 1 recipe Caramelized Hazelnut Brittle (page 181) or |
| 2 eggs | purchased nut brittle, broken into pieces (optional) |

**1** Grease and lightly flour thirty-six 1¾-inch muffin cups, twelve 2½-inch muffin cups, or four 3½-inch muffin cups or line muffin cups with paper bake cups. Set pan(s) aside. In a medium bowl stir together flour, baking powder, pumpkin pie spice, salt, and baking soda; set aside.

**2** Preheat oven to 350°F. In a large bowl combine eggs, sugar, and oil; beat with an electric mixer on medium speed until combined. Alternately add flour mixture and pumpkin to sugar mixture, beating just until mixture is combined.

**3** Spoon batter into the prepared muffin cups, filling each two-thirds full. Bake in the preheated oven until a toothpick inserted in the center of each cake comes out clean. Allow 12 to 15 minutes for 1¾-inch muffin cups, 20 to 25 minutes for 2½-inch cups, or 25 to 30 minutes for 3½-inch cups. Cool in muffin cups on a wire rack for 5 minutes. Using a table knife or small metal spatula, loosen edges; carefully remove cakes from muffin cups. Cool completely on wire rack.

**4** Frost cakes with Creamy Frosting. If desired, arrange shards of Caramelized Hazelnut Brittle on top of cakes. Makes 36 (1¾-inch) cakes, 12 (2½-inch), or 4 (3½-inch).

Per 1¾-inch cake: 153 cal., 8 g total fat (2 g sat. fat), 11 mg chol., 54 mg sodium, 20 g carbo., 0 g fiber, 1 g pro.

**Good to Know** If you have any leftover brittle, chop it and use it as a topping for cake or ice cream. Or make a batch and eat it as candy—or give it as a hostess gift. (Everyone will be so impressed.)

**Ask Mom** How do I grease a baking pan/dish? p. 59 / How do I line a pan with foil? p. 58 / How do I measure flour? p. 54 / How do I measure liquids? p. 55 / How do I measure sugar? p. 55 / What are chopped nuts? p. 34 / What is baking powder? p. 30, 319 / What is baking soda? p. 30, 319 / What is canned pumpkin? p. 302 / What is cooking oil? p. 28 / What is pumpkin pie spice? p. 36, 37 / What's that flour? p. 31 / What's that nut? p. 34–35

**CAN I USE OTHER NUTS IN THE BRITTLE?** You can use almost any kind of chopped nut you like or have on hand. Almonds, walnuts, pecans, peanuts—even pistachios—will work just fine in this recipe.

**1**

**2**

**3**

## Caramelized Hazelnut Brittle

1. Line a large baking sheet with foil; butter foil and set aside. In a small saucepan melt 2 teaspoons butter over low heat. Stir in ⅓ cup chopped hazelnuts (filberts); keep warm over low heat. Place 1 cup granulated sugar in a heavy 12-inch skillet; heat over medium-high heat until sugar begins to melt, shaking skillet occasionally to heat sugar evenly. Reduce heat to medium-low; cook until sugar is melted and golden (photo 1), stirring only as necessary after sugar begins to melt. This should take 12 to 15 minutes.

2. Turn off heat or remove skillet from heat. Quickly stir in the warm chopped hazelnuts and butter (photo 2).

3. Immediately pour the mixture onto the prepared baking sheet, allowing syrup to flow and distributing nuts evenly. Cool completely. Break candy into shardlike pieces. Store in a tightly covered container in a cool dry place for up to 1 month.

(2) Skill Level

**Good to Know** The finished cupcakes will likely have a slight indentation in the top from having a peanut butter cup baked in the middle of them—but that's OK, helpful even. The indentation makes a perfect cradle for the jam.

# Peanut Butter Cupcakes

1⅓ cups all-purpose flour
⅔ cup graham cracker crumbs
1 tablespoon baking powder
1 cup creamy peanut butter
⅓ cup shortening
1⅓ cups sugar
2 eggs

1 teaspoon vanilla
1 cup milk
24 bite-size chocolate-covered peanut butter cups, unwrapped
Raspberry or strawberry jam

**1** Preheat oven to 350°F. Line twenty-four 2½-inch muffin cups with paper bake cups (photo 1, page 177); set aside. In a medium bowl stir together flour, graham cracker crumbs, and baking powder (photo 2, page 136); set aside.

**2** In a very large mixing bowl beat peanut butter and shortening with an electric mixer on medium speed until combined. Gradually add sugar, beating on medium speed until well combined. Beat in eggs and vanilla. Alternately add flour mixture and milk to peanut butter mixture, beating on low speed after each addition just until combined.

**3** Spoon a rounded tablespoon batter into each prepared muffin cup (below). Place 1 peanut butter cup in each muffin cup on top of the batter (below). Spoon remaining batter into muffin cups to cover peanut butter cups (below). Bake in the preheated oven about 18 minutes or until a wooden toothpick inserted near edges comes out clean (cupcakes may have a slight indentation). Cool cupcakes in muffin cups on wire racks for 5 minutes. Remove cupcakes from muffin cups; cool thoroughly on wire racks. Spoon a small amount of jam on top of each cupcake (below). Makes 24 cupcakes.

Per cupcake: 295 cal., 15 g total fat (5 g sat. fat), 21 mg chol., 139 mg sodium, 38 g carbo., 2 g fiber, 6 g pro.

**1** Spoon a rounded tablespoon of batter into each paper-lined muffin cup. Use a thin rubber scraper to scrape batter from spoon.

**2** Place a miniature peanut butter cup on top of the batter in each muffin cup.

**3** Spoon the remaining batter over the peanut butter cups. Gently spread the batter to completely cover the candy.

**4** The cupcakes sink slightly during baking. Drop a spoonful of jam into each indentation in the cupcakes.

**Ask Mom** How do I make cracker/cookie crumbs? p. 129 / How do I measure flour? p. 54 / How do I measure liquids? p. 55 / How do I measure peanut butter? p. 55 / How do I measure shortening? p. 55 / How do I measure sugar? p. 55 / What is baking powder? p. 30, 319 / What is vanilla? p. 128 / What's that flour? p. 31

# luscious
## CHEESECAKES
## & SHORTCAKES

**These two classic desserts lend themselves to all kinds of innovations with toppings and fillings—seasonal fruits, nuts, and chocolate.**

6

**Bars, Cherry Cheesecake** ① ....................................185

**Bars, Key Lime Cheesecake** ① ................................186

**Caramel Apples and Cranberries** ② ...........................197

**Cheesecake-Baking Basics** ................................188–189

## CHEESECAKES

Blueberry Cheesecake ② ...............................191

Café au Lait Cheesecake ③ ............................194

Caramel-Peanut Cheesecake ② .......................190

Cheesecake Supreme ② ...............................187

Chocolate Chip Cheesecake ② ........................190

Chocolate Marble Cheesecake ② ....................187

Cookie Cheesecake ② ...............................190

Cranberry-Gingersnap Cheesecake ② ..................191

Espresso Cheesecake ② ...............................191

Honey-Mango Cheesecake ② ..........................190

Lemon-Ginger Cheesecake ② ..........................191

Maple-Dried Fruit Cheesecake ② ......................190

Orange-Ginger Baby Cheesecakes ② ...................196

Orange-Hazelnut Cheesecake ② ......................191

Raspberry Cheesecake ② ...........................190

Sour Cream-Pumpkin Cheesecake ③ ..................192

Spinach-Blue Cheese Cheesecake ③ ..................195

Strawberry-Fudge Cheesecake ② .....................191

**Pomegranate Sauce** ② ........................................187

## SHORTCAKES

Caramel Apples and Cranberry Pecan Shortcakes ② .......197

Chocolate-Raspberry Shortcakes ② ....................200

Mixed Berry Shortcake Croutons ② ....................198

Mixed Fruit Shortcakes ② ..............................198

Peanutty Ice Cream Shortcakes ③ .....................202

Strawberry Lemon-Poppy Seed Shortcakes ② ............199

Strawberry Shortcakes ② ............................199

Whole Shortcake ② ...................................198

**Ingredient Info**
Maraschino cherries
are available with
or without stems. If
you buy them with
stems, they're easily
plucked off. To drain
the cherries, pour into
a colander or sieve,
then turn onto a paper
towel-lined plate and
pat them dry with
another paper towel.

# Cherry Cheesecake Bars

    2  cups finely crushed vanilla wafers
   ⅓  cup butter, melted
    1  10-ounce jar maraschino cherries
    2  8-ounce packages cream cheese, softened
    1  cup sugar
    5  egg whites, lightly beaten

**1** Preheat oven to 350°F. Line a 13×9×2-inch baking pan with foil, extending foil over edges of pan; set aside.

**2** For crust, in a medium bowl combine crushed vanilla wafers and melted butter (photo 1, page 188). Press crust mixture evenly into the bottom of the prepared baking pan. Bake crust in the preheated oven for 10 minutes.

**3** Meanwhile, drain cherries well, reserving 2 tablespoons of the cherry liquid. Remove stems from cherries (below). Finely chop cherries (below); set aside.

**4** For filling, in a large mixing bowl beat cream cheese and sugar with an electric mixer on medium speed until combined (photo 4, page 188). Stir in chopped cherries, egg whites, and reserved cherry liquid until well combined (below).

**5** Pour filling evenly over crust. Bake for 20 to 25 minutes or until center appears set (photo 10, page 189). Cool in pan on a wire rack for 1 hour. Cover and chill for 4 to 24 hours. Cut into bars. Makes 32 bars.

**Per bar:** 157 cal., 9 g total fat (5 g sat. fat), 21 mg chol., 96 mg sodium, 18 g carbo., 0 g fiber, 2 g pro.

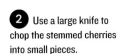

**1** After draining the cherries on paper towels, pull out the stems.

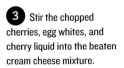

**2** Use a large knife to chop the stemmed cherries into small pieces.

**3** Stir the chopped cherries, egg whites, and cherry liquid into the beaten cream cheese mixture.

**Ask Mom** How do I line a pan with foil? p. 58 / How do I make cracker/cookie crumbs? p. 129 / How do I measure butter? p. 55 / How do I measure sugar? p. 55 / How do I soften cream cheese? p. 57 / How do I store cheesecake? p. 68, 193 / How do I use a sieve? p. 65 / How do I work with eggs? p. 26–27

# Key Lime Cheesecake Bars

1 cup finely crushed pretzel sticks
2 tablespoons sugar
½ cup butter, melted
2 8-ounce packages cream cheese, softened
⅔ cup sugar

1 teaspoon vanilla
3 eggs, lightly beaten
3 tablespoons bottled key lime juice* or regular lime juice
½ teaspoon finely shredded lime peel
¼ cup chopped salted pistachio nuts

**1** Preheat oven to 350°F. Grease the bottom of a 9×9×2-inch baking pan; set aside.

**2** For crust, in a medium bowl combine crushed pretzels and the 2 tablespoons sugar; stir in butter (photo 1, page 188). Press crust mixture evenly into the bottom of the prepared baking pan. Bake in the preheated oven for 10 minutes. Cool on a wire rack while preparing filling.

**3** For filling, in a large mixing bowl beat cream cheese, the ⅔ cup sugar, and vanilla with an electric mixer on medium speed until combined (photo 4, page 188). Stir in eggs (photo 7, page 188). Stir in lime juice and lime peel.

**4** Pour filling evenly over crust; sprinkle with nuts. Bake for 20 to 25 minutes or until center appears set (photo 10, page 189). Cool in pan on a wire rack for 1 hour. Cover and chill for 4 to 24 hours (top will crack slightly). Cut into bars. Makes 15 to 20 bars.

*Note: Look for bottled key lime juice in the juice aisle of your supermarket.

**Per bar:** 254 cal., 19 g total fat (11 g sat. fat), 92 mg chol., 276 mg sodium, 17 g carbo., 0 g fiber, 4 g pro.

**Ask Mom** How do I grease a baking pan? p. 59 / How do I juice a lemon/lime? p. 44, 45 / How do I make cracker/cookie crumbs? p. 129 / How do I measure butter? p. 55 / How do I measure sugar? p. 55 / How do I shred lemon/lime/orange peel? p. 45, 105 / How do I soften cream cheese? p. 57 / How do I store cheesecake? p. 68, 193 / How do I work with eggs? p. 26–27 / What are chopped nuts? p. 34 / What are key limes? p. 258 / What is vanilla? p. 128 / What's that nut? p. 34–35

# Cheesecake Supreme

1½ cups finely crushed graham crackers

¼ cup finely chopped walnuts

1 tablespoon sugar

½ teaspoon ground cinnamon (optional)

½ cup butter, melted

3 8-ounce packages cream cheese, softened

1 cup sugar

2 tablespoons all-purpose flour

1 teaspoon vanilla

¼ cup milk

3 eggs, lightly beaten

½ teaspoon finely shredded lemon peel (optional)

1 recipe Pomegranate Sauce or Raspberry Sauce (page 60) (optional)

**1** Preheat oven to 375°F. For crust, in a bowl combine crushed graham crackers, walnuts, the 1 tablespoon sugar, and, if desired, the cinnamon; stir in melted butter (photo 1, page 188). Press crumb mixture onto the bottom and about 2 inches up the sides of an 8- or 9-inch springform pan (photos 2–3, page 188); set aside.

**2** For filling, in a large mixing bowl beat cream cheese, the 1 cup sugar, flour, and vanilla with an electric mixer on medium speed until combined (photo 4, page 188). Beat in milk until smooth (photos 5–6, page 188). Stir in eggs and, if desired, lemon peel (photo 7, page 188).

**3** Pour filling into crust-lined pan (photo 8, page 188); place pan in a shallow baking pan (photo 9, page 189). Bake in the preheated oven for 40 to 45 minutes for the 8-inch pan, 35 to 40 minutes for the 9-inch pan, or until a 2½-inch area around the outside edges appears set when gently shaken (photo 10, page 189).

**4** Cool in pan on a wire rack for 15 minutes. Loosen crust from sides of pan (photo 4, page 194); cool for 30 minutes more. Remove sides of pan (photo 11, page 189); cool cheesecake for 2 hours on rack. Cover and chill for at least 4 hours before serving. If desired, serve with Pomegranate Sauce. Makes 12 slices.

Per slice: 426 cal., 32 g total fat (17 g sat. fat), 138 mg chol., 303 mg sodium, 29 g carbo., 1 g fiber, 8 g pro.

**Chocolate Marble Cheesecake:** Prepare as above, except omit lemon peel. Melt 4 ounces semisweet chocolate; stir melted chocolate into half of the filling. Pour plain filling into crust; pour chocolate filling into crust. Use a knife or narrow metal spatula to gently marble and spread the fillings evenly (photo 3, page 143).

**Pomegranate Sauce:** In a medium saucepan bring one 16-ounce bottle pomegranate juice to boiling; reduce heat and boil gently, uncovered, for 10 to 12 minutes or until reduced to 1 cup. Stir together ¼ cup packed brown sugar and 1 tablespoon cornstarch; stir into juice. Cook and stir until thickened and bubbly. Cook and stir for 2 minutes more. Transfer to a medium bowl; cover surface with clear plastic wrap. Cool to room temperature. Cover and chill until serving time.

**Flavor Changes**
Cheesecake is incredibly versatile. See pages 190–191 for a dozen ways to create a whole new cheesecake with crust change-ups, stir-ins, and toppings.

**Ask Mom** How do I cut cheesecake? p. 193 / How do I make cracker crumbs? p. 129 / How do I measure butter/liquids/sugar? p. 55 / How do I measure flour? p. 54 / How do I shred lemon/lime/orange peel? p. 45, 105 / How do I soften cream cheese? p. 57 / How do I store cheesecake? p. 68, 193 / How do I work with eggs? p. 26–27 / What are chopped nuts? p. 34 / What is a springform pan? p. 16, 17 / What is cinnamon? p. 36 / What is vanilla? p. 128 / What's that flour? p. 31 / What's that nut? p. 34–35

# Cheesecake-Baking Basics

## Cheesecake suffers from the misconception that it's tricky and temperamental. Not true. Here's how to make a silky-textured, perfect cheesecake every time.

Let your ingredients stand at room temperature for 30 minutes before baking. You'll get more volume from the eggs, and the cream cheese will be softened so it blends better with the other ingredients. Thorough blending is especially important when it comes to the cheese and sugar. Be sure they're smooth before liquids such as eggs and milk are added. Once the batter thins, it becomes difficult to smooth out lumps. And while you want some volume from the eggs, you don't want to overbeat the batter after adding them. Overbeating incorporates too much air, which can cause the cheesecake to puff a lot, then fall and crack. Overbaking can also cause cracking. Check it at the minimum baking time. It's done when the center appears nearly set. A 1-inch spot in the center will jiggle slightly when the cheesecake is done (it firms up as the cake cools). Don't check it by poking it with a knife or toothpick—you want a smooth surface. Set a timer for the exact cooling time specified. When time's up, carefully loosen the crust from the pan. If you wait, it might start to pull away from the sides and crack.

**1** Add the melted butter to the crust ingredients, stirring until all the ingredients are moistened.

**2** Use your fingers to make sure the crust is an even thickness on the bottom and up the sides of the springform pan.

**3** Use a small measuring cup to press the crumbs firmly onto the bottom and up the sides of the pan.

**4** Beat the softened cream cheese and sugar (and sometimes flavorings) on medium speed until the mixture is light and fluffy.

**5** Use low speed on your electric mixer to slowly beat the milk into the cream cheese mixture.

**6** Use a higher speed to beat the filling just until it's creamy and smooth.

**7** Use a spatula to gently stir the eggs into the filling.

**8** Carefully transfer the filling to the crust-lined pan; spread evenly with a rubber spatula.

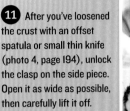

**11** After you've loosened the crust with an offset spatula or small thin knife (photo 4, page 194), unlock the clasp on the side piece. Open it as wide as possible, then carefully lift it off.

**9** Place the filled springform pan on a shallow baking pan just in case some of the butter leaks out of the crust.

**10** To check for doneness, gently shake the pan. If the filling appears nearly set, it's done. The center will firm up as it cools.

**12** For nice clean slices, cut the cheesecake using a nonserrated knife with a thin blade. Before cutting each slice, dip the knife in hot water and wipe it dry with a towel.

**DON'T GO WITH THE OVERFLOW.** When you're pressing the crust into the pan, be sure it's slightly taller than the level of the filling so that the finished cheesecake fits comfortably in the crust and doesn't spill over the sides.

## Chocolate Chip Cheesecake

¾ cup miniature semisweet chocolate pieces

White and/or milk chocolate curls

Prepare Cheesecake Supreme (page 187) as directed, except stir miniature chocolate pieces into filling. Top each slice with chocolate curls.

## Raspberry Cheesecake

Fresh raspberries

Seedless raspberry preserves, warmed

Prepare Cheesecake Supreme (page 187) as directed. To serve, stir raspberries gently into warm preserves; spoon over each slice.

## Cookie Cheesecake

1½ cups finely crushed chocolate sandwich cookies

Chopped chocolate sandwich cookies

Prepare Cheesecake Supreme (page 187) as directed, except substitute crushed sandwich cookies for the graham crackers in the crust. Top each slice with chopped sandwich cookies.

## Caramel-Peanut Cheesecake

Caramel-flavor ice cream topping, warmed

¾ cup chopped cocktail peanuts

Prepare Cheesecake Supreme (page 187) as directed. To serve, stir peanuts into warm ice cream topping; spoon over each slice.

## Honey-Mango Cheesecake

Fresh mango slices

Honey, warmed

Prepare Cheesecake Supreme (page 187) as directed. Top each slice with mango slices and warm honey.

## Maple-Dried Fruit Cheesecake

Snipped dried fruit (such as apricots or cherries)

Maple syrup, warmed

Prepare Cheesecake Supreme (page 187) as directed. To serve, stir dried fruit into warm maple syrup; spoon over each slice.

## Lemon-Ginger Cheesecake

⅓ cup finely chopped crystallized ginger
Purchased lemon curd

Prepare Cheesecake Supreme (page 187) as directed, except stir crystallized ginger into filling. Top each slice with lemon curd.

## Strawberry-Fudge Cheesecake

Hot fudge-flavor ice cream topping, warmed
Sliced fresh strawberries

Prepare Cheesecake Supreme (page 187) as directed, except pour warm ice cream topping over top of chilled cheesecake. Top each slice with sliced strawberries.

## Cranberry-Gingersnap Cheesecake

1½ cups finely crushed gingersnaps
Cranberry chutney

Prepare Cheesecake Supreme (page 187) as directed, except substitute crushed gingersnaps for the graham crackers in the crust. Top each slice with cranberry chutney.

## Blueberry Cheesecake

¾ cup blueberries
Whipped cream

Prepare Cheesecake Supreme (page 187) as directed, except pour half the filling into the crust-lined pan. Sprinkle blueberries evenly over filling; pour remaining filling evenly over blueberries. Top each slice with whipped cream.

## Orange-Hazelnut Cheesecake

Orange or ginger marmalade
Coarsely chopped hazelnuts (filberts), toasted

Prepare Cheesecake Supreme (page 187) as directed. Top each slice with marmalade and hazelnuts.

## Espresso Cheesecake

2 teaspoons instant espresso coffee powder
Whipped cream
Chopped chocolate-covered coffee beans

Prepare Cheesecake Supreme (page 187) as directed, except stir espresso powder into milk. Top each slice with whipped cream and coffee beans.

# Sour Cream-Pumpkin Cheesecake

II graham cracker squares
½ cup pecan halves
¼ cup sugar
3 tablespoons butter, melted
3 8-ounce packages cream cheese, softened
I cup sugar
I tablespoon cornstarch
2 teaspoons pumpkin pie spice

I teaspoon vanilla
I 15-ounce can pumpkin
2 tablespoons whipping cream
4 eggs, lightly beaten
I 16-ounce carton dairy sour cream
2 tablespoons sugar
2 teaspoons vanilla

**1** Preheat oven to 375°F. For crust, in a food processor combine graham cracker squares, pecan halves, the ¼ cup sugar, and melted butter. Cover and process until combined (below). Press crumb mixture into the bottom of a 9×3-inch springform pan (photos 2–3, page 188).

**2** For filling, beat cream cheese, the 1 cup sugar, cornstarch, pumpkin pie spice, the 1 teaspoon vanilla, and ¼ teaspoon *salt* with an electric mixer until combined (photo 4, page 188). Beat in pumpkin and whipping cream (photos 5–6, page 188). Stir in eggs (photo 7, page 188). Pour filling into crust-lined pan (photo 8, page 188); place in a shallow baking pan (photo 9, page 189). Bake in the preheated oven about 50 minutes or until center appears nearly set when gently shaken (photo 10, page 189). Meanwhile, stir together sour cream, the 2 tablespoons sugar, and the 2 teaspoons vanilla; spread over cheesecake. Return to oven and bake for 5 minutes more.

**3** Cool in pan on a wire rack for 15 minutes. Loosen crust from sides of pan (photo 4, page 194); cool for 30 minutes more. Remove sides of pan (photo 11, page 189); cool cheesecake for 2 hours on rack. Cover and chill for at least 4 hours before serving. If desired, garnish with *pomegranate seeds* (below), *orange wedges,* and/or *pecan halves.* Makes 12 to 16 slices.

Per slice: 484 cal., 35 g total fat (2I g sat. fat), I6I mg chol., 3I2 mg sodium, 35 g carbo., I g fiber, I0 g pro.

**1** Place crust ingredients in a food processor fitted with the blade attachment. Process using on/off pulses until finely crushed and moistened.

**2** Cut a pomegranate vertically in half; gently break into sections. Be careful because the red juices will stain!

**3** Place the sections in a bowl of water. Push the seeds out of each section into the water. The tasty seeds will sink to the bottom of the bowl.

**4** Scoop the spongy pith out of the water. Pour the water out of the bowl over a sieve to catch the seeds.

**Ask Mom** How do I measure butter? p. 55 / How do I measure sugar? p. 55 / How do I soften cream cheese? p. 57 / How do I store cheesecake? p. 68, 193 / How do I work with eggs? p. 26–27 / What is a springform pan? p. 16, 17 / What is canned pumpkin? p. 302 / What is pumpkin pie spice? p. 36, 37 / What is vanilla? p. 128 / What is whipping cream? p. 24 / What's that nut? p. 34–35

# HOW DO I CUT A PERFECT SLICE OF CHEESECAKE?

Part of the appeal of cheesecake is that it's creamy—which can make it cling to the knife when you're cutting it. To make a clean cut, simply run the knife under warm water and wipe it dry between slices.

Cheesecake has to be chilled for storage, of course. Cover a whole cake, a partial cake, or individual pieces thoroughly with plastic wrap. Cheesecake will stay fresh in the refrigerator for up to 3 days.

# Café au Lait **Cheesecake**

| | |
|---|---|
| 1¾ cups finely crushed chocolate cookies | 2 tablespoons coffee liqueur or water |
| ⅓ cup butter, melted | 3 8-ounce packages cream cheese, softened |
| 2 ounces semisweet chocolate, chopped | 1 cup sugar |
| 2 tablespoons water | 2 tablespoons all-purpose flour |
| 1 tablespoon instant espresso coffee powder or regular instant coffee crystals | 1 teaspoon vanilla |
| | 4 eggs, lightly beaten |

**1** For crust, in a bowl combine the crushed cookies and melted butter (photo 1, page 188). Press crumb mixture onto the bottom and about 2 inches up the sides of an 8-inch springform pan (photos 2–3, page 188). Chill crust until needed.

**2** In a small saucepan combine chopped chocolate, water, and coffee powder. Cook and stir over low heat until chocolate starts to melt. Remove from heat, stirring until smooth. Stir in coffee liqueur; cool.

**3** Preheat oven to 350°F. For filling, in a large mixing bowl beat cream cheese, sugar, flour, and vanilla with an electric mixer until combined (photo 4, page 188). Stir in eggs (photo 7, page 188). Reserve 2 cups of the filling; cover and chill. Stir cooled chocolate mixture into the remaining filling just until combined. Pour chocolate mixture into crust-lined pan (below).

**4** Bake in the preheated oven about 30 minutes or until sides are set (center will be soft-set) (below). Remove reserved filling from refrigerator 10 minutes before needed. Carefully pour reserved filling in a ring around the outside edges of the chocolate mixture (below). Gently spread evenly over entire surface. Bake for 15 to 20 minutes more or until center appears nearly set when gently shaken (photo 10, page 189). Cool in pan on a wire rack for 10 minutes. Loosen sides of pan (below); cool for 30 minutes more. Remove sides of pan (photo 11, page 189); cool cheesecake for 2 hours on rack. Cover and chill for 4 to 24 hours before serving. Makes 12 slices.

Per slice: 424 cal., 29 g total fat (17 g sat. fat), 146 mg chol., 333 mg sodium, 35 g carbo., 2 g fiber, 8 g pro.

**1** Carefully pour the chocolate portion of the filling into the crust-lined springform pan.

**2** Gently pull out the oven rack to see if the sides are set and the center soft-set.

**3** Carefully pour the reserved filling around the outside edges (where the chocolate mixture is set).

**4** Run an off-set spatula or thin knife between the crust and the pan to loosen the cheesecake before releasing the sides of the pan.

**Ask Mom** How do I chop chocolate? p. 33 / How do I cut cheesecake? p. 193 / How do I make cracker/cookie crumbs? p. 129 / How do I measure butter? p. 55 / How do I measure flour? p. 54 / How do I measure sugar? p. 55 / How do I soften cream cheese? p. 57 / How do I store cheesecake? p. 68, 193 / How do I work with eggs? p. 26–27 / What is a springform pan? p. 16, 17 / What is semisweet/bittersweet chocolate? p. 32 / What is vanilla? p. 128 / What's that flour? p. 31

# Spinach-Blue Cheese Cheesecake

- 1 cup chopped walnuts, toasted
- ¼ cup all-purpose flour
- 2 tablespoons butter, melted
- 2 tablespoons grated Parmesan cheese
- 2 tablespoons finely chopped shallot
- 2 cloves garlic, minced
- 1 tablespoon olive oil or cooking oil
- 1 10-ounce package frozen chopped spinach, thawed and well drained (below)
- 2 8-ounce packages cream cheese, softened
- 2 tablespoons all-purpose flour
  Few dashes bottled hot pepper sauce
- 2 eggs, lightly beaten
- 1 cup finely crumbled blue cheese (4 ounces) (below)

**1** Preheat oven to 375°F. In a blender or food processor combine walnuts, the ¼ cup flour, melted butter, and Parmesan cheese. Cover and process or blend until very finely chopped (below). Press crust mixture into the bottom of a 9-inch springform pan (photos 2–3, page 188). Bake in the preheated oven about 8 minutes or until light brown. Cool crust on a wire rack.

**2** In a small skillet cook shallot and garlic in hot oil over medium heat until tender; remove from heat. Stir in spinach; set aside.

**3** Beat the cream cheese, the 2 tablespoons flour, hot pepper sauce, ¼ teaspoon *salt*, and ¼ teaspoon *ground black pepper* with an electric mixer until combined (photo 4, page 188). Stir in eggs (photo 7, page 188). Stir in spinach mixture and blue cheese (below). Pour filling into crust-lined pan; place pan in a shallow baking pan (photos 8–9, page 188). Bake about 20 minutes or until center appears nearly set when gently shaken (photo 10, page 189). Cool in pan on a wire rack for 15 minutes. Loosen sides of pan (photo 11, page 189); cool for 30 minutes more. Remove sides of pan (photo 4, page 194); cool cheesecake for 2 hours on rack. Cover and chill for at least 4 hours or overnight. To serve, let cheesecake stand at room temperature for 30 minutes. Serve with *assorted crackers* and, if desired, *pear* or *apple slices*. Makes 16 to 20 appetizer slices.

Per slice: 221 cal., 20 g total fat (9 g sat. fat), 69 mg chol., 273 mg sodium, 5 g carbo., 1 g fiber, 7 g pro.

**1** In a blender combine the walnuts, flour, butter, and Parmesan cheese. Cover and blend until very finely chopped.

**2** Put the thawed spinach in a fine-mesh sieve and press with the back of a spoon to remove all the liquid that you can.

**3** Crumble the blue cheese into small pieces with your fingers.

**4** Stir the spinach mixture and the crumbled blue cheese into the beaten cream cheese mixture.

**Ask Mom** How do I cut cheesecake? p. 193 / How do I measure butter? p. 55 / How do I measure flour? p. 54 / How do I mince garlic? p. 21 / How do I soften cream cheese? p. 57 / How do I store cheesecake? p. 68, 193 / How do I toast nuts? p. 34 / How do I work with eggs? p. 26–27 / What are chopped nuts? p. 34 / What is a springform pan? p. 16, 17 / What is cooking oil? p. 28 / What's that flour? p. 31 / What's that nut? p. 34–35

# Orange-Ginger Baby Cheesecakes

¾ cup finely crushed gingersnaps (about fourteen 1¾-inch cookies)

1 tablespoon packed brown sugar

3 tablespoons butter, melted

1 8-ounce package cream cheese, softened

½ cup orange marmalade

1 egg yolk

1 tablespoon all-purpose flour

**1** Preheat oven to 350°F. For crust, in a small bowl combine crushed cookies, brown sugar, and melted butter (photo 1, page 188). Divide crumb mixture evenly among sixteen 1¾-inch muffin cups. Press crumb mixture onto the bottom and up sides of each cup. Bake in the preheated oven for 5 minutes.

**2** Meanwhile, for filling, in a medium mixing bowl beat cream cheese, ¼ cup of the marmalade, egg yolk, and flour with an electric mixer on medium speed until combined (photo 4 page 188). Divide filling evenly among muffin cups (below). Bake about 15 minutes or until a knife inserted in the centers comes out clean (below).

**3** Cool in pans on a wire rack (centers will dip slightly). Carefully remove cheesecakes from muffin cups (below). Top each cheesecake with about ½ teaspoon of the remaining marmalade (below). Serve at once or cover and chill for up to 24 hours. Makes 16 servings.

**Make-ahead directions:** Bake cheesecakes as directed but do not top with remaining marmalade. Place cheesecakes in a freezer container. Cover and freeze for up to 3 months. To serve, thaw overnight in refrigerator. Top with marmalade just before serving.

Per serving: 127 cal., 8 g total fat (5 g sat. fat), 34 mg chol., 104 mg sodium, 13 g carbo., 0 g fiber, 2 g pro.

**1** Use a measuring teaspoon to spoon some of the filling into each of the baked crusts.

**2** Insert the tip of a table knife into the cheesecake centers. The knife will come out clean if the cheesecakes are fully cooked.

**3** Run the tip of the knife around the muffin cups and lift the cheesecakes out.

**4** Spoon the remaining marmalade onto each cheesecake, filling the indentation.

**Ask Mom** How do I make cracker/cookie crumbs? p. 129 / How do I measure butter? p. 55 / How do I measure flour? p. 54 / How do I measure sugar? p. 55 / How do I soften cream cheese? p. 57 / How do I work with eggs? p. 26–27 / What's that flour? p. 31

# Caramel Apples and
## Cranberry Pecan Shortcakes

2 cups all-purpose flour

½ cup finely ground toasted pecans

¼ cup sugar

2 teaspoons baking powder

½ teaspoon ground cinnamon

¼ teaspoon salt

¼ teaspoon ground nutmeg

½ cup cold butter, cut up

⅔ cup milk

1 egg, lightly beaten

2 teaspoons finely shredded orange peel

1 teaspoon vanilla

1 recipe Caramel Apples and Cranberries

1 recipe Sweetened Whipped Cream (page 25)

**1** Preheat oven to 450°F. Lightly grease a baking sheet; set aside. In a large bowl combine flour, pecans, sugar, baking powder, cinnamon, salt, and nutmeg. Using a pastry blender, cut in butter until mixture resembles coarse crumbs. Make a well in center of flour mixture. In a small bowl combine milk, egg, orange peel, and vanilla. Add to flour mixture all at once, stirring with a fork just until moistened (photos 2–3, page 199).

**2** Drop dough into 8 to 10 mounds onto the prepared baking sheet (photo 2, page 326); flatten each mound with the back of a spoon until about ¾ inch thick. Bake in the preheated oven about 10 minutes or until golden. Transfer shortcakes to a wire rack and let cool for 10 minutes.

**3** To serve, cut shortcakes in half horizontally. Spoon most of the Caramel Apples and Cranberries over shortcake bottoms. Replace shortcake tops. Top with remaining Caramel Apples and Cranberries. Serve with Sweetened Whipped Cream. Makes 8 to 10 servings.

Caramel Apples and Cranberries: In a very large nonstick skillet melt ¼ cup butter. Add 8 cups sliced, unpeeled red and/or green apples (about 8 medium) and ⅓ cup dried cranberries. Cook over medium heat for 3 minutes, stirring occasionally. Sprinkle apples with 1 tablespoon sugar and ⅛ teaspoon ground cinnamon. Cook and stir for 1 to 2 minutes more or until apples are crisp-tender. Add 2 tablespoons apple cider, stirring to combine.

Per serving: 496 cal., 29 g total fat (15 g sat. fat), 94 mg chol., 311 mg sodium, 55 g carbo., 5 g fiber, 6 g pro.

**Ask Mom** How do I cut in butter? p. 56 / How do I grease a baking pan? p. 59 / How do I grind nuts? p. 34 / How do I measure butter/liquids/sugar? p. 55 / How do I measure flour? p. 54 / How do I slice apples? p. 38, 39 / How do I shred orange peel? p. 45, 105 / How do I toast nuts? p. 34 / How do I work with eggs? p. 26–27 / What is baking powder? p. 30, 319 / What is cinnamon/nutmeg? p. 36–37 / What is vanilla? p. 128 / What's that dried fruit? p. 41 / What's that nut? p. 34–35

# ONE SHORTCAKE, SO MANY WAYS.

The same shortcake dough can be shaped and filled to create three deliciously different desserts. Make a whole cake, individual cakes—or charm guests with baby-size shortcakes tucked into a bowl of fresh berries.

1

2

3

1. **Whole Shortcake:** Prepare as on page 199, except spread dough evenly in a greased 8×1½-inch round baking pan. Bake in the preheated oven for 18 to 20 minutes or until a wooden toothpick inserted near the center comes out clean. Cool in pan for 10 minutes. Remove from pan and cool completely. Split in half horizontally. To serve, spoon half of the strawberries and half of the Sweetened Whipped Cream over bottom layer. Replace top layer. Top with remaining strawberries and whipped cream; cut into wedges.

2. **Mixed Fruit Shortcakes:** Prepare as on page 199, except substitute 5 cups mixed fruit (raspberries or sliced peaches, nectarines, bananas, or strawberries) for the 5 cups sliced strawberries.

3. **Mixed Berry Shortcake Croutons:** Prepare as on page 199, except drop dough into 24 mounds onto prepared baking sheet. Bake in the preheated oven for 6 to 8 minutes or until golden. Substitute 5 cups mixed berries (blueberries, raspberries, and/or blackberries) for the 5 cups sliced strawberries.

# Strawberry Shortcakes

1½ cups all-purpose flour
¼ cup sugar
1 teaspoon baking powder
¼ teaspoon salt
¼ teaspoon baking soda
⅓ cup cold butter, cut up

1 egg, lightly beaten
½ cup dairy sour cream
2 tablespoons milk
5 cups sliced strawberries
3 tablespoons sugar
1 recipe Sweetened Whipped Cream (page 25)

**1** Preheat oven to 400°F. Lightly grease a baking sheet; set aside. In a food processor combine flour, the ¼ cup sugar, the baking powder, salt, and baking soda; add butter. Cover and process until mixture resembles coarse crumbs (below).\*Transfer to a medium bowl. Make a well in center of flour mixture. Combine egg, sour cream, and milk. Add to flour mixture all at once, stirring with a fork just until moistened (below).

**2** Drop dough into 8 mounds onto the prepared baking sheet (photo 2, page 326). Bake in the preheated oven for 12 to 15 minutes or until golden. Transfer shortcakes to a wire rack and let cool. Meanwhile, combine 4 cups of the strawberries and the 3 tablespoons sugar. If desired, use a potato masher to mash berries slightly; set aside.

**3** To serve, cut shortcakes in half horizontally. Spoon strawberry mixture and Sweetened Whipped Cream over shortcake bottoms. Replace shortcake tops. Top with remaining sliced strawberries. Makes 8 shortcakes.

\*Note: Or use a pastry blender to cut butter into flour, sugar, baking powder, salt, and soda.

**Strawberry Lemon-Poppy Seed Shortcakes:** Prepare as above, except stir in 1 tablespoon poppy seeds and 1 teaspoon finely shredded lemon peel after processing the butter.

Per shortcake: 373 cal., 23 g total fat (14 g sat. fat), 93 mg chol., 226 mg sodium, 39 g carbo., 3 g fiber, 5 g pro.

**1** Add butter to flour mixture in a food processor fitted with the blade attachment. Process using on/off pulses until the mixture resembles coarse crumbs.

**2** Pour the sour cream mixture into the flour mixture all at once.

**3** Stir with a fork just until the flour mixture is moistened. Do not overstir.

**Ask Mom** How do I cut in butter/shortening? p. 56 / How do I grease a baking pan/dish? p. 59 / How do I measure butter? p. 55 / How do I measure flour? p. 54 / How do I measure sugar? p. 55 / How do I wash fresh berries? p. 42 / How do I work with eggs? p. 26–27 / What is a food processor? p. 20 / What is a pastry blender? p. 10, 11 / What is baking powder? p. 30, 319 / What is baking soda? p. 30, 319 / What's that flour? p. 31

# Chocolate-Raspberry Shortcakes

2 cups all-purpose flour
½ cup packed brown sugar
½ cup unsweetened cocoa powder
2 teaspoons baking powder
½ teaspoon salt
½ cup cold butter, cut up
2 ounces bittersweet or semisweet chocolate, finely chopped
1 egg, lightly beaten
½ cup buttermilk or sour milk
1 tablespoon buttermilk
1 tablespoon coarse sugar
3 cups raspberries and/or sliced strawberries
3 tablespoons granulated sugar
1 cup whipping cream
¼ cup dairy sour cream
½ teaspoon vanilla

1 Preheat oven to 400°F. Lightly grease a baking sheet; set aside. In a large bowl combine flour, brown sugar, cocoa powder, baking powder, and salt. Using a pastry blender, cut in butter until mixture resembles coarse crumbs. Add chopped chocolate; toss to combine. Make a well in center of flour mixture. In a small bowl combine egg and the ½ cup buttermilk. Add to flour mixture all at once, stirring with a spoon just until moistened (photos 1–2, page 201).

2 Turn dough out onto a well-floured surface. Gently knead dough for 10 to 12 strokes or until nearly smooth (photo 3, page 201). Pat or lightly roll dough until ½ inch thick (photo 4, page 201). Cut dough with a floured 3-inch round cutter into 6 to 8 biscuits (photo 5, page 201). Reroll scraps as necessary.

3 Place dough circles 1 inch apart on the prepared baking sheet. Brush tops with the 1 tablespoon buttermilk; sprinkle with coarse sugar. Bake in the preheated oven for 12 to 15 minutes or until light brown. Transfer shortcakes to a wire rack and let cool.

4 Meanwhile, combine berries and 2 tablespoons of the granulated sugar. Cover and let stand for 1 hour. In a medium bowl combine the whipping cream, sour cream, the remaining 1 tablespoon granulated sugar, and vanilla. Beat with an electric mixer on medium speed until soft peaks form.

5 To serve, cut shortcakes in half horizontally. Spoon berry mixture and whipped cream mixture over shortcake bottoms. Replace shortcake tops. Makes 6 to 8 shortcakes.

Per shortcake: 660 cal., 38 g total fat (21 g sat. fat), 137 mg chol., 454 mg sodium, 71 g carbo., 6 g fiber, 10 g pro.

**Ask Mom** How do I chop chocolate? p. 33 / How do I cut in butter? p. 56 / How do I grease a baking pan? p. 59 / How do I make sour milk? p. 24 / How do I measure butter/liquids/sugar/flour? p. 54–55 / How do I wash berries? p. 42 / How do I whip cream? p. 25–26 / How do I work with eggs? p. 26–27 / What is baking powder? p. 30, 319 / What is buttermilk? p. 24 / What is coarse sugar? p. 29 / What is cocoa powder? p. 170 / What is bittersweet chocolate? p. 32 / What is vanilla? p. 128

**HOW DO I SPLIT THE SHORTCAKES?** Use a serrated knife (such as a bread knife) to easily cut the shortcakes in half horizontally. A regular knife—no matter how sharp—is likely to crumble the shortcakes rather than slice neatly through them.

**1** Use a wooden spoon to push the flour mixture against the sides of the bowl to make a well. Pour buttermilk mixture into well.

**2** Stir the buttermilk mixture into the flour mixture just until the dough starts to hold together.

**3** To knead, fold dough in half toward you. Gently press the edges together with the heel of your hand. Give dough a quarter turn and repeat.

**4** Use your hands to pat (or a rolling pin to gently roll) out the dough until it is ½ inch thick.

**5** Using a scalloped-edge cookie or biscuit cutter gives your shortcakes a little bit of flair without any fuss. Every other cut or so, dip the cutter in flour to keep it from sticking to the dough.

# Peanutty Ice Cream Shortcakes

2 cups all-purpose flour

2 tablespoons granulated sugar

1 tablespoon baking powder

½ teaspoon salt

⅓ cup creamy honey-roasted peanut butter

2 tablespoons shortening

⅔ cup milk

3 cups vanilla, chocolate, or other favorite flavor ice cream, softened (below)

1½ cups chocolate-covered peanuts

¾ cup coarsely chopped pecans, toasted

Powdered sugar

**1** Preheat oven to 425°F. Lightly grease a baking sheet; set aside. In a large bowl combine flour, granulated sugar, baking powder, and salt. Using a pastry blender, cut in peanut butter and shortening until mixture resembles coarse crumbs. Make a well in center of flour mixture. Add milk all at once, stirring with a fork just until moistened (photos 1–2, page 201).

**2** Turn dough out onto a lightly floured surface. Knead dough for 4 to 6 strokes or just until dough holds together (photo 3, page 201). Pat or lightly roll dough until ½ inch thick (photo 4, page 201). Cut dough with a floured 3½-inch round cutter into 6 biscuits (photo 5, page 201).

**3** Place dough circles 1 inch apart on the prepared baking sheet. Bake in the preheated oven for 10 to 12 minutes or until golden brown. Transfer shortcakes to a wire rack and let cool.

**4** To serve, cut shortcakes in half horizontally. In a large bowl stir together ice cream, chocolate-covered peanuts, and pecans. Spoon ice cream mixture over shortcake bottoms. Replace shortcake tops. Sprinkle with powdered sugar. Makes 6 shortcakes.

Per shortcake: 778 cal., 48 g total fat (16 g sat. fat), 74 mg chol., 443 mg sodium, 76 g carbo., 6 g fiber, 17 g pro.

To soften ice cream, place in a large chilled bowl. Press ice cream against sides of bowl with a wooden spoon until soft but not melted.

**Ask Mom** How do I grease a baking pan/dish? p. 59 / How do I measure flour? p. 54 / How do I measure liquids? p. 55 / How do I measure peanut butter? p. 55 / How do I measure sugar? p. 55 / How do I toast nuts? p. 34 / What are chopped nuts? p. 34 / What is baking powder? p. 30, 319 / What is powdered sugar? p. 29 / What's that flour? p. 31 / What's that nut? p. 34–35

# anytime
# DESSERTS

**Crown a great meal with a warm and comforting fruit cobbler, crisp, bread pudding, airy soufflé—or crème brûlée.**

7

## COBBLERS & CRISPS

Apple Cobbler ② .................................. 209
Blueberry Cobbler ② ............................ 209
Blueberry Crisp ① .............................. 206
Cherry Cobbler ② ............................... 208
Cherry Crisp ① ................................. 206
Fruit Crisp ① .................................. 206
Rhubarb Cobbler ② ............................. 209
Rhubarb Crisp ① ............................... 206
Peach Cobbler ② ............................... 209
Pear Cobbler ② ................................ 209

## FRUIT DESSERTS

Apple-Cranberry Dessert ① ...................... 205
Dessert Oven Pancake ① ........................ 211
Strawberry Soufflé ③ .......................... 217
Triple-Berry Pudding Cake ③ .................... 210

**Heavenly White-in-White Meringues ③** ........ 212

## PUDDINGS & CUSTARDS

Amaretto Crème Brûlée ③ ....................... 218
Banana Caramel Custard ③ ...................... 222
Bread Pudding with Whiskey Sauce ② ............ 215
Chocolate Bread Pudding ② ..................... 216
Chocolate Flan ③ ............................... 224
Crème Brûlée ③ ................................ 218
Maple Crème Brûlée ③ .......................... 218
Raspberry Crème Brûlée ③ ...................... 221
Triple-Berry Pudding Cake ③ .................... 210
White Chocolate Pudding ③ ..................... 212

**Whiskey Sauce ②** ........................... 215
**White Dipped Almonds ①** .................... 212

# Apple-Cranberry Dessert

I 12-ounce package fresh or frozen cranberries or one 16-ounce package frozen unsweetened pitted tart red cherries*

I cup chopped, peeled, cored cooking apple

I tablespoon butter, cut up

⅔ cup sugar

½ cup chopped walnuts or pecans

I egg, lightly beaten

⅓ cup butter, melted

½ cup sugar

⅓ cup all-purpose flour

Vanilla ice cream

**1** Preheat oven to 325°F. Grease the bottom of an 8×8×2-inch baking dish. Toss the cranberries and apple together in the pan. Dot cranberry mixture with the 1 tablespoon butter. Sprinkle evenly with the ⅔ cup sugar and the chopped walnuts. Set aside.

**2** In a small bowl whisk together the egg, melted butter, the ½ cup sugar, and the flour until well combined. Pour evenly over cranberry mixture.

**3** Bake in the preheated oven about 1 hour or until top is golden brown and filling is bubbly. Cool on a wire rack for at least 30 minutes. Serve warm or at room temperature with vanilla ice cream. Makes 6 servings.

*Note: If using frozen cranberries, do not thaw before tossing with the apple. If using frozen cherries, let stand at room temperature for 30 minutes before tossing with the apple.

Per serving: 540 cal., 27 g total fat (13 g sat. fat), 99 mg chol., 157 mg sodium, 72 g carbo., 4 g fiber, 6 g pro.

**Ask Mom** How do I core and slice/chop apples? p. 38, 39 / How do I grease a baking pan/dish? p. 59 / How do I measure butter? p. 55 / How do I measure flour? p. 54 / How do I measure sugar? p. 55 / How do I work with eggs? p. 26–27 / What are chopped nuts? p. 34 / What does it mean to dot? p. 69 / What is a good baking/cooking apple? p. 39, 287 / What's that flour? p. 31 / What's that nut? p. 34–35

# Fruit Crisp

5 cups sliced, peeled cooking apples, pears, peaches, or apricots or frozen unsweetened peach slices

2 to 4 tablespoons granulated sugar

½ cup regular rolled oats

½ cup packed brown sugar

¼ cup all-purpose flour

¼ teaspoon ground nutmeg, ginger, or cinnamon

¼ cup butter

¼ cup chopped nuts or flaked coconut

Vanilla ice cream (optional)

**1** Preheat oven to 375°F. If fruit is frozen, thaw but do not drain. Place fruit in a 2-quart square baking dish. Stir in the granulated sugar.

**2** For topping, in a medium bowl stir together the oats, brown sugar, flour, and nutmeg. Using a pastry blender, cut in butter until mixture resembles coarse crumbs. Stir in the nuts. Sprinkle topping over fruit.

**3** Bake in the preheated oven for 30 to 35 minutes (40 minutes for thawed frozen fruit) or until fruit is tender (photo, page 207) and topping is golden. If desired, serve warm with ice cream. Makes 6 servings.

**Per serving:** 319 cal., 13 g total fat (6 g sat. fat), 22 mg chol., 92 mg sodium, 53 g carbo., 5 g fiber, 3 g pro.

**Blueberry Crisp:** Prepare as above, except substitute 5 cups fresh or frozen blueberries for the sliced fruit. Use 4 tablespoons granulated sugar and add 3 tablespoons all-purpose flour to the berry mixture.

**Cherry Crisp:** Prepare as above, except substitute 5 cups fresh or frozen unsweetened pitted tart red cherries for the sliced fruit. Increase granulated sugar to ½ cup and add 3 tablespoons all-purpose flour to the cherry mixture.

**Rhubarb Crisp:** Prepare as above, except substitute 5 cups fresh or frozen unsweetened sliced rhubarb for the fruit. Increase granulated sugar to ¾ cup and add 3 tablespoons all-purpose flour to the rhubarb mixture.

**Flavor Changes** This one simple recipe yields a dessert for every taste, occasion, and season. Simply by varying the fruit, spice, and choice of nuts or coconut in the topping, it can be completely different every time you make it. Good combinations to try: apples, cinnamon, and walnuts; blueberries, ginger, and almonds; apricots, ginger, and pistachio nuts; and peaches, nutmeg, and coconut. (And don't stop there.)

**Ask Mom** Can I use quick-cooking oats instead of regular rolled oats? p. 351 / How do I peel, core, and slice pears? p. 46, 47 / How do I measure butter/sugar? p. 55 / How do I measure flour? p. 54 / How do I peel and slice apples? p. 38, 39 / How do I peel peaches? p. 43 / How do I prepare rhubarb? p. 49, 117 / How do I wash fresh berries? p. 42 / What are chopped nuts? p. 34 / What is a good cooking apple? p. 39, 287 / What is cinnamon/ginger/nutmeg? p. 36, 37 / What's that flour? p. 31

# ICE CREAM AND OTHER OPTIONS. Good cooks know that much of the pleasure of eating is about contrast—cold, creamy ice cream melting over warm fruit crisp, for instance. Ice cream is a natural with this dessert, but you can top it with cream or milk too.

**Is it done yet?** In general you can tell when a crisp is cooked when the fruit—whatever it happens to be—is tender and the topping is golden. Some fruits, such as raspberries, start out tender and make a juicier filling. Those crisps are usually done when the filling is bubbly. With firmer fruit, such as apples, the crisp is done when a fork or knife easily pierces the fruit in the center of the dish. When it's ready, set out the ice cream for a few minutes to soften slightly and allow the juices of the crisp to thicken a bit before serving.

Desserts

# Cherry Cobbler

| | |
|---|---|
| 1 cup all-purpose flour | 6 cups fresh or frozen unsweetened pitted tart red cherries |
| 2 tablespoons sugar | 1 cup sugar |
| 1½ teaspoons baking powder | 2 tablespoons cornstarch |
| ¼ teaspoon salt | 1 egg |
| ½ teaspoon ground cinnamon (optional) | ¼ cup milk |
| ¼ cup cold butter | Vanilla ice cream (optional) |

**1** Preheat oven to 400°F. For topping, in a medium bowl stir together flour, the 2 tablespoons sugar, the baking powder, salt, and, if desired, cinnamon. Using a pastry blender, cut in butter until mixture resembles coarse crumbs; set aside.

**2** For filling, in a large saucepan combine the cherries, the 1 cup sugar, and the cornstarch (below). Cook over medium heat until cherries release their juice, stirring occasionally. Continue to cook, stirring constantly, over medium heat until thickened and bubbly (below). Keep filling hot over low heat.

**3** In a small bowl stir together egg and milk. Add egg mixture to flour mixture, stirring just until moist (below). Transfer hot filling to a 2-quart square baking dish. Using a spoon, immediately drop flour mixture into six mounds on top of filling (below).

**4** Bake in the preheated oven for 20 to 25 minutes or until topping is golden brown. If desired, serve warm with ice cream. Makes 6 servings.

Per serving: 386 cal., 10 g total fat (5 g sat. fat), 58 mg chol., 236 mg sodium, 73 g carbo., 3 g fiber, 5 g pro.

**1** Place the cherries, sugar, and cornstarch in a saucepan. Using a wooden spoon, stir until well mixed.

**2** Cook over medium heat, stirring occasionally, until the cherries get juicy. Stir constantly until the liquid thickens and bubbles.

**3** Stir the egg mixture and flour mixture together just until combined. It will be lumpy.

**4** Use a flatware tablespoon to scoop up flour mixture. Use a second spoon to push mixture onto the cherry filling in six mounds.

**Ask Mom** How do I cut in butter/shortening? p. 56 / How do I measure butter? p. 55 / How do I measure flour? p. 54 / How do I measure liquids? p. 55 / How do I measure sugar? p. 55 / What is a pastry blender? p. 10, 11 / What is baking powder? p. 30, 319 / What is cinnamon? p. 36 / What's that flour? p. 31

**1**

**2**

**3**

1. **Blueberry or Peach Cobbler:** Prepare as on page 208, except, for filling, in a saucepan combine ⅓ to ⅔ cup sugar, ¼ cup water, and I tablespoon cornstarch. Stir in 5 cups fresh or frozen blueberries or unsweetened peach slices. Cook and stir until slightly thickened and bubbly.

2. **Rhubarb Cobbler:** Prepare as on page 208, except substitute fresh or frozen sliced rhubarb for the cherries.

3. **Apple or Pear Cobbler:** Prepare as on page 208, except, for filling, in a saucepan combine 6 cups sliced, cored, and peeled cooking apples or pears; ⅓ to ½ cup sugar; and I tablespoon lemon juice. Bring to boiling, stirring occasionally once fruit begins to release its juice; reduce heat. Simmer, covered, for 5 minutes or until fruit is almost tender, stirring occasionally. Stir together 2 tablespoons water and I tablespoon cornstarch; add to filling. Cook and stir until thickened and bubbly.

# Triple-Berry Pudding Cake

I cup fresh or frozen blueberries, thawed
I cup fresh or frozen raspberries, thawed
½ cup fresh or frozen cranberries, thawed
I cup all-purpose flour
⅔ cup granulated sugar
1½ teaspoons baking powder
¼ teaspoon salt
½ cup milk

2 tablespoons butter, melted
I teaspoon vanilla
¾ cup boiling water
⅓ cup granulated sugar
⅓ cup packed brown sugar
¼ cup butter, melted
½ cup sliced almonds

**1** Preheat oven to 350°F. Grease a 9×9×2-inch baking pan. Arrange blueberries, raspberries, and cranberries in the prepared pan; set aside.

**2** In a medium mixing bowl stir together flour, the ⅔ cup granulated sugar, the baking powder, and salt. Add milk, the 2 tablespoons butter, and the vanilla; stir well. Spoon batter over berries in pan; carefully spread batter evenly over berries (below).

**3** In a glass measuring cup stir together boiling water and the ⅓ cup sugar; pour evenly over batter (below). Bake in the preheated oven about 40 minutes or until top is brown and edges are bubbly. Meanwhile, in a small bowl stir together brown sugar, the ¼ cup butter, and the almonds.

**4** Remove cake from oven. Spoon almond mixture evenly over cake (below). Preheat broiler and carefully adjust oven rack so top of cake will be 4 to 5 inches from heat (below). Broil cake for 1 to 2 minutes or just until golden. Cool on a wire rack for 30 minutes. Serve cake warm. Makes 8 servings.

Per serving: 335 cal., 14 g total fat (5 g sat. fat), 25 mg chol., 194 mg sodium, 50 g carbo., 4 g fiber, 4 g pro.

**1** Spoon the batter in mounds over the berries in pan. Using a rubber scraper, carefully spread the batter evenly over the berries.

**2** Carefully pour the boiling water mixture all over the batter.

**3** Sprinkle the almond mixture in an even layer over the baked cake.

**4** Adjust the oven rack so the top of the cake will be 4 to 5 inches from the heating element of the broiler.

**Ask Mom** How do I grease a baking pan/dish? p. 59 / How do I measure butter? p. 55 / How do I measure flour? p. 54 / How do I measure liquids? p. 55 / How do I measure sugar? p. 55 / How do I wash fresh berries? p. 42 / What is baking powder?

# Dessert Oven Pancake

²/₃ cup whipping cream
⅓ cup milk
3 eggs
⅓ cup all-purpose flour
¼ cup sugar
2 tablespoons butter, melted

2 teaspoons vanilla
2 teaspoons finely shredded lemon peel
⅛ teaspoon salt
2½ cups thinly sliced plums or pears
2 tablespoons sugar
1 recipe Sweetened Whipped Cream (page 25) (optional)

**1** Preheat oven to 375°F. Generously grease a 9-inch pie plate; set aside.

**2** In a medium mixing bowl combine cream, milk, eggs, flour, the ¼ cup sugar, the butter, vanilla, 1 teaspoon of the lemon peel, and the salt. Beat with an electric mixer on low speed until batter is smooth.

**3** Pour about half of the batter into the prepared pie plate. Arrange plums on top. Sprinkle with the remaining 1 teaspoon lemon peel. Carefully pour remaining batter over plums. Sprinkle with the 2 tablespoons sugar.

**4** Bake in the preheated oven for 50 to 55 minutes or until puffed and light brown. Cool on a wire rack for 15 minutes. (The pancake will fall as it cools.) Serve warm. If desired, serve with Sweetened Whipped Cream. Makes 8 servings.

Per serving: 206 cal., 13 g total fat (7 g sat. fat), 115 mg chol., 95 mg sodium, 20 g carbo., 1 g fiber, 4 g pro.

**Ask Mom**   How do I core and slice pears? p. 46, 47  /  How do I grease a baking pan/dish? p. 59  /  How do I measure butter? p. 55  /  How do I measure flour? p. 54  /  How do I measure liquids? p. 55  /  How do I measure sugar? p. 55  /  How do I shred lemon/lime/orange peel? p. 45, 105  /  What is vanilla? p. 128  /  What is whipping cream? p. 24  /  What's that flour? p. 31

**(3) Skill Level**

**Good to Know** The hour the meringues spend in the oven with the heat off allows them to dry out completely without burning. Don't be tempted to open the oven door to admire your meringues before the hour is up—the cooldown will make them chewy instead of signature crisp.

# Heavenly White-in-White
## Meringues

 3  egg whites
¼  teaspoon cream of tartar
 I  cup sugar
¼  cup ground sliced almonds
 I  recipe White Chocolate Pudding
 I  recipe White Dipped Almonds (optional)

**1** Place egg whites in a medium mixing bowl; let stand at room temperature for 30 minutes. Line two baking sheets with parchment paper. Draw eight 3-inch circles on each paper; turn papers over (photo 1, page 213); set aside. Preheat oven to 300°F.

**2** Add cream of tartar to egg whites. Beat with an electric mixer on medium speed until soft peaks form (tips curl). Add sugar, 1 tablespoon at a time, beating on high speed until stiff peaks form (tips stand straight) and sugar is almost dissolved. Fold in almonds (photo 2, page 213).

**3** Evenly spread egg white mixture over circles on paper on the prepared pans (photo 3, page 213). Place pans in the preheated oven; turn off oven. Let meringues dry in oven for 1 hour. Remove from oven. Transfer meringues to a wire rack and let cool.*

**4** To serve, spoon 2 teaspoons of the White Chocolate Pudding on each serving plate (this will help keep meringues in place). Place one meringue on top. Top meringue with 2 to 3 tablespoons of the pudding (photo 8, page 213). Top with a second meringue. If desired, garnish with White Dipped Almonds. Serve immediately. Makes 8 servings.

*Note: To store meringues, place cooled meringues in an airtight container; cover. Store at room temperature for up to 3 days.

White Chocolate Pudding: In a medium bowl beat 2 egg yolks with a fork; set aside. In a medium heavy saucepan stir together ¼ cup sugar and 4 teaspoons cornstarch. Stir in 1½ cups milk (photo 4, page 213). Cook and stir over medium heat until thickened and bubbly. Cook and stir for 2 minutes more. Remove from heat. Gradually stir 1 cup of the milk mixture into egg yolks (photo 5, page 213). Add egg yolk mixture to milk mixture in saucepan (photo 6, page 213). Bring to a gentle boil; reduce heat. Cook and stir for 2 minutes more. Remove from heat. Stir in 4 ounces white baking chocolate, chopped; 1 tablespoon butter; and 1 teaspoon vanilla until melted (photo 7, page 213). Pour pudding into a bowl. Cover and chill for 2 to 24 hours. Stir before assembling meringues. (If pudding has any lumps, strain it through a fine-mesh sieve before serving.)

White Dipped Almonds: In a small saucepan heat and stir 2 ounces white baking chocolate until melted. Dip blanched whole almonds in melted chocolate. Place on a baking sheet lined with waxed paper. Chill until set. To store, place in an airtight container; cover. Refrigerate or freeze.

Per serving: 339 cal., 13 g total fat (7 g sat. fat), 64 mg chol., 75 mg sodium, 49 g carbo., I g fiber, 6 g pro.

**Ask Mom** How do I add egg yolks to a hot filling? p. 247 / How do I grind nuts? p. 34 / How do I measure liquids? p. 55 / How do I measure sugar? p. 55 / How do I melt chocolate? p. 32, 33 / How do I use a sieve? p. 65 / How do I work with eggs? p. 26–27 / What is a fine-mesh sieve? p. 10, 65 / What is parchment paper? p. 21, 69 / What is white chocolate? p. 32 / What's that nut? p. 34–35

**1** After drawing circles on paper, turn the paper over on the baking sheet. The circles will show through the paper.

**2** Using a rubber scraper, gently fold ground almonds into beaten egg white mixture. Be careful not to deflate.

**3** Evenly divide egg white mixture among circles on prepared paper. Spread mixture to edges of circles.

**4** Gradually stir the milk into the sugar mixture. Stir until the sugar is dissolved and the mixture bubbles.

**5** To prevent the yolks from curdling, stir a small amount of hot milk mixture into the yolks.

**6** Stir the warmed egg yolks into the hot milk mixture in the saucepan. Cook and stir for 2 minutes more.

**7** Off the heat, stir the chopped chocolate, butter, and vanilla into the pudding until melted and smooth.

**8** Just before serving, use a little pudding to "glue" a meringue to each serving plate. Then top with more pudding and a second meringue.

**WHAT IF I DON'T WANT WHISKEY SAUCE?** There are lots of options for topping this hearty bread pudding. You can finish it off with Sweetened Whipped Cream (page 25), a splash of cream or milk—or even a purchased caramel sauce.

# Bread Pudding With Whiskey Sauce

5 cups French bread cubes (½-inch cubes)
½ cup raisins, dried cherries, or dried cranberries
½ cup chopped toasted pecans
⅓ cup flaked coconut, toasted
2 eggs
2¼ cups milk

½ cup sugar
¼ cup butter, melted
1 tablespoon vanilla
¾ teaspoon ground cinnamon
¼ teaspoon ground nutmeg
1 recipe Whiskey Sauce (optional)

**1** Preheat oven to 300°F. Arrange bread cubes in a single layer in a shallow baking pan. Bake in the preheated oven for 10 to 15 minutes or until golden brown, stirring once. Remove from oven. Increase oven temperature to 350°F. Place bread cubes in an ungreased 2-quart square baking dish. Sprinkle raisins, pecans, and coconut over bread cubes; set aside.

**2** In a large bowl lightly beat eggs. Whisk in the milk, sugar, butter, vanilla, cinnamon, and nutmeg. Pour egg mixture over bread mixture (below). Use the back of a large spoon to gently push down on the bread cubes, making sure the bread absorbs the egg mixture (below).

**3** Bake in the preheated oven about 50 minutes or until top is brown and evenly puffed (below). Cool on a wire rack for 30 to 45 minutes. Serve warm. If desired, serve with Whiskey Sauce. Makes 9 servings.

**Per serving:** 268 cal., 14 g total fat (6 g sat. fat), 65 mg chol., 196 mg sodium, 31 g carbo., 2 g fiber, 6 g pro.

Whiskey Sauce: In a medium saucepan whisk together half of a 14-ounce can sweetened condensed milk (⅔ cup), one 5-ounce can evaporated milk, and 3 egg yolks. Whisk mixture over medium heat for 6 to 8 minutes or until mixture is slightly thickened and just begins to boil (below). Remove from heat. Stir in 3 tablespoons whiskey. Cover and keep warm.

**1** Pour the egg mixture all over the bread mixture. Try to coat all the bread.

**2** To ensure that the bread is completely coated, use the back of a spoon to press bread into egg mixture.

**3** When done, the bread pudding should be brown and puffed all over.

**4** Using a whisk to prevent lumps, stir the sauce over medium heat until thickened and just bubbly.

**Ask Mom** How do I measure butter? p. 55 / How do I measure liquids? p. 55 / How do I measure sugar? p. 55 / How do I toast coconut? p. 40 / How do I work with eggs? p. 26–27 / What are chopped nuts? p. 34 / What is cinnamon? p. 36 / What is evaporated milk? p. 24 / What is nutmeg? p. 37 / What is sweetened condensed milk? p. 24 / What is vanilla? p. 128 / What's that dried fruit? p. 41 / What's that nut? p. 34–35

# Chocolate Bread Pudding

8 ounces brioche or challah bread

⅓ cup butter, melted

1½ cups whipping cream

½ cup milk

6 ounces bittersweet or semisweet chocolate, finely chopped, or 1 cup semisweet chocolate pieces

6 egg yolks

⅓ cup sugar

4 ounces bittersweet or semisweet chocolate, coarsely chopped

Vanilla ice cream (optional)

**1** Preheat oven to 300°F. Cut bread into ½-inch cubes (you should have about 6 cups) (below). In a large bowl toss bread cubes with melted butter. Arrange buttered bread cubes in a single layer in a shallow baking pan. Bake in the preheated oven for 10 to 15 minutes or until golden brown, stirring once. Set aside.

**2** In a medium saucepan combine cream, milk, and the 6 ounces finely chopped chocolate. Heat and stir over medium heat until chocolate melts. In a large bowl whisk together egg yolks and sugar. Gradually whisk cream mixture into egg yolks (below). Stir in toasted bread cubes (below). Cover and chill for at least 2 hours or overnight.

**3** Preheat oven to 325°F. Lightly butter a 2-quart square baking dish. Stir the 4 ounces coarsely chopped chocolate into the chilled bread mixture. Pour bread mixture into the prepared dish. Place dish in a roasting pan. Place roasting pan on rack in oven. Pour boiling water into the roasting pan around baking dish to a depth of 1 inch (below). Bake in the preheated oven about 55 minutes or until evenly puffed and top is set.

**4** Carefully remove baking dish from water. Cool on a wire rack about 1 hour. If desired, serve warm pudding with vanilla ice cream. Makes 8 servings.

Per serving: 582 cal., 46 g total fat (26 g sat. fat), 268 mg chol., 190 mg sodium, 43 g carbo., 3 g fiber, 8 g pro.

**1** Using a serrated bread knife, cut bread into about ½-inch cubes.

**2** To prevent the egg yolks from curdling, slowly whisk the hot cream mixture into the yolks.

**3** Add the toasted bread cubes to the chocolate mixture, stirring gently to coat cubes completely.

**4** Don't risk sloshing hot water into the pudding. Put the roasting pan in the oven, then add water to the pan.

**Ask Mom** How do I chop chocolate? p. 33 / How do I grease a baking pan/dish? p. 59 / How do I measure butter? p. 55 / How do I measure liquids? p. 55 / How do I measure sugar? p. 55 / How do I work with eggs? p. 26–27 / What is a water bath? p. 219 / What is semisweet/bittersweet chocolate? p. 32 / What is whipping cream? p. 24

# Strawberry **Soufflé**

5 egg whites
Butter
Sugar
2 cups sliced fresh strawberries

¼ to ⅓ cup sugar
4 teaspoons cornstarch
½ cup sugar
Strawberry- or chocolate-flavor syrup

**1** Place egg whites in a large mixing bowl; let stand at room temperature for 30 minutes. Grease six 1-cup soufflé dishes or 10-ounce custard cups with butter. Sprinkle dishes with sugar to coat, shaking out any excess sugar. Place dishes in a shallow baking pan; set aside.

**2** Meanwhile, in a medium bowl stir together strawberries and the ¼ to ⅓ cup sugar. Let stand about 15 minutes or until strawberries become juicy. In a blender or food processor combine strawberry mixture and the cornstarch. Cover and blend until smooth. Set aside.

**3** Preheat oven to 350°F. Beat egg whites with an electric mixer on medium speed until soft peaks form (tips curl). Add the ½ cup sugar, 1 tablespoon at a time, beating on high speed until stiff peaks form (tips stand straight) and sugar is almost dissolved.

**4** With a rubber scraper, push beaten egg whites to one side of the bowl. Pour strawberry mixture into the bottom of the bowl. Carefully stir a little of the beaten egg whites into the strawberry mixture, then fold the two mixtures together (there should be a few pink streaks remaining). Spoon strawberry mixture evenly into the prepared dishes.

**5** Bake in the preheated oven for 15 to 18 minutes or until a knife inserted near the centers comes out clean. Serve immediately with strawberry- or chocolate-flavor syrup. Makes 6 servings.

Per serving: 248 cal., 2 g total fat (1 g sat. fat), 4 mg chol., 70 mg sodium, 57 g carbo., 1 g fiber, 3 g pro.

SPRINT TO THE TABLE. Make sure everyone is ready and waiting—soufflés start to deflate almost immediately after they are taken out of the oven.

# Crème Brûlée

1¾  cups half-and-half or light cream

  5  egg yolks, lightly beaten

⅓  cup sugar

  1  teaspoon vanilla

⅛  teaspoon salt

¼  cup sugar

**1** Preheat oven to 325°F. In a small heavy saucepan heat half-and-half over medium-low heat just until bubbly (photo 1, page 219). Remove from heat; set aside.

**2** Meanwhile, in a medium bowl combine egg yolks, the ⅓ cup sugar, the vanilla, and salt. Beat with a wire whisk just until combined (photo 2, page 219). Slowly whisk the hot half-and-half into the egg mixture (photo 3, page 219).

**3** Place six 4-ounce ramekins or 6-ounce custard cups in a 13×9×2-inch baking dish or pan. Pour egg mixture evenly into ramekins (photo 4, page 219). Place baking dish on rack in oven. Pour boiling water into the baking dish until water is halfway up the sides of the ramekins (photo 5, page 219).

**4** Bake in the preheated oven for 30 to 40 minutes or until a knife inserted near the centers comes out clean. Carefully remove ramekins from water. Cool on a wire rack. Cover and chill for at least 1 hour or for up to 8 hours.

**5** Before serving, let custards stand at room temperature for 20 minutes. Meanwhile, in a 8-inch heavy skillet heat the ¼ cup sugar over medium-high heat until sugar begins to melt, shaking the skillet occasionally for even melting (photo 6, page 219). Do not stir. When sugar starts to melt, reduce heat to low; cook about 5 minutes more or until all sugar is melted and golden brown, stirring with a wooden spoon (photo 7, page 219).

**6** Quickly drizzle the caramelized sugar over each crème brûlée (photo 8, page 219). (If sugar starts to harden, return skillet to heat, stirring until melted.) Serve immediately. Makes 6 servings.

**Per dessert:** 209 cal., 12 g total fat (6 g sat. fat), 197 mg chol., 84 mg sodium, 22 g carbo., 0 g fiber, 4 g pro.

Amaretto Crème Brûlée: Prepare as above, except stir 2 tablespoons amaretto, crème de cacao, or coffee liqueur into the egg yolk mixture.

Maple Crème Brûlée: Prepare as above, except reduce the sugar to 3 tablespoons and stir 2 tablespoons pure maple syrup or maple-flavor syrup and 1 teaspoon maple extract (optional) into egg yolk mixture.

**Good to Know** The traditional method for creating the crunchy caramel topping on crème brûlée is to use a kitchen torch. This recipe calls for the sugar to be caramelized on the stovetop, then drizzled over the top of the custards—so you can make this much-beloved dessert even if you don't own a kitchen torch.

**WHY BAKE IN WATER?** The method of cooking in a hot water bath—which the French call *bain-marie*—surrounds the custards (and other delicate foods) with gentle heat, which prevents them from curdling. Foods can be cooked this way in the oven or on the stovetop.

**1** Half-and-half can easily burn onto the bottom of the pan, so heat it over medium-low heat just until bubbly.

**2** After the half-and-half is hot, set it aside while whisking the egg yolks and sugar together.

**3** Slowly pour the hot half-and-half into the egg mixture while constantly whisking the mixture.

**4** Use a half-cup measure to evenly pour egg mixture into the ramekins.

**5** Place baking dish with ramekins in the oven, then pour boiling water into the dish until it is halfway up ramekin sides.

**6** Heat sugar in a heavy skillet over medium-high heat. Shake skillet occasionally for even melting but do not stir until the sugar starts to melt.

**7** When sugar starts to melt, stir occasionally with a wooden spoon until completely melted and golden brown.

**8** Using a flatware spoon, drizzle melted sugar over crème brûlée. It hardens quickly, so move fast.

**HOW DO I SPLIT A VANILLA BEAN?** Although the pod has wonderful flavor, the seeds have even more of it. Lay the bean on a flat surface and with the tip of a paring knife cut into—but not all the way through— the length of the bean. Gently open before using.

If you want to serve these fruited custards at room temperature rather than cold out of the refrigerator, let them stand on the counter for 30 minutes before serving.

# Raspberry Crème Brûlée

     2  cups whipping cream
     1  4-inch vanilla bean,* split lengthwise (below)
     5  egg yolks, lightly beaten
    ½  cup sugar
    ¾  cup fresh raspberries or sliced small strawberries
        Raspberries or strawberries (optional)

**1** Preheat oven to 325°F. In a medium heavy saucepan heat cream and vanilla bean over medium-low heat about 15 minutes or just until bubbly (do not boil), stirring often. Remove from heat and let steep for 15 minutes. Remove and discard the vanilla bean.

**2** In a medium mixing bowl combine egg yolks and sugar. Beat with an electric mixer on low speed just until mixture is pale yellow and thick. Gradually whisk about half of the cream mixture into the egg mixture (photo 3, page 219). Pour egg mixture into the remaining cream mixture, stirring until completely combined. Set aside.

**3** Place eight 4-ounce ramekins or six 6-ounce custard cups in a 13×9×2-inch baking pan. Add 5 raspberries or strawberry slices to each ungreased ramekin. Pour egg mixture evenly into the ramekins (photo 4, page 219). Place baking dish on rack in oven. Pour boiling water into the baking dish until water is halfway up the sides of the ramekins (photo 5, page 219).

**4** Bake in the preheated oven about 60 minutes or until custard is set. Carefully remove ramekins from water. Cool on a wire rack for 30 minutes. Cover and chill for 1 hour or for up to 8 hours. If desired, garnish each crème brûlée with additional raspberries or strawberries. Makes 8 servings.

*Note: Or substitute 2 teaspoons vanilla extract. If using the vanilla extract, heat whipping cream just until warm; do not cook until bubbly and do not steep. Add vanilla to the warm cream.

Per serving: 292 cal., 25 g total fat (15 g sat. fat), 210 mg chol., 28 mg sodium, 15 g carbo., 1 g fiber, 3 g pro.

**Ingredient Info** Vanilla beans are actually the dried seedpod of a species of orchid. There are two types of vanilla beans—Bourbon and Tahitian. Bourbon beans are long and thin, with thick, oily skin and lots of seeds. They have a strong vanilla scent and flavor. Tahitian beans are shorter and fatter, with fewer seeds and a fruitier, more floral aroma. Which one you choose is a matter of personal preference. Look for vanilla beans that are a little oily to the touch, very fragrant, and slightly flexible. Avoid those that look brittle or dried out.

**Ask Mom** How do I measure liquids? p. 55 / How do I measure sugar? p. 55 / How do I wash fresh berries? p. 42 / How do I work with eggs? p. 26–27 / What does steep mean? p. 69 / What is a custard cup? p. 13 / What is a ramekin? p. 19 / What is a water bath? p. 219 / What is vanilla? p. 128 / What is whipping cream? p. 24

# Banana Caramel **Custard**

1½ cups sugar
 6 eggs
 3 cups eggnog
 2 teaspoons vanilla
 ⅛ teaspoon salt
 2 tablespoons butter
 ⅛ teaspoon ground cinnamon
 I or 2 ripe but firm bananas, sliced ¼ to ½ inch thick

**1** Preheat oven to 350°F. Place rack in center of oven.

**2** In a 10-inch heavy skillet heat ½ cup of the sugar over medium-high heat until sugar begins to melt, shaking the skillet occasionally for even melting (photo 1, page 223). Do not stir. When sugar starts to melt, reduce heat to low; cook about 5 minutes more or until all sugar is melted and golden brown, stirring with a wooden spoon (photos 2–3, page 223). Immediately pour caramelized sugar into a 10-cup soufflé dish;* tilt to coat the entire bottom of the dish (photo 4, page 223).

**3** In a large bowl lightly beat the eggs. Whisk in the remaining 1 cup sugar, the eggnog, vanilla, and salt until well combined. Pour eggnog mixture into the prepared soufflé dish (photo 5, page 223). Place dish in a large deep roasting pan. Place roasting pan on rack in oven. Pour boiling water into the roasting pan around dish to a depth of 2 inches (photo 4, page 217).

**4** Bake in the preheated oven about 1¼ hours or until a knife inserted near the center comes out clean (custard will not appear set when gently shaken). Cool custard in roasting pan on a wire rack for 15 minutes. Carefully remove baking dish from water. Cool on a wire rack for 2 hours. Cover and chill overnight or for up to 2 days.

**5** Just before serving, run a thin metal spatula or sharp knife around edges of custard in dish (photo 6, page 223). Invert a serving plate over dish; turn dish and plate over together (photo 7, page 223). Remove dish. Set custard aside.

**6** In a large skillet melt butter. Stir in cinnamon. Add banana slices. Cook for 4 to 6 minutes or until golden, using a metal turner to turn slices once halfway through cooking. Arrange bananas over custard on serving plate. Spoon some of the caramel sauce over the bananas (photo 8, page 223). Makes 10 to 12 servings.

***Note:** Briefly warm the soufflé dish in the oven so the caramel mixture spreads over the bottom more easily.

Per serving: 296 cal., II g total fat (6 g sat. fat), I78 mg chol., I29 mg sodium, 44 g carbo., 0 g fiber, 7 g pro.

## CAN I USE LIGHT EGGNOG? You can. The custard won't taste quite as rich as it does made with regular eggnog, but it will save you some calories and a few fat grams. Just don't use soy-based nog!

**Ask Mom** How do I measure butter? p. 55 / How do I measure liquids? p. 55 / How do I measure sugar? p. 55 / What is a soufflé dish? p. I9 / What is a water bath? p. 2I9 / What is cinnamon? p. 36 / What is vanilla? p. I28

**1** Place sugar in a heavy skillet over medium-high heat. Shake skillet occasionally until sugar starts to melt.

**2** Once the sugar starts to melt, you can use a wooden spoon to stir it for even melting and browning.

**3** Heat the melted sugar just until it turns golden brown, stirring often. Once it's done, get it off the heat.

**4** Immediately pour caramelized sugar in a warmed soufflé dish. Tilt dish to coat entire bottom.

**8** Top the custard with hot banana slices. Spoon any caramel sauce left in the soufflé dish over the custard, as well as any sauce left in the skillet.

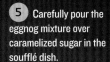
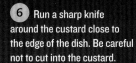

**5** Carefully pour the eggnog mixture over caramelized sugar in the soufflé dish.

**6** Run a sharp knife around the custard close to the edge of the dish. Be careful not to cut into the custard.

**7** Place a serving dish over the soufflé dish. Quickly turn the plate and dish over together; remove the dish.

**3** Skill Level

# Chocolate **Flan**

¾ cup sugar
8 ounces bittersweet chocolate, chopped
4 cups milk
8 eggs

¾ cup sugar
½ teaspoon ground cinnamon
Pomegranate seeds (optional)

**1** Preheat oven to 325°F. In a 10-inch heavy skillet heat ¾ cup sugar over medium-high heat until sugar begins to melt, shaking the skillet occasionally for even melting (photo 6, page 219). Do not stir. When sugar starts to melt, reduce heat to low; cook about 5 minutes more or until all sugar is melted and golden brown, stirring with a wooden spoon (photo 7, page 219). Immediately pour melted sugar into a 9-inch round cake pan;* tilt to coat the entire bottom of the pan (photo 4, page 223). Set aside for at least 10 minutes.

**2** In a large heavy saucepan heat and stir chocolate over low heat until melted. Gradually whisk in milk; heat and stir over medium heat until smooth. Remove from heat; set aside.

**3** In a large bowl lightly beat eggs. Whisk the warm chocolate mixture, the remaining ¾ cup sugar, and the cinnamon into eggs. Pour chocolate mixture into cake pan. Place cake pan in a roasting pan. Place roasting pan on rack in oven. Pour boiling water into the roasting pan around cake pan to a depth of 1 inch (photo 4, page 216).

**4** Bake in the preheated oven for 45 to 50 minutes or until a knife inserted near the center comes out clean. Carefully remove cake pan from water. Cool slightly on a wire rack. Cover and chill for 6 to 24 hours.

**5** To unmold, run a sharp knife around edges of flan in pan (photo 6, page 223). Invert a serving plate over pan; turn pan and plate over together (photo 7, page 223). Remove pan. If desired, garnish with pomegranate seeds. Makes 12 servings.

*Note: Be sure to use a pan that is 2 inches deep. A pan that is 1½ inches deep will not hold all of the egg mixture. And briefly warm the pan in oven so the caramel mixture spreads over the bottom more easily.

Per serving: 282 cal., 12 g total fat (6 g sat. fat), 148 mg chol., 80 mg sodium, 39 g carbo., 2 g fiber, 8 g pro.

**Ask Mom** How do I chop chocolate? p. 33 / How do I measure liquids? p. 55 / How do I measure sugar? p. 55 / How do I melt chocolate? p. 32, 33 / How do I prepare a pomegranate? p. 192 / What is a water bath? p. 219 / What is cinnamon? p. 36 / What is semisweet/bittersweet chocolate? p. 32

# perfect
## PIES & TARTS

**Whatever form it takes—a homey, dome-shape pie or a thin, elegant tart—there are few combinations better than rich, buttery pastry and a really great filling.**

8

## CHILLED & FROZEN PIES

Caramel-Pecan French Silk Pie ③ ....................... 246

Chocolate-Mascarpone Raspberry Pie ② ............... 244

Lemon Meringue Pie ③ ............................... 248

Peppermint-Fudge Pie ② ............................. 250

## CREAM & CUSTARD PIES

Banana Cream Pie ③ ................................. 232

Best Pumpkin Pie ② .................................. 240

Chocolate Pecan Pie ② .............................. 238

Coconut Cream Pie ③ ................................ 232

Dark Chocolate Cream Pie ③ ......................... 232

Pecan Pie ② ......................................... 238

Vanilla Cream Pie ③ ................................. 232

## CRUSTS & PASTRY

Almond Pastry ② ...................................... 261

Baked Pastry Shell ② ................................ 227

Baked Pastry Tart Shell ② ........................... 227

Chocolate Crumb Crust ② ............................ 250

Coconut-Macadamia Nut Pastry ③ ..................... 258

decorative edges for, ............................242–243

Pastry for Double-Crust Pie ② ....................... 230

Pastry for Lattice-Top Pie ② ......................... 230

Pastry for Single-Crust Pie ② ........................ 227

Quick Lattice-Top ② ................................. 230

Rich Tart Pastry ② ................................... 260

## FRUIT PIES

Berry Pie ② .......................................... 233

Caramel Apple Pie ② ................................. 235

Fool-Your-Family Peach Pie ① ........................ 234

Lattice Cherry Pie ③ ................................. 236

Mixed Berry Cream Pie ② ............................ 239

Peach Pie ② ......................................... 233

Rhubarb Pie ② ....................................... 233

**How do I make a basic fruit pie?** ................................233

**How do I make a basic pie?** ...........................228–229

**How do I make a cream pie?** ...................................232

## QUICHES & TARTS

Brown Butter Tart ② ................................. 260

Dried Pear and Chocolate-Caramel Tart ③ .............. 262

Ham and Cheese Quiche ③ ............................ 253

Key Lime Tart ③ ..................................... 258

Peach-Almond Tart ② ................................. 261

Triple Onion Appetizer Tart ② ........................ 255

Two-Cheese Vegetable Quiche ③ ...................... 254

Winter Vegetable Tarts with Bacon and Goat Cheese ② .... 256

## TOPPINGS

Cranberry-Pecan Caramel Topper ② .................... 240

Crumb Topping ① .................................... 262

Meringue for Pie ③ .................................. 248

Peppermint Whipped Cream ② ......................... 251

White Chocolate Topping ② ........................... 244

# Pastry for Single-Crust Pie

1¼ cups all-purpose flour

¼ teaspoon salt

⅓ cup shortening

4 to 5 tablespoons cold water

**1** In a medium bowl stir together flour and salt. Using a pastry blender, cut in shortening until pieces are pea size (photo 1, page 228).

**2** Sprinkle 1 tablespoon of the water over part of the flour mixture; gently toss with a fork. Push moistened pastry to the side of the bowl. Repeat moistening flour mixture, using 1 tablespoon of the water at a time, until all of the flour mixture is moistened (photo 2, page 228). Form pastry into a ball (photo 3, page 228).

**3** On a lightly floured surface, use your hands to slightly flatten pastry. Roll pastry from center to edges into a circle about 12 inches in diameter (photo 4, page 228).

**4** Wrap pastry circle around rolling pin (photo 5, page 229). Unroll pastry into a 9-inch pie plate (photo 6, page 229). Ease pastry into pie plate without stretching it (photo 7, page 229).

**5** Trim pastry to ½ inch beyond edge of pie plate (photo 8, page 229). Fold under extra pastry (photo 9, page 229). Crimp edge as desired (pages 242–243). Do not prick pastry. Fill and bake as directed in recipes. Makes 8 slices (1 piecrust).

Per slice regular, food processor, pastry shell, or pastry tart shell variations: 140 cal., 9 g total fat (2 g sat. fat), 0 mg chol., 073 mg sodium, 14 g carbo., 0 g fiber, 2 g pro.

Food Processor Directions: Place steel blade in food processor bowl. Add flour, salt, and shortening. Cover and process with on/off turns until most of flour mixture resembles cornmeal but a few larger pieces remain. With food processor running, quickly add 3 tablespoons water through feed tube. Stop processor as soon as all of the water is added; scrape down sides. Process with two on/off turns (mixture may not all be moistened). Remove dough from bowl; shape into a ball. Continue with Step 3.

Baked Pastry Shell: Prepare as above, except prick bottom and sides of pastry with a fork (photo 11, page 229). Line pastry with a double thickness of foil (photo 12, page 229). Bake in a 450°F oven for 8 minutes. Remove foil. Bake for 5 to 6 minutes more or until golden. Cool on a wire rack.

Baked Pastry Tart Shell: Prepare as above through Step 3. Wrap pastry circle around the rolling pin. Unroll pastry into a 10-inch tart pan that has a removable bottom. Ease pastry into pan without stretching it. Press pastry into fluted sides of tart pan and trim edges (photos 1–4, page 259). Prick pastry with a fork (photo 5, page 259). Line pastry with a double thickness of foil (photo 12, page 229). Bake in a 450°F oven for 8 minutes. Remove foil. Bake for 6 to 8 minutes more or until golden. Cool on a wire rack.

**Good to Know** Recipe for an instant pie: Bake and cool a single-crust pie shell, then fill it with your favorite flavor of pudding and top it off with whipped cream.

**Ask Mom** How do I measure flour? p. 54 / How do I measure shortening? p. 55 / What is a food processor? p. 20 / What is a pastry blender? p. 10, 11 / What is a tart pan? p. 10, 259 / What's that flour? p. 31

# How do I make a basic pie?

Pie is defined by the presence of crust. Great pie depends on tender, flaky crust. Here are a few hints to help you achieve pie perfection every time you bake.

The mantra about the need to measure accurately for successful baking applies to piecrust this way: Too much flour or water makes tough pastry, while too much shortening makes it crumble. Measure carefully and add water gradually—the colder, the better. Ice-cold water (add a couple of ice cubes) won't melt the bits of shortening, which is what creates pockets (flakiness) in piecrust during baking. If the fat melts, your piecrust will be dense and tough.

Once the dough is rolled out, it is an admittedly tricky proposition getting it into the pie plate. The easiest way is to roll it around the rolling pin (photos 5–6, page 229), then gently unroll it across the plate, easing it in as you go. If you wind up with a tear in the crust, patch it with a pastry scrap before adding the filling. Moisten the underside of the scrap with a little water to get it to stick. Above all, use a gentle touch and don't overwork the dough.

**4** Flour the rolling surface just enough to keep the dough from sticking. Roll dough with a floured rolling pin from center to edge. Use light, even strokes to form a 12-inch circle with an even thickness.

**1** Use a pastry blender to cut the shortening into the flour mixture. Work just until the pieces are the size of small peas.

**2** Sprinkle cold water, 1 tablespoon at a time, over part of the flour mixture; toss gently with a fork. Push to side of bowl. Repeat until all the flour mixture is evenly moistened.

**3** After all the flour is moistened, use your hands to gently press and form the dough into a ball.

HOW DO I ROLL MY PIECRUST EVENLY? **To get a crust that is uniform in thickness, place the dough on a lightly floured surface, then roll from the center out to the edges, all of the way around the circle.**

**5** For easy transfer to the pie plate, wrap the pastry around the rolling pin.

**6** Holding the rolling pin over the pie plate, unroll the pastry starting at one side of the pie plate.

**7** Ease the pastry into the pie plate without stretching it. Lightly press the pastry over the bottom and sides of the pie plate.

**8** Use kitchen scissors to trim the excess dough to ½ inch beyond edge of pie plate.

**9** To build up the edge of the pie shell, fold the extra ½ inch of pastry under so it is even with the rim of the pie plate.

**10** To create a fluted edge, place a finger against the inside edge of the pastry and, using the thumb and index finger of the other hand, press the pastry around the finger.

**11** If the pastry is to be baked without a filling, prick the bottom and sides all over with a fork. This will prevent the pastry from shrinking while it bakes.

**12** Line the pastry shell with a double layer of regular foil or a single layer of heavy-duty foil. The foil prevents the crust from shrinking or losing its shape while it bakes.

# Pastry for Double-Crust Pie

2¼ cups all-purpose flour

¾ teaspoon salt

⅔ cup shortening

8 to 10 tablespoons cold water

**1** In a medium bowl stir together flour and salt. Using a pastry blender, cut in shortening until pieces are pea size (photo 1, page 228).

**2** Sprinkle 1 tablespoon of the water over part of the flour mixture; gently toss with a fork. Push moistened pastry to side of bowl. Repeat moistening flour mixture, using 1 tablespoon of the water at a time, until all of the flour mixture is moistened (photo 2, page 228). Divide pastry in half; form each half into a ball (photo 3, page 228).

**3** On a lightly floured surface, use your hands to slightly flatten one pastry ball. Roll pastry from center to edges into a circle about 12 inches in diameter (photo 4, page 228).

**4** Wrap pastry around rolling pin (photo 5, page 229). Unroll pastry into a 9-inch pie plate (photo 6, page 229). Ease pastry into pie plate without stretching it (photo 7, page 229). Transfer desired filling to pastry-lined pie plate (photo 1, page 231). Trim pastry even with rim of pie plate (photo 2, page 231).

**5** Roll remaining pastry ball into a circle about 12 inches in diameter. Cut slits in pastry (photo 3, page 231). Place pastry circle on filling; trim to ½ inch beyond edge of plate (photos 4–5, page 231). Fold top pastry under bottom pastry (photo 6, page 231). Crimp edge as desired (pages 242–243). Bake as directed in recipes. Makes 8 slices (2 piecrusts).

**Pastry for Lattice-Top Pie:** Prepare as above, except trim bottom pastry to ½ inch beyond edge of pie plate. Roll out remaining pastry and cut into ½-inch-wide strips (photo 1, page 236). Transfer desired filling to pastry-lined pie plate (photo 1, page 231). Weave strips over filling in a lattice pattern (photo 2, page 236). Press ends of strips into bottom pastry rim. Fold bottom pastry over strip ends (photo 3, page 236); seal and crimp edge (photo 4, page 236). Bake as directed in recipes.

**Quick Lattice-Top:** Prepare Pastry for Lattice-Top Pie as above, except instead of weaving strips over filling, lay half of the pastry strips on filling at 1-inch intervals. Give pie a quarter turn; arrange remaining strips perpendicular to the first strips.

Per slice regular or lattice variation: 269 cal., 17 g total fat (4 g sat. fat), 0 mg chol., 219 mg sodium, 25 g carbo., 1 g fiber, 3 g pro.

**WHY CUT SLITS IN THE TOP CRUST?** It looks pretty, but it's primarily for a practical reason. The slits allow steam to escape during baking, which does two things: It prevents the fruit juices from bubbling over, and it keeps the crust from getting soggy.

**Ask Mom** How do I measure flour? p. 54 / How do I measure shortening? p. 55 / What does crimp mean? p. 69 / What is a pastry blender? p. 10, 11 / What's that flour? p. 31

**2** Use a sharp knife to trim the pastry even with the rim of the pie plate. Trim after adding the filling so it doesn't pull the pastry down into the pie plate.

**1** Transfer the filling to the pastry-lined pie plate.

**3** Use a sharp knife to cut slits near the center of the top pastry to allow steam to escape during baking.

**4** Wrap the top pastry around the rolling pin and unroll onto the filled pie, being careful not to stretch the pastry.

**5** Use kitchen scissors to trim the edge of the top pastry ½ inch beyond the rim of the pie plate.

**6** Lift the bottom pastry edge away from the pie plate and fold the extra top pastry under it.

**7** For a rope edge, pinch the pastry edge by pushing forward on a slant with your bent index finger and pulling back with your thumb.

**Good to Know** When you're making any double-crust fruit pie, make sure you evenly distribute the fruit in the bottom crust, or someone will get a nearly fruitless piece of pie (and you don't want that!).

# How do I make a cream pie?

## Custardy, vanilla-scented cream pie can be served plain or flavored with chocolate, coconut, or bananas.

Prepare Baked Pastry Shell (page 227) as directed. Separate egg yolks from whites for 4 eggs; set whites aside for meringue. For filling, in a medium saucepan combine ¾ cup sugar and ¼ cup cornstarch. Gradually stir in 2½ cups half-and-half, light cream, or milk. Cook and stir over medium-high heat until thickened and bubbly; reduce heat. Cook and stir 2 minutes more. Remove from heat. Slightly beat the egg yolks with a fork. Gradually stir about 1 cup of the hot filling into yolks. Add egg yolk mixture to hot filling in saucepan. Bring to a gentle boil; reduce heat. Cook and stir for 2 minutes more. Remove from heat. Stir in 1 tablespoon butter and 1½ teaspoons vanilla; keep filling warm. Preheat oven to 325°F. Prepare meringue (see box at right). Pour warm filling into Baked Pastry Shell. Spread meringue over warm filling; seal to edge (photo 4, page 248). Bake for 30 minutes. Cool on a wire rack for 1 hour. Chill for 3 to 6 hours before serving; cover for longer storage. Makes 8 slices.

### Meringue for Pie

In a large mixing bowl combine 4 egg whites, I teaspoon vanilla, and ½ teaspoon cream of tartar. Beat with an electric mixer on medium speed about I minute or until soft peaks form (tips curl). Gradually add ½ cup sugar, I tablespoon at a time, beating on high speed about 5 minutes or until mixture forms stiff, glossy peaks (tips stand straight) (photos 1–3, page 248).

Dark Chocolate Cream Pie: Prepare as at left, except increase sugar to 1 cup. Stir in 3 ounces chopped unsweetened chocolate with the half-and-half.

Coconut Cream Pie: Prepare as at left, except stir in 1 cup flaked coconut with the butter and vanilla. Sprinkle another ⅓ cup flaked coconut over meringue before baking.

Banana Cream Pie: Prepare as at left, except before adding filling, arrange 3 medium bananas, sliced (about 2¼ cups), over bottom of pie shell.

**Safe Storage** Cream pies are called "refrigerator" pies for a reason. All the rich eggs and cream make them vulnerable to spoilage. To store a cream pie, cover with plastic wrap and refrigerate up to 2 days. (They don't hold up if frozen.)

# How do I make a basic fruit pie?

## With one pastry recipe, a few simple ingredients, and fresh, seasonal fruit, you can pick your pie.

Prepare Pastry for Double-Crust Pie (page 230) as directed. Line a 9-inch pie plate with a pastry circle (photos 5–7, page 229). In a large bowl combine the sugar, thickener, and flavoring for desired fruit filling, according to the amounts given below. Stir in fruit; toss gently until coated. (If using frozen fruit, let mixture stand about 45 minutes or until fruit is partially thawed but still icy.) Preheat oven to 375°F. Transfer fruit filling to the pastry-lined pie plate (photo 1, page 231). Trim bottom pastry to edge of pie plate (photo 2, page 231). Cut slits in remaining pastry circle; place on filling and seal (photos 3–6, page 231). Crimp edges as desired (pages 242–243). If desired, brush top pastry with milk and sprinkle with additional sugar (photos 2–3, page 234). To prevent overbrowning, cover edge of pie with foil (photos 1–3, page 240). Bake in the preheated oven for 25 minutes (or 50 to 60 minutes for frozen fruit). Remove foil. Bake pie for 20 to 30 minutes more or until filling is bubbly and pastry is golden. Cool on a wire rack.

**Peach Pie:** Combine ½ to ¾ sugar, 2 tablespoons quick-cooking tapioca, ¼ teaspoon ground cinnamon, and ¼ teaspoon ground nutmeg. Stir in 6 cups thinly sliced, peeled peaches or frozen unsweetened peaches. Let stand 20 minutes, stirring occasionally.

**Rhubarb Pie:** Combine ¾ cup sugar, ⅓ cup all-purpose flour, and ½ teaspoon ground cinnamon. Stir in 6 cups fresh or frozen rhubarb.

**Berry Pie:** If using raspberries or blackberries, combine ¾ to I cup sugar, ⅓ cup all-purpose flour, and 2 teaspoons finely shredded lemon peel. If using blueberries, combine ⅔ to ¾ cup sugar and 3 tablespoons all-purpose flour. Stir in 5 cups fresh or frozen raspberries, blackberries, or blueberries.

**Shopping Savvy** Look for the tiny cutters used to cut decorative holes in the top crust of this pie at specialty cookware shops. You can use either a small cookie cutter or a cutter used to make canapés (bite-size, open-face appetizer sandwiches).

**1** Skill Level

# Fool-Your-Family
## Peach Pie

1   15-ounce package rolled refrigerated unbaked piecrusts (2 crusts)
1   21-ounce can peach pie filling
1½  cups fresh blueberries
⅓   cup slivered almonds, toasted
1   tablespoon milk
2   teaspoons coarse sugar or granulated sugar
1   recipe Sweetened Whipped Cream (page 25) or vanilla ice cream (optional)

**1** Let refrigerated piecrusts stand at room temperature according to package directions. Meanwhile, for filling, in a large bowl stir together pie filling, blueberries, and almonds.

**2** Preheat oven to 375°F. Line a 9-inch pie plate with 1 of the piecrusts (photos 5–7, page 229). Transfer filling to pastry-lined pie plate (photo 1, page 231). Trim bottom pastry to edge of pie plate (photo 2, page 231). Using a 1-inch round cutter, cut 3 holes in center of remaining piecrust (below); place on filling and seal (photos 4–6, page 231). Crimp edge as desired (pages 242–243). Brush top pastry with milk (below); sprinkle with sugar (below).

**3** To prevent overbrowning, cover edge of pie with foil (below). Bake in the preheated oven for 25 minutes. Remove foil. Bake for 25 to 30 minutes more or until top is golden and filling is bubbly. Cool on a wire rack. If desired, serve with Sweetened Whipped Cream or ice cream. Makes 8 servings.

Per serving: 355 cal., 17 g total fat (6 g sat. fat), 10 mg chol., 212 mg sodium, 48 g carbo., 2 g fiber, 3 g pro.

**1** Use small decorative cutters to cut out pieces of pastry. These cuts will allow steam to escape.

**2** For a nicely glazed, browner top crust, brush the pastry with a little milk.

**3** After brushing with milk, sprinkle the top crust with a little bit of sugar.

**4** To protect the edges of the piecrust from getting too brown, cover it with foil. Loosely mold the foil over the pie's edge (see page 240).

**Ask Mom** How do I measure sugar? p. 55 / How do I store pie? p. 68 / How do I toast nuts? p. 34 / How do I wash fresh berries? p. 42 / What does crimp mean? p. 69 / What is coarse sugar? p. 29 / What is granulated sugar? p. 29 / What's that nut? p. 34–35

② Skill Level

# Caramel Apple Pie

1 recipe Pastry for Double-Crust Pie (page 230)
or one 15-ounce package rolled refrigerated
unbaked piecrusts (2 crusts)

½ cup packed brown sugar

3 tablespoons all-purpose flour

1 teaspoon ground cinnamon

6 cups thinly sliced, peeled cooking apples

½ cup chopped pecans (optional)

¼ cup caramel-flavor ice cream topping

**1** Prepare and roll out Pastry for Double-Crust Pie or let refrigerated piecrusts stand at room temperature according to package directions. Line a 9-inch pie plate with a pastry circle (photos 5–7, page 229); set aside.

**2** Preheat oven to 375°F. For filling, in a large bowl stir together brown sugar, flour, cinnamon, and ⅛ teaspoon *salt*. Stir in apples and, if desired, pecans; toss gently until coated. Transfer filling to pastry-lined pie plate (photo 1, page 231). Trim bottom pastry to edge of pie plate (photo 2, page 231). Cut slits in remaining pastry circle (photo 3, page 231); place on filling and seal (photos 4–6, page 231). Crimp edge as desired (pages 242–243).

**3** To prevent overbrowning, cover edge of pie with foil (photos 1–3, page 240). Bake in the preheated oven for 30 minutes. Remove foil. Bake about 30 minutes more or until top is golden and filling is bubbly. Cool on a wire rack. To serve, drizzle each serving with ice cream topping. Makes 8 servings.

Per serving: 397 cal., 17 g total fat (4 g sat. fat), 0 mg chol., 211 mg sodium, 58 g carbo., 3 g fiber, 3 g pro.

**Ingredient Info** It's worth seeking out (and shelling out a few extra pennies for) a quality caramel topping to use in this pie so that the sauce is not too thin.

**Ask Mom**  How do I measure flour? p. 54 / How do I measure sugar? p. 55 / How do I peel and slice apples? p. 38, 39 / How do I store pie? p. 68 / What are chopped nuts? p. 34 / What does crimp mean? p. 69 / What does drizzle mean? p. 69, 85 / What is a good baking/cooking apple? p. 39, 287 / What is cinnamon? p. 36 / What's that flour? p. 31 / What's that nut? p. 34–35

# Lattice Cherry Pie

| | |
|---|---|
| 1 recipe Pastry for Double-Crust Pie (page 230) or one 15-ounce package rolled refrigerated unbaked piecrusts (2 crusts) | ¼ cup cornstarch |
| | ½ teaspoon ground cinnamon |
| | 1 tablespoon butter |
| 2 14½-ounce cans pitted tart red cherries (water pack) | ½ teaspoon almond extract |
| 1½ cups sugar | |

**1** Prepare and roll out Pastry for Double-Crust Pie or let refrigerated piecrusts stand at room temperature according to package directions. Line a 9-inch pie plate with a pastry circle (photos 5–7, page 229). Roll out remaining pastry and cut into ½-inch-wide strips (below).

**2** Preheat oven to 375°F. For filling, drain cherries, reserving the liquid from one of the cans (discard liquid from the other can). In a medium saucepan combine sugar, cornstarch, and cinnamon. Gradually stir in reserved cherry liquid. Cook and stir over medium-high heat just until bubbly. Remove from heat; stir in cherries, butter, and almond extract.

**3** Transfer filling to the pastry-lined pie plate (photo 1, page 231). Trim pastry to ½ inch beyond edge of pie plate (photo 8, page 229). Weave pastry strips in a lattice pattern (below). Press ends of strips into bottom pastry rim (below). Fold bottom pastry over strip ends; seal and crimp edge (below).

**4** To prevent overbrowning, cover edge of pie with foil (photos 1–3, page 240). Bake in the preheated oven for 35 minutes. Remove foil. Bake for 20 to 25 minutes more or until top is golden and filling is bubbly. Cool on a wire rack. Makes 8 servings.

**Per serving:** 488 cal., 18 g total fat (5 g sat. fat), 4 mg chol., 237 mg sodium, 78 g carbo., 2 g fiber, 2 g pro.

**1** With a sharp knife, cut the dough into strips about ½ inch wide. Use a ruler for straight and even strips.

**2** Working from the center out, lay one pastry strip horizontally on top of the filling; lay the next strip vertically on top of the first. Continue alternating strips horizontally, then vertically.

**3** Trim pastry strips even with edge of bottom pastry; press strip ends into bottom pastry to seal.

**4** Fold the bottom pastry over the ends of the lattice strips. Crimp as desired (pages 242–243).

**Ask Mom** How do I measure butter? p. 55 / How do I measure sugar? p. 55 / How do I store pie? p. 68 / What does crimp mean? p. 69 / What is cinnamon? p. 36

# CAN I PUT A LATTICE CRUST ON ANY FRUIT PIE?

The main consideration is the cooked texture of the fruit you're using. Berries, cherries, and peaches cook down, allowing for a smooth lattice top. Apples stay chunkier, which can cause a bumpier crust.

Lattice crust may look complicated, but this no-weave version of the traditional lattice gives you the same effect with less effort and confusion.

② Skill Level

**Good to Know** The gooey filling that so sweetly suspends the pecans in this pie after it's baked is liquid before it's baked. Be very careful when you move the pie from the countertop to the oven to avoid splashing and spilling it over the edge of the crust.

# Chocolate Pecan Pie

1  recipe Pastry for Single-Crust Pie (page 227) or ½ of a 15-ounce package rolled refrigerated unbaked piecrusts (1 crust)

3  eggs, lightly beaten

1  cup light-colored corn syrup

⅔  cup sugar

⅓  cup butter, melted

1  teaspoon vanilla

1¼  cups pecan halves or chopped macadamia nuts

½  cup semisweet chocolate pieces

**1** Preheat oven to 350°F. Prepare and roll out Pastry for Single-Crust Pie or let refrigerated piecrust stand at room temperature according to package directions. Line a 9-inch pie plate with the pastry circle and trim (photos 1–9, pages 228–229). Crimp edge as desired (pages 242–243).

**2** For filling, in a medium bowl combine eggs, corn syrup, sugar, butter, and vanilla; mix well. Stir in pecan halves.

**3** Pat semisweet chocolate pieces onto bottom of pastry shell (below). Pour filling over chocolate pieces (below). To prevent overbrowning, cover edge of pie with foil (photos 1–3, page 240). Bake in the preheated oven for 25 minutes. Remove foil. Bake for 20 to 25 minutes more or until a knife inserted near the center comes out clean (below). Cool on a wire rack. Cover and chill within 2 hours. Makes 8 servings.

Per serving: 581 cal., 33 g total fat (9 g sat. fat), 101 mg chol., 205 mg sodium, 71 g carbo., 2 g fiber, 7 g pro.

**Pecan Pie:** Prepare as above, except omit the semisweet chocolate pieces.

**①** Lightly pat the chocolate pieces evenly onto the bottom of the pastry shell.

**②** Carefully pour the filling over the chocolate pieces.

**③** To test for doneness, insert a knife near center of filling. When done, the knife will come out clean.

**Ask Mom** How do I measure butter? p. 55 / How do I measure liquids? p. 55 / How do I measure sugar? p. 55 / How do I store pie? p. 68 / How do I work with eggs? p. 26–27 / What does crimp mean? p. 69 / What is semisweet/bittersweet chocolate? p. 32 / What is vanilla? p. 128 / What's that nut? p. 34–35

**Good to Know** If you need a Mixed Berry Cream Pie—now—you can skip making the homemade pastry. Buy a frozen pie shell and bake it according to the package directions, then proceed with the rest of the recipe.

**②** Skill Level

# Mixed Berry Cream Pie

- I recipe Baked Pastry Shell (page 227)
- 6 cups fresh blackberries, blueberries, and/or raspberries*
- I cup sugar
- 2 tablespoons all-purpose flour
- I tablespoon lemon juice
- I 8-ounce carton dairy sour cream
- 3 tablespoons all-purpose flour
- ¼ teaspoon salt
- ½ cup fine dry bread crumbs
- 3 tablespoons packed brown sugar
- 2 tablespoons butter, melted

**1** Prepare Baked Pastry Shell; set aside. In a large bowl toss berries with ¼ cup of the sugar, the 2 tablespoons flour, and lemon juice. Transfer berry mixture to Baked Pastry Shell (below). In a medium bowl combine sour cream, the remaining ¾ cup sugar, the 3 tablespoons flour, and salt. Spoon sour cream mixture over berry mixture in pie shell (below).

**2** Preheat oven to 375°F. In a small bowl combine bread crumbs, brown sugar, and butter. Sprinkle crumb mixture evenly over sour cream mixture (below). To prevent overbrowning, cover edge of pie with foil (photos 1–3, page 240). Place pie on a baking sheet. Bake in the preheated oven about 50 minutes or until juices are clear. Cool on a wire rack. Chill at least 3 hours before serving. Makes 8 servings.

*Note: Do not use more than 3 cups raspberries in the berry mixture. Because raspberries are very juicy, using more than 3 cups may make the crust soggy.

Per serving: 463 cal., 23 g total fat (10 g sat. fat), 47 mg chol., 361 mg sodium, 62 g carbo., 7 g fiber, 5 g pro.

**1** Carefully transfer the berry filling to the cooled prebaked pastry shell.

**2** Spoon the sour cream mixture evenly over the berry filling.

**3** Sprinkle the crumb topping evenly over the top of the pie.

# Best Pumpkin Pie

I recipe Pastry for Single-Crust Pie (page 227)
I 15-ounce can pumpkin
¾ cup sugar
I to I¼ teaspoons ground cinnamon
½ to I teaspoon ground ginger
½ teaspoon salt
¼ to ½ teaspoon ground nutmeg

¼ to ½ teaspoon ground cloves
3 eggs, lightly beaten
I¼ cups milk
I recipe Cranberry-Pecan Caramel Topper (optional)
I recipe Sweetened Whipped Cream (page 25) (optional)

**1** Preheat oven to 375°F. Prepare and roll out Pastry for Single-Crust Pie. Line a 9-inch pie plate with the pastry circle and trim (photos 1–9, pages 228–229). Crimp edge as desired (pages 242–243).

**2** For filling, combine pumpkin, sugar, cinnamon, ginger, salt, nutmeg, and cloves. Add eggs; whisk together lightly until combined. Gradually add milk; stir just until combined.

**3** Pour filling into pastry shell. To prevent overbrowning, cover edge of pie with foil (below). Bake in the preheated oven for 30 minutes. Remove foil. Bake for 25 to 30 minutes more or until a knife inserted near the center comes out clean (photo 3, page 238). Cool on a wire rack. Cover and chill within 2 hours.

**4** To serve, if desired, top with Cranberry-Pecan Caramel Topper and/or Sweetened Whipped Cream. Makes 8 servings.

Per serving: 283 cal., 12 g total fat (3 g sat. fat), 82 mg chol., 263 mg sodium, 40 g carbo., 2 g fiber, 6 g pro.

Cranberry-Pecan Caramel Topper: In a medium bowl combine ⅓ cup dried cranberries and 3 tablespoons brandy or apple juice; let stand for 15 minutes. Stir in 1½ cups pecan halves, toasted, and ¼ cup caramel-flavor ice cream topping. Serve immediately or cover and chill for up to 1 week. Bring to room temperature before serving.

**1** To protect the edges of a piecrust from overbrowning, tear off a 12-inch square of aluminum foil; fold it into quarters.

**2** Cut a 7- to 7½-inch circle out of the center of the foil.

**3** Unfold the foil and place it on the pie, loosely molding the foil over the edges.

**Ask Mom** How do I measure liquids? p. 55 / How do I measure sugar? p. 55 / How do I store pie? p. 68 / How do I work with eggs? p. 26–27 / What are cloves? p. 36 / What does crimp mean? p. 69 / What is canned pumpkin? p. 302 / What is cinnamon? p. 36 / What is ginger? p. 36

You can use any kind of milk—from nonfat on up to whole milk—in this holiday classic, but it will be much richer and creamier if you use whole milk.

# On the Edge
## Make your crusted dessert stand out with a special edge.

## Cutout edge

Roll out pastry scraps very thin. Use a fluted pastry wheel, knife, or hors d'oeuvre cutter to cut pastry into desired shapes. Flatten edge of pastry shell slightly; brush with water. Arrange cutouts on edge of pastry shell and press lightly to secure.

## Rope edge

Crimp around edge of pastry by pinching it. When pinching, push forward on a slant with a bent finger and pull back with your thumb.

## Tabbed edge

Use kitchen scissors to snip $\frac{1}{2}$-inch slits into pastry about $\frac{1}{2}$ inch apart along edge. For a little bit different look, press every other tab in the opposite direction.

## Criss-cross edge

Flatten edge of pastry slightly.
Lightly press the tines of a fork
into pastry, switching angles every
other pressing.

## Petal edge

Crimp pastry as directed on page
229, photo 10. Press the tines of
a fork lightly into the center of
each flute.

## Scallop edge

Crimp pastry as directed on page
229, photo 10. Press the bowl of
a spoon lightly into the center of
each flute.

# Chocolate-Mascarpone Raspberry Pie

1 recipe Baked Pastry Shell (page 227)
1 8-ounce carton mascarpone cheese
6 ounces bittersweet chocolate, chopped
½ cup powdered sugar
2 tablespoons raspberry liqueur

1 cup whipping cream
2 cups fresh raspberries
⅓ cup seedless raspberry jam, melted and cooled slightly
1 recipe White Chocolate Topping (optional)

**1** Prepare Baked Pastry Shell; set aside. For filling, in a medium saucepan combine mascarpone cheese, chocolate, and powdered sugar. Cook and stir over medium-low heat until chocolate melts and mixture is smooth. Remove saucepan from heat; stir in liqueur. Let the filling cool to room temperature.

**2** In a medium chilled mixing bowl beat whipping cream with an electric mixer on medium speed until soft peaks form. Stir about ½ cup of the whipped cream into the cooled filling. Fold in remaining whipped cream just until combined. Carefully spoon filling into Baked Pastry Shell, spreading evenly. Cover and chill for 3 to 24 hours or until set.

**3** Just before serving, gently stir the 2 cups raspberries into the jam (below). Spoon the raspberry mixture over filling (below). If desired, top each serving with White Chocolate Topping. Makes 10 servings.

**Per serving:** 559 cal., 42 g total fat (23 g sat. fat), 93 mg chol., 100 mg sodium, 44 g carbo., 3 g fiber, 9 g pro.

**White Chocolate Topping:** In a small heavy saucepan heat and stir 2 ounces chopped white baking chocolate and ¼ cup whipping cream until chocolate melts and mixture is smooth; cool. In a medium chilled mixing bowl beat ⅔ cup whipping cream with an electric mixer on medium speed until mixture mounds but does not form peaks; turn off mixer. Add white chocolate mixture; beat on low speed just until stiff peaks form (tips stand straight).

**1** Use a spatula to gently stir the raspberries into the melted raspberry jam.

**2** Spoon the raspberry mixture evenly over the chocolate filling.

**Ingredient Info** Mascarpone cheese is a buttery, double- or triple-cream cheese from the Lombardy region of Italy. It's the same cheese that makes tiramisu—that Italian coffee-and-chocolate-flavor dessert—so rich and delicious. Look for it in the specialty cheese section of your supermarket.

**Ask Mom** How do I chop chocolate? p. 33 / How do I store pie? p. 68 / How do I wash fresh berries? p. 42 / What are soft peaks? p. 26 / What are stiff peaks? p. 26 / What does fold mean? p. 65 / What is powdered sugar? p. 29 / What is semisweet/ bittersweet chocolate? p. 32 / What is whipping cream? p. 24 / What is white chocolate? p. 32

**CAN I USE FROZEN RASPBERRIES?** Fresh is really the only choice. Raspberries lose their shape in the freezing/thawing process—and you don't want smushed berries on your pie. Be sure to use seedless jam too so that the berries look smooth and glossy.

You'll get neat, clean slices of pie through this fudgy filling if you run your knife under warm water and wipe it dry before you make each cut.

# Caramel-Pecan French Silk Pie

1 recipe Baked Pastry Shell (page 227)
1 cup whipping cream
1 cup semisweet chocolate pieces
⅓ cup butter
⅓ cup sugar
2 egg yolks, lightly beaten

3 tablespoons crème de cacao or whipping cream
1 cup caramel-flavor ice cream topping
¾ cup coarsely chopped pecans or almonds, toasted
⅔ cup whipping cream
Chocolate curls (optional)

**1** Prepare Baked Pastry Shell; set aside.

**2** In a medium heavy saucepan combine the 1 cup whipping cream, chocolate pieces, butter, and sugar. Cook and stir over low heat about 10 minutes or until chocolate melts. Remove saucepan from heat. Gradually stir half of the hot mixture into the beaten egg yolks (photo 1, page 247). Return egg mixture to saucepan (photo 2, page 247). Cook over medium-low heat about 5 minutes, stirring constantly, until mixture is slightly thickened and begins to bubble (photo 3, page 247). Remove from heat. (Mixture may appear to separate.) Stir in crème de cacao. Place the saucepan in a bowl of ice water about 20 minutes, stirring occasionally, until mixture stiffens and becomes hard to stir (photo 4, page 247).

**3** Meanwhile, spread ice cream topping in bottom of Baked Pastry Shell (photo 5, page 247); sprinkle pecans evenly over ice cream topping (photo 6, page 247).

**4** Transfer cooled chocolate mixture to a large mixing bowl. Beat with an electric mixer on medium to high speed for 2 to 3 minutes or until light and fluffy (photo 7, page 247). Spread chocolate mixture over pecans (photo 8, page 247). Cover and chill for 5 to 24 hours.

**5** To serve, in a chilled medium mixing bowl beat the ⅔ cup whipping cream with an electric mixer on medium speed until soft peaks form; spread over top of pie (below). If desired, garnish with chocolate curls. Makes 8 to 10 servings.

Per serving: 725 cal, 50 g total fat (23 g sat. fat), 142 mg chol., 294 mg sodium, 70 g carbo., 3 g fiber, 7 g pro.

An offset spatula, like the one shown here, allows you to get the blade of the spreader perfectly flat against the top of the pie. Use it to make swirls in the cream for a pretty effect.

**Ask Mom** How do I measure butter? p. 55 / How do I measure liquids? p. 55 / How do I measure sugar? p. 55 / How do I store pie? p. 68 / How do I toast nuts? p. 34 / How do I work with eggs? p. 26–27 / What are chopped nuts? p. 34 / What are soft peaks? p. 26 / What is semisweet/bittersweet chocolate? p. 32 / What is whipping cream? p. 24 / What's that nut? p. 34–35

**WHY ADD ONLY HALF OF THE HOT FILLING TO THE EGG YOLKS?** By combining only part of the filling with the yolks and then pouring it all back into the pan, you allow the eggs to acclimate to the heat—so you don't wind up with scrambled eggs in your filling.

**1** Stir constantly as you pour about half of the hot chocolate mixture into the beaten egg yolks.

**2** Return all of the egg yolk and chocolate mixture to the saucepan.

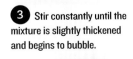

**3** Stir constantly until the mixture is slightly thickened and begins to bubble.

**4** Place the saucepan in a bowl of ice water and stir occasionally. The chocolate mixture will stiffen and become hard to stir.

**5** Use an offset spatula to spread the ice cream topping over the bottom of the baked pastry shell.

**6** Sprinkle the coarsely chopped pecans over the ice cream topping.

**7** Beat the cooled chocolate mixture until it's light and fluffy.

**8** Carefully spread the chocolate mixture over the pecans and ice cream topping in the pastry shell.

# Lemon Meringue Pie

1 recipe Baked Pastry Shell (page 227)
2 cups sugar
¼ cup cornstarch
4 teaspoons finely shredded lemon peel
1¼ cups water

¾ cup lemon juice
9 egg yolks, lightly beaten
⅓ cup butter, cut up
1 recipe Meringue for Pie

**Good to Know** Don't cry over your pie: Work lightning-fast to get the meringue spread onto the piping-hot pie filling. This helps the underside of the meringue to cook at the same rate as the top of it, so it won't form a layer of water between the meringue and filling (called "weeping").

**1** Prepare Baked Pastry Shell; set aside. For filling, in a 2-quart saucepan stir together sugar and cornstarch. Stir in lemon peel, water, and lemon juice. Cook and stir over medium heat until thickened and bubbly. Remove saucepan from heat. Stir half of the hot lemon mixture into the beaten egg yolks (photo 1, page 247). Return egg mixture to saucepan (photo 2, page 247). Cook, stirring constantly, over medium heat until mixture comes to a gentle boil. Cook and stir for 2 minutes more. Remove saucepan from heat. Add butter pieces, stirring until melted. Cover filling; keep warm.

**2** Preheat oven to 325°F. Prepare Meringue for Pie. Spread hot filling into Baked Pastry Shell. Immediately spread meringue over filling, carefully sealing to edge of pastry (below). Using the back of a spoon, add high peaks to the meringue (photo, page 249). Bake in the preheated oven for 30 minutes. Cool on a wire rack for 1 hour. Chill for 5 to 6 hours before serving; cover for longer storage. Makes 8 servings.

**Meringue for Pie:** Allow 5 egg whites to stand at room temperature for 30 minutes. In a very large mixing bowl combine egg whites, 1 teaspoon vanilla, and ½ teaspoon cream of tartar. Beat with an electric mixer on medium speed until soft peaks form (tips curl) (below). Gradually add 1 cup sugar, 1 tablespoon at a time, beating on high speed about 6 minutes more or until mixture forms stiff, glossy peaks (tips stand straight) and sugar dissolves (below).

Per serving: 601 cal., 22 g total fat (9 g sat. fat), 256 mg chol., 173 mg sodium, 97 g carbo., 1 g fiber, 6 g pro.

**1** Beat the egg white mixture about 1 minute or until the tips of the peaks bend over in soft curls when the beaters are lifted.

**2** Gradually add sugar, 1 tablespoon at a time, beating on high speed.

**3** Continue beating on high speed until the sugar dissolves and the glossy peaks stand up straight when the beaters are lifted.

**4** Spread the meringue over the hot filling, sealing it to the edge of the pastry to prevent it from shrinking while it bakes.

**Ask Mom** How do I juice a lemon? p. 44, 45 / How do I measure butter? p. 55 / How do I measure liquids? p. 55 / How do I measure sugar? p. 55 / How do I shred lemon peel? p. 45, 105 / How do I work with eggs? p. 26–27

**WHAT IS BEADING?** Small water droplets that can develop on meringue are the result of steam from the filling pushing up through it. Most evaporates, but some collects in the peaks and pushes through. Minimize beading by not overbaking your pie.

Use a spoon to swirl and twist the meringue into curlicued peaks. They'll turn a beautiful golden color when baked, creating a textured, gorgeous crown of meringue.

# Peppermint-**Fudge Pie**

**Good to Know** This ice cream pie—and all other ice cream pies, really—will cut much more easily if you use a sharp knife that's been run under hot water and dried before cutting each slice.

- 1 recipe Chocolate Crumb Crust
- 1 cup sugar
- 1 5-ounce can (⅔ cup) evaporated milk
- 2 tablespoons butter
- 2 ounces unsweetened chocolate, chopped
- 1 teaspoon vanilla
- 2 pints (4 cups) peppermint ice cream
- 1 recipe Peppermint Whipped Cream (page 251)

**1** Prepare Chocolate Crumb Crust; set aside. For fudge sauce, in a small saucepan combine the 1 cup sugar, the evaporated milk, butter, and chocolate. Cook and stir over medium heat until bubbly; reduce heat. Boil gently for 4 to 5 minutes or until mixture is thickened and reduced to 1½ cups, stirring occasionally. Remove from heat; stir in vanilla. If necessary, beat until smooth with a wire whisk or rotary beater. Spread about half of the warm fudge sauce over the cooled Chocolate Crumb Crust; freeze until set. Set remaining fudge sauce aside.

**2** In a chilled bowl stir ice cream until softened (page 202); spread over fudge sauce layer (below). Freeze about 2 hours or until set. Pipe remaining fudge sauce over ice cream (below); spread evenly. Top with Peppermint Whipped Cream (below). Freeze for at least 6 hours or until set. Remove sides of springform pan (photo 11, page 189). If desired, sprinkle with crushed *striped round peppermint candies* just before serving. Makes 12 servings.

Chocolate Crumb Crust: Preheat oven to 375°F. Lightly coat an 8-inch springform pan with nonstick cooking spray; set aside. In a medium bowl combine 1 cup finely crushed vanilla wafers (about 22 cookies), ⅓ cup powdered sugar, and 3 tablespoons unsweetened cocoa powder. Stir in 3 tablespoons butter, melted. Pat crust mixture firmly into the bottom of prepared pan. Bake in the preheated oven for 7 to 8 minutes or until crust is firm. Cool in pan on a wire rack.

Per serving: 439 cal., 26 g total fat (16 g sat. fat), 77 mg chol., 142 mg sodium, 49 g carbo., 1 g fiber, 4 g pro.

**1** Carefully spread the softened peppermint ice cream over the fudge sauce.

**2** Put remaining fudge sauce in a resealable plastic bag. Snip a tiny hole in corner of bag; pipe sauce over ice cream. Spread evenly with a spatula.

**3** Spoon the Peppermint Whipped Cream over the top; spread evenly.

**Ask Mom** How do I chop chocolate? p. 33 / How do I make cookie crumbs? p. 128 / How do I measure butter? p. 55 / How do I measure sugar? p. 55 / How do I soften ice cream? p. 202 / What is a springform pan? p. 16, 17 / What is cocoa powder? p. 170 / What is evaporated milk? p. 24 / What is powdered sugar? p. 29 / What is unsweetened chocolate? p. 32 / What is vanilla? p. 128

**HOW FAR AHEAD CAN I MAKE THIS PIE?** Most ice cream pies—wrapped tightly in plastic and put in a 2-gallon freezer bag—can be stored in the freezer for up to 1 month. This one, because of the whipped-cream topping, can be made only up to 2 days ahead.

To make the Peppermint Whipped Cream, beat 1½ cups whipping cream in a chilled mixing bowl with an electric mixer on medium speed until stiff peaks form. Fold in ¼ cup crushed striped round peppermint candies (about 10).

**WHY DO I HAVE TO LET THE QUICHE STAND BEFORE CUTTING IT?** The 10-minute waiting period allows the custard to set and firm up as it cools slightly so that when you cut the quiche the wedges stay neat and the custard doesn't run.

This colorful quiche is a great dish to serve at a brunch or luncheon. With a crisp green salad, some crusty bread, and a glass of white wine, it makes a welcome Sunday evening supper too.

# Ham and Cheese Quiche

    1 recipe Baked Pastry Tart Shell (page 227)
½ cup shredded Italian cheese blend
½ cup finely chopped red sweet pepper
½ cup finely chopped smoked cooked ham
    1 tablespoon thinly sliced green onion or 1½ teaspoons snipped fresh chives
1½ teaspoons all-purpose flour
¼ teaspoon dried Italian seasoning, crushed
⅛ teaspoon salt
⅛ teaspoon ground black pepper
    4 eggs, lightly beaten
½ cup half-and-half, light cream, or milk

**1** Prepare Baked Pastry Tart Shell; set aside.

**2** Preheat oven to 325°F. In a medium bowl combine cheese, sweet pepper, ham, green onion, flour, Italian seasoning, salt, and pepper; pour into Baked Pastry Tart Shell.

**3** In the same bowl beat together eggs and half-and-half. Pour egg mixture over ham mixture in pastry shell. Bake for 25 to 30 minutes or until a knife inserted near the center comes out clean (photo 3, page 238). Let stand for 10 minutes before serving. Remove sides of tart pan (photo 8, page 259) Cut into wedges. Makes 8 servings.

**Per serving:** 243 cal., 15 g total fat (5 g sat. fat), 121 mg chol., 306 mg sodium, 17 g carbo., 1 g fiber, 7 g pro.

**Ingredient Info** Depending on the brand you buy, an Italian cheese blend is generally some combination of shredded mozzarella, provolone, Asiago, Parmesan, and Romano cheeses. You can buy a blend, or you can use ¼ cup each of any two of those cheeses in shredded form to make the ½ cup called for in the recipe.

**Ask Mom** How do I measure flour? p. 54 / How do I measure liquids? p. 55 / How do I seed and chop sweet peppers? p. 52 / How do I slice green onions? p. 51 / How do I snip fresh herbs? p. 49 / How do I work with eggs? p. 26–27 / What's that flour? p. 31

# Two-Cheese Vegetable Quiche

1 recipe Baked Pastry Shell (page 227)
½ cup shredded Swiss cheese (below)
½ cup shredded cheddar cheese (below)
½ cup shredded carrot
⅓ cup sliced green onion (3)
1 tablespoon all-purpose flour

4 eggs
1 10.75-ounce can condensed cream of broccoli soup
½ cup milk
⅛ teaspoon garlic powder
⅛ teaspoon ground black pepper

**1** Prepare Baked Pastry Shell; set aside.

**2** Preheat oven to 325°F. For filling, in a medium bowl toss together Swiss cheese, cheddar cheese, carrot, green onion, and flour; set aside. In a large bowl beat eggs with a fork. Stir in soup, milk, garlic powder, and pepper; stir in cheese mixture.

**3** Pour filling into Baked Pastry Shell (below). Bake in the preheated oven for 50 to 55 minutes or until a knife inserted near the center comes out clean (photo 3, page 238). If necessary, cover edge of crust with foil to prevent overbrowning (below). Let stand for 10 minutes before serving. Cut into wedges. Makes 6 servings.

**Per serving:** 375 cal., 23 g total fat (8 g sat. fat), 163 mg chol., 545 mg sodium, 29 g carbo., 2 g fiber, 11 g pro.

**1** Hold a cheese shredder over a piece of waxed paper and push the chunk of cheese downward.

**2** Carefully pour the quiche filling into the prebaked pastry shell.

**3** To protect the crust from getting too brown, loosely mold the foil over the edges (see page 240).

**Ask Mom** How do I measure liquids? p. 55 / How do I shred carrots? p. 48 / How do I slice green onions? p. 51 / What is garlic powder? p. 36 / Why do I have to let quiche stand before cutting it? p. 252

**2** Skill Level

# Triple Onion Appetizer Tart

½ of a 15-ounce package rolled refrigerated
   unbaked piecrusts (I crust)

¼ cup butter

1 Vidalia onion (or other sweet onion),
   halved and thinly sliced

1 large leek, halved lengthwise and thinly sliced

2 shallots, thinly sliced

1 teaspoon sugar

¾ teaspoon salt

½ teaspoon ground nutmeg

½ teaspoon ground black pepper

1 3-ounce package cream cheese, cubed
   and softened

¾ cup shredded Swiss cheese
   (photo I, page 254)

¾ cup shredded Monterey Jack cheese
   with jalapeño peppers
   (photo I, page 254)

3 eggs, lightly beaten

⅔ cup whipping cream

**1** Let refrigerated piecrust stand at room temperature according to package directions. Line a 9-inch pie plate with piecrust (photos 5–7, page 229); set aside.

**2** Preheat oven to 375°F. In a 12-inch skillet melt butter over medium heat; add onion, leek, shallot, sugar, salt, nutmeg, and pepper. Cook about 8 minutes or until vegetables are tender but not brown, stirring occasionally. Reduce heat; stir in cream cheese until melted. Stir in Swiss cheese and Monterey Jack cheese until combined.

**3** In a large bowl combine eggs and whipping cream. Gradually stir in onion mixture until combined. Pour onion mixture into pastry shell. Fold edge of crust over filling, pleating as necessary (photo 5, page 257).

**4** Bake in the preheated oven about 40 minutes or until crust and top are golden brown and a knife inserted near the center comes out clean (photo 3, page 238). Cool on a wire rack for 15 to 20 minutes; cut into wedges. Makes 16 appetizer servings.

Per serving: 203 cal., 16 g total fat (9 g sat. fat), 79 mg chol., 256 mg sodium, 10 g carbo., 0 g fiber, 5 g pro.

> Be sure you use a Vidalia, Walla Walla, or some other sweet yellow onion in this tart. White onions have their uses, but they have a harsher flavor that can overtake everything else in the dish.

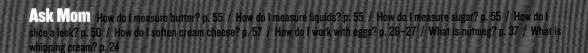

**Ask Mom** How do I measure butter? p. 55 / How do I measure liquids? p. 55 / How do I measure sugar? p. 55 / How do I slice a leek? p. 50 / How do I soften cream cheese? p. 57 / How do I work with eggs? p. 26–27 / What is nutmeg? p. 37 / What is whipping cream? p. 24

# Winter Vegetable Tarts with
# Bacon and Goat Cheese

7½ cups winter vegetables, peeled, seeded as necessary,
and cut into bite-size pieces (such as butternut squash,
sweet potatoes, red onions, potatoes, parsnips, carrots,
turnips, and/or rutabagas)

4 slices thick-sliced bacon, cut into 1-inch pieces

3 tablespoons olive oil or cooking oil

2 tablespoons snipped fresh thyme

1 cup crumbled goat cheese (4 ounces)

1 tablespoon balsamic vinegar

4 cloves garlic, minced

1 15-ounce package rolled refrigerated
unbaked piecrusts (2 crusts)

Fresh thyme sprigs (optional)

**1** In a very large bowl toss prepared vegetables with bacon, 2 tablespoons of the oil, thyme, ¼ teaspoon *salt*, and ¼ teaspoon *ground black pepper*; spread evenly in a 15×10×1-inch baking pan. Set baking pan on the lowest oven rack of a cold oven. Turn oven to 425°F. Roast vegetables about 35 minutes or until golden brown and tender, stirring every 10 minutes. Remove vegetables from oven; stir in ¾ cup of the goat cheese, vinegar, and garlic (photo 1, page 257). Set vegetable mixture aside. Leave oven on; adjust oven racks to lower-middle and upper positions.

**2** Meanwhile, let refrigerated piecrusts stand at room temperature according to package directions. Line 2 baking sheets with parchment paper; set aside.

**3** Roll one of the piecrusts into a 12- to 13-inch square (photo 2, page 257); cut into 4 squares (photo 3, page 257). Arrange pastry squares on 1 of the prepared baking sheets (crusts may touch). Repeat with remaining piecrust, placing remaining pastry squares on second prepared baking sheet. Spoon vegetable mixture into center of each dough square, leaving about a 1-inch border (photo 4, page 257). Fold pastry over vegetable mixture (photo 5, page 257). Sprinkle exposed vegetable mixture with the remaining ¼ cup goat cheese.

**4** Bake in the preheated oven about 20 minutes or until tarts are golden brown, rotating baking sheets between oven racks after 10 minutes. Drizzle with the remaining 1 tablespoon oil. Serve warm. If desired, garnish with thyme sprigs. Makes 8 tarts.

Make-ahead directions: Prepare as directed through Step 4. Let cool on wire racks, uncovered, for up to 2 hours. Preheat oven to 300°F. Reheat tarts in preheated oven about 10 minutes or until warm.

**Per tart:** 479 cal., 31 g total fat (11 g sat. fat), 24 mg chol., 517 mg sodium, 43 g carbo., 3 g fiber, 7 g pro.

## WHAT KIND OF GOAT CHEESE SHOULD I USE?
Goat cheese (also called chèvre, French for "goat") ranges in texture from moist and creamy to dry and semifirm, depending on how long it's aged. A medium-texture cheese will crumble most easily for use in this recipe.

**Ask Mom** How do I crumble cheese? p. 195, 335 / How do I mince garlic? p. 21 / How do I snip fresh herbs? p. 49 / How do I use a rolling pin? p. 61, 228 / What is cooking oil? p. 28

1  After roasting the vegetables, gently stir in goat cheese, vinegar, and garlic.

2  Roll the piecrusts out into 12- to 13-inch squares (they don't have to be perfect squares).

3  Use a sharp knife to cut each piecrust into 4 squares.

5  Fold the pastry up over the vegetable mixture, pleating and tucking as you go.

4  Spoon some of the vegetable mixture onto each square; leave a 1-inch border around the perimeter.

# Key Lime **Tart**

l recipe Coconut-Macadamia Nut Pastry

4 egg yolks

l 14-ounce can sweetened condensed milk

l teaspoon finely shredded lime peel

½ cup lime juice (10 to 12 key limes or 4 to 6 Persian limes) or bottled key lime juice

Few drops green food coloring (optional)

l recipe Sweetened Whipped Cream (page 25)

Toasted coconut (optional)

Chopped macadamia nuts (optional)

**1** Prepare Coconut-Macadamia Nut Pastry. Preheat oven to 450°F. On a lightly floured surface, roll pastry from center to edges into a circle about 12 inches in diameter. Transfer pastry to a 10-inch tart pan that has a removable bottom (photo 1, page 259). Press pastry into fluted sides of tart pan (photo 2, page 259); trim edges (photo 3, page 259). Prick pastry with a fork (photo 5, page 259). Line pastry with a double thickness of foil (photo 12, page 229), letting foil hang over the edges of the pan to cover the edges of the crust. Bake in the preheated oven for 8 minutes. Remove foil. Bake for 6 to 8 minutes more or until golden. Cool on a wire rack. Reduce oven temperature to 350°F.

**2** For filling, in a medium bowl beat egg yolks with a wire whisk or fork. Gradually whisk in sweetened condensed milk (photo 6, page 259); add lime peel, lime juice, and, if desired, food coloring. Mix well (mixture will thicken slightly).

**3** Pour filling into baked tart shell (photo 7, page 259). Place on a baking sheet. To prevent over-browning, cover edges of pastry with foil (photos 1–3, page 240). Bake for 15 to 20 minutes or until set. Remove foil. Cool on a wire rack for 1 hour. Chill for 2 to 3 hours before serving.

**4** To serve, remove sides of tart pan (photo 8, page 259); cut into wedges. Top with Sweetened Whipped Cream, and, if desired, coconut and macadamia nuts. Makes 8 servings.

Coconut-Macadamia Nut Pastry: In a medium bowl stir together 1¼ cups all-purpose flour and ¼ cup sugar. Using a pastry blender, cut in ½ cup cold butter until pieces are pea size. Stir in ¼ cup finely chopped coconut, toasted, and 2 tablespoons finely chopped macadamia nuts. In a small bowl whisk together 2 egg yolks and 1 tablespoon cold water. Gradually stir egg yolk mixture into flour mixture. Using your fingers, gently knead pastry just until a ball forms. Wrap pastry in plastic wrap; chill for 30 to 60 minutes or until pastry is easy to handle.

Make-ahead directions: Prepare as above through Step 3. Cover and chill for up to 2 days. Continue as directed in Step 4.

Per serving: 540 cal., 33 g total fat (19 g sat. fat), 236 mg chol., 175 mg sodium, 55 g carbo., 2 g fiber, 8 g pro.

Ingredient Info Despite their diminutive size, key limes actually pack more punch than their larger, more commonly available cousins—Persian limes. Key limes are about the size of a walnut and are more tart, bitter, and intensely flavored than Persian limes. Either kind works fine in this recipe, but if you can find them, key limes will give your tart a more authentic Floridian flavor.

**Ask Mom** How do I measure/cut in butter? p. 55–56 / How do I juice a lime? p. 44, 45 / How do I measure flour? p. 54 / How do I shred lime peel? p. 45, 105 / How do I store pie? p. 68 / How do I toast coconut? p. 40 / How do I use a rolling pin? p. 61, 228 / How do I work with eggs? p. 26–27 / What are key limes? p. 258 / What is a lightly floured surface? p. 60 / What is a tart pan? p. 16, 259 / What is sweetened condensed milk? p. 24 / What's that flour? p. 31 / What's that nut? p. 34–35

**WHY DOES THE BOTTOM OF THE PAN NEED TO BE REMOVABLE?** Mostly it's for serving and presentation. Unlike a deep and slant-sided pie pan, a tart pan is straight-sided and shallow—which makes it difficult to cut the tart if it remains in the pan.

**1** Gently ease the pastry circle into the tart pan without stretching it.

**2** Press the pastry into the fluted sides of the pan.

**3** Trim the excess pastry by pressing through it along the top edges of the pan.

**4** If the tender pastry tears, patch it with a pastry scrap. Moisten the underside of the scrap with a little water so it stays in place.

**5** Prick the bottom and sides of the pastry generously with a fork to prevent it from shrinking while it bakes.

**6** Use a wire whisk to stir the sweetened condensed milk into the beaten egg yolks.

**7** Carefully pour the filling into the baked tart shell.

**8** To remove the sides of the tart pan, place the tart on a can and let the sides drop to the counter.

# Brown Butter Tart

| | |
|---|---|
| 1 recipe Rich Tart Pastry | 1 vanilla bean, split lengthwise, or 1 teaspoon vanilla |
| 3 eggs | ¾ cup butter |
| 1¼ cups sugar | 3 cups assorted mixed berries or assorted cut-up fresh fruit |
| ½ cup all-purpose flour | |

**1** Prepare Rich Tart Pastry. On a lightly floured surface, roll pastry from center to edges into a circle about 12 inches in diameter (photo 4, page 228). Transfer pastry to a 10-inch tart pan that has a removable bottom (photo 1, page 259). Press pastry into fluted sides of tart pan (photo 2, page 259); trim edges (photo 3, page 259). Set aside.

**2** Preheat oven to 350°F. For filling, in a large bowl lightly beat eggs with a fork. Stir in sugar, flour, and, if using, liquid vanilla; set aside.

**3** In a medium heavy saucepan combine the vanilla bean, if using, and butter (below). Cook over medium-high heat until the butter turns the color of light brown sugar (below). Remove pan from heat; remove and discard vanilla bean. Slowly add the butter to the egg mixture, stirring until combined. Pour filling into pastry-lined tart pan. Bake in the preheated oven about 35 minutes or until top is crisp and golden. Cool on a wire rack for 1 to 2 hours. Cover and chill within 2 hours.

**4** To serve, remove sides of tart pan (photo 8, page 259); cut into wedges. Serve with berries and, if desired, whipped cream. Makes 12 servings.

Rich Tart Pastry: In a medium bowl stir together 1¼ cups all-purpose flour and ¼ cup sugar. Using a pastry blender, cut in ½ cup cold butter until pieces are pea size. In a small bowl whisk together 2 egg yolks and 1 tablespoon cold water. Gradually stir egg yolk mixture into flour mixture. Using your fingers, gently knead pastry just until a ball forms. If necessary, cover with plastic wrap and chill for 30 to 60 minutes or until pastry is easy to handle.

Per serving: 365 cal., 2 g total fat (13 g sat. fat), 138 mg chol., 156 mg sodium, 40 g carbo., 3 g fiber, 4 g pro.

**1** Place the butter in a heavy saucepan. Stir constantly as the butter heats.

**2** Continue to stir as the butter becomes light brown in color and has a nutty aroma.

**Ask Mom** How do I cut in butter/? p. 56 / How do I measure butter? p. 55 / How do I measure flour? p. 54 / How do I measure sugar? p. 55 / How do I wash fresh berries? p. 42 / What is a lightly floured surface? p. 60 / What is a pastry blender? p. 10, 11 / What is a tart pan? p. 16, 259 / What is a vanilla bean? p. 69, 220 / What is vanilla? p. 128 / What's that flour? p. 31

# Peach-Almond **Tart**

| | |
|---|---|
| 1 recipe Almond Pastry | 1 cup fresh raspberries |
| ¾ cup almond paste | 3 tablespoons apricot jam |
| 1 egg white, lightly beaten | 2 tablespoons sliced almonds |
| ½ cup packed brown sugar or granulated sugar | Milk |
| 2 cups peeled sliced fresh peaches or sliced fresh apricots | Coarse sugar (optional) |

**1** Prepare Almond Pastry. On a lightly floured surface, roll two-thirds of the pastry from center to edges into a circle about 12 inches in diameter (photo 4, page 228). Transfer pastry to an 11-inch tart pan that has a removable bottom (photo 1, page 259). Press pastry into fluted sides of tart pan (photo 2, page 259); trim edges (photo 3, page 259). Roll remaining pastry to ⅛-inch thickness; cut into ½-inch-wide strips (photo 1, page 236).

**2** Preheat oven to 375°F. In a small bowl crumble almond paste; stir in egg white and brown sugar. Spread or gently pat into bottom of pastry-lined tart pan. In a bowl toss together peaches, raspberries, and jam. Spoon fruit mixture into tart pan; sprinkle with almonds.

**3** Weave pastry strips in a lattice pattern (photo 2, page 236). Press ends of strips against the pan to seal. Lightly brush pastry strips with milk, and, if desired, sprinkle with coarse sugar (photos 2–3, page 234).

**4** Bake in the preheated oven about 1 hour or until crust is golden. Cool on a wire rack for 30 to 60 minutes. To serve, remove sides of tart pan (photo 8, page 259); cut into wedges. Makes 8 servings.

**Almond Pastry:** In a medium bowl stir together 2 cups all-purpose flour, ½ cup ground almonds, 1 tablespoon sugar, and ½ teaspoon salt. Using a pastry blender, cut in ¾ cup cold butter and 3 tablespoons shortening until pieces are pea size (photo 1, page 228). Sprinkle 1 tablespoon cold water over part of the flour mixture; gently toss with a fork. Push moistened pastry to the side of the bowl. Repeat moistening flour mixture, using 1 tablespoon water at a time (about 4 tablespoons more), until all of the flour mixture is moistened (photo 2, page 228). Using your fingers, gently knead pastry just until a ball forms. Flatten pastry into a disc. Wrap pastry in plastic wrap; chill for 2 to 24 hours or until pastry is easy to handle.

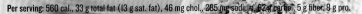

Per serving: 560 cal., 33 g total fat (13 g sat. fat), 46 mg chol., 285 mg sodium, 62 g carbo, 5 g fiber, 8 g pro.

**Ask Mom** How do I cut in butter? p. 56 / How do I grind nuts? p. 34 / How do I measure flour? p. 54 / How do I measure sugar? p. 55 / How do I peel peaches? p. 43 / How do I wash fresh berries? p. 42 / How do I work with eggs? p. 26–27 / What is a lightly floured surface? p. 60 / What is a pastry blender? p. 10, 11 / What is almond paste? p. 69, 288 / What is coarse sugar? p. 29 / What is granulated sugar? p. 29 / What's that flour? p. 31 / What's that nut? p. 34–35

# Dried Pear and Chocolate-Caramel Tart

½ of a 15-ounce package rolled refrigerated unbaked piecrusts (1 crust)

4 3-ounce packages dried pears, cut into ¼-inch-wide strips

1 12-ounce can pear nectar

2 tablespoons packed brown sugar

½ teaspoon ground cinnamon

¼ teaspoon ground nutmeg

1 recipe Crumb Topping

1 ounce bittersweet or semisweet chocolate, coarsely chopped

⅓ cup caramel-flavor ice cream topping

**1** Preheat oven to 450°F. Let refrigerated piecrust stand at room temperature according to package directions. Transfer piecrust to a 9-inch tart pan that has a removable bottom (photo 1, page 259). Press pastry into fluted sides of tart pan (photo 2, page 259); trim pastry even with rim of pan (photo 3, page 259). Line unpricked pastry with a double thickness of foil (photo 12, page 229). Bake in the preheated oven for 8 minutes. Remove foil. Bake for 2 to 3 minutes more or until golden. Cool on a wire rack. Reduce oven temperature to 375°F.

**2** Meanwhile, in a medium saucepan combine dried pears and pear nectar. Bring to boiling; reduce heat. Simmer, covered, for 5 minutes. Stir in brown sugar, cinnamon, and nutmeg. Simmer, uncovered, for 5 to 8 minutes more or until mixture is thickened. Spoon pear mixture evenly into baked tart shell; sprinkle with Crumb Topping.

**3** Bake about 30 minutes or until topping is golden brown. Cool on a wire rack for 20 minutes; sprinkle with chocolate. Cool completely.

**4** To serve, remove sides of tart pan (photo 8, page 259). Cut into wedges; drizzle each serving with ice cream topping. Makes 8 servings.

Crumb Topping: In a small bowl combine ½ cup rolled oats, ½ cup packed brown sugar, and ¼ teaspoon salt. Using a pastry blender, cut in ⅓ cup cold butter until mixture resembles coarse crumbs.

Per serving: 460 cal., 17 g total fat (8 g sat. fat), 23 mg chol., 292 mg sodium, 81 g carbo., 4 g fiber, 3 g pro.

**Ask Mom** Can I use quick-cooking oats instead of regular rolled oats? p. 351 / How do I chop chocolate? p. 33 / How do I cut in butter/shortening? p. 56 / How do I measure sugar? p. 55 / What does drizzle mean? p. 69, 85 / What is a pastry blender? p. 10, 11 / What is a tart pan? p. 16, 259 / What is cinnamon? p. 36 / What is nutmeg? p. 37 / What is semisweet/bittersweet chocolate? p. 32

# pastry shop
# SPECIALTIES

**With a few simple recipes for cream puffs and a few clever tricks with prepared phyllo, you'll be turning out treats that look and taste like they were made by a pro.**

9

Apple Dumpling Roll-Ups ① .................................... 286

## CREAM PUFFS
Chocolate Cream Puffs ① ............................. 265
Cream Puffs ① ....................................... 265
Manchego Cheese Appetizer Puffs ① .................. 270

Croissants, Easy Chocolate-Almond ② ...................... 288

How do I make cream puffs?............................266–267

## MINI PUFFS
Blue Cheese & Pear Mini Puffs ① ........................ 268
Chicken Salad Mini Puffs ① ............................ 269
Chocolate-Strawberry Mini Puffs ① ..................... 269
Crab Salad Mini Puffs ① .............................. 268
Fruit Sorbet Mini Puffs ① ............................ 268
Ice Cream Mini Puffs ① ............................... 268
Mini Puffs ① ......................................... 265
Salad Mini Puffs ① ................................... 269
Scrambled Egg Mini Puffs ① ........................... 269
Smoked Salmon Mini Puffs ① ........................... 269
Southwestern Mini Puffs ① ............................ 268
Spinach-Artichoke Mini Puffs ① ....................... 268
Tropical Mini Puffs ① ................................ 269

## PHYLLO PASTRIES
Creamy Pumpkin Strudels ③ .......................... 283
Fresh Berry Napoleons ② .............................280
Mushroom-Cheese Appetizer Bundles ③ ................ 284
Pistachio-Apricot Cups ② ............................ 279
Spinach and Feta Phyllo Triangles ② ................... 285

## PUFF PASTRIES
Brie en Croûte with Apricots and Almonds ② ............ 276
Brie en Croûte with Cherries and Pecans ② ............. 276
Lemon-Pistachio Bites ① ...............................271
Raspberry Danish Rosettes ③ ......................... 272
Spinach-Prosciutto Palmiers ③ ....................... 278
White Chocolate and Berries Dessert Pastries ③ ......... 275

**1** Skill Level

# Cream **Puffs**

  1 cup water
  ½ cup butter
  ⅛ teaspoon salt
  1 cup all-purpose flour
  4 eggs
  3 cups whipped cream, pudding, or ice cream
   Cocoa powder or powdered sugar (optional)

**1** Preheat oven to 400°F. Lightly grease a baking sheet; set aside.

**2** In a medium saucepan combine water, butter, and salt. Bring to boiling. Add flour all at once, stirring vigorously (photos 1–2, page 266). Cook and stir until mixture forms a ball (photo 3, page 266). Remove from heat. Cool for 10 minutes.

**3** Add eggs, one at a time, beating well with a wooden spoon after each addition (photos 4–5, page 266).

**4** Drop dough into 12 mounds onto prepared baking sheet (photo 6, page 266). Bake in the preheated oven for 30 to 35 minutes or until golden brown and firm. Transfer cream puffs to a wire rack; let cool.

**5** Cut off the top one-third of each cream puff (photo 7, page 266); remove soft dough from inside (photo 8, page 266). Fill with whipped cream. Replace tops. If desired, sift cocoa powder over tops (page 267). Makes 12 cream puffs.

Per cream puff: 238 cal., 21 g total fat (12 g sat. fat), 134 mg chol., 140 mg sodium, 9 g carbo., 0 g fiber, 4 g pro.

Chocolate Cream Puffs: Prepare as above, except add 2 tablespoons sugar to the saucepan with the water, butter, and salt. Stir 3 tablespoons unsweetened cocoa powder into the flour before adding the flour to the butter mixture.

Mini Puffs: Prepare as above, except drop dough by rounded teaspoons 2 inches apart onto one of two prepared baking sheets. Bake one sheet at a time in a 400°F oven about 25 minutes or until golden brown and firm (keep remaining dough covered while first batch bakes). Cool, split, and fill as in Steps 4 and 5. Makes about 30 mini puffs.

Good to Know It's crucial to let the cooked dough cool exactly 10 minutes before adding the eggs so that it's just the right temperature. If it's too hot, the eggs will cook in the dough, creating lumps of "scrambled" eggs. If it's too cold, the eggs won't incorporate into the dough. After beating in the eggs, the dough will be sticky and glossy—perfect for making cream puffs.

# How do I make cream puffs?

Although they sound fussy (in French, they're *choux à la pâtisserie*), they're not difficult to make if you use a precise method. Your friends will be so impressed.

Perfect cream puffs are crisp, tender, airy pillows of pastry. Achieving those results depends on a few key factors. One: Add the flour all at once to the water-butter mixture as soon as it is at a rolling boil so that the starch swells and soaks up all of the liquid. This gives the dough the structure it needs to puff up. Two: Use large eggs and add them one at a time after cooling the cooked dough for 10 minutes. Three: Be sure the puffs are golden brown, firm, and dry before you take them out of the oven. You will be rewarded with supreme satisfaction (you're a French pastry chef!). One of the coolest things about cream puffs is that they can be a vessel for sweet or savory fillings. See pages 268–269 for some great ideas.

**1** As soon as the butter melts and the water boils, add the flour all at once. (Leave saucepan on heat.)

**2** Vigorously stir in the flour with a wooden spoon.

**3** Cook and stir until the mixture forms a ball that doesn't separate. Remove saucepan from heat.

**4** After cooling the dough 10 minutes, add the eggs, one at a time.

**5** After adding each egg, beat the dough until it becomes thick, smooth, and slightly sticky.

**6** Drop dough onto the greased baking sheet. For evenly shaped puffs, avoid going back and adding more dough to the mounds.

**7** Once the puffs are cool enough to handle, use a serrated knife to cut the top one-third off each puff with a gentle sawing motion.

**8** Use a fork to carefully remove the moist, soft dough from inside each cream puff.

## How do I dust with powdered sugar?

A fine-mesh sieve is the perfect tool for sifting powdered sugar, cocoa powder, and spices such as cinnamon (or any combination of the three) over the top of baked goods for decoration and a little added flavor or sweetness. Just place whatever you're sifting in the sieve, then move it over the baked goods evenly, gently tapping the side of the sieve as you go.

If you prefer a clean serving platter, dust the cream puffs before you place them on it. Dusting them on the platter creates a pretty effect, though—rings of cocoa powder or powdered sugar around each puff.

## Crab Salad Mini Puffs

Purchased crab salad

Prepare Mini Puffs (page 265) as directed. Spoon about 1 tablespoon crab salad into the bottom of each puff; replace tops.

## Blue Cheese & Pears Mini Puffs

Chopped pears
Crumbled blue cheese
Chopped walnuts, toasted
Honey

Prepare Mini Puffs (page 265) as directed. Combine desired amounts of pears, blue cheese, and walnuts. Spoon about 1 tablespoon of the pear mixture into the bottom of each puff. Replace tops; drizzle with honey.

## Fruit Sorbet Mini Puffs

Raspberry, mango, and/or lemon sorbet

Prepare Mini Puffs (page 265) as directed. Spoon or scoop desired fruit sorbet into the bottom of each puff; replace tops.

## Spinach-Artichoke Mini-Puffs

Purchased spinach-artichoke dip, warmed
Chopped roasted red sweet peppers, drained

Prepare Mini Puffs (page 265) as directed. Spoon about 1 tablespoon spinach-artichoke dip into the bottom of each puff; top with roasted sweet pepper pieces. Replace tops.

## Ice Cream Mini Puffs

Coffee ice cream or your favorite ice cream
Purchased or homemade hot fudge sauce, warmed

Prepare Mini Puffs (page 265) as directed. Spoon or scoop ice cream into the bottom of each puff; replace tops. Drizzle hot fudge sauce over the tops.

## Southwestern Mini Puffs

Chopped grape tomatoes
Chopped avocado
Snipped fresh cilantro
Fresh lime wedges

Prepare Mini Puffs (page 265) as directed. Combine desired amounts of tomatoes, avocado, and cilantro; drizzle with a squeeze of lime. Spoon desired amount into bottom of each puff; replace tops.

## Scrambled Egg Mini Puffs

1 recipe Mini Puffs
Scrambled eggs
Salsa
Crumbled cooked bacon

Prepare Mini Puffs (page 265) as directed. Spoon about 1 tablespoon scrambled eggs into the bottom of each puff. Top with salsa; sprinkle with bacon. Replace tops.

## Smoked Salmon Mini Puffs

Tub-style cream cheese with chives and onion
Thinly sliced smoked salmon
Fresh dill sprigs

Prepare Mini Puffs (page 265) as directed. Pipe or spoon about 1 tablespoon cream cheese into bottom of each puff; top with a piece of salmon and a sprig of dill. Replace tops.

## Tropical Mini Puffs

Chopped fresh pineapple
Chopped macadamia nuts, toasted
Shredded coconut, toasted
Caramel-flavor ice cream topping, warmed

Prepare Mini Puffs (page 265) as directed. Combine desired amounts of pineapple, nuts, and coconut; spoon into bottom of each puff. Replace tops; drizzle with topping.

## Chocolate-Strawberry Mini Puffs

Prepared chocolate mousse or chocolate pudding
Coarsely chopped fresh strawberries

Prepare Mini Puffs (page 265) as directed. Spoon about 1 tablespoon chocolate mousse into the bottom of each puff; replace tops. Serve with strawberries.

## Salad Mini Puffs

Grated Parmesan cheese
Baby salad greens
Vinaigrette salad dressing
Sunflower seeds, toasted
Shredded Parmesan cheese

Prepared Mini Puffs (page 265) as directed, except before baking sprinkle with grated Parmesan cheese. Combine desired amounts of salad greens, salad dressing, sunflower seeds, and shredded Parmesan cheese. Fill bottoms of each puff with salad mixture; replace tops.

## Chicken Salad Mini Puffs

Purchased curried or regular chicken salad

Prepare Mini Puffs (page 265) as directed. Spoon about 1 tablespoon chicken salad into bottom of each puff; replace tops.

# Manchego Cheese Appetizer Puffs

¾ cup water

⅓ cup butter

¼ teaspoon garlic salt

⅛ teaspoon ground nutmeg

¾ cup all-purpose flour

3 eggs

¾ cup finely shredded Manchego cheese (3 ounces)

½ cup finely snipped dried apricots or ½ cup finely chopped membrillo (quince paste)

**1** Preheat oven to 400°F. Lightly grease two large baking sheets; set aside.

**2** In a medium saucepan combine water, butter, garlic salt, and nutmeg. Bring to boiling. Add flour all at once, stirring vigorously (photos 1–2, page 266). Cook and stir until mixture forms a ball (photo 3, page 266). Remove from heat. Cool for 10 minutes.

**3** Add eggs, one at a time, beating well with a wooden spoon after each addition (photos 4–5, page 266). Stir in ½ cup of the cheese and the apricots.

**4** Place dough in a pastry bag fitted with a large star tip. Pipe dough (about 1 tablespoon each) into 40 mounds onto prepared baking sheets. (Or drop dough by small spoonfuls onto prepared baking sheets [photo 6, page 266].) Sprinkle with the remaining ¼ cup cheese.

**5** Bake in the preheated oven on separate oven racks for 16 to 18 minutes or until golden brown, rotating baking sheets between oven racks halfway through baking. Serve warm. Makes 40 puffs.

**Make-ahead directions:** Prepare as above through Step 4. Freeze dough mounds on baking sheets about 1 hour or until firm. Transfer to a covered freezer container. Freeze for up to 1 month. To bake, preheat oven to 400°F. Arrange frozen dough mounds on greased baking sheets. Bake in the preheated oven for 18 to 20 minutes or until golden brown.

**Per puff:** 38 cal., 2 g total fat (I g sat. fat), 21 mg chol., 51 mg sodium, 3 g carbo., 0 g fiber, I g pro.

## What is Manchego cheese?

As Parmigiano-Reggiano is to Italy, Manchego is to Spain—its defining and most famous cheese. Manchego is a semifirm sheep's milk cheese, made exclusively from the milk of Manchego sheep that nibble on grasses from the plains of La Mancha. It is most commonly available in two forms: curado, aged 3 to 6 months, and viejo, aged for I year. The longer it's aged, the stronger the flavor—which is rich, mellow, slightly salty, and a little piquant. It's a great snacking cheese and melts beautifully.

**Ask Mom** How do I fill a pastry bag? p. 66 / How do I grease a baking pan? p. 59 / How do I measure butter? p. 55 / How do I measure flour? p. 54 / How do I measure liquids? p. 55 / How do I shred cheese? p. 21, 254 / How do I snip dried fruit or preserves? p. 41, 102 / What is nutmeg? p. 37 / What's that dried fruit? p. 41 / What's that flour? p. 31

1 Skill Level

**Ingredient Info** Crème fraîche is a very thick French version of sour cream. It's available in the specialty dairy section of most supermarkets. If you can't find it, you can substitute sour cream, as long as it's regular, not reduced-fat.

# Lemon-Pistachio **Bites**

½ of a 17.3-ounce package frozen puff pastry (1 sheet), thawed

⅓ cup purchased lemon curd

¼ cup purchased crème fraîche

¼ teaspoon finely shredded lemon peel

1 tablespoon finely chopped pistachio nuts

**1** Preheat oven to 400°F. Line a baking sheet with parchment paper; set aside.

**2** Unfold puff pastry; flatten and smooth the pastry sheet (photo 1, page 272). Cut puff pastry sheet crosswise and lengthwise into sixths to make thirty-six 1½-inch squares (below). Place squares 1 inch apart on prepared baking sheet.

**3** Bake in the preheated oven for 13 to 15 minutes or until pastry is puffed and golden brown. Remove pastry shells from baking sheet. Cool completely on wire racks.

**4** Hollow out a small circle in the center of each cooled pastry shell, leaving the bottom of the shell intact (below). For filling, in a small bowl combine lemon curd, crème fraîche, and lemon peel.

**5** Just before serving, transfer filling to a small resealable plastic bag. Seal bag and snip off a small corner. Pipe about ¾ teaspoon of the filling into each pastry shell (below). Sprinkle nuts over filled pastries (below). Makes 36 bites.

**Make-ahead directions:** Prepare as above through Step 3. Place shells in a covered airtight container. Store at room temperature for 24 hours or freeze for up to 3 months. If frozen, thaw pastry shells at room temperature before filling.

**Per bite:** 47 cal., 3 g total fat (0 g sat. fat), 4 mg chol., 30 mg sodium, 5 g carbo., 0 g fiber, 0 g pro.

**1** Using a fluted pastry wheel or sharp knife, cut the pastry sheet crosswise into six strips, then lengthwise into six strips.

**2** Using a ¼-teaspoon measuring spoon or a small melon baller, scoop out the center of each pastry shell, leaving the bottom intact.

**3** Squeeze the plastic bag, pushing the filling through the hole into each pastry shell.

**4** Finish the pastries by sprinkling each one with chopped pistachio nuts.

**③ Skill Level**

# Raspberry Danish **Rosettes**

½ of a 17.3-ounce package frozen puff pastry (1 sheet), thawed

3 tablespoons seedless raspberry jam

Coarsely chopped almonds or pistachio nuts

**1** Preheat oven to 400°F. On a lightly floured surface, unfold thawed puff pastry; flatten and smooth the pastry sheet (below).

**2** Cut pastry into 12 equal strips (below). Roll up one end (about 1½ inches) of one of the strips (below). Hold the coiled part upright (below). Twist and wrap the rest of the dough strip around the coiled center (below). Tuck end of strip under the rosette (below). Repeat with remaining pastry strips. Place rosettes 1½ inches apart on an ungreased baking sheet (below).

**3** Bake in the preheated oven about 15 minutes or until golden brown. Remove from oven. Brush rosettes with jam (below); sprinkle with nuts. Cool slightly on a wire rack; serve warm. Makes 12 rosettes.

**Per rosette:** 120 cal., 8 g total fat (0 g sat. fat), 0 mg chol., 90 mg sodium, 12 g carbo., 0 g fiber, 1 g pro.

**①** Use a rolling pin to lightly roll out the creases in the sheet of puff pastry.

**②** Use a pizza cutter to cut the pastry sheet into 12 strips.

**③** Roll up the first 1½ inches of each strip.

**④** Hold the rolled part upright so the rest of the dough strip is on its side.

**⑤** Twist and wrap the rest of the dough strip around the coiled center to make a rosette.

**⑥** Tuck the end of the dough strip under the finished rosette.

**⑦** Arrange the rosettes on an ungreased baking sheet.

**⑧** Use a pastry brush to brush the warm rosettes with raspberry jam.

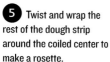
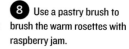

**WHAT'S PUFF PASTRY?** It's a buttery, flaky, multilayered pastry that has multiple uses, including croissants, Napoleons, and as a wrapping for cheese such as baked Brie. It comes prepared (lucky you!). Look for it in the freezer case of your supermarket.

These delightful little bites can easily change flavor. Try brushing them with different kinds of jam—strawberry, peach, and apricot—and even orange marmalade.

# HOW DO I SPLIT THE PASTRY FOR FILLING? The best way to split the baked pastries is with the tines of a fork. If you try to use a knife, you'll likely crush the pastry rather than split it neatly.

You can assemble these dessert pastries ahead of time but not too far ahead. Let them chill for no more than an hour or they'll get soggy. If you're in a real time pinch, you can use a box of white chocolate pudding for the filling .

# White Chocolate and
# Berries Dessert Pastries

½ cup sugar

2 tablespoons cornstarch or ¼ cup all-purpose flour

2 cups milk

4 egg yolks, lightly beaten

4 ounces white baking chocolate or white-flavored candy coating, chopped

2 teaspoons butter

½ of a 17.3-ounce package frozen puff pastry (1 sheet), thawed

2 cups fresh berries (such as raspberries, blueberries, and/or sliced strawberries)

Powdered sugar (optional)

**1** For filling, in a medium heavy saucepan stir together sugar and cornstarch. Stir in milk. Cook and stir over medium heat until bubbly. Cook and stir for 2 minutes more. Remove saucepan from heat. Gradually stir half of the milk mixture into the beaten egg yolks. Return egg yolk mixture to saucepan. Bring to a gentle boil; reduce heat. Cook and stir for 2 minutes more. Remove saucepan from heat; add white chocolate and butter, stirring until melted. Pour filling into a medium bowl; cover surface with plastic wrap. Chill for at least 2 hours or for up to 24 hours. (Do not stir during chilling.)

**2** Preheat oven to 425°F. On a lightly floured surface, unfold puff pastry. Using a sharp knife, cut pastry along creases into thirds; cut each third crosswise to make a total of 6 rectangles.

**3** Transfer pastry rectangles to an ungreased baking sheet. Bake in the preheated oven about 10 minutes or until golden brown. Remove from baking sheet; cool on a wire rack.

**4** To assemble, split pastry rectangles in half horizontally. Place pastry bottoms on dessert plates. Spoon filling and berries over pastry bottoms. Top with pastry tops. If desired, cover and chill for up to 1 hour. If desired, sift powdered sugar over the top just before serving (page 267). Makes 6 pastries.

**Make-ahead directions:** Prepare as above through Step 3. Place pastries in a covered airtight container. Store at room temperature for up to 24 hours.

Per pastry: 474 cal., 25 g total fat (7 g sat. fat), 153 mg chol., 222 mg sodium, 55 g carbo., 2 g fiber, 8 g pro.

**Good to Know** The white chocolate filling for these pastries has to be made at least 2 hours (and up to 24 hours) ahead and then chilled. To keep the filling from forming a "skin" on its surface during chilling, put the plastic wrap directly on the surface of the filling. A little bit of it will stick to the plastic—but that's better than having it form a film.

**Ask Mom** How do I add egg yolks to a hot filling? p. 247 / How do I dust with powdered sugar? p. 267 / How do I measure butter? p. 55 / How do I measure flour? p. 54 / How do I measure liquids? p. 55 / How do I measure sugar? p. 55 / How do I wash fresh berries? p. 42 / How do I work with eggs? p. 26–27 / What is a lightly floured surface? p. 60 / What is candy coating? p. 32 / What is powdered sugar? p. 29 / What is puff pastry? p. 273 / What is white chocolate? p. 32 / What's that flour? p. 31

# Brie en Croûte with
# Cherries and Pecans

½ of a 17.3-ounce package frozen puff pastry (1 sheet), thawed

½ cup chopped pecans

⅓ cup snipped dried tart cherries

2 tablespoons honey

2 4.5-ounce rounds Brie cheese

1 egg, lightly beaten

1 tablespoon water

Apple slices, pear slices, and/or seedless grapes

**1** Preheat oven to 375°F. Line a baking sheet with parchment paper; set aside. On a lightly floured surface, unfold puff pastry; flatten and smooth the pastry sheet (photo 1, page 272). Roll pastry into a 16×10-inch rectangle. Cut two 8-inch circles from pastry rectangle (photo 1, page 277); set trimmings aside.

**2** In a small bowl combine pecans, dried cherries, and honey. Divide cherry mixture between the 2 pastry circles (photo 2, page 277). Place 1 cheese round on top of each cherry mixture, pressing down to spread cherry mixture (photo 3, page 277). Bring pastry up around cheese to enclose it completely, pleating and pinching edges to cover and seal (photos 4–5, page 277). Place rounds, sealed sides down, on prepared baking sheet. In a small bowl combine egg and water with a fork; set aside.

**3** Cut reserved pastry trimmings into desired shapes (photo 6, page 277). Brush egg mixture onto wrapped cheese rounds; top with pastry shapes and brush again (photo 7, page 277).

**4** Bake in the preheated oven for 20 to 25 minutes or until pastry is deep golden brown. Let stand for 10 minutes before serving. Serve with fruit. Makes 12 servings.

**Per serving:** 220 cal., 16 g total fat (4 g sat. fat), 39 mg chol., 217 mg sodium, 14 g carbo., 1 g fiber, 6 g pro.

**Brie en Croûte with Apricots and Almonds:** Prepare as above, except substitute chopped almonds or hazelnuts (filberts) for the pecans, finely snipped dried apricots for the dried cherries, and apricot preserves for the honey.

HOW DO I MAKE DECORATIVE PASTRY SHAPES? If you don't think you're the Picasso of pastry and would prefer to not work with a knife, use a small cookie, canapé, or aspic (a kind of savory jelly) cutter. Look for them in specialty cookware shops or online.

**1** Using an 8-inch plate or cake pan as a pattern, carefully cut two circles from the dough rectangle.

**2** Spoon the cherry mixture into the very center of each dough circle.

**3** Press cheese round down into the cherry mixture so it spreads out slightly.

**4** Gently bring the edges of the pastry up and over the cheese round, folding and pleating as necessary.

**5** Pinch the pastry together to seal. Trim off any excess pastry so it's not too thick on the bottom.

**6** Using a sharp knife, cut the pastry trimmings into desired small shapes.

**7** After brushing the pastry with the egg mixture, arrange the pastry cutouts on top; brush cutouts again.

The best tool for serving this yummy, melty, pastry-encased cheese is a small knife or spreader. Be sure to let the cheese stand for 10 minutes before serving so it isn't too runny.

# Spinach-Prosciutto **Palmiers**

½ of a 17.3-ounce package frozen puff pastry (1 sheet), thawed

⅓ cup refrigerated basil pesto

½ of a 10-ounce package frozen chopped spinach, thawed and well drained

¾ cup roasted red sweet peppers, drained and finely chopped

¼ cup grated Parmesan cheese

2 ounces thinly sliced prosciutto or thinly sliced cooked ham

1 egg, lightly beaten

1 tablespoon water

Grated Parmesan cheese (optional)

**1** Preheat oven to 400°F. Line a very large baking sheet with parchment paper; set aside. On a lightly floured surface, unfold puff pastry; flatten and smooth the pastry sheet (photo 1, page 272). Roll pastry into an 11-inch square. Spread pesto on the puff pastry square, leaving a ½-inch border on all sides (below); top with spinach and roasted red peppers. Sprinkle with the ¼ cup Parmesan cheese; cover with prosciutto (below). Lightly press ingredients down into pastry with your fingers.

**2** Beginning on one side, roll pastry up; stop in the middle. Beginning on the opposite side, roll pastry up until the two rolls of dough meet and touch in the center (below). Cut pastry roll crosswise into sixteen ½-inch-thick slices (below).

**3** Place slices on prepared baking sheet. In a small bowl combine egg and water with a fork; brush over slices. If desired, sprinkle with additional Parmesan cheese. Bake in the preheated oven about 20 minutes or until pastry is puffed and golden brown. Serve warm or at room temperature. Makes 16 palmiers.

**Per palmier:** 129 cal., 10 g total fat (0 g sat. fat), 15 mg chol., 195 mg sodium, 7 g carbo., 0 g fiber, 3 g pro.

**1** Use an offset spatula to spread the pesto evenly over the rolled-out puff pastry.

**2** Lay the thin slices of prosciutto evenly over the top of the other ingredients.

**3** Roll one side of the pastry tightly and evenly to the center; repeat on the other side.

**4** Using a thin serrated knife in a sawing motion, cut the filled and shaped puff pastry dough into slices.

**Ask Mom** How do I drain spinach? p. 195, 285 / How do I use a rolling pin? p. 61, 228 / How do I work with eggs? p. 26–27 / What is a lightly floured surface? p. 60 / What is parchment paper? p. 21, 69 / What is prosciutto? p. 324 / What is puff pastry? p. 273

**Shopping Savvy**
During the holiday/
entertaining season,
these handy little
phyllo dough shells
will likely be on display
in the specialty foods
or cheese section of
your supermarket. All
other times of the year,
look for them in the
freezer case.

(1) Skill Level

# Pistachio-Apricot Cups

2 2.1-ounce packages baked miniature phyllo dough shells (30)
3 tablespoons orange juice
2 tablespoons butter
3 tablespoons snipped dried apricots
¼ cup sugar
2 tablespoons honey
1 egg white, lightly beaten
¼ teaspoon ground cardamom
½ cup coarsely chopped, lightly salted, dry roasted pistachio nuts

**1** Preheat oven to 350°F. Place phyllo shells in a 15×10×1-inch baking pan (below); set aside.

**2** For filling, in a small saucepan heat orange juice and butter until butter melts and mixture just comes to boiling, stirring occasionally. Remove saucepan from heat; stir in apricots. Cover and let stand for 10 minutes. Stir in sugar, honey, egg white, and cardamom; stir in nuts (below). Spoon filling into phyllo shells (below).

**3** Bake in the preheated oven for 12 to 15 minutes or until filling is bubbly and pastry is golden. Transfer shells to a wire rack (below); cool completely. Makes 30 cups.

**Make-ahead directions:** Prepare as above; cool completely. Place shells in a single layer in a covered airtight container. Refrigerate for up to 2 days or freeze for up to 3 months. Thaw shells, if frozen, before serving.

Per cup: 56 cal., 3 g total fat (1 g sat. fat), 2 mg chol., 26 mg sodium, 7 g carbo., 0 g fiber, 1 g pro.

**1** Arrange the phyllo shells in a shallow baking pan (or place them in 1¾-inch muffin cups) to catch any drips.

**2** Stir the coarsely chopped pistachio nuts into the apricot mixture.

**3** Spoon the apricot filling into the phyllo shells, filling each shell nearly full.

**4** Use a spatula to transfer the baked shells to a wire rack for cooling.

**Ask Mom** How do I juice an orange? p. 45 / How do I measure butter? p. 55 / How do I measure sugar? p. 55 / How do I snip dried fruit or preserves? p. 41, 102 / How do I work with eggs? p. 26–27 / What are chopped nuts? p. 34 / What is cardamom? p. 36 / What's that dried fruit? p. 41 / What's that nut? p. 34–35

② Skill Level

**Ingredient Info**
Phyllo dough is a little tricky to work with, but the results are so wonderful and impressive, it's worth the effort. It dries out easily, so it's important to keep it covered with plastic wrap and a slightly damp kitchen towel at all times.

# Fresh Berry Napoleons

    8  sheets frozen phyllo dough (14×9-inch rectangles), thawed
    ¼  cup butter, melted
    ¼  cup coarse sugar
    ⅓  cup whipping cream
    ¼  cup purchased lemon curd
  2½  cups mixed fresh berries (such as blueberries, raspberries, and/or sliced strawberries)
    1  recipe Sweetened Whipped Cream (page 25)

**1** Preheat oven to 350°F. Unfold phyllo dough (below). Place 1 sheet of phyllo dough on a work surface (below). (Keep remaining phyllo dough covered to prevent it from drying out [below]; remove sheets as needed.) Brush phyllo lightly with some of the butter (below); sprinkle lightly with some of the sugar (photo 5, page 281). Top with another sheet of phyllo dough. Brush with butter and sprinkle with sugar. Repeat with remaining phyllo, butter, and sugar.

**2** Cut the phyllo stack crosswise into eight 1¾-inch-wide strips. Cut each strip crosswise into 4 rectangles (photo 7, page 281). (There should be a total of 32 rectangles.) Transfer rectangles to ungreased baking sheets. Bake in the preheated oven for 10 to 12 minutes or until golden brown. Remove from baking sheets; cool on wire racks (There will be 2 extra phyllo rectangles to use in case any break.)

**3** Meanwhile, in a chilled medium mixing bowl beat whipping cream and lemon curd with an electric mixer on medium speed until mixture thickens and mounds slightly.

**4** To serve, place about 1 teaspoon of the lemon curd mixture on each dessert plate. Top with 1 phyllo rectangle, top side down (photo 8, page 281). Spread with another teaspoon lemon curd mixture; top with some of the berries. Add another phyllo rectangle, top side down. Top with another teaspoon lemon curd mixture and more berries. Add another phyllo rectangle, top side up. Top each with Sweetened Whipped Cream. Makes 10 Napoleons.

**Per Napoleon:** 248 cal., 16 g total fat (10 g sat. fat), 57 mg chol., 104 mg sodium, 26 g carbo., 2 g fiber, 2 g pro.

**①** Thaw frozen phyllo dough in the refrigerator while it's still wrapped and sealed. Carefully unfold the thawed dough.

**②** As you transfer sheets to your work surface, be careful not to lift the sheet too high; the phyllo may tear from its weight.

**③** Keep the phyllo sheets moist by covering them with plastic wrap topped with a damp towel.

**④** Work quickly to coat phyllo sheets with melted butter when stacking them.

**Ask Mom** How do I measure butter? p. 55 / How do I wash fresh berries? p. 42 / How do I work with phyllo dough? p. 280, 282 / What is coarse sugar? p. 29 / What is lemon curd? p. 119 / What is phyllo dough? p. 281 / What is whipping cream? p. 24

**WHAT'S PHYLLO DOUGH?** If you've ever had the rich Greek pastry called baklava, you know: tissue-thin, crisp, delicate leaves of pastry. You can get it fresh at Greek markets and frozen in most supermarkets. Once it's opened, you need to use it in 2 or 3 days.

**5** Sprinkle buttered phyllo sheet with some of the coarse sugar.

**6** Place another phyllo sheet on top and repeat until you have all 8 sheets layered.

**7** Use a pizza cutter to cut the stack of phyllo sheets crosswise into 8 strips; cut each strip into 4 rectangles.

**8** Begin assembling the Napoleons by spooning about 1 teaspoon of the lemon curd mixture on each plate. Top with a phyllo rectangle, sugared side down.

The butter that's brushed on each sheet of phyllo before stacking is what creates the crispy layers of pastry.

**HOW DO I THAW FROZEN PHYLLO?** You can keep frozen phyllo in the freezer for up to 1 year after you buy it. To thaw, put the package, unopened, in the refrigerator overnight, then use it up within a few days. Phyllo turns brittle if you try to refreeze it.

This pumpkin-filled pastry makes a great option to pumpkin pie for the holidays. Just one crispy, creamy bite and there will be no complaints about the missing pie—guaranteed.

Skill Level

# Creamy Pumpkin **Strudels**

½ of a 15-ounce can (¾ cup) canned pumpkin*
¼ cup packed brown sugar
¼ teaspoon ground cinnamon
⅛ teaspoon ground ginger
⅛ teaspoon ground nutmeg
12 sheets frozen phyllo dough (14×9-inch rectangles), thawed
½ cup butter, melted
¾ cup granulated sugar
1 tablespoon ground cinnamon
1 cup chopped pecans
½ of an 8-ounce package cream cheese, cut into 12 pieces
  Whipped cream (optional)

**1** Line a large baking sheet with parchment paper; set aside. For filling, in a small bowl combine pumpkin, brown sugar, the ¼ teaspoon cinnamon, ginger, and nutmeg. Set filling aside.

**2** Preheat oven to 400°F. Unfold phyllo dough (photo 1, page 280). Place 2 sheets of phyllo on top of one another on a work surface (photo 2, page 280). (Keep phyllo dough covered to prevent it from drying out [photo 3, page 280]; remove sheets as needed.) Brush top phyllo sheet with some of the butter (photo 4, page 280). Combine granulated sugar and the 1 tablespoon cinnamon; sprinkle 2 tablespoons of the cinnamon-sugar mixture over the brushed phyllo (photo 5, page 281). Sprinkle with about 2 tablespoons of the pecans.

**3** Cut the 2 layered sheets of phyllo lengthwise to create 2 long strips. Place a piece of cream cheese about 2 inches from an end of each dough strip. Spoon a measuring tablespoon of the filling on top of each cream cheese piece.

**4** To shape, fold bottom edge of phyllo up and over the filling. Roll up to enclose filling, folding in sides as you roll. Place rolls, seam sides down, on the prepared baking sheet. Brush with some of the butter. Repeat with the remaining phyllo dough, cinnamon-sugar mixture, pecans, cream cheese, and filling to make a total of 12 strudels. Sprinkle any remaining sugar-cinnamon mixture over top of strudels.

**5** Bake in the preheated oven about 15 minutes or until golden brown. Serve warm. If desired, serve with whipped cream. Makes 12 strudels.

*Note: Transfer the remaining pumpkin to an airtight container and refrigerate for up to 1 week or freeze for up to 3 months.

Make-ahead directions: Prepare as above; cool completely. Place strudels in a covered airtight container; refrigerate overnight. To reheat, preheat oven to 400°F. Lightly coat a baking sheet with nonstick cooking spray. Place strudels on prepared baking sheet. Bake in the preheated oven about 10 minutes or until centers are warm.

**Ask Mom** How do I measure butter? p. 55 / How do I measure sugar? p. 55 / How do I work with phyllo dough? p. 280, 282 / What are chopped nuts? p. 34 / What is canned pumpkin? p. 302 / What is cinnamon? p. 36 / What is ginger? p. 36 / What is granulated sugar? p. 29 / What is nutmeg? p. 37 / What is parchment paper? p. 21, 69 / What is phyllo dough? p. 281 / What's that nut? p. 34–35

# Mushroom-Cheese
# Appetizer Bundles

1½ cups chopped fresh mushrooms
1 tablespoon butter
1 5.2-ounce container semisoft cheese with garlic and herb
½ of a 3-ounce package cream cheese, softened

1 teaspoon Worcestershire sauce
⅓ cup chopped walnuts, toasted
12 sheets frozen phyllo dough (14×9-inch rectangles), thawed
½ cup butter, melted

**1** For filling, in a large skillet cook and stir mushrooms in the 1 tablespoon hot butter over medium heat for 4 to 5 minutes or until mushrooms are tender and liquid has evaporated. Set mushrooms aside. Beat together semisoft cheese, cream cheese, and Worcestershire sauce with an electric mixer until smooth; fold in cooked mushrooms and walnuts. Set filling aside.

**2** Preheat oven to 375°F. Unfold phyllo dough (photo 1, page 280). Place 1 sheet of phyllo dough on a work surface (photo 2, page 280). (Keep remaining phyllo dough covered to prevent it from drying out [photo 3, page 280]; remove sheets as needed.) Brush lightly with some of the butter (photo 4, page 280). Top with another sheet of phyllo dough; brush with butter. Repeat with 2 more sheets of phyllo and more butter. Cut phyllo stack lengthwise into thirds; cut crosswise into fourths (below). (There should be a total of 12 squares.)

**3** Place a rounded teaspoon of the filling in the center of each square (below). Bring the 4 corners of each square together and pinch to seal (below). Repeat with remaining phyllo dough, butter, and filling to make a total of 36 bundles. Arrange on a large ungreased baking sheet. Brush any remaining butter over the bundles. Bake in the preheated oven for 10 to 12 minutes or until golden. Serve warm. Makes 36 bundles.

**Make-ahead directions:** Prepare as above through Step 3, except do not bake. Cover and refrigerate for up to 4 hours. Preheat oven to 375°F. Continue as directed in Step 3.

Per bundle: 62 cal., 6 g total fat (3 g sat. fat), 13 mg chol., 41 mg sodium, 2 g carbo., 0 g fiber, 1 g pro.

**1** Use a fluted pastry wheel to cut the stack of phyllo lengthwise into thirds and crosswise into fourths.

**2** Spoon a teaspoon of the filling into the center of each phyllo square.

**3** Bring two opposite corners of the phyllo squares together.

**4** Bring the remaining 2 opposite corners together and pinch firmly to seal.

**Ask Mom** How do I measure butter? p. 55 / How do I soften cream cheese? p. 57 / How do I toast nuts? p. 34 / How do I work with phyllo dough? p. 280, 282 / What are chopped nuts? p. 34 / What is phyllo dough? p. 281 / What's that nut? p. 34–35

# Spinach and Feta Phyllo Triangles

1 cup chopped onion

2 cloves garlic, minced

2 tablespoons butter

2 10-ounce packages frozen chopped spinach, thawed and well drained (below)

1½ cups crumbled feta cheese (6 ounces)

1 cup cottage cheese

2 eggs, lightly beaten

3 tablespoons snipped fresh dill or 1 tablespoon dried dill

2 teaspoons finely shredded lemon peel

⅔ cup butter, melted

24 sheets frozen phyllo dough (14×9-inch rectangles), thawed

**1** For filling, in a large skillet cook and stir onion and garlic in the 2 tablespoons hot butter until onion is tender. Remove skillet from heat. Stir in spinach, feta cheese, cottage cheese, eggs, dill, and lemon peel. Set filling aside.

**2** Preheat oven to 325°F. Brush a 13×9×2-inch baking pan with some of the ¾ cup melted butter. Unfold phyllo dough (photo 1, page 280). Layer 12 of the phyllo sheets in the baking pan, generously brushing each sheet with butter as you layer. (Keep phyllo dough covered to prevent it from drying out [photo 3, page 280]; remove sheets as needed.)

**3** Carefully spread filling evenly over phyllo in pan. Layer remaining phyllo sheets on top of filling, brushing each sheet with melted butter as you layer (below). Drizzle top phyllo sheet with remaining butter. Cut into 24 squares; cut each square into a triangle (below).

**4** Bake in the preheated oven about 45 minutes or until golden. Cool in pan on a wire rack for 20 minutes. Recut triangles (below); serve warm. Makes 48 triangles.

**Make-ahead directions:** Prepare as above through Step 1. Transfer filling to a covered airtight container. Refrigerate for up to 24 hours. Continue as directed in Step 2.

Per triangle: 66 cal., 5 g total fat (3 g sat. fat), 22 mg chol., 134 mg sodium, 3 g carbo., 0 g fiber, 2 g pro.

**1** Place spinach in a fine-mesh sieve. Using the back of a spoon, push against the spinach to force out as much liquid as you can.

**2** Layer the 12 remaining phyllo sheets on top of the filling, brushing each with butter as you go.

**3** Use a sharp knife to cut through all the layers to make 24 squares; cut each square diagonally in half to make 48 triangles.

**4** After baking and cooling for 20 minutes, use the sharp knife to recut the triangles.

**Ask Mom** How do I chop an onion? p. 51 / How do I crumble cheese? p. 195 / How do I grease a baking pan? p. 59 / How do I measure butter? p. 55 / How do I mince garlic? p. 21 / How do I shred lemon/lime/orange peel? p. 45, 105 / How do I snip fresh herbs? p. 49 / How do I work with eggs? p. 26–27 / How do I work with phyllo dough? p. 280, 282 / What does drizzle mean? p. 69, 85 / What is phyllo dough? p. 281

# Apple Dumpling **Roll-Ups**

½ cup apple juice

⅓ cup packed brown sugar

2 tablespoons butter

2 tablespoons granulated sugar

1 teaspoon ground cinnamon

1 large cooking apple, peeled if desired, cored, and cut into 8 wedges

1 8-ounce package (8) refrigerated crescent rolls

1 teaspoon coarse sugar or granulated sugar

Vanilla or cinnamon ice cream (optional)

**1** Preheat oven to 375°F. Lightly grease a 2-quart square baking dish; set aside. In a small saucepan cook and stir apple juice, brown sugar, and butter over medium-low heat until butter melts and sugar dissolves. Set aside.

**2** In a medium bowl stir together the granulated sugar and the cinnamon. Add apple wedges; toss to coat evenly. Unroll dough and separate at perforations into 8 triangles. Place a coated apple wedge along the shortest side of each dough triangle. Roll up dough around apple wedges toward the point. Arrange roll-ups in prepared baking dish. Slowly drizzle apple juice mixture over roll-ups, coating evenly; sprinkle with coarse sugar.

**3** Bake in the preheated oven for 25 to 30 minutes or until golden brown and apples are tender. Cool for 30 minutes. If desired, serve with ice cream. Makes 8 roll-ups.

**Per roll-up:** 201 cal., 9 g total fat (4 g sat. fat), 8 mg chol., 245 mg sodium, 28 g carbo., 1 g fiber, 2 g pro.

**Good to Know** This old-fashioned comfort-food dessert gets a modern makeover when made with convenient refrigerated crescent rolls. Use regular crescents—not reduced-fat—and don't be alarmed when you open them (they let off a minor explosion when the under-pressure contents are released). Crescent rolls are more often used in savory dishes, but with the addition of sugar and cinnamon, they sure are sweet.

**Ask Mom** How do I grease a baking pan? p. 59 / How do I measure butter? p. 55 / How do I measure liquids? p. 55 / How do I measure sugar? p. 55 / How do I peel and core apples? p. 38, 39 / How do I peel and slice apples? p. 38, 39 / What does drizzle mean? p. 69, 85 / What is a good baking/cooking apple? p. 39, 287 / What is cinnamon? p. 36 / What is coarse sugar? p. 29 / What is granulated sugar? p. 29

**WHAT'S A COOKING APPLE?** Most apple varieties are good eaten out of hand and in salads. But some apple types hold up to heat better than others—they keep their shape and don't take on a mealy texture. See page 39 to identify apples that are good for cooking.

A bit of apple peel peeking out of the pastry adds a little color to this shortcut version of a traditional dessert. If you prefer your apples paler, peel them (page 38).

(2) Skill Level

# Easy Chocolate-Almond Croissants

½ of an 8-ounce can almond paste, cut up (below)

¼ cup whipping cream

4 ounces semisweet or bittersweet chocolate, finely chopped

I 8-ounce package (8) refrigerated crescent rolls

I egg, lightly beaten

I tablespoon water

¼ cup sliced almonds

I tablespoon powdered sugar

**Ingredient Info**
Almond paste is a blend of ground blanched almonds, sugar, and glycerin—a syrupy alcohol that adds moistness. Look for it in the baking aisle of your supermarket. Wrap any leftovers tightly in plastic wrap and refrigerate for up to I month.

**1** Preheat oven to 350°F. Lightly grease a baking sheet; set aside. In a medium mixing bowl combine almond paste pieces and 1 tablespoon of the whipping cream; beat until nearly smooth (below). Continue beating in whipping cream, 1 tablespoon at a time, until nearly smooth. Stir in chocolate.

**2** Unroll dough and separate at perforations into eight triangles. Spoon almond paste mixture onto the shortest side of each dough triangle; spread slightly. Starting at the shortest side of each triangle, roll up dough around filling toward the point (below); shape into crescent shapes (below). Place croissants, pointed sides down, on prepared baking sheet.

**3** In a small bowl combine egg and water with a fork. Brush dough lightly with egg mixture; sprinkle with almonds. Bake in the preheated oven for 15 to 17 minutes or until golden brown. Transfer croissants to a wire rack; cool slightly. Sift powdered sugar over croissants (page 267); serve warm. Makes 8 croissants.

Per croissant: 296 cal., I9 g total fat (6 g sat. fat), 37 mg chol., 26I mg sodium, 28 g carbo., 2 g fiber, 6 g pro.

**1** Use a sharp knife to cut the almond paste into small pieces.

**2** Beat the almond paste pieces and whipping cream together with an electric mixer on medium speed.

**3** Roll the dough up around the filling, rolling toward the opposite point.

**4** Curve in the ends of each triangle to make a crescent shape.

# quick-as-can-be
# MUFFINS &
# BREADS

**Whether it's basketful of muffins for breakfast or a slice of something sweet for coffee break, quick breads satisfy in a flash.**

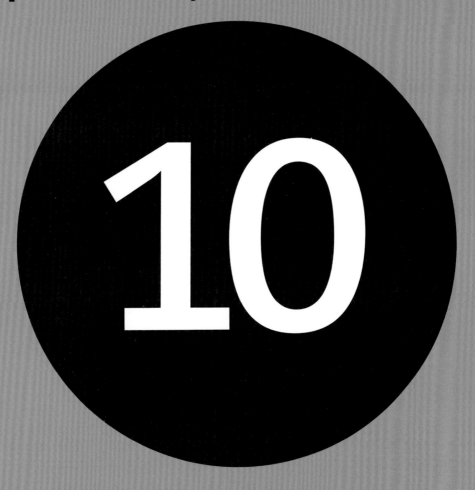

10

## COFFEE CAKES

Blueberry Streusel Coffee Cake ② .......................314

Coconut-Pecan Coffee Cake ② .......................312

Cream Cheese-Berry Coffee Cake ② ...................313

Walnut-Pear Sour Cream Coffee Cake ③ ...............316

## FROSTINGS & TOPPINGS

Coconut-Pecan Topping ② ...........................312

Maple Icing ① ......................................300

Powdered Sugar Icing ① .............................314

Streusel-Nut Topping ① .............................308

Streusel Topping ① ..................................291

**How do I make a basic muffin?**..........................292–293

## MUFFINS

Almond-Cherry Muffins ① .............................295

Almond-Pear Muffins ① ..............................295

Banana-Coconut Muffins ① ...........................295

Banana Crunch Muffins ② ............................298

Blueberry-Lemon Muffins ① ..........................295

Caramel Apple Muffins ① ............................295

Carrot-Ginger Muffins ① .............................295

Carrot-Pineapple Muffins ① ..........................296

Corn Muffins ② .....................................311

Cranberry Muffins ① ................................295

Gingerbread-Sour Cream Muffins ② ...................297

Lemon Curd-Oat Muffins ② ..........................299

Lemon-Poppy Seed Muffins ② ........................295

Maple Bran Muffins ② ...............................300

Mocha Muffins ① ...................................295

Muffins ① ..........................................291

Oatmeal Muffins ① ..................................295

Peanut Butter Muffins ① .............................295

Pecan-Date Muffins ① ...............................395

Pumpkin-Praline Muffins ② ..........................302

## QUICK BREADS

Apple Pie Bread ② ..................................308

Banana Bread ② ....................................304

Banana-Chocolate Bread ② ..........................304

Banana-Coconut Bread ② ............................304

Chocolate-Cashew Bread ② ..........................303

Cinnamon-Nut Bread ② ..............................306

Corn Bread ② ......................................311

Double Corn Bread ② ...............................310

Green Chile Corn Bread ② ...........................310

Green Onion-Bacon Corn Bread ② ....................310

Quick Seed Bread ② ................................307

Sweet Pepper Corn Bread ② .........................310

Toffee-Almond Banana Bread ② ......................304

# Muffins

1¾ cups all-purpose flour
⅓ cup sugar
2 teaspoons baking powder
¼ teaspoon salt
1 egg
¾ cup milk
¼ cup cooking oil
1 recipe Streusel Topping (optional)

**1** Preheat oven to 400°F. Grease twelve 2½-inch muffin cups or line with paper bake cups (photos 1–2, page 292); set aside. In a medium bowl stir together the flour, sugar, baking powder, and salt. Make a well in the center of the flour mixture (photo 3, page 292); set aside.

**2** In a small bowl beat egg with a fork; stir in milk and oil. Add egg mixture to flour mixture all at once (photo 4, page 292); stir just until moistened (batter should be lumpy) (photo 5, page 293). Spoon batter into the prepared muffin cups, filling each two-thirds full (photo 6, page 293). If desired, sprinkle Streusel Topping evenly over batter (photo 7, page 293).

**3** Bake in the preheated oven for 18 to 20 minutes or until golden and a wooden toothpick inserted in the centers comes out clean. Cool in muffin cups on a wire rack for 5 minutes. Remove muffins from cups (photo 8, page 293). Serve warm. Makes 12 muffins.

Per muffin: 136 cal., 5 g total fat (1 g sat. fat), 19 mg chol., 128 mg sodium, 19 g carbo., 0 g fiber, 3 g pro.

**Streusel Topping:** In a small bowl stir together 3 tablespoons all-purpose flour, 3 tablespoons packed brown sugar, and ¼ teaspoon ground cinnamon. Using a pastry blender, cut in 2 tablespoons cold butter until mixture resembles coarse crumbs. Stir in 2 tablespoons chopped pecans or walnuts.

**Good to Know** Having muffins in the freezer is like having money in the bank. To freeze muffins, put them in resealable plastic bags for up to 3 months. To reheat from the frozen state, wrap them in heavy foil. Heat them in a 300°F oven for 12 to 15 minutes for mini muffins, 15 to 18 minutes for standard-size muffins, and 25 to 30 minutes for jumbo-size muffins.

**Flavor Changes** Muffins are fun to make because their flavoring is so flexible. This basic muffin recipe can be amended in all kinds of ways. See page 295 for inspiration.

**Ask Mom** How do I cut in butter/shortening? p. 56 / How do I measure flour? p. 54 / How do I measure liquids? p. 55 / How do I measure sugar? p. 55 / How do I store baked goods? p. 68 / What is a pastry blender? p. 10, 11 / What is baking powder? p. 30, 319 / What is cinnamon? p. 36 / What is cooking oil? p. 28 / What's that flour? p. 31

# How do I make a basic muffin?

## No matter how they're flavored, all muffins are made using the method below. The most important thing to remember: Don't overmix or they'll be tough.

Muffins really are simple to make. But there are a few things you should know to have success in your muffin-making endeavors.

Muffin batter can't really be made ahead. Once you have it mixed, get it in the oven immediately. Batters that use baking powder and baking soda need to be baked right away so that their leavening power isn't lost. When you're filling the muffin cups, fill them two-thirds to three-fourths full. If you fill them too full, you'll have flat muffin tops instead of nicely domed ones. The color of those tops is an indicator of when the muffins are done—look for them to be nice and golden. Let them cool in the muffin cups only for the time specified in the recipe or your muffins might get soggy.

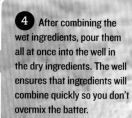

**4** After combining the wet ingredients, pour them all at once into the well in the dry ingredients. The well ensures that ingredients will combine quickly so you don't overmix the batter.

**1** Grease muffin cups by brushing the bottoms and sides with shortening or softened butter. You could also lightly coat them with nonstick cooking spray.

**2** If you're taking your muffins somewhere, paper liners are the way to go. Just drop them in the muffin cups.

**3** Stir together all the dry ingredients in a bowl. Use the wooden spoon to make a hole or well in the center.

**5** Use a wooden spoon to stir together the wet and dry ingredients just until they are combined. It's OK if the batter looks lumpy.

**6** Spoon the muffin batter into the prepared muffin cups. The recipe will state whether to fill them two-thirds or three-fourths full.

**7** After filling the muffin cups, sprinkle any toppings over the batter. Sprinkle it evenly so it stays on top instead of sinking into the muffin.

**8** Let the baked muffins cool in the muffin cups on a wire rack just until they are cool enough to remove (about 5 minutes). Use a butter knife to lift muffins from the cups so you can grab them and place them on the wire rack to finish cooling or in a basket for eating right away.

# One Muffin, 12 Ways

With just a few ingredient switches and swap-outs, one simple recipe yields a dozen different muffins—at least one for every taste or occasion.

## Caramel Apple Muffins

½ teaspoon ground cinnamon
¾ cup shredded, peeled tart apple
½ cup toffee bits

Prepare Muffins (page 291) as directed, except stir cinnamon into flour mixture. Fold shredded apple and toffee bits into batter.

## Lemon-Poppy Seed Muffins

1 tablespoon poppy seeds
2 teaspoons finely shredded lemon peel
Lemon curd (optional)

Prepare Muffins (page 291) as directed, except stir poppy seeds and lemon peel into flour mixture. If desired, serve warm muffins with lemon curd.

## Carrot-Ginger Muffins

¾ cup shredded carrot
½ cup raisins
1 tablespoon finely chopped crystallized ginger

Prepare Muffins (page 291) as directed, except fold shredded carrot, raisins, and chopped ginger into batter.

## Almond-Pear Muffins

¼ teaspoon almond extract
¾ cup chopped, peeled pear
Chopped almonds

Prepare Muffins (page 291) as directed, except stir almond extract into egg mixture. Fold chopped pear into batter and use chopped almonds in Streusel Topping.

## Oatmeal Muffins

¾ cup regular rolled oats
½ teaspoon ground cinnamon, apple pie spice, or pumpkin pie spice

Prepare Muffins (page 291) as directed, except reduce flour to 1⅓ cups. Stir oats and cinnamon into flour mixture.

## Mocha Muffins

2 teaspoons instant espresso powder
⅔ cup miniature semisweet chocolate pieces

Prepare Muffins (page 291) as directed, except stir espresso powder into egg mixture. Fold chocolate pieces into batter.

## Almond-Cherry Muffins

⅓ cup snipped dried tart cherries
⅓ cup chopped toasted almonds

Prepare Muffins (page 291) as directed, except fold cherries and almonds into batter.

## Peanut Butter Muffins

¾ cup peanut butter-flavor baking pieces

Prepare Muffins (page 291) as directed, except fold peanut butter-flavor baking pieces into batter.

## Banana-Coconut Muffins

¾ cup chopped banana
½ cup toasted flaked coconut (page 40)

Prepare Muffins (page 291) as directed, except fold banana and coconut into batter.

## Blueberry-Lemon Muffins

¾ cup fresh or frozen blueberries
1 tablespoon finely shredded lemon peel

Prepare Muffins (page 291) as directed, except fold blueberries and lemon peel into batter.

## Cranberry Muffins

¾ cup coarsely chopped cranberries
1 tablespoon sugar

Prepare Muffins (page 291) as directed, except toss together cranberries and sugar, then fold cranberry mixture into batter.

## Pecan-Date Muffins

¾ cup chopped dates
⅓ cup chopped toasted pecans

Prepare Muffins (page 291) as directed, except fold dates and pecans into batter.

( 1 ) Skill Level

**Ingredient Info**
Shelled pumpkin
seeds—also called
pepitas—add a
delicate, nutty flavor
and crunch to these
good-morning muffins.
If you can't find them
at your supermarket,
look for them at a
healthfood store or
Mexican market.

# Carrot-Pineapple **Muffins**

1¾ cups all-purpose flour

½ cup sugar

2 teaspoons baking powder

¼ teaspoon salt

¼ teaspoon ground cinnamon (optional)

2 tablespoons shelled pumpkin seeds or dry-roasted
shelled sunflower kernels

1 egg

½ cup milk

¼ cup cooking oil

⅓ cup finely shredded carrot

1 8-ounce can crushed pineapple, drained

**1** Preheat oven to 400°F. Lightly grease twelve 2½-inch muffin cups or line with paper bake cups (photos 1–2, page 292); set aside.

**2** In a medium bowl stir together the flour, sugar, baking powder, salt, and, if desired, cinnamon (photo 3, page 292). Stir in pumpkin seeds. In another medium bowl beat egg with a fork; stir in milk and oil. Stir in carrot and pineapple. Add egg mixture to flour mixture all at once (photo 4, page 292); stir just until moistened (batter should be lumpy) (photo 5, page 293). Spoon batter into the prepared muffin cups, filling each two-thirds full (photo 6, page 293).

**3** Bake in the preheated oven for 18 to 20 minutes or until golden and a wooden toothpick inserted in the centers comes out clean. Cool in muffin cups on a wire rack for 5 minutes. Remove muffins from cups (photo 8, page 293). Serve warm. Makes 12 muffins.

Per muffin: 175 cal., 6 g total fat (1 g sat. fat), 18 mg chol., 122 mg sodium, 27 g carbo., 1 g fiber, 2 g pro.

# Gingerbread-Sour Cream Muffins

**Good to Know** A spoonful of Sweetened Whipped Cream (page 25) or lemon curd is the traditional gingerbread topper. The sweet-tart taste of lemon curd is delicious with these spicy muffins.

    2  cups all-purpose flour
    1  tablespoon finely chopped fresh ginger or 1 teaspoon ground ginger
    2  teaspoons baking powder
  3/4  teaspoon ground allspice or ground cinnamon
  1/4  teaspoon baking soda
  1/4  teaspoon salt
  1/4  cup butter
    1  egg
    1  8-ounce carton dairy sour cream
  1/3  cup milk
  1/4  cup packed brown sugar
  1/4  cup mild-flavor molasses
    2  tablespoons granulated sugar
    2  tablespoons finely chopped crystallized ginger

**1** Preheat oven to 400°F. Grease bottoms of twelve 2½-inch muffin cups (photo 1, page 292); set aside.

**2** In a medium bowl stir together the flour, ginger, baking powder, allspice, baking soda, and salt (photo 3, page 292). Using a pastry blender, cut in butter until mixture resembles coarse crumbs. Make a well in the center of the flour mixture; set aside.

**3** In another medium bowl beat egg with a fork; stir in sour cream, milk, brown sugar, and molasses. Add egg mixture to flour mixture all at once (photo 4, page 292); stir just until moistened (batter should be lumpy) (photo 5, page 293). Spoon batter into the prepared muffin cups, filling each three-fourths full (photo 6, page 293). In a small bowl stir together the granulated sugar and crystallized ginger; sprinkle evenly over batter.

**4** Bake in the preheated oven for 18 to 20 minutes or until golden and a wooden toothpick inserted in the centers comes out clean. Cool in muffin cups on a wire rack for 5 minutes. Remove muffins from cups (photo 8, page 293). Serve warm. Makes 12 muffins.

**Per muffin:** 211 cal., 9 g total fat (5 g sat. fat), 37 mg chol., 168 mg sodium, 30 g carbo., 1 g fiber, 4 g pro.

## MAKE MINE MINI. Almost any standard-size muffin recipe can be adjusted to be made in a mini-muffin pan or in a jumbo-size pan. Bake mini muffins about 8 minutes less than a standard muffin. Bake jumbo muffins in a 350°F oven about 30 minutes.

**Ask Mom** How do I measure butter? p. 55 / How do I measure flour? p. 54 / How do I measure liquids? p. 55 / How do I measure sugar? p. 55 / How do I reheat muffins? p. 291 / How do I store baked goods? p. 68 / What is allspice? p. 36 / What is baking powder? p. 30, 319 / What is baking soda? p. 30, 319 / What is cinnamon? p. 36 / What is fresh ginger? p. 48 / What is ginger? p. 36 / What is granulated sugar? p. 29 / What's that flour? p. 31

# Banana Crunch **Muffins**

¼ cup all-purpose flour

¼ cup granulated sugar

2 tablespoons cold butter

¼ cup chopped pecans

2 cups all-purpose flour

½ cup granulated sugar

⅓ cup packed brown sugar

1½ teaspoons baking soda

¼ teaspoon salt

¼ teaspoon ground cinnamon

¼ teaspoon ground nutmeg

½ cup cold butter

1 egg

1 cup mashed banana (3 medium)

⅓ cup milk

**1** Preheat oven to 375°F. Grease twelve 2½-inch muffin cups or line with paper bake cups (photos 1–2, page 292); set aside. For topping, in a small bowl stir together the ¼ cup flour and the ¼ cup granulated sugar. Using a pastry blender, cut in the 2 tablespoons butter until mixture resembles coarse crumbs. Stir in pecans; set aside.

**2** In a medium bowl stir together the 2 cups flour, the ½ cup granulated sugar, the brown sugar, baking soda, salt, cinnamon, and nutmeg (photo 3, page 292). Using a pastry blender, cut in the ½ cup butter until mixture resembles coarse crumbs. Make a well in the center of the flour mixture; set aside.

**3** In a small bowl beat egg with a fork; stir in banana and milk. Add egg mixture to flour mixture all at once (photo 4, page 292); stir just until moistened (batter should be lumpy) (photo 5, page 293). Spoon batter into the prepared muffin cups, filling each three-fourths full (photo 6, page 293). Sprinkle topping evenly over batter (photo 7, page 293).

**4** Bake in the preheated oven for 16 to 18 minutes or until golden and a wooden toothpick inserted in the centers comes out clean. Cool in muffin cups on a wire rack for 5 minutes. Remove muffins from cups (photo 8, page 293). Serve warm. Makes 12 muffins.

Per muffin: 285 cal., 12 g total fat (7 g sat. fat), 45 mg chol., 285 mg sodium, 42 g carbo., 1 g fiber, 2 g pro.

**Ask Mom** How do I cut in butter? p. 56 / How do I mash bananas? p. 40 / How do I measure butter? p. 55 / How do I measure flour? p. 54 / How do I measure liquids? p. 55 / How do I measure sugar? p. 55 / How do I reheat muffins? p. 291 / How do I store baked goods? p. 68 / What are chopped nuts? p. 34 / What is a pastry blender? p. 10, 11 / What is baking soda? p. 30, 319 / What is cinnamon? p. 36 / What is granulated sugar? p. 29 / What is nutmeg? p. 37 / What's that flour? p. 31 / What's that nut? p. 34–35

# Lemon Curd-Oat Muffins

I cup all-purpose flour

I cup regular rolled oats

½ cup granulated sugar

I tablespoon baking powder

I tablespoon poppy seeds

I tablespoon finely shredded lemon peel

¼ teaspoon salt

I egg

¾ cup milk

¼ cup cooking oil

⅓ cup purchased lemon curd

Powdered sugar

**1** Preheat oven to 375°F. Grease twelve 2½-inch muffin cups or line with paper bake cups (photos 1–2, page 292); set aside. In a medium bowl stir together the flour, oats, granulated sugar, baking powder, poppy seeds, lemon peel, and salt (photo 3, page 292). Make a well in the center of the flour mixture; set aside.

**2** In a small bowl beat egg with a fork; stir in milk and oil. Add egg mixture to flour mixture all at once (photo 4, page 292); stir just until moistened (batter should be lumpy) (photo 5, page 293). Spoon batter into the prepared muffin cups, filling each two-thirds full (photo 6, page 293). Spoon about 1 teaspoon of the lemon curd on top of the batter in each cup (below).

**3** Bake in the preheated oven for 15 to 20 minutes or until tops are light brown. Cool in muffin cups on a wire rack for 5 minutes. Remove muffins from cups (photo 8, page 293). Sift powdered sugar over warm muffins. Serve warm. Makes 12 muffins.

**Per muffin:** 180 cal., 6 g total fat (I g sat. fat), 25 mg chol., 159 mg sodium, 29 g carbo., 2 g fiber, 3 g pro.

**1** Pretty, blue-gray poppy seeds add beautiful speckles, a nutty flavor, and a tiny bit of crunch to these yummy, lemony muffins.

**2** Using a measuring teaspoon and flatware spoon, drop lemon curd onto the top of the batter in each cup.

**Ask Mom** Can I use quick-cooking oats instead of regular oats? p. 351 / How do I dust with powdered sugar? p. 267 / How do I measure flour? p. 54 / How do I measure liquids? p. 55 / How do I measure sugar? p. 55 / How do I reheat muffins? p. 291 / How do I shred lemon/lime peel? p. 45, 105 / How do I store baked goods? p. 68 / What is baking powder? p. 30, 319 / What is cooking oil?

(2) Skill Level

**Ingredient Info**
Pure maple syrup
has a more intense
taste than maple-
flavor syrup—and a
correspondingly higher
price tag. Although
some maple-flavor
syrup lists pure maple
syrup as an ingredient,
it can also simply
be corn syrup that
contains some artificial
maple extract and
brown coloring.

# Maple Bran Muffins

1⅔ cups buttermilk or sour milk

2 cups whole bran cereal

1 cup whole wheat flour

1¾ teaspoons baking powder

½ teaspoon ground cinnamon

¼ teaspoon baking soda

2 eggs, lightly beaten

⅓ cup packed brown sugar

¼ cup pure maple syrup or maple-flavor syrup

3 tablespoons cooking oil

¾ cup mixed dried fruit bits and/or raisins

1 recipe Maple Icing (optional)

**1** Preheat oven to 350°F. Lightly grease twelve to sixteen 2½-inch muffin cups (photo 1, page 292); set aside.

**2** In a large bowl stir buttermilk into bran cereal; let stand for 5 to 10 minutes or until cereal has softened. In a small bowl stir together the flour, baking powder, cinnamon, and baking soda (photo 3, page 292); set aside.

**3** Stir eggs, brown sugar, syrup, and oil into bran mixture. Add flour mixture to bran mixture; stir just until combined (photo 5, page 293). Stir in dried fruit bits. Spoon batter into the prepared muffin cups, filling each three-fourths full (photo 6, page 293).

**4** Bake in the preheated oven for 25 to 30 minutes or until a wooden toothpick inserted in the centers comes out clean. Cool in muffin cups on a wire rack for 5 minutes. Remove muffins from cups (photo 8, page 293). If desired, drizzle with Maple Icing. Serve warm. Makes 12 to 16 muffins.

Per muffin: 179 cal., 5 g total fat (1 g sat. fat), 37 mg chol., 144 mg sodium, 33 g carbo., 5 g fiber, 5 g pro.

Maple Icing: In a small bowl stir together ⅓ cup powdered sugar and ¼ teaspoon maple flavoring. Stir in enough milk (1 to 2 teaspoons) to make an icing of drizzling consistency.

## What's whole bran cereal?

Bran is the flaky, brown, high-in-fiber outer layer of grains such as wheat or oats that is removed during the milling process. You can buy wheat and oat bran in the store—and you can buy commercial cereals that are made up primarily of bran in its raw, unprocessed form. Whole bran cereals can take the form of either "shreds" or flakes. Shreds are probably a better choice for baking; they break down more easily than a flaked cereal but still give the muffins a great wheaty texture.

**Ask Mom** How do I make sour milk? p. 24 / How do I measure flour? p. 54 / How do I measure sugar? p. 55 / How do I reheat muffins? p. 291 / How do I store baked goods? p. 68 / How do I work with eggs? p. 26–27 / What does drizzle mean? p. 69, 85 / What is baking powder? p. 30, 319 / What is baking soda? p. 30, 319 / What is buttermilk? p. 24 / What is cinnamon? p. 36 / What

**PICK A NEW FRUIT.** Dried fruit of almost any kind adds flavor, chewiness, and good nutrition to these hearty muffins. Try snipped whole dates or snipped dried apricots, dried cherries, and dried cranberries, or even snipped dried mangoes.

When drizzling the icing, keep the stream directly over the top of the muffins, stopping a little short of the edges. Since the muffins are served warm, the icing will melt and run down the sides.

# Pumpkin-Praline **Muffins**

⅓ cup packed brown sugar

2 tablespoons dairy sour cream

⅔ cup chopped pecans, toasted

2 cups all-purpose flour

2 teaspoons baking powder

I teaspoon ground cinnamon

½ teaspoon baking soda

¼ teaspoon salt

¼ teaspoon ground nutmeg

⅛ teaspoon ground cloves

I egg

¾ cup buttermilk or sour milk

¾ cup canned pumpkin

⅔ cup packed brown sugar

⅓ cup butter, melted

**1** Preheat oven to 375°F. Grease twelve 2½-inch muffin cups or line with paper bake cups (photos 1–2, page 292); set aside. For topping, in a small bowl stir together the ⅓ cup brown sugar and the sour cream; stir in pecans (below). Set aside.

**2** In a medium bowl stir together the flour, baking powder, cinnamon, baking soda, salt, nutmeg, and cloves (photo 3, page 292). Make a well in the center of the flour mixture; set aside. In another medium bowl lightly beat egg with a fork; stir in buttermilk, pumpkin, the ⅔ cup brown sugar, and the melted butter. Add pumpkin mixture to flour mixture all at once (photo 4, page 292); stir just until moistened (batter should be lumpy) (photo 5, page 293). Spoon batter into the prepared muffin cups, filling each three-fourths full (photo 6, page 293). Spoon topping evenly over batter (below).

**3** Bake for 20 to 25 minutes or until golden brown and a wooden toothpick inserted in the centers comes out clean. Cool in muffin cups on a wire rack for 5 minutes. Remove muffins from cups (photo 8, page 293). Serve warm. Makes 12 muffins.

Per muffin: 250 cal., II g total fat (4 g sat. fat), 32 mg chol., 2I5 mg sodium, 36 g carbo., 2 g fiber, 2 g pro.

**1** The topping for these muffins is a little different because the mixture is wet. The topping will be gooey.

**2** Use two flatware spoons to evenly top the batter. Push the topping off one spoon with the second.

**Ingredient Info** Be sure you use plain pumpkin puree in this recipe—not pumpkin pie filling, which is already spiced and sweetened. You'll have some pumpkin left over. You can discard it—or save it for another use. It freezes just fine in a tightly sealed container.

**Ask Mom** How do I make sour milk? p. 24 / How do I measure butter? p. 55 / How do I measure flour? p. 54 / How do I measure sugar? p. 55 / How do I reheat muffins? p. 29I / How do I store baked goods? p. 68 / What are chopped nuts? p. 34 / What are cloves? p. 36 / What is baking powder? p. 30, 3I9 / What is baking soda? p. 30, 3I9 / What is buttermilk? p. 24 / What is cinnamon? p. 36 / What is nutmeg? p. 37 / What's that flour? p. 3I / What's that nut? p. 34–35

# Chocolate-Cashew Bread

2 cups all-purpose flour
½ cup sugar
1 tablespoon baking powder
½ teaspoon salt
1 egg
¾ cup milk

½ cup cooking oil
1⅓ cups semisweet chocolate pieces
1 cup chopped cashews or hazelnuts (filberts)
1½ teaspoons shortening
Coarsely chopped cashews or hazelnuts (filberts) (optional)

**1** Preheat oven to 350°F. Grease the bottom and ½ inch up the sides of an 8×4×2-inch loaf pan (photo 1, page 305); set aside.

**2** In a large bowl stir together the flour, sugar, baking powder, and salt (photo 3, page 292). Make a well in the center of the flour mixture; set aside. In a medium bowl beat egg with a fork; stir in milk and oil. Add egg mixture to flour mixture all at once (photo 4, page 292); stir just until moistened (batter should be lumpy) (photo 5, page 293). Fold in 1 cup of the chocolate pieces and the 1 cup cashews. Spread batter evenly in the prepared pan.

**3** Bake in the preheated oven for 50 to 55 minutes or until a wooden toothpick inserted near the center comes out clean. Cool in pan on a wire rack for 10 minutes. Remove from pan (photo 3, page 305). Cool completely on wire rack. Wrap and store bread overnight before slicing (photo 4, page 305).

**4** Before serving, in a small saucepan heat and stir the remaining ⅓ cup chocolate pieces and the shortening until smooth. Drizzle melted chocolate over loaf. If desired, sprinkle additional coarsely chopped cashews on top. Let stand until chocolate is set. Makes 1 loaf (14 slices).

**Per slice:** 301 cal., 18 g total fat (5 g sat. fat), 16 mg chol., 148 mg sodium, 33 g carbo., 2 g fiber, 5 g pro.

If you decide to sprinkle additional nuts on top of the bread, do it before the chocolate sets—and only on the chocolate—so they have something on which to stick.

**Ask Mom** How do I measure flour/liquids/sugar? p. 54, 55 / How do I melt chocolate? p. 32, 33 / How do I remove quick breads from pans? p. 60 / How do I store baked goods? p. 68 / What does drizzle mean? p. 69, 85 / What is baking powder? p. 30, 319 / What is cooking oil? p. 28 / What is semisweet chocolate? p. 32 / What's that flour? p. 31 / What's that nut? p. 34-35 / Why is there a crack in my bread? p. 305 / Why remove bread from the pan to cool? p. 350 / Why wait a day to slice quick bread? p. 309

# Banana **Bread**

**Good to Know**
Bananas mash most
easily when they're
a little overripe—a
little more black than
yellow. To mash several
bananas at once in
a large bowl, use a
potato masher.

  2  cups all-purpose flour
1½  teaspoons baking powder
 ½  teaspoon baking soda
 ¼  teaspoon salt
 ¼  teaspoon ground cinnamon
 ⅛  teaspoon ground nutmeg
  2  eggs
1½  cups mashed banana (4 medium)
  I  cup sugar
 ½  cup cooking oil or melted butter
 ½  cup chopped walnuts

**1** Preheat oven to 350°F. Grease the bottom and ½ inch up the sides of a 9×5×3-inch loaf pan (photo 1, page 305) or two 7½×3½×2-inch loaf pans; set aside.

**2** In a large bowl stir together the flour, baking powder, baking soda, salt, the cinnamon, and nutmeg (photo 3, page 292). Make a well in the center of the flour mixture; set aside. In a medium bowl beat eggs with a fork; stir in banana, sugar, and oil. Add egg mixture to flour mixture all at once (photo 4, page 292); stir just until moistened (batter should be lumpy) (photo 5, page 293). Fold in walnuts. Spread batter evenly in the prepared pan(s).

**3** Bake in the preheated oven for 55 to 60 minutes for 9×5×3-inch pan (40 to 45 minutes for 7½×3½×2-inch pans) or until a wooden toothpick inserted near the center comes out clean. (If necessary, cover bread loosely with foil the last 15 minutes of baking to prevent overbrowning.) Cool in pan on a wire rack for 10 minutes. Remove from pan (photo 3, page 305). Cool completely on wire rack. Wrap and store bread overnight before slicing (photo 4, page 305). Makes 1 loaf (14 slices).

**Per slice:** 24I cal., II g total fat (I g sat. fat), 30 mg chol., 123 mg sodium, 32 g carbo., I g fiber, 2 g pro.

Banana-Chocolate Bread: Prepare as directed, except omit the walnuts and fold in ⅔ cup miniature semisweet chocolate pieces.

Banana-Coconut Bread: Prepare as directed, except substitute chopped macadamia nuts for the walnuts and fold in ½ cup flaked coconut.

Toffee-Almond Banana Bread: Prepare as directed, except substitute chopped almonds for the walnuts and fold in ⅔ cup toffee pieces.

**Ask Mom** How do I mash bananas? p. 40 / How do I measure flour/butter/sugar? p. 54, 55 / How do I remove quick breads from pans? p. 60 / How do I store baked goods? p. 68 / What are toffee pieces? p. 90 / What is baking powder/soda? p. 30, 319 / What is cinnamon/nutmeg? p. 36, 37 / What is cooking oil? p. 28 / What is semisweet chocolate? p. 32 / What's that flour? p. 31 / What's that nut? p. 34-35 / Why remove bread from the pan to cool? p. 350 / Why wait a day to slice quick bread? p. 309

**CAN I PREVENT CRACKS IN MY BREAD?** Probably not. The cracks in the tops of quick breads are simply a result of rapidly rising batter. They're completely normal. Tunnels in the center of the bread can result from overmixing—but not the cracks on top.

**1** Use a brush to lightly spread vegetable shortening over the bottom and ½ inch up the sides of the loaf pan.

**2** If you loosely covered the bread with foil to prevent overbrowning, remove it when you take the bread out to cool.

**3** Run a spatula or butter knife between the pan sides and the loaf to loosen loaf. Invert pan to remove loaf.

**4** After the bread is cooled, wrap it in plastic wrap, then in foil to keep it from drying out.

**Good to Know** A large glass measuring cup—4 cups or larger—makes a great vessel for mixing up quick breads. The handle makes it easy to pick up and pour and the spout helps control the flow of batter to keep things neat and tidy.

# Cinnamon-Nut Bread

1⅓ cups sugar

½ cup finely chopped toasted pecans or walnuts

2 teaspoons ground cinnamon

2 cups all-purpose flour

1 teaspoon baking powder

½ teaspoon salt

1 egg

1 cup milk

⅓ cup cooking oil

**1** Preheat oven to 350°F. Grease and flour the bottom and ½ inch up the sides of a 9×5×3-inch loaf pan (photo 1, page 305); set aside. In a small bowl stir together ⅓ cup of the sugar, the pecans, and cinnamon; set aside.

**2** In a large bowl stir together the remaining 1 cup sugar, the flour, baking powder, and salt (photo 3, page 292). In a medium bowl beat egg with a fork; stir in milk and oil. Add egg mixture to flour mixture all at once (photo 4, page 292); stir just until moistened (batter should be lumpy) (photo 5, page 293).

**3** Spread half of the batter in prepared pan. Sprinkle with half of the cinnamon mixture. Repeat with remaining batter and cinnamon mixture (below). Using a wide rubber scraper, cut down through batter and pull up in a circular motion to marble the cinnamon mixture (below).

**4** Bake in the preheated oven for 55 to 60 minutes or until a wooden toothpick inserted near the center comes out clean. Cool in pan on a wire rack for 10 minutes. Remove from pan (photo 3, page 305). Cool completely on wire rack. Wrap and store bread overnight before slicing (photo 4, page 305). Makes 1 loaf (14 slices).

**1** Layer the batter and cinnamon mixture so it's easier to swirl together.

**2** Top the last of the batter with the remaining half of the cinnamon mixture.

**3** Use a rubber scraper to cut through the batter and swirl it for a marbled look.

**Ask Mom** How do I measure flour? p. 54 / How do I measure liquids/sugar? p. 55 / How do I remove quick breads from pans? p. 60 / How do I store baked goods? p. 68 / How do I toast nuts? p. 34 / What are chopped nuts? p. 34 / What is baking powder? p. 30, 319 / What is cinnamon? p. 36 / What is cooking oil? p. 28 / What's that flour? p. 31 / What's that nut? p. 34–35 / Why is there a crack in my bread? p. 305 / Why remove bread from the pan to cool? p. 350 / Why wait a day to slice quick bread? p. 309

# Quick Seed Bread

- 1½ cups all-purpose flour
- ½ cup whole wheat flour
- ¾ cup packed brown sugar
- ½ cup dry roasted shelled sunflower kernels
- ⅓ cup ground flaxseed
- 2 tablespoons whole flaxseeds
- 2 tablespoons sesame seeds
- 2 tablespoons poppy seeds
- 1 teaspoon baking powder
- ½ teaspoon baking soda
- 1 egg
- 1¼ cups buttermilk or sour milk*
- ¼ cup cooking oil
- 4 teaspoons whole flaxseeds, sesame seeds, poppy seeds, and/or shelled sunflower kernels

**1** Preheat oven to 350°F. Grease the bottom and ½ inch up the sides of a 9×5×3-inch loaf pan (photo 1, page 305); set aside.

**2** In a large bowl stir together the flours, brown sugar, sunflower kernels, ground flaxseeds, the 2 tablespoons whole flaxseeds, the 2 tablespoons sesame seeds, the 2 tablespoons poppy seeds, the baking powder, baking soda, and ½ teaspoon *salt* (photo 3, page 292). Make a well in the center of the flour mixture; set aside. In a medium bowl beat egg with a fork; stir in buttermilk and oil. Add egg mixture to flour mixture all at once (photo 4, page 292); stir just until moistened (batter should be lumpy) (photo 5, page 293). Spread batter evenly in the prepared pan. Sprinkle with the 4 teaspoons seeds.

**3** Bake in the preheated oven for 45 to 55 minutes or until a wooden toothpick inserted near the center comes out clean. Cool in pan on a wire rack for 10 minutes. Remove from pan (photo 3, page 305). Cool completely on wire rack. Wrap and store bread overnight before slicing (photo 4, page 305). Makes 1 loaf (14 slices).

*Note: For 1¼ cups sour milk, place ¾ teaspoon lemon juice or vinegar in a measuring cup. Add milk for 1¼ cups total liquid; stir. Let stand 5 minutes.

**Per slice:** 219 cal., 10 g total fat (1 g sat. fat), 16 mg chol., 180 mg sodium, 29 g carbo., 3 g fiber, 5 g pro.

A mix of crunchy seeds adds taste, texture, and a nutritional boost to this yummy bread. Flaxseeds are loaded with heart-healthy omega-3 fatty acids, and sunflower seeds with antioxidant vitamin E.

**Good to Know** Make
cleanup easy: Place a
sheet of waxed paper
under the cooling
rack to catch any of
the streusel topping
that falls off the bread
when it's removed from
the pan.

# Apple Pie Bread

½ cup butter, softened

I cup sugar

¼ cup buttermilk or sour milk*

2 teaspoons baking powder

2 eggs

I teaspoon vanilla

2 cups all-purpose flour

½ teaspoon salt

2 cups shredded, peeled apple (about 4 medium)

I cup chopped walnuts or pecans

½ cup raisins

I recipe Streusel-Nut Topping

**1** Preheat oven to 350°F. Grease the bottom and ½ inch up the sides of a 9×5×3-inch loaf pan (photo 1, page 305); set aside.

**2** In a large mixing bowl beat butter with an electric mixer on medium to high speed for 30 seconds. Beat in sugar until combined. Add buttermilk and baking powder; beat until combined. Beat in eggs and vanilla. Add flour and salt; beat just until combined. Stir in apple, walnuts, and raisins. Spread batter evenly in the prepared pan. Sprinkle Streusel-Nut Topping evenly over batter.

**3** Bake in the preheated oven for 60 to 65 minutes or until a wooden toothpick inserted near the center comes out clean. Cool in pan on a wire rack for 10 minutes. Remove from pan (photo 3, page 305). Cool completely on wire rack. Wrap and store bread overnight before slicing (photo 4, page 305). Makes 1 loaf (14 servings).

*Note: To make ¼ cup sour milk, place ¾ teaspoon lemon juice or vinegar in a glass measuring cup. Add enough milk to make ¼ cup total liquid; stir. Let stand for 5 minutes before using.

Streusel-Nut Topping: In a small bowl stir together ¼ cup packed brown sugar and 3 tablespoons all-purpose flour. Using a pastry blender, cut in 2 tablespoons cold butter until mixture resembles coarse crumbs. Stir in ⅓ cup chopped walnuts or pecans.

**Per serving:** 326 cal., 17 g total fat (6 g sat. fat), 52 mg chol., 193 mg sodium, 42 g carbo., 2 g fiber, 5 g pro.

**WHY WAIT A DAY TO SLICE?** Quick breads require a little patience. The day they're baked, they're just too soft to slice. If you try, they'll break and crumble. Store them tightly wrapped for a day and they'll firm up enough to slice cleanly and easily.

The best tool for slicing quick breads is a large serrated knife. Cut the loaf in ½-inch-thick slices. If you're serving a large crowd, it's probably best to cut the slices in half vertically.

**WHAT KIND OF CORNMEAL IS BEST?** It depends on what you like. You can use cornmeal made from yellow, white, or blue corn—and it can be ground fine, medium, or coarse. The latter choice will give your corn bread a little bit of a pleasantly crunchy texture.

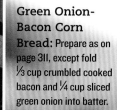

**Green Onion-Bacon Corn Bread:** Prepare as on page 3ll, except fold ⅓ cup crumbled cooked bacon and ¼ cup sliced green onion into batter.

**Double Corn Bread:** Prepare as on page 3ll, except fold ½ cup frozen whole kernel corn, thawed, into the batter.

**Green Chile Corn Bread:** Prepare as on page 3ll, except fold I cup shredded cheddar cheese or Monterey Jack cheese (4 ounces) and one 4-ounce can diced green chile peppers, drained, into the batter.

**Sweet Pepper Corn Bread:** Prepare as on page 3ll, except fold ½ cup chopped red sweet pepper into the batter.

# Corn Bread

| | |
|---|---|
| 1 cup all-purpose flour | 1 tablespoon butter |
| ¾ cup cornmeal | 2 eggs |
| 2 to 3 tablespoons sugar | 1 cup milk |
| 2½ teaspoons baking powder | ¼ cup cooking oil or melted butter |
| ¾ teaspoon salt | |

**1** Preheat oven to 400°F. In a medium bowl stir together the flour, cornmeal, sugar, baking powder, and salt (photo 3, page 292); set aside.

**2** Add the 1 tablespoon butter to an 8×8×2-inch baking pan (below), a 9×1½-inch round baking pan, or a 10-inch cast-iron skillet. Place pan in the preheated oven about 3 minutes or until butter melts. Remove pan from oven (below); swirl butter to coat bottom and sides of pan.

**3** Meanwhile, in a small bowl beat eggs with a fork; stir in milk and oil. Add egg mixture to flour mixture all at once (photo 4, page 292); stir just until moistened (batter should be lumpy) (photo 5, page 293). Pour batter into hot pan (below). Bake for 15 to 20 minutes or until a wooden toothpick inserted near the center comes out clean. Serve warm. Makes 8 to 10 servings.

Per serving: 219 cal., 10 g total fat (3 g sat. fat), 60 mg chol., 390 mg sodium, 26 g carbo., 1 g fiber, 5 g pro.

**Corn Muffins:** Prepare as above, except omit the 1 tablespoon butter. Spoon batter into 12 greased 2½-inch muffin cups, filling each two-thirds full (photo 6, page 293). Bake in the preheated oven about 15 minutes or until light brown and a wooden toothpick inserted in the centers comes out clean. Makes 12 muffins.

 **1** Instead of greasing the pan for corn bread, add 1 tablespoon of butter to the baking pan.

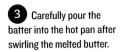 **2** Melt the butter in the pan in the oven. Starting with a hot pan ensures crisp edges on the corn bread.

**3** Carefully pour the batter into the hot pan after swirling the melted butter.

**Ask Mom** How do I measure butter? p. 55 / How do I measure flour? p. 54 / How do I measure liquids? p. 55 / How do I measure sugar? p. 55 / How do I store baked goods? p. 68 / What is baking powder? p. 30, 319 / What is cooking oil? p. 28 / What's that flour? p. 31

# Coconut-Pecan Coffee Cake

½ cup butter, softened
1 cup granulated sugar
2 teaspoons baking powder
½ teaspoon baking soda
¼ teaspoon salt

2 eggs
1 teaspoon vanilla
2¼ cups all-purpose flour
1 8-ounce carton dairy sour cream
1 recipe Coconut-Pecan Topping

**1** Preheat oven to 350°F. Grease and flour a 9-inch springform pan; set aside. In a large mixing bowl beat butter with an electric mixer on medium to high speed for 30 seconds. Add the sugar, baking powder, baking soda, and salt. Beat until well combined (below), scraping sides of bowl occasionally. Add eggs, one at a time, beating well after each addition (below). Beat in vanilla. Add flour and sour cream alternately to butter mixture, beating on low speed after each addition just until combined.*

**2** Spread half of the batter in the prepared pan. Sprinkle with half of the Coconut-Pecan Topping (below). Spoon remaining cake batter in mounds over coconut mixture (below); carefully spread evenly. Sprinkle with remaining Coconut-Pecan Topping.

**3** Bake in the preheated oven about 65 minutes or until a wooden toothpick inserted near the center comes out clean. If necessary, cover cake with foil for the last 15 to 20 minutes of baking to prevent overbrowning. Cool in pan on a wire rack for 20 minutes. Run a thin knife around edge of cake. Remove sides of pan. Cool for 30 minutes more. Serve warm. Makes 12 servings.

*Note: If batter is too thick for the mixer, use a wooden spoon to beat in flour and sour cream.

Coconut-Pecan Topping: In a large bowl stir together 1 cup all-purpose flour, 1 cup packed brown sugar, and 1 teaspoon ground cinnamon. Using a pastry blender, cut in ½ cup cold butter until mixture resembles coarse crumbs. Stir in ¾ cup semisweet chocolate pieces, ½ cup flaked coconut, and ½ cup chopped pecans.

Per serving: 561 cal., 29 g total fat (16 g sat. fat), 85 mg chol., 325 mg sodium, 71 g carbo., 3 g fiber, 6 g pro.

**1** Beat sugar, baking powder, baking soda, and salt into butter until fluffy.

**2** Beat in eggs, one at a time, making sure they are well incorporated.

**3** Spread half the batter in the pan and sprinkle evenly with half the coconut mixture.

**4** The remaining batter is easier to spread if spooned in mounds on coconut mixture.

**Ask Mom** How do I cut in butter? p. 56 / How do I grease and flour a pan? p. 59 / How do I measure flour/butter/sugar? p. 54, 55 / How do I soften butter? p. 28, 76 / How do I store baked goods? p. 68 / What are chopped nuts? p. 34 / What is a pastry blender? p. 10, 11 / What is a springform pan? p. 16, 17 / What is baking powder/baking soda? p. 30, 319 / What is cinnamon? p. 36 / What is semisweet chocolate? p. 32 / What is vanilla? p. 128 / What's that flour? p. 31 / What's that nut? p. 34-35

# Cream Cheese-Berry Coffee Cake

1 8-ounce package cream cheese or reduced-fat cream cheese (Neufchâtel), softened
1 cup granulated sugar
½ cup butter, softened
1¾ cups all-purpose flour
2 eggs
¼ cup milk
1 teaspoon baking powder
½ teaspoon baking soda
½ teaspoon vanilla
¼ teaspoon salt
½ cup seedless red raspberry jam*
Sifted powdered sugar

**1** Preheat oven to 350°F. Grease a 13×9×2-inch baking pan; set aside.

**2** In a large mixing bowl beat cream cheese, granulated sugar, and butter with electric mixer on medium speed until smooth. Add ¾ cup of the flour, the eggs, milk, baking powder, baking soda, vanilla, and salt. Beat about 1 minute or until combined. Beat in the remaining 1 cup flour on low speed just until combined. Spread batter evenly in the prepared pan. In a small bowl stir jam until nearly smooth (below). Spoon jam in eight to ten mounds on top of batter in pan (below). Using a thin spatula or knife, swirl preserves into batter (below).

**3** Bake in the preheated oven for 30 to 35 minutes or until a wooden toothpick inserted near the center comes out clean (below). Cool in pan on a wire rack for 30 minutes. Dust top of cake with powdered sugar. Serve warm. Makes 24 servings.

**\*Note:** If desired, substitute different fruit preserves, such as strawberry or apricot, for the raspberry jam.

Per serving: 158 cal., 8 g total fat (4 g sat. fat), 39 mg chol., 127 mg sodium, 20 g carbo., 0 g fiber, 2 g pro.

**1** Use a spoon to stir the jam to make it smooth and slightly runny.

**2** Spoon the jam in mounds all over the top of the batter in the pan.

**3** Use a butter knife or spatula to cut through the jam and pull it into the batter in swirls.

**4** When testing for doneness, be sure to stick the toothpick in an area where there is no jam.

**Ask Mom** How do I dust with powdered sugar? p. 267 / How do I measure butter? p. 55 / How do I measure flour? p. 54 / How do I measure liquids? p. 55 / How do I measure sugar? p. 55 / How do I soften cream cheese? p. 57 / How do I store baked goods? p. 68 / What is baking powder? p. 30, 319 / What is baking soda? p. 30, 319 / What is powdered sugar? p. 29 / What is vanilla? p. 128 / What's that flour? p. 31

**Good to Know** If you're using frozen blueberries, you want to avoid bleeding blueberry juice into the batter. The best way to do this is to thaw them in a colander set over a bowl at room temperature for about 1 hour. Use the berries and discard the juice.

**2** Skill Level

# Blueberry Streusel
# Coffee Cake

- 1½ cups packed brown sugar
- 1 cup coarsely chopped nuts
- 4 teaspoons ground cinnamon
- 1 8-ounce carton dairy sour cream
- 1 teaspoon baking soda
- ¾ cup granulated sugar
- ½ cup butter, softened
- 3 eggs
- 1 teaspoon vanilla
- 2 cups all-purpose flour
- 1½ teaspoons baking powder
- 2 cups fresh or frozen blueberries, thawed
- 1 recipe Powdered Sugar Icing

**1** Preheat oven to 350°F. For topping, in a small bowl stir together the brown sugar, nuts, and cinnamon. Set aside. In another small bowl stir together the sour cream and baking soda. Set aside. Grease a 13×9×2-inch baking pan; set aside.

**2** In a large mixing bowl beat granulated sugar and butter with an electric mixer on medium speed until well mixed (photo 1, page 312). Beat in eggs and vanilla. Beat in flour and baking powder until well mixed. Add the sour cream mixture; beat until combined.

**3** Spread half of the batter evenly in prepared pan (photo 1, page 315). Sprinkle blueberries over batter (photo 2, page 315). Sprinkle half of the topping over the blueberries (photo 3, page 315). Drop remaining batter into large mounds on top of filling. Carefully spread batter over the topping and blueberries (photo 4, page 315). Sprinkle the remaining topping over batter.

**4** Bake in the preheated oven for 35 to 40 minutes or until a wooden toothpick inserted near the center comes out clean. Drizzle with Powdered Sugar Icing. Serve warm or let cool on a wire rack. Makes 16 servings.

**Powdered Sugar Icing:** In a small bowl stir together ½ cup powdered sugar, 2 teaspoons milk, and ¼ teaspoon vanilla. Stir in enough additional milk, 1 teaspoon at a time, to make an icing of drizzling consistency.

**Per serving:** 345 cal., 14 g total fat (6 g sat. fat), 61 mg chol., 184 mg sodium, 51 g carbo., 2 g fiber, 4 g pro.

**Ask Mom** How do I grease a baking pan? p. 59 / How do I measure butter/sugar? p. 55 / How do I measure flour? p. 54 / How do I soften butter? p. 28, 76 / How do I store baked goods? p. 68 / How do I wash fresh berries? p. 42 / What are chopped nuts? p. 34 / What does drizzle mean? p. 69, 85 / What is baking powder/baking soda? p. 30, 319 / What is cinnamon? p. 36 / What is granulated sugar/powdered sugar? p. 29 / What is vanilla? p. 128 / What's that flour? p. 31 / What's that nut? p. 34–35

**TOPPING-PROOF TESTING.** When testing for doneness with a toothpick or cake tester, look for a spot where there isn't a lot of chunky topping. If there is some batter on the toothpick, the chunky stuff (like nuts) can scrape it off, which renders your test inaccurate.

**1** Spoon half the batter into the prepared pan and spread it out evenly using a spatula or rubber scraper.

**2** Sprinkle the blueberries evenly over the surface of the batter in the pan.

**3** Sprinkle half the topping mixture over the blueberries, making sure to fill in any gaps.

**4** Spoon the remaining batter over the blueberries and topping in mounds. Use a spatula to carefully spread batter into an even layer.

You can swap raspberries for blueberries in this coffee cake. Use an equal amount of fresh raspberries or frozen raspberries, thawed, using the same method (above and page 314).

# Walnut-Pear Sour
## Cream Coffee Cake

- 1 cup broken walnuts
- ⅓ cup packed brown sugar
- 1 teaspoon ground cinnamon
- ¼ cup cold butter
- ⅓ cup all-purpose flour
- 2 medium pears, peeled, cored, and sliced (about 2 cups)
- 2 teaspoons lemon juice
- 1¾ cups all-purpose flour
- ¾ teaspoon baking powder

- ½ teaspoon baking soda
- ¼ teaspoon salt
- ½ cup butter, softened
- 1 cup granulated sugar
- 1 teaspoon vanilla
- 2 eggs
- 1 8-ounce carton dairy sour cream
- ½ cup broken walnuts (optional)
- 1 recipe Sweetened Whipped Cream (page 25) (optional)

**1** Preheat oven to 350°F. Grease a 9-inch springform pan or a 9×9×2-inch baking pan; set aside. In a small bowl stir together the 1 cup walnuts, the brown sugar, and cinnamon. For topping, in a second small bowl, using a pastry blender, cut the ¼ cup butter into the ⅓ cup flour until mixture resembles coarse crumbs. Stir in ¾ cup of the nut mixture. Set topping and the remaining nut mixture aside.

**2** In a small bowl toss pears with lemon juice; set aside. In a medium bowl stir together the 1¾ cups flour, the baking powder, baking soda, and salt; set aside. In a large mixing bowl beat the ½ cup butter with an electric mixer on medium to high speed for 30 seconds. Beat in the granulated sugar and vanilla (photo 1, page 312). Add eggs, one at a time, beating well after each addition (photo 2, page 312). Add flour mixture and sour cream alternately to egg mixture, beating on low speed after each addition until combined.

**3** Spread two-thirds of the batter evenly in the prepared pan. Sprinkle with reserved nut mixture (photo 3, page 312). Layer pears over nut mixture. Spoon remaining batter in mounds over pears (photo 4, page 312); carefully spread evenly. Sprinkle with the reserved topping.

**4** Bake in the preheated oven for 10 minutes. If desired, sprinkle with the ½ cup walnuts. Bake for 45 to 50 minutes more or until a wooden toothpick inserted near the center comes out clean. Cool in pan on a wire rack for 10 minutes. Run a thin metal spatula or knife around edge of cake. Remove sides of springform pan, if using. Cool for at least 1 hour. If desired, serve warm with Sweetened Whipped Cream. Makes 12 servings.

**Per serving:** 396 cal., 23 g total fat (10 g sat. fat), 75 mg chol., 260 mg sodium, 45 g carbo., 2 g fiber, 5 g pro.

**Ask Mom** How do I peel, core, and slice pears? p. 46, 47 / How do I grease a baking pan? p. 59 / How do I juice a lemon/lime? p. 44, 45 / How do I measure butter? p. 55 / How do I measure flour? p. 54 / How do I measure sugar? p. 55 / How do I soften butter? p. 28, 76 / How do I store baked goods? p. 68 / What is a springform pan? p. 16, 17 / What is baking powder/baking soda? p. 30, 3I9 / What is cinnamon? p. 36 / What is vanilla? p. 128 / What's that flour? p. 3I / What's that nut? p. 34–35

# scrumptious
## SCONES &
## BISCUITS

Sweet or savory, buttery biscuits and scones add a special element to breakfast, lunch, dinner, and dessert (chocolate scone, anyone?).

11

## BISCUITS

Biscuits Supreme ② . . . . . . . . . . . . . . . . . . . . . . . . . . . . . . . . 319
Buttermilk Biscuits ② . . . . . . . . . . . . . . . . . . . . . . . . . . . . . . 319
Drop Biscuits Supreme ② . . . . . . . . . . . . . . . . . . . . . . . . . . . 319
Herbed Cheese and Bacon Biscuits ② . . . . . . . . . . . . . . . . 323
Lemon-Blueberry Biscuits ① . . . . . . . . . . . . . . . . . . . . . . . . 326
Prosciutto Biscuits ② . . . . . . . . . . . . . . . . . . . . . . . . . . . . . . 325
Savory Biscuit Sticks ② . . . . . . . . . . . . . . . . . . . . . . . . . . . . 322

**Flax Soda Bread** ② . . . . . . . . . . . . . . . . . . . . . . . . . . . . . . . . 336
**How do I make a basic biscuit?** . . . . . . . . . . . . . . . . . . . . . . . 320-321
**Lemon Glaze** ① . . . . . . . . . . . . . . . . . . . . . . . . . . . . . . . . . . . 326

## SCONES

Almond-Spice Scones ② . . . . . . . . . . . . . . . . . . . . . . . . . . . . 330
Apple-Cheddar Scones ② . . . . . . . . . . . . . . . . . . . . . . . . . . . 330
Apple-Cinnamon Scones ② . . . . . . . . . . . . . . . . . . . . . . . . . . 330
Apricot Scones ② . . . . . . . . . . . . . . . . . . . . . . . . . . . . . . . . . 330
Bacon-Onion Scones ② . . . . . . . . . . . . . . . . . . . . . . . . . . . . 330
Cherry Scones ② . . . . . . . . . . . . . . . . . . . . . . . . . . . . . . . . . 330
Chocolate-Coconut Scones ② . . . . . . . . . . . . . . . . . . . . . . . 330
Cranberry-Pistachio Scones ② . . . . . . . . . . . . . . . . . . . . . . . 330
Double Chocolate Scones ② . . . . . . . . . . . . . . . . . . . . . . . . . 334
Fresh Cranberry-Chocolate Scones ② . . . . . . . . . . . . . . . . . 333
Fresh Cranberry-Orange Scones ② . . . . . . . . . . . . . . . . . . . 333
Fresh Cranberry-Pecan Scones ② . . . . . . . . . . . . . . . . . . . . 333
Fresh Cranberry Scones ② . . . . . . . . . . . . . . . . . . . . . . . . . . 332
Ginger-Pear Scones ② . . . . . . . . . . . . . . . . . . . . . . . . . . . . . 330
Gorgonzola Cheese and Green Onion Scones ② . . . . . . . . . . 335
Maple-Oat Scones ② . . . . . . . . . . . . . . . . . . . . . . . . . . . . . . 330
Pecan-Date Scones ② . . . . . . . . . . . . . . . . . . . . . . . . . . . . . 330
Scones ② . . . . . . . . . . . . . . . . . . . . . . . . . . . . . . . . . . . . . . . 328
Zucchini Scones ② . . . . . . . . . . . . . . . . . . . . . . . . . . . . . . . . 330

# Biscuits **Supreme**

3 cups all-purpose flour

1 tablespoon baking powder

1 tablespoon sugar

1 teaspoon salt

¾ teaspoon cream of tartar

¾ cup cold butter or ½ cup cold butter plus ¼ cup shortening

1 cup milk

**1** Preheat oven to 450°F. In a large bowl stir together the flour, baking powder, sugar, salt, and cream of tartar (photo 1, page 320). Using a pastry blender, cut in butter until mixture resembles coarse crumbs (photo 2, page 320). Make a well in the center of the flour mixture (photo 3, page 320). Add milk to flour mixture all at once (photo 4, page 320). Using a fork, stir just until moistened (photo 5, page 321).

**2** Turn dough out onto a lightly floured surface (photo 6, page 321). Knead dough by folding and gently pressing it for four to six strokes or just until dough holds together (photos 7–8, page 321). Pat or lightly roll dough until ¾ inch thick (photos 9–10, page 321). Using a floured 2½-inch biscuit cutter, cut out dough, rerolling scraps as necessary (photos 11–12, page 321). Place biscuits 1 inch apart on an ungreased baking sheet.

**3** Bake in the preheated oven for 10 to 14 minutes or until golden. Remove biscuits from baking sheet; serve warm. Makes 12 biscuits.

**Drop Biscuits Supreme:** Prepare as above through Step 1, except increase the milk to 1¼ cups. Using a large spoon or small ice cream scoop, drop dough into 12 mounds onto a greased baking sheet (photo 2, page 326). Bake as above. Makes 12 biscuits.

**Buttermilk Biscuits:** Prepare as above, except for rolled-dough biscuits, substitute 1¼ cups buttermilk or sour milk for the 1 cup milk. For drop biscuits, substitute 1½ cups buttermilk or sour milk for the 1¼ cups milk.

**Per biscuit:** 227 cal., 13 g total fat (6 g sat. fat), 34 mg chol., 350 mg sodium, 24 g carbo., 1 g fiber, 4 g pro.

**Good to Know** If baking powder, baking soda, or cream of tartar appears lumpy, sift through a fine-mesh sieve before you use it. (Biting into a ball of baking powder tends to puts a damper on your biscuit-eating bliss.)

**Ask Mom** How do I grease and flour a pan? p. 59 / How do I make sour milk? p. 24 / How do I measure butter? p. 55 / How do I measure flour? p. 54 / How do I measure liquids? p. 55 / How do I measure shortening? p. 55 / What is a lightly floured surface? p. 60 / What is a pastry blender? p. 10, 11 / What is baking powder? p. 30, 319 / What is buttermilk? p. 24 / What's that flour? p. 31

# How do I make a basic biscuit?

**Delicious with pork chops at dinner and with eggs for Sunday brunch, light, tender, flaky biscuits are a breeze to make with a few basic techniques.**

The first rule of biscuit baking: Mix gently and carry a big spoon. You want to be sure the dry ingredients are well blended to evenly distribute the leavening before you cut in the fat (whether that's shortening or butter) and add the liquid. Mix the fat and flour only until the mixture resembles coarse crumbs (bits of fat create the airy pockets in the biscuits) and mix in the liquid only until everything is moistened. Turn the dough onto a lightly floured surface, then knead the dough by folding and pressing just 10 to 12 times. Overworked dough makes tough biscuits. Gently handled dough makes ethereal biscuits. If you like a soft crust, place biscuits close together on the baking sheet; if you like them crisp, place about 1 inch apart.

**4** Pour the milk into the well in the flour mixture all at once. There is no need to work it in slowly.

**1** In a large mixing bowl or batter bowl stir together all of the dry ingredients.

**2** Cut in the butter and shortening by repeatedly pushing through them with a pastry blender until they look like coarse crumbs.

**3** Push the flour mixture to the sides of the bowl, making a hole or well.

Making a well in the dry ingredients and pouring all of the liquid in at once helps the dry and wet ingredients to blend with the least amount of mixing—which makes the tenderest biscuits.

**5** Use a fork to stir together the dry and wet ingredients. A fork combines it all without overworking the dough.

**6** Spread a little flour out onto a work surface, then push the sticky dough out of the bowl onto the floured surface.

**7** Coat your hands with flour and gently press the dough together, adding just enough flour so the dough is workable.

**8** Gently knead the dough by folding and pressing it until the dough is uniform and holds together nicely.

**11** When cutting out biscuits, push down quickly and firmly on the cutter. A clean cut ensures high-rising biscuits and flaky layers.

**9** Pat the dough into an even thickness on the floured surface. Don't work it too much or it will be tough.

**10** The biscuit dough should be about ¾ inch thick. Use a ruler to check.

**12** Gently reroll the scraps to cut out more biscuits. Remember, the more you work the dough, the less tender they will be.

**A CLEVER WAY TO CUT.** Most biscuits are cut with a 2½-inch biscuit cutter, but if you don't have one, you can use the rim of a similar-size drinking glass. Dip the rim in flour before each cut to keep the biscuit from sticking to the glass.

② Skill Level

**Good to Know**
Cumin—a spice used generously in Mexican and Latin cooking—has an earthy, warm, pungent flavor. It comes both ground and in whole-seed forms. Crush the cumin seeds in a mortar and pestle, or place them in a small plastic bag and roll a rolling pin over the top.

# Savory Biscuit Sticks

 2 cups all-purpose flour
 2 tablespoons sugar
 2 teaspoons baking powder
 ¼ teaspoon baking soda
 1¼ teaspoons cracked black pepper
 ¼ teaspoon garlic powder
 6 tablespoons cold butter
 ½ cup finely shredded Asiago cheese (2 ounces)
 1 egg, lightly beaten
 ½ cup buttermilk or sour milk
    Buttermilk or sour milk
 ¾ teaspoon cumin seeds, crushed

**1** Preheat oven to 450°F. In a large bowl stir together the flour, sugar, baking powder, baking soda, ¼ teaspoon of the pepper, and the garlic powder (photo 1, page 320). Using a pastry blender, cut in butter until mixture resembles coarse crumbs (photo 2, page 320). Stir in cheese. Make a well in the center of the flour mixture (photo 3, page 320); set aside. In a small bowl stir together the egg and the ½ cup buttermilk. Add the egg mixture all at once to the flour mixture (photo 4, page 320). Using a fork, stir just until moistened (photo 5, page 321).

**2** Turn dough out onto a lightly floured surface (photo 6, page 321). Knead dough by folding and gently pressing it for four to six strokes or just until dough holds together (photos 7–8, page 321). Pat or lightly roll dough into a 12×6-inch rectangle (photo 9, page 321). Brush top lightly with additional buttermilk. Sprinkle rectangle evenly with the remaining 1 teaspoon pepper and the cumin seeds; press lightly into dough. Cut rectangle crosswise into twenty-four 6-inch-long strips. Place dough strips 1 inch apart on an ungreased baking sheet.

**3** Bake in the preheated oven about 8 minutes or until golden. Remove biscuit sticks from baking sheet; serve warm or cool on a wire rack.* Makes 24 biscuit sticks.

*Note: Cooled biscuit sticks can be wrapped in foil and stored at room temperature for up to 2 days. To serve, preheat oven to 350°F. Unwrap biscuit sticks and place on a baking sheet. Bake in the preheated oven for 5 to 7 minutes or until heated through.

Per 2 biscuit sticks: 164 cal., 9 g total fat (5 g sat. fat), 40 mg chol., 223 mg sodium, 18 g carbo., 1 g fiber, 4 g pro.

**Ask Mom** How do I make sour milk? p. 24 / How do I measure butter? p. 55 / How do I measure flour? p. 54 / How do I shred cheese? p. 21, 254 / How do I work with eggs? p. 26–27 / What is a lightly floured surface? p. 60 / What is baking powder? p. 30, 319 / What is baking soda? p. 30, 319 / What is buttermilk? p. 24 / What's that flour? p. 31

# Herbed Cheese
# And Bacon Biscuits

best kind of bacon for these biscuits is a regular or thin-cut style. It crumbles more easily and delicately than thick-cut bacon. Thick-cut works and tastes just fine too— your crumbles will just be bigger.

- 2 slices bacon
- ½ cup chopped red onion
- 3 cups all-purpose flour
- 1 tablespoon baking powder
- 1 teaspoon sugar
- ½ teaspoon salt
- ¼ teaspoon ground black pepper
- 1 5.2-ounce package semisoft cheese with garlic and herbs
- 1 cup half-and-half or light cream

**1** Preheat oven to 450°F. In a large skillet cook bacon over medium heat for 8 to 10 minutes or until crisp, turning occasionally. Remove bacon from skillet and drain on paper towels; reserve drippings in skillet. Crumble bacon; set aside. Cook onion in bacon drippings over medium heat for 4 to 5 minutes or until tender and beginning to brown. Remove from heat; set aside.

**2** In a large bowl stir together the flour, baking powder, sugar, salt, and pepper (photo 1, page 320). Using a pastry blender, cut in cheese until mixture resembles coarse crumbs (photo 2, page 320). Stir in bacon and onion. Make a well in the center of the flour mixture (photo 3, page 320). Add half-and-half all at once (photo 4, page 320). Using a fork, stir just until mixture is moistened (photo 5, page 321).

**3** Turn dough out onto a lightly floured surface (photo 6, page 321). Knead dough by folding and gently pressing for four to six strokes or just until dough holds together (photos 7–8, page 321). Pat or lightly roll dough until ¾ inch thick (photos 9–10, page 321). Using a floured 2½-inch biscuit cutter, cut out dough, rerolling scraps as necessary (photos 11–12, page 321). Place biscuits 1 inch apart on an ungreased baking sheet.

**4** Bake in the preheated oven about 10 minutes or until golden. Remove biscuits from baking sheet; serve warm. Makes 10 to 12 biscuits.

Per biscuit: 261 cal., 11 g total fat (6 g sat. fat), 28 mg chol., 262 mg sodium, 31 g carbo., 1 g fiber, 7 g pro.

Semisoft cheese serves as the fat in these luscious biscuits. To most easily incorporate it into the flour mixture, cut it into chunks with a butter knife before adding it to the bowl.

**Ask Mom** How do I chop an onion? p. 51 / How do I measure flour? p. 54 / What is a lightly floured surface? p. 60 / What is baking powder? p. 30, 319 / What is half-and-half? p. 24 / What is light cream? p. 24 / What's that flour? p. 31

**SAY "CIAO" OR "HOWDY!"** Made with prosciutto and provolone, these biscuits take on an Italian accent—made with ham and cheddar, they become Southern-style comfort food.

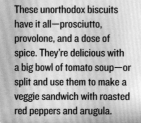

These unorthodox biscuits have it all—prosciutto, provolone, and a dose of spice. They're delicious with a big bowl of tomato soup—or split and use them to make a veggie sandwich with roasted red peppers and arugula.

## What is prosciutto?

It's ham, with a paradigm shift. In Italian, the word itself means "ham," although it's not created or eaten like American ham. Prosciutto is a ham that has been seasoned, salt-cured, air-dried, and pressed—but not smoked. True prosciutto comes from the region of Parma in Italy (hence it's also called Parma ham), but there is some very good American-made proscuitto. Prosciutto is almost always served in paper-thin slices. Wrapped around slices of ripe cantaloupe, ripe figs, or cold roasted asparagus, it makes a great appetizer.

**② Skill Level**

# Prosciutto **Biscuits**

1⅓ cups all-purpose flour

1 teaspoon baking powder

1 teaspoon fennel seeds, crushed

½ teaspoon sugar

¼ teaspoon salt

¼ teaspoon baking soda

6 tablespoons cold butter, cut up

½ cup shredded provolone or sharp cheddar cheese (2 ounces)

1 ounce thinly sliced prosciutto or cooked ham, finely chopped (about ⅓ cup)

½ cup milk

**1** Preheat oven to 425°F. In a medium bowl stir together the flour, baking powder, fennel seeds, sugar, salt, and baking soda (photo 1, page 320). Using a pastry blender, cut in butter until mixture resembles coarse crumbs (photo 2, page 320). Stir in cheese and prosciutto. Make a well in the center of the flour mixture (photo 3, page 320). Add milk all at once (photo 4, page 320). Using a fork, stir just until mixture is moistened (photo 5, page 321).

**2** Turn dough out onto a lightly floured surface (photo 6, page 321). Knead dough by folding and gently pressing for four to six strokes or just until dough holds together (photos 7–8, page 321). Pat or lightly roll dough into a 9×5-inch rectangle (below). Using a long knife or pizza cutter, cut dough lengthwise in half, then crosswise into fourths, making 8 rectangles (below). Place rectangles 1 inch apart on an ungreased baking sheet.

**3** Bake in the preheated oven for 12 to 14 minutes or until golden. Remove biscuits from baking sheet; serve warm. Makes 8 biscuits.

Per biscuit: 187 cal., 11 g total fat (7 g sat. fat), 31 mg chol., 368 mg sodium, 16 g carbo., 1 g fiber, 5 g pro.

**Ingredient Info**
Fennel seeds have a licoricelike flavor. They are in large part what gives Italian sausage that great, savory flavor. In fact fennel is delicious paired with all kinds of pork—like the prosciutto in these biscuits. Crush the seeds in a mortar and pestle or put them in a plastic bag and roll a rolling pin over the top.

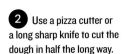
**1** Gently roll the dough into a 9×5-inch rectangle. Use a ruler to check the measurements.

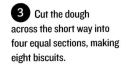
**2** Use a pizza cutter or a long sharp knife to cut the dough in half the long way.

**3** Cut the dough across the short way into four equal sections, making eight biscuits.

**Ask Mom** How do I measure butter? p. 55 / How do I measure flour? p. 54 / How do I measure liquids? p. 55 / How do I shred cheese? p. 21, 254 / What is a lightly floured surface? p. 60 / What is baking powder? p. 30, 319 / What's that flour? p. 31

# Lemon-Blueberry Biscuits

2 cups all-purpose flour
⅓ cup granulated sugar
2 teaspoons baking powder
½ teaspoon baking soda
¼ teaspoon salt
¼ cup cold butter

1 egg, lightly beaten
1 6-ounce carton lemon lowfat yogurt
2 tablespoons milk
1 teaspoon finely shredded lemon peel
1 cup fresh or frozen unsweetened blueberries
1 recipe Lemon Glaze

**1** Preheat oven to 400°F. Lightly grease a large baking sheet; set aside. In a large bowl stir together the flour, sugar, baking powder, baking soda, and salt (photo 1, page 320). Using a pastry blender, cut in butter until mixture resembles coarse crumbs (photo 2, page 320). Make a well in the center of the flour mixture; set aside (photo 3, page 320).

**2** In a small bowl stir together the egg, yogurt, milk, and lemon peel. Add egg mixture to flour mixture all at once (photo 4, page 320). Using a fork, stir just until moistened (photo 5, page 321). Fold in blueberries (below). Drop about ¼ cup dough for each biscuit (or use a small ice cream scoop) onto the prepared baking sheet (below).

**3** Bake in the preheated oven for 12 to 15 minutes or until golden brown (below). Transfer biscuits to a wire rack. Drizzle Lemon Glaze over warm biscuits. Serve warm. Makes about 12 biscuits.

**Lemon Glaze:** In a small bowl stir together 1 cup powdered sugar, 1 teaspoon finely shredded lemon peel, 1 teaspoon vanilla, and enough lemon juice (3 to 4 teaspoons) to make a glaze of drizzling consistency (below).

Per biscuit: 159 cal., 4 g total fat (2 g sat. fat), 23 mg chol., 147 mg sodium, 28 g carbo., 1 g fiber, 1 g pro.

**1** Gently fold the blueberries into the dough by pulling the dough up and over the berries.

**2** Use a small ice cream scoop to easily drop the sticky dough onto a greased baking sheet.

**3** The biscuits are done when they are golden brown all over. Transfer them to a wire rack to drizzle with glaze before serving.

**4** Stir together all the glaze ingredients until smooth. Add more lemon juice if needed so glaze drizzles easily from a spoon.

**Ask Mom** How do I cut in butter? p. 56 / How do I grease a baking pan? p. 59 / How do I juice a lemon? p. 44, 45 / How do I measure butter? p. 55 / How do I measure flour? p. 54 / How do I measure sugar? p. 55 / How do I shred lemon peel? p. 45, 105 / How do I wash fresh berries? p. 42 / How do I work with eggs? p. 26–27 / What does drizzle mean? p. 69, 85 / What is baking powder/baking soda? p. 30, 319 / What is powdered sugar? p. 29 / What is vanilla? p. 128 / What's that nut? p. 34–35

**CAN I FREEZE THESE BISCUITS?** You can—just don't glaze them. After they've cooled, wrap them in foil and put them in a plastic freezer bag. To reheat, put the foil-wrapped biscuits in a 300°F oven for 20 to 25 minutes—then glaze them.

The lemon glaze adds extra lemon flavor to these perfect-for-tea biscuits, but you can simply give them a dusting of powdered sugar instead.

# Scones

| | |
|---|---|
| 2 ½ cups all-purpose flour | 2 eggs, lightly beaten |
| 2 tablespoons sugar | ¾ cup whipping cream |
| 1 tablespoon baking powder | ½ cup dried currants or snipped raisins |
| ¼ teaspoon salt | Whipping cream or milk |
| ⅓ cup cold butter | Coarse or granulated sugar |

**1** Preheat oven to 400°F. In a large bowl stir together the flour, the 2 tablespoons sugar, the baking powder, and salt (photo 1, page 320). Using a pastry blender, cut in butter until mixture resembles coarse crumbs (photo 2, page 320). Make a well in the center of the flour mixture (photo 3, page 320); set aside.

**2** In a medium bowl stir together the eggs, the ¾ cup whipping cream, and the currants. Add egg mixture to flour mixture all at once (photo 4, page 320). Using a fork, stir just until moistened (photo 5, page 321).

**3** Turn dough out onto a lightly floured surface (photo 6, page 321). Knead dough by folding and gently pressing it for 10 to 12 strokes or until dough is nearly smooth (below). Divide dough in half. Pat or lightly roll half of the dough into a 6-inch circle (below). Cut into 6 wedges (below). Repeat with the remaining dough.

**4** Place wedges 2 inches apart on an ungreased baking sheet. Brush wedges with additional whipping cream and sprinkle with coarse sugar (below).

**5** Bake in the preheated oven for 12 to 14 minutes or until golden. Remove scones from baking sheet; serve warm. Makes 12 scones.

Per scone: 229 cal., 12 g total fat (7 g sat. fat), 71 mg chol., 165 mg sodium, 26 g carbo., 1 g fiber, 4 g pro.

**1** On a floured work surface, gently knead the dough by pushing and folding it until it is almost smooth.

**2** Pat half of the dough into a 6-inch circle. Press against the sides of the circle so it is uniformly thick.

**3** Use a long sharp knife to cut the circle into six equal-size wedges.

**4** Brush the tops of the wedges with cream, then sprinkle them with coarse or regular sugar.

**Ask Mom** How do I measure butter? p. 55 / How do I measure flour? p. 54 / How do I measure liquids? p. 55 / How do I snip dried fruit or preserves? p. 41, 102 / How do I work with eggs? p. 26–27 / What is a lightly floured surface? p. 60 / What is a pastry blender? p. 10, 11 / What is baking powder? p. 30, 319 / What is coarse sugar? p. 29 / What is granulated sugar? p. 29 / What is whipping cream? p. 24 / What's that dried fruit? p. 41 / What's that flour? p. 31

**A CHANGE OF SHAPE.** Instead of wedges, you can make these scones round or square. Just pat the dough ¾ inch thick, then cut into squares with a sharp knife—or use a round cutter to cut dough into circles, rerolling scraps as necessary.

This may be the classic English scone—buttery, flaky, and studded with currants—but there's no end to the flavoring possibilities, both sweet and savory. See pages 332–333 for some ideas.

## Cherry Scones

- ½ cup dried sweet cherries, snipped
- 1½ teaspoons finely shredded lemon peel
- ¼ teaspoon ground nutmeg

Prepare Scones (page 328) as directed, except omit currants. Stir cherries, lemon peel, and nutmeg into the flour mixture. If desired, sprinkle a little ground nutmeg on top of scones with the sugar.

## Maple-Oat Scones

- ½ cup quick-cooking rolled oats
- ¼ cup pure maple syrup Quick-cooking rolled oats

Prepare Scones (page 328) as directed, except substitute ½ cup oats for ¼ cup of the flour and substitute maple syrup for ¼ cup of the whipping cream. Sprinkle tops of scones with additional oats instead of sugar.

## Almond-Spice Scones

- ⅓ cup chopped toasted almonds
- ¼ teaspoon ground cinnamon

Prepare Scones (page 328) as directed, except stir almonds and cinnamon into the flour mixture.

## Apricot Scones

- ½ cup snipped dried apricots
- ¼ teaspoon almond extract Sliced almonds

Prepare Scones (page 328) as directed, except substitute apricots for currants. Stir almond extract into the egg mixture and sprinkle tops of scones with almonds instead of sugar.

## Apple-Cheddar Scones

- ½ cup shredded tart apple
- ⅓ cup shredded sharp cheddar cheese

Prepare Scones (page 328) as directed, except omit currants. Stir apple and cheese into the egg mixture.

## Pecan-Date Scones

- ⅓ cup chopped dates
- ¼ cup chopped toasted pecans

Prepare Scones (page 328) as directed, except omit currants. Stir dates and pecans into the flour mixture.

## Ginger-Pear Scones

- ½ cup snipped dried pear
- 2 tablespoons finely chopped crystallized ginger

Prepare Scones (page 328) as directed, except omit currants. Stir pear and ginger into the egg mixture.

## Bacon-Onion Scones

- ⅓ cup sliced green onion
- ⅓ cup crumbled crisp-cooked bacon

Prepare Scones (page 328) as directed, except omit currants. Stir onion and bacon into the flour mixture. Do not sprinkle scones with sugar.

## Apple-Cinnamon Scones

- ½ cup shredded, peeled tart apple
- ⅓ cup cinnamon-flavor baking pieces

Prepare Scones (page 328) as directed, except omit currants. Stir apple and cinnamon pieces into the egg mixture.

## Chocolate-Coconut Scones

- ¾ unsweetened coconut milk
- ⅓ cup flaked coconut, toasted
- ⅓ cup miniature semisweet chocolate pieces

Prepare Scones (page 328) as directed, except omit currants. Substitute coconut milk for whipping cream and stir coconut and chocolate pieces into the flour mixture.

## Cranberry-Pistachio Scones

- ⅓ cup dried cranberries
- ⅓ cup chopped pistachios

Prepare Scones (page 328) as directed, except substitute cranberries for currants and stir pistachios into the flour mixture.

## Zucchini Scones

- ½ cup shredded zucchini
- ⅓ cup grated Romano or Parmesan cheese

Prepare Scones (page 328) as directed, except omit currants. Stir zucchini into the egg mixture and Romano cheese into the flour mixture. Do not sprinkle scones with sugar.

# One Scone, 12 Ways

Nibble a sweet scone with your morning o.j. and a savory one with your evening soup. With a few tweaks, one basic recipe makes a dozen different scones.

# Fresh Cranberry Scones

2¼ cups all-purpose flour

2 tablespoons sugar

1 tablespoon baking powder

¼ teaspoon salt

1½ cups fresh cranberries, finely chopped

2 tablespoons honey

1 cup whipping cream

1 egg, lightly beaten

1 tablespoon water

1 tablespoon sugar

**Good to Know** Fresh cranberries give these scones a pretty, pale pink hue—and lip-puckering tartness. They're great spread with lemon curd.

**1** Preheat oven to 375°F. In a large bowl stir together the flour, 2 tablespoons sugar, the baking powder, and ¼ teaspoon salt (photo 1, page 320). Make a well in the center of the flour mixture (photo 3, page 320); set aside.

**2** In a medium bowl stir together cranberries and honey; stir in whipping cream. Add cranberry mixture to flour mixture. Using a fork, stir just until moistened (photo 5, page 321).

**3** Turn dough out onto a lightly floured surface (photo 6, page 321). Knead dough by folding and gently pressing it for 10 to 12 strokes or until dough is nearly smooth (photo 1, page 328). Pat or lightly roll dough into an 8-inch circle (photo 2, page 328). Cut into 8 wedges (photo 3, page 328). Place wedges 1 inch apart on an ungreased baking sheet. In a small bowl whisk together egg and water. Lightly brush wedges with egg mixture and sprinkle tops with 1 tablespoon sugar (photo 4, page 328).

**4** Bake in the preheated oven for 20 to 25 minutes or until golden. Remove scones from baking sheet; serve warm. Makes 8 scones.

**Per scone:** 300 cal., 12 g total fat (7 g sat. fat), 68 mg chol., 184 mg sodium, 42 g carbo., 2 g fiber, 6 g pro.

The best way to chop fresh cranberries is to put them in the bowl of a food processor, then cover and pulse several times until finely chopped.

**Ask Mom** How do I chop chocolate? p. 33 / How do I chop cranberries? p. 43 / How do I juice an orange and shred orange peel? p. 45, 105 / How do I measure flour/liquids? p. 54, 55 / How do I toast nuts? p. 34 / How do I work with eggs? p. 26–27 / What is a lightly floured surface? p. 60 / What is baking powder? p. 30, 319 / What is powdered sugar? p. 29 / What is pure maple syrup? p. 300 / What is bittersweet chocolate? p. 32 / What is vanilla? p. 128 / What is whipping cream? p. 24 / What's that flour? p. 31

**CAN I USE FROZEN CRANBERRIES IF FRESH AREN'T AVAILABLE?** Fresh cranberries do have a fairly short window in the marketplace—usually just around the holidays. To use frozen cranberries, thaw completely, then make sure they're well drained before chopping.

1. **Fresh Cranberry-Pecan Scones:** Prepare as on page 336, except stir ⅔ cup coarsely chopped toasted pecans into the cranberry mixture. For icing, in a small bowl stir together I cup powdered sugar, 2 tablespoons pure maple syrup, and ¼ teaspoon vanilla. Stir in milk, I teaspoon at a time, to make icing of drizzling consistency. Drizzle icing over scones.

2. **Fresh Cranberry-Orange Scones:** Prepare as on page 336, except stir I½ teaspoons finely shredded orange peel into the cranberry mixture. For icing, in a small bowl stir together I cup powdered sugar, I tablespoon orange juice, and ¼ teaspoon vanilla. Stir in additional orange juice, I teaspoon at a time, to make icing of drizzling consistency. Drizzle icing over scones.

3. **Fresh Cranberry-Chocolate Scones:** Prepare as on page 336, except stir ⅔ cup (3 ounces) coarsely chopped bittersweet chocolate into the cranberry mixture. For icing, drizzle 2 ounces melted bittersweet chocolate over scones.

# Double Chocolate Scones

2 cups all-purpose flour
½ cup granulated sugar
⅓ cup unsweetened cocoa powder
1 tablespoon baking powder
½ teaspoon salt
⅓ cup cold butter
1 egg, lightly beaten

½ cup whipping cream
1 teaspoon vanilla
1 cup miniature semisweet chocolate pieces
½ cup chopped pecans, toasted (optional)
Whipping cream (optional)
Coarse sugar (optional)

**1** Preheat oven to 400°F. Line a large baking sheet with parchment paper; set aside. In a large bowl stir together the flour, granulated sugar, cocoa powder, baking powder, and salt (photo 1, page 320). Using a pastry blender, cut in butter until mixture resembles coarse crumbs (photo 2, page 320). Make a well in the center of the flour mixture (photo 3, page 320); set aside.

**2** In a small bowl stir together the egg, the ½ cup whipping cream, and the vanilla. Add egg mixture to flour mixture all at once (photo 4, page 320). Add chocolate pieces and, if desired, the pecans. Using a fork, stir just until moistened (photo 5, page 321).

**3** Turn dough out onto a lightly floured surface (photo 6, page 321). Knead dough by folding and gently pressing it for 10 to 12 strokes or until dough is nearly smooth (photo 1, page 328). Divide dough in half. Pat or lightly roll half of the dough into a 4½-inch circle about 1 inch thick (photo 2, page 328). Cut into 6 wedges (photo 3, page 328). Repeat with remaining dough. Place wedges 1 inch apart on the prepared baking sheet. If desired, brush wedges with additional whipping cream and sprinkle with coarse sugar (photo 4, page 328).

**4** Bake in the preheated oven for 12 to 14 minutes or until bottoms are light brown. Remove scones from baking sheet. Serve warm. Makes 12 scones.

Per scone: 312 cal., 15 g total fat (9 g sat. fat), 45 mg chol., 168 mg sodium, 39 g carbo., 1 g fiber, 5 g pro.

**Ask Mom** How do I measure flour? p. 54 / How do I measure liquids/sugar? p. 55 / How do I work with eggs? p. 26–27 / What are chopped nuts? p. 34 / What is a pastry blender? p. 10, 11 / What is baking powder? p. 30, 319 / What is coarse sugar? p. 29 / What is cocoa powder? p. 170 / What is granulated sugar? p. 29 / What is parchment paper? p. 21, 69 / What is semisweet chocolate? p. 32 / What is vanilla? p. 128 / What is whipping cream? p. 24 / What's that flour? p. 31 / What's that nut? p. 34–35

**2** Skill Level

# Gorgonzola Cheese and
## Green Onion Scones

2 cups all-purpose flour

2 tablespoons thinly sliced green onion (1)

2 teaspoons baking powder

¼ teaspoon baking soda

¼ teaspoon salt

¼ teaspoon ground black pepper

1 egg, lightly beaten

½ cup crumbled Gorgonzola cheese or other blue cheese (2 ounces)

½ cup buttermilk or sour milk

1 egg white, lightly beaten

1 tablespoon water

**1** Preheat oven to 400°F. Line a large baking sheet with parchment paper; set aside. In a medium bowl stir together the flour, green onion, baking powder, baking soda, salt, and pepper (photo 1, page 320). Make a well in the center of the flour mixture (photo 3, page 320); set aside.

**2** In a small bowl stir together the whole egg, cheese, and buttermilk. Add egg mixture to flour mixture all at once (photo 4, page 320). Using a fork, stir just until moistened (photo 5, page 321).

**3** Turn dough out onto a lightly floured surface (photo 6, page 321). Knead dough by folding and gently pressing it for 10 to 12 strokes or until dough is nearly smooth (photo 1, page 328). Divide dough in half. Pat or lightly roll half of the dough into a 5-inch circle (photo 2, page 328). Cut into 6 wedges (photo 3, page 328) or 3-inch circles or squares. Repeat with the remaining dough.

**4** Place wedges 1 inch apart on the prepared baking sheet. In a small bowl stir together the egg white and water. Lightly brush wedges with egg white mixture.

**5** Bake in the preheated oven for 15 to 18 minutes or until golden. Remove scones from baking sheet; serve warm. Makes 12 scones.

Per scone: 105 cal., 2 g total fat (1 g sat. fat), 22 mg chol., 221 mg sodium, 17 g carbo., 1 g fiber, 4 g pro.

To avoid getting your hands messy while crumbling the Gorgonzola, hold the wedge over the measuring cup and chunk the cheese off into it with a fork. The veining helps the cheese crumble easily.

**Ask Mom** How do I make sour milk? p. 24 / How do I measure flour? p. 54 / How do I slice green onions? p. 51 / How do I work with eggs? p. 26–27 / What is baking powder? p. 30, 319 / What is baking soda? p. 30, 319 / What is buttermilk? p. 24 / What is

# Flax Soda Bread

| | |
|---|---|
| 1 cup unbleached all-purpose flour | 3 tablespoons cold butter |
| ¾ cup whole wheat flour or rye flour | 2 eggs, lightly beaten |
| ½ cup ground flax seeds* | ¾ cup buttermilk or sour milk |
| ¾ teaspoon baking powder | 2 tablespoons honey |
| ½ teaspoon baking soda | ¼ cup whole flaxseeds |
| ½ teaspoon salt | 1 egg, lightly beaten |

**1** Preheat oven to 375°F. Lightly grease a baking sheet; set aside. In a large bowl stir together the all-purpose flour, whole wheat flour, ground flaxseeds, baking powder, baking soda, and salt (photo 1, page 320). Using a pastry blender, cut in butter until mixture resembles coarse crumbs (photo 2, page 320). Make a well in the center of the flour mixture (photo 3, page 320); set aside.

**2** In a small bowl stir together the 2 eggs, the buttermilk, and honey. Add egg mixture to flour mixture all at once (photo 4, page 320). Using a fork, stir just until moistened (photo 5, page 321). Stir in whole flaxseeds. (Dough will be sticky.)

**3** Turn dough out onto a well-floured surface. With well-floured hands, knead dough by folding and gently pressing it for 10 to 12 strokes or until dough is nearly smooth (below). On the prepared baking sheet pat the dough into a 7-inch oval loaf (below). With a sharp knife cut a 4-inch cross, ¼ inch deep, on the top of the loaf (below). Lightly brush with the remaining egg.

**4** Bake in the preheated oven for 30 to 35 minutes or until a wooden toothpick inserted near the center comes out clean. Remove bread from baking sheet (below); serve warm. Makes 12 to 16 servings.

*Note: Flaxseeds can usually be found in the baking aisle or health food section of your supermarket. Grind them in a coffee or spice grinder, food processor, or blender.

Per serving: 166 cal., 7 g total fat (3 g sat. fat), 16 mg chol., 227 mg sodium, 20 g carbo., 3 g fiber, 6 g pro.

**1** This dough is sticky, so make sure the work surface and your hands are well floured when kneading.

**2** Transfer the kneaded dough to a greased baking sheet. Pat it into an oval that is 7 inches long.

**3** Using a sharp knife, cut a 4-inch cross in the top of the oval that is ¼ inch deep.

**4** Transfer the baked bread to a wire rack to cool slightly before cutting. Serve the bread warm.

**Ask Mom** How do I grease a baking pan/dish? p. 59 / How do I make sour milk? p. 24 / How do I measure butter? p. 55 / How do I measure flour? p. 54 / How do I work with eggs? p. 26–27 / What is a pastry blender? p. 10, 11 / What is baking powder?

# your daily
# BREADS

Feel a true sense of triumph as you watch your first loaf of yeast bread rise and get crusty in the oven. Then taste it, sliced and slathered with butter.

12

**Batter Bread, Oatmeal** ① ...................................... 339

**Breadsticks, Pine Nut and Herb Twirled** ① .....................354

**Buns, Wasabi Shrimp-Stuffed** ② ............................... 353

**Country-Style Semolina Bread** ③ ...............................344

## FILLINGS & TOPPERS
Caramelized Onion Topper ① ........................... 348

Focaccia Topper ② ..................................... 340

Pretzel Topper ② ...................................... 340

Seasoned Bread Filling ② ............................. 340

**Focaccia, Cross-Culture** ② ...................................... 341

**Focaccia, Onion-Sage** ② ........................................ 348

**Galette, Potato Pancetta** ③ ..................................... 355

**How do I make basic yeast breads?** .......................342–343

## ICINGS
Cream Cheese Icing ① ................................. 361

Orange Icing ① ........................................ 362

Vanilla Icing ① ........................................ 361

**Pretzels, Salt and Pepper Baked** ② ............................ 341

## ROLLS
Cheddar Honey-Nut Rolls ① ............................. 347

Florentine-Feta Rolls ② ................................ 352

Pesto Roll-Ups ① ...................................... 347

Refrigerator Dinner Rolls ③ ........................... 349

Seeded Pull-Aparts ① .................................. 347

Three-Grain Cloverleaf Rolls ③ ........................ 351

**Seasoned Bread** ② .............................................. 341

## SWEET BREADS & ROLLS
Caramel-Pecan Rolls ③ ................................ 361

Cinnamon and Chocolate Rolls ③ ...................... 361

Cinnamon Rolls ③ ..................................... 359

Cranberry-Orange Tea Ring ③ .......................... 362

Easy Cinnamon Rolls ② ................................ 361

Easy Cinnamon Spirals ① .............................. 358

PB and Apple Rolls ① .................................. 347

Spiced Maple Pull-Aparts ② ........................... 356

**1** Skill Level

# Oatmeal Batter Bread

| | |
|---|---|
| 1 cup warm milk (105°F to 115°F) | 1 tablespoon cooking oil |
| ¼ cup honey or packed brown sugar | ½ teaspoon salt |
| 1 package active dry yeast | ¾ cup whole wheat flour |
| 1¾ cups all-purpose flour | ½ cup rolled oats |
| 1 egg, lightly beaten | |

**1** In a large mixing bowl combine milk, honey, and yeast, stirring until yeast dissolves. Let stand for 5 minutes. Meanwhile, grease an 8×4×2-inch loaf pan; set pan aside.

**2** Add flour, egg, oil, and salt to yeast mixture. Beat with an electric mixer on low speed until combined. Beat for 3 minutes on high speed, scraping bowl occasionally. Using a wooden spoon, stir in whole wheat flour and oats until combined. Spoon batter into prepared loaf pan, spreading evenly. Cover; let dough rise in a warm place until double in size (about 45 minutes).

**3** Preheat oven to 350°F. Bake in the preheated oven about 40 minutes or until bread sounds hollow when lightly tapped. If necessary to prevent overbrowning, cover top of bread with foil for the last 10 to 15 minutes of baking. Immediately remove bread from pan. Cool on a wire rack. Makes 1 loaf (12 slices).

Per slice: 166 cal., 3 g total fat (1 g sat. fat), 19 mg chol., 113 mg sodium, 31 g carbo., 2 g fiber, 5 g pro.

# WHAT IF MY BREAD DOESN'T RISE? That could be due to a couple of things. First make sure your yeast is fresh (check the expiration date). Then be sure the warm water is between 120°F and 130°F. Too hot, and the yeast dies; too cold, and it doesn't get activated.

Seasoned Bread

Cross-Culture Focaccia

Salt and Pepper Baked Pretzels

**Seasoned Bread Filling:** In a small bowl combine ⅓ cup refrigerated dried-tomato pesto or purchased kalamata olive tapenade and 2 tablespoons grated Parmesan cheese.

**Focaccia Topper:** Sprinkle dough with 1 cup shredded Mexican-style four cheese blend. Very thinly slice 1 large tomato; arrange slices on top of cheese.

**Pretzel Topper:** In a small bowl combine 1½ teaspoons coarse salt and 1 teaspoon garlic pepper.

**Good to Know**
Some yeast bread recipes call for the dough to rest for a few minutes before the shaping and second rising. This allows the gluten (the stuff that makes the dough snap back when pulled) to relax, so the dough is easier to work with.

 **Skill Level**

# 3-Way Bread Dough

3 to 3½ cups all-purpose flour
1 package active dry yeast
1¼ cups warm water (120°F to 130°F)
¼ cup butter, melted, or olive oil
½ cup yellow cornmeal or whole wheat flour
1 recipe Seasoned Bread Filling, Focaccia Topper, or Pretzel Topper (page 340)

**1** In a large mixing bowl combine 1½ cups of the all-purpose flour, yeast, and 1½ teaspoons *salt*. Add the warm water and 3 tablespoons of the melted butter. Beat with an electric mixer for 30 seconds, scraping sides of bowl constantly. Beat on high speed for 3 minutes. Using a wooden spoon, stir in the cornmeal and as much of the remaining all-purpose flour as you can (photos 1–5, pages 342–343).

**2** Turn dough out onto a lightly floured surface. Knead in enough of the remaining all-purpose flour to make a moderately stiff dough that is smooth and elastic (6 to 8 minutes total). Shape dough into a ball. Place dough in a lightly greased bowl, turning once. Cover; let dough rise in a warm place until double (30 to 45 minutes). Punch dough down (photos 6–10, page 343).

**Seasoned Bread:** Cover dough; let rest for 10 minutes. Meanwhile, grease a 9×5×3-inch loaf pan; set aside. On a lightly floured surface, roll dough into a 16×9-inch rectangle. Brush with the remaining 1 tablespoon melted butter. Spread Seasoned Bread Filling over dough, leaving a 1-inch border on one of the short sides. Roll up rectangle, starting from the filled short side. Pinch dough to seal seam and ends. Place loaf in prepared pan. Cover; let dough rise in a warm place until nearly double in size (about 30 minutes). Preheat oven to 375°F. Bake in the preheated oven for 35 to 40 minutes or until bread sounds hollow when lightly tapped. Immediately remove bread from pan. Cool on a wire rack; serve warm or at room temperature. Makes 1 loaf (12 slices).

Per slice: 196 cal., 7 g total fat (3 g sat. fat), 11 mg chol., 384 mg sodium, 29 g carbo., 2 g fiber, 5 g pro.

**Cross-Culture Focaccia:** Cover dough; let rest for 10 minutes. Meanwhile, grease a 12-inch pizza pan. Press dough evenly into prepared pan. Cover; let dough rise in a warm place until double in size (about 30 minutes). Preheat oven to 400°F. With your fingers, press deep indentations in the dough 1 inch apart (photo 2, page 348). Brush with the remaining 1 tablespoon melted butter. Bake in the preheated oven for 15 minutes. Follow directions for Focaccia Topper. Bake about 15 minutes more or until bottom crust is golden brown. Immediately transfer focaccia to a wire rack; cool slightly. Cut into wedges; serve warm. Makes 12 servings.

Per serving: 206 cal., 7 g total fat (5 g sat. fat), 19 mg chol., 386 mg sodium, 29 g carbo., 1 g fiber, 6 g pro.

**Salt and Pepper Baked Pretzels:** Cover dough; let rest for 10 minutes. Meanwhile, lightly grease 2 baking sheets; set aside. On a lightly floured surface, roll dough into a 14×8-inch rectangle. Cut into eight 14×1-inch strips. Gently pull the strips into 16-inch ropes. Shape each pretzel by crossing one end of a rope over the other to form a circle, overlapping about 4 inches from each end. Take one end of dough in each hand and twist once at the point where the dough overlaps. Carefully lift each end across to the edge of the circle opposite it. Tuck ends under edges to make a pretzel shape. Moisten ends and press to seal. Place pretzels on prepared baking sheets. Cover; let pretzels rise in a warm place until nearly double in size (about 30 minutes). Preheat oven to 375°F. Brush with the remaining 1 tablespoon melted butter. Sprinkle with Pretzel Topper. Bake in the preheated oven for 20 to 24 minutes or until golden brown. Immediately remove pretzels from baking sheets. Cool on wire racks. Makes 8 pretzels.

Per pretzel: 252 cal., 7 g total fat (4 g sat. fat), 15 mg chol., 817 mg sodium, 42 g carbo., 2 g fiber, 6 g pro.

**Ask Mom** How do I grease a baking pan/dish? p. 59 / How do I measure butter? p. 55 / How do I measure flour? p. 54 / How do I measure liquids? p. 55 / How do I store baked goods? p. 68 / How do I work with bread dough? p. 62, 63 / What is a lightly floured surface? p. 60 / What is yeast? p. 63 / What kind of cornmeal is best? p. 310 / What's that flour? p. 31 / Why remove bread

# How do I make basic yeast bread?

Making homemade bread is truly one of the most rewarding things you can do—and it's not as difficult as it might seem, if you're just a little bit careful.

The most crucial first step is coddling the yeast just a bit. (See Step 2, below, for tips.) If your yeast doesn't work right, you wind up with a brick instead of a loaf of bread. The same thing can happen if you add too much flour during mixing and kneading. Start with the minimum amount of flour given in a recipe and knead in just enough—and certainly don't use more than the maximum! You can proof (raise) your dough in a draft-free place between 80°F and 85°F until double for the first rise and nearly double for the second. (Your bread will rise higher, called "oven spring," if you stop short of doubling the second time.) Your unheated oven, fitted with a large pan of hot water on the lower rack, is an ideal spot.

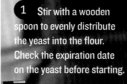

**1** Stir with a wooden spoon to evenly distribute the yeast into the flour. Check the expiration date on the yeast before starting.

**2** Check the temperature of the liquid (it may be water and/or milk) with an instant-read thermometer. If it's too hot, the yeast will die and your bread won't rise. If it's too cold, the yeast won't activate and your bread won't rise either.

**3** Add the warm water and melted butter to the flour mixture all at once.

**WHAT'S THE DIFFERENCE BETWEEN MODERATELY SOFT AND MODERATELY STIFF DOUGH?** Moderately soft dough is slightly sticky and used for rich, sweet breads. It requires 3 to 5 minutes of kneading. Moderately stiff dough—used for most nonsweet breads—is not sticky, is slightly firm to the touch, and requires 6 to 8 minutes of kneading.

**6** To knead, fold dough over and push down with the heel of your hand. Turn, fold dough over, and push down again. Repeat this process over and over.

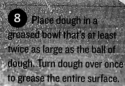

**4** Beat with an electric mixer on low to medium speed. Scrape sides of bowl to make sure all the flour and yeast are moistened.

**5** Use the wooden spoon to stir in as much of the remaining flour as you can.

**7** Knead until the dough is smooth and elastic; shape it into a ball.

**8** Place dough in a greased bowl that's at least twice as large as the ball of dough. Turn dough over once to grease the entire surface.

**9** Cover dough with plastic wrap that's been sprayed with nonstick cooking spray. This prevents the dough from sticking to the plastic as it rises to the top of the bowl.

**10** Punch dough down by pushing your fist into the center. Then use your fingers to pull the edges into the center.

343

Yeast Breads

# Country-Style Semolina Bread

1 cup warm water (105°F to 115°F)

½ cup warm milk (105°F to 115°F)

2 tablespoons honey or sugar

1 package active dry yeast

3 cups bread flour

1 cup semolina flour

¼ cup olive oil

1 teaspoon sea salt

2 tablespoons coarse cornmeal

**1** In a large mixing bowl combine water, milk, honey, and yeast. Let stand for 10 to 15 minutes or until foamy (photo 1, page 345). Add 2 cups of the bread flour. Beat with the electric mixer on low speed for 4 minutes. Cover bowl; let stand for 30 minutes to 2 hours.

**2** Using a wooden spoon, stir in the semolina flour, 2 tablespoons of the olive oil, the salt, and as much of the remaining 1 cup bread flour as you can (photo 2, page 345). Turn dough out onto a lightly floured surface. Knead in enough of the remaining bread flour to make a soft, fairly sticky dough (3 to 5 minutes total) (photo 3, page 345). Brush a large bowl with 1 tablespoon of the remaining oil. Transfer dough to oiled bowl, turning once to grease surface (photo 8, page 343). Cover (photo 9, page 343); let dough rise in a warm place until double in size (about 1 hour).

**3** Turn dough out onto a floured surface; divide dough in half. Cover and let rest for 15 minutes. Sprinkle a large baking sheet with the cornmeal. Shape dough by gently pulling each portion into a ball, tucking edges under (photo 4, page 345). Place dough balls on the baking sheet. Flatten each dough ball slightly to about 6 inches in diameter (photo 5, page 345). Brush tops of loaves with the remaining 1 tablespoon olive oil (photo 6, page 345). Let dough rise until nearly double (20 to 30 minutes).

**4** Preheat oven to 450°F. With a very sharp knife, make 3 or 4 cuts about ¼ inch deep across each loaf (photo 7, page 345). Place a shallow baking pan on the bottom rack of the preheated oven; fill with about ½ inch of boiling water. Place baking sheet on the middle rack of the oven. Working quickly, heavily mist the inside of the oven, including the bread, with water (photo 8, page 345).

**5** Bake in the preheated oven for 25 to 30 minutes or until the internal temperature of the bread registers 200°F with an instant-read thermometer, covering bread with foil the last 10 minutes of baking to prevent overbrowning. Immediately remove loaves from baking sheet. Cool on wire racks. Makes 2 loaves (16 slices).

**Per slice:** 179 cal., 4 g total fat (1 g sat. fat), 1 mg chol., 105 mg sodium, 30 g carbo., 1 g fiber, 5 g pro.

**Ask Mom** How do I measure flour? p. 54 / How do I measure liquids? p. 55 / How do I store baked goods? p. 68 / What is a lightly floured surface? p. 60 / What is yeast? p. 63 / What's that flour? p. 31

**WHAT'S SEMOLINA FLOUR?** Also known as farina, semolina is what's left of the milled wheat kernels after the finer, silkier flour has been sifted out. It's commonly used to make pasta and hot cereal. It lends a crunchy texture to this Italian-style bread.

**1** After standing for 10 to 15 minutes, the yeast mixture will look foamy.

**2** Use a wooden spoon to stir in the semolina flour, olive oil, salt, and as much of the remaining bread flour as you can.

**3** After kneading bread flour into the dough, you should have a soft dough that is rather sticky.

**4** To shape the dough, gently pull it into a ball; tuck the edges underneath.

**5** Flatten the dough balls directly on a baking sheet that's been sprinkled with cornmeal.

**6** After flattening the dough into a circle that's about 6 inches in diameter, brush with remaining olive oil.

**7** Just before baking, use a very sharp knife to make three or four ¼-inch-deep slashes on top of each loaf.

**8** Use a spray bottle filled with water to mist the inside of the preheated oven; mist the bread loaves too. The moisture will give your bread a nice, crisp crust.

**HOW DO I USE FROZEN BREAD DOUGH?** A 1-pound loaf of dough takes between 6 and 12 hours to thaw in the refrigerator. Take it from the freezer the day before you want to use it. You can substitute white dough for the whole wheat in any of these recipes.

Seeded Pull-Aparts

PB and Apple Rolls

Cheddar Honey-Nut Rolls

Pesto Roll-Ups

# Frozen Whole Wheat Bread Dough Fix-ups

**Seeded Pull-Aparts:** Thaw one 16-ounce loaf frozen whole wheat bread dough. Divide bread dough into 12 portions; roll each portion into a ball (photos 2–3, page 349). In a small bowl lightly beat 1 egg white and 1 tablespoon water with a fork. In a shallow bowl combine 2 tablespoons flaxseeds; 3 tablespoons sesame seeds, toasted; 2 tablespoons poppy seeds; and 1 tablespoon cumin seeds, toasted. Brush top of each dough ball with egg white mixture; dip in seed mixture. Arrange rolls in a lightly greased 9×1½-inch round baking pan. Cover; let rolls rise in a warm place until nearly double in size (30 to 60 minutes). Preheat oven to 375°F. Bake in the preheated oven for 20 to 25 minutes or until tops sound hollow when lightly tapped. Immediately invert rolls onto a wire rack; serve warm or at room temperature. Makes 12 rolls.

Per roll: 129 cal., 4 g total fat (0 g sat. fat), 0 mg chol., 217 mg sodium, 19 g carbo., 2 g fiber, 6 g pro.

**PB and Apple Rolls:** Thaw one 16-ounce loaf frozen whole wheat bread dough. Divide bread dough into 12 portions; roll each portion into a ball (photos 2–3, page 349). In a small bowl combine ½ cup finely chopped, peeled apple; ¼ cup peanut butter; and 1 tablespoon apple jelly. Flatten each dough ball into a 3-inch circle. Spoon a rounded teaspoon of the apple mixture into center of each dough circle. Bring sides of dough up around apple mixture; pinch edges of dough to seal. Place dough balls, seam sides down, in a lightly greased 9×9×2-inch baking pan. Cover; let rolls rise in a warm place until nearly double in size (30 to 60 minutes). Preheat oven to 375°F. Bake in the preheated oven for 20 to 25 minutes or until tops are golden brown. Immediately remove rolls from pan; serve warm. Makes 12 rolls.

Per roll: 136 cal., 4 g total fat (1 g sat. fat), 0 mg chol., 235 mg sodium, 21 g carbo., 2 g fiber, 6 g pro.

**Cheddar Honey-Nut Rolls:** Thaw one 16-ounce loaf frozen whole wheat bread dough. For filling, in a small bowl combine ⅓ cup shredded reduced-fat cheddar cheese; ¼ cup finely chopped pecans or walnuts, toasted; and 1 tablespoon honey. On a lightly floured surface, roll bread dough into a 12-inch circle. Cut dough into 12 wedges. Spoon a rounded teaspoon of the filling onto the wide end of each wedge. Beginning at the wide end of each wedge, roll up dough toward the point, enclosing the filling. Place rolls, point sides down, 2 to 3 inches apart on a large parchment paper- or foil-lined baking sheet. Cover; let rolls rise in a warm place until nearly double in size (30 to 60 minutes). Preheat oven to 375°F. Bake in the preheated oven for 12 to 15 minutes or until golden brown. Immediately remove rolls from baking sheet; serve warm. Cover and chill any leftover rolls. Makes 12 rolls.

Per roll: 129 cal., 4 g total fat (1 g sat. fat), 3 mg chol., 240 mg sodium, 20 g carbo., 2 g fiber, 6 g pro.

**Pesto Roll-Ups:** Thaw one 16-ounce loaf frozen whole wheat bread dough. On a lightly floured surface, roll bread dough into a 12×8-inch rectangle. Spread ⅓ cup purchased basil pesto over dough rectangle to within 1 inch of long sides. Chop ⅓ cup bottled roasted red sweet peppers; drain and pat dry with paper towels. Sprinkle roasted peppers over pesto. Roll up dough, starting from a long side; seal seam. Cut roll crosswise into 12 pieces (photo 4, page 359). Place each piece in a lightly greased 2½-inch muffin cup (photo 4, page 352). Cover; let rolls rise in a warm place until nearly double in size (30 to 60 minutes). Preheat oven to 375°F. Bake in the preheated oven for 20 to 25 minutes or until tops are golden brown. Immediately remove rolls from muffin cups; serve warm. Cover and chill any leftover rolls. Makes 12 rolls.

Per roll: 146 cal., 6 g total fat (0 g sat. fat), 1 mg chol., 261 mg sodium, 19 g carbo., 2 g fiber, 5 g pro.

**Ask Mom** How do I grease a baking pan/dish? p. 59 / How do I line a pan with foil? p. 58 / How do I measure peanut butter? p. 55 / How do I peel and core apples? p. 38, 39 / How do I reheat rolls? p. 350 / How do I shred cheese? p. 21, 254 / How do I store baked goods? p. 68 / How do I work with bread dough? p. 62, 63 / What is parchment paper? p. 21, 69 / Why remove bread from the pan to cool? p. 350

# Onion-Sage Focaccia

2⅓ to 3 cups all-purpose flour
1 package active dry yeast
2 teaspoons dried Italian seasoning, crushed
1¼ cups warm water (120°F to 130°F)
2 tablespoons olive oil

½ cup semolina flour
Nonstick cooking spray
1 recipe Caramelized Onion Topper
1 tablespoon snipped fresh sage or 1 teaspoon dried sage, crushed

**1** In a large mixing bowl combine 1½ cups of the all-purpose flour, the yeast, Italian seasoning, and 1 teaspoon *salt*. Add the water and 2 tablespoons of the oil. Beat with an electric mixer for 30 seconds, scraping bowl. Beat on high speed for 3 minutes. Stir in semolina flour and as much of the remaining all-purpose flour as you can (photos 1–5, pages 342–343 ). Turn dough out onto a lightly floured surface. Knead in enough of the remaining all-purpose flour to make a moderately soft dough that is smooth and elastic (3 to 5 minutes total). Shape dough into a ball. Place dough in a lightly greased bowl, turning once to grease surface. Cover; let dough rise in a warm place until double in size (45 to 60 minutes) (photos 6–9, page 343).

**2** Punch dough down (photo 10, page 343); let rest 10 minutes. Grease a 15×10×1-inch baking pan. Place dough in prepared pan. Gently pull and stretch dough into pan (below). Lightly coat dough with cooking spray. Cover loosely with plastic wrap; let rise in a warm place until nearly double (about 30 minutes). Press deep indentations in dough 1½ to 2 inches apart (below).

**3** Preheat oven to 450°F. Bake in the preheated oven for 15 minutes. Spread Caramelized Onion Topper over top of focaccia. Sprinkle with sage; press gently into focaccia. Bake for 4 to 5 minutes more or until golden brown. Immediately transfer focaccia to a wire rack; cool slightly. Cut into rectangles; serve warm. Makes 16 to 24 servings.

**Caramelized Onion Topper:** In a medium skillet heat 2 tablespoons olive oil over medium-low heat; add 2 cups coarsely chopped onion. Cook, covered, for 10 minutes, stirring frequently. Stir in 1 teaspoon packed brown sugar and ¼ teaspoon salt. Cook, uncovered, over medium-high heat for 4 to 5 minutes more or until onion is light brown, stirring frequently.

Per serving: 126 cal., 4 g total fat (1 g sat. fat), 0 mg chol., 184 mg sodium, 20 g carbo., 1 g fiber, 3 g pro.

**1** Use your fingertips to pull and stretch the dough into the baking pan.

**2** Press your fingertips about ½ inch deep into the dough to make indentations.

**Ask Mom** How do I chop an onion? p. 51 / How do I grease a baking pan/dish? p. 59 / How do I measure flour? p. 54 / How do I measure liquids? p. 55 / How do I store baked goods? p. 68 / How do I work with bread dough? p. 62, 63 / What is a lightly floured surface? p. 60 / What is yeast? p. 63 / What's that flour? p. 31 / Why remove bread from the pan to cool? p. 350

**3** Skill Level

# Refrigerator Dinner Rolls

  1 package active dry yeast
  ¾ cup warm water (105°F to 115°F)
  ½ cup sugar
  ½ cup packaged instant mashed potatoes
  ½ cup butter, softened
  2 eggs
  3½ to 4 cups all-purpose flour

**Good to Know** Chilling the dough in the refrigerator arrests, or nearly stops, the dough from rising. This means you can store it in the fridge for up to 3 days, taking it out whenever you want fresh-baked bread. The rolls take 2 to 3 hours to rise because the dough has to slowly come to room temperature.

**1** In a large bowl dissolve yeast in warm water. Let stand about 10 minutes or until bubbly. Using a wooden spoon, stir in sugar, instant mashed potatoes, butter, eggs, and ¾ teaspoon *salt*. Gradually stir in as much of the flour as you can (photo 5, page 343).

**2** Turn dough out onto a lightly floured surface. Knead in enough of the remaining flour to make a moderately stiff dough that is smooth and elastic (6 to 8 minutes total). Shape dough into a ball. Place dough in a lightly greased bowl, turning once. Cover bowl with plastic wrap and a kitchen towel (photos 6–9, page 343). Chill for at least 8 hours or up to 3 days.

**3** Grease 2 large baking sheets or twenty-four 2½-inch muffin cups (photo 1, page 292); set aside. Punch down dough (photo 10, page 343). Turn out onto a lightly floured surface. Divide dough in half. Divide each half of dough into 12 pieces (24 pieces total) Shape each piece into a ball (below). Place balls 2 inches apart on prepared baking sheets or in prepared muffin cups. Flatten balls slightly if using baking sheets. Cover; let rolls rise in a warm place until nearly double in size (2 to 3 hours).

**4** Preheat oven to 375°F. Bake in the preheated oven about 15 minutes or until golden brown. Immediately remove rolls from baking sheets or muffin cups. Cool slightly on wire racks; serve warm or at room temperature. Makes 24 rolls.

**Per roll:** 127 cal., 4 g total fat (3 g sat. fat), 28 mg chol., 108 mg sodium, 19 g carbo., 1 g fiber, 3 g pro.

**1** Divide dough in half; divide each half into 12 pieces.

**2** Shape each piece of dough into a ball.

**3** To make a smooth top, pull the edges of each dough ball under.

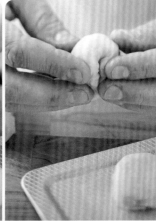

**Ask Mom** How do I grease and flour a pan? p. 59 / How do I measure butter? p. 55 / How do I measure flour? p. 54 / How do I measure liquids? p. 55 / How do I measure sugar? p. 55 / How do I reheat rolls? p. 350 / How do I soften butter? p. 28, 76 / How do I store baked goods? p. 68 / How do I work with bread dough? p. 62, 63 / What is a lightly floured surface? p. 60 / What is yeast?

## WHY REMOVE BREAD FROM THE PAN TO COOL?
If you leave bread and rolls in the pans to cool, condensation forms between the pan and the bread, resulting in soggy bread. Putting it on a wire rack allows air to circulate around it, cooling it faster.

To reheat dinner rolls, wrap in foil and place in a 325°F oven about 10 minutes or until heated through. If they're frozen, wrap in foil and heat them about 30 minutes or until heated through.

# Three-Grain Cloverleaf Rolls

2 cups warm water (105°F to 115°F)
2 packages active dry yeast
1 teaspoon sugar
½ cup sugar
½ cup cooking oil
2 eggs, lightly beaten

1½ teaspoons salt
1 cup rye flour
½ cup regular rolled oats
½ cup whole bran cereal (page 300)
4¼ to 4¾ cups all-purpose flour

**1** In a large mixing bowl combine 1 cup of the warm water, yeast, and the 1 teaspoon sugar. Let stand for 5 minutes or until yeast dissolves and mixture is bubbly on top. Using a wooden spoon, stir the remaining 1 cup warm water, the ½ cup sugar, the oil, eggs, and salt into yeast mixture. Add rye flour, oats, and bran cereal, stirring to combine. Let stand for 5 minutes.

**2** Add 2 cups of the all-purpose flour to the yeast mixture. Beat with an electric mixer on low to medium speed for 30 seconds, scraping sides of bowl constantly (photo 4, page 343). Beat on high speed for 3 minutes. Using the wooden spoon, stir in as much of the remaining all-purpose flour as you can (photo 5, page 343).

**3** Turn dough out onto a lightly floured surface. Knead in enough of the remaining flour to make a moderately stiff dough that is smooth and elastic (8 to 10 minutes total). Dough may be sticky. Shape dough into a ball. Place dough in a lightly greased bowl, turning once to grease surface. Cover; let dough rise in a warm place until double in size (about 1 hour) (photos 6–9, page 343).

**4** Punch dough down (photo 10, page 343). Turn out onto a lightly floured surface. Divide dough in half. Cover; let rest for 10 minutes. Meanwhile, grease twenty-four 2½-inch muffin cups (photo 1, page 292); set aside.

**5** Divide each dough half into 2 portions. Divide each portion into 18 pieces (72 pieces total). Shape each piece into a ball (photos 1–3, page 349). Place 3 balls in each prepared muffin cup, smooth sides up. Cover; let rolls rise in a warm place until double (about 30 minutes).

**6** Preheat oven to 375°F. Bake in the preheated oven about 12 minutes or until golden brown. Immediately remove rolls from muffin cups. Cool on wire racks. Makes 24 rolls.

Per roll: 172 cal., 6 g total fat (1 g sat. fat), 18 mg chol., 156 mg sodium, 27 g carbo., 2 g fiber, 4 g pro.

Ingredient Info Oats come in three basic forms: regular rolled oats (sometimes called "old-fashioned" oats, they're oat grains that are steamed and then rolled flat); quick-cooking oats, which are rolled and then processed into smaller pieces to cook very quickly; and steel-cut oats (sometimes called Irish oats), which are hulled oat grains that have not been rolled at all but simply chopped into small pieces. They are very nutty and chewy. For the right texture in these wholesome rolls, be sure to use regular rolled oats. Be sure to use the kind of oats called for in a recipe—they're generally not interchangeable.

**Ask Mom** Can I use quick-cooking oats instead of regular rolled oats? p. 351 / How do I measure flour? p. 54 / How do I measure liquids? p. 55 / How do I measure sugar? p. 55 / How do I store baked goods? p. 68 / How do I work with bread dough? p. 62, 63 / How do I work with eggs? p. 26–27 / What is a lightly floured surface? p. 60 / What is cooking oil? p. 28 / What is yeast? p. 63 / What's that flour? p. 31 / Why remove bread from the pan to cool? p. 350

**2** Skill Level

# Florentine-Feta Rolls

| | |
|---|---|
| 4 green onions, finely chopped | ¼ teaspoon ground black pepper |
| 2 cloves garlic, minced | 1 13.8-ounce package refrigerated pizza dough |
| 2 tablespoons olive oil | ¼ cup crumbled feta cheese |
| 1 6-ounce package fresh baby spinach | 2 tablespoons pine nuts, toasted |
| ¼ cup snipped fresh basil | 1 tablespoon butter, melted |
| ½ teaspoon salt | ¼ cup finely shredded Parmesan cheese |

**1** Grease twelve 2½-inch muffin cups (photo 1, page 292); set aside. In a large skillet cook green onion and garlic in 1 tablespoon of the hot oil until tender. Add spinach and basil. Cook and stir just until spinach wilts (below). Set spinach mixture aside to cool. Drain off excess liquid (there should be no remaining liquid). Stir in salt and pepper.

**2** Preheat oven to 375°F. On a well-floured surface, unroll the pizza dough and shape into a 12×8-inch rectangle. Brush dough with the remaining 1 tablespoon oil. Spread spinach mixture over dough, leaving a 1-inch border on one of the long sides (below). Sprinkle feta cheese and pine nuts over spinach mixture. Roll up rectangle, starting from the filled long side (below). Pinch dough to seal seam.

**3** Using a thin serrated knife in a sawing motion, cut rolled rectangle into 12 equal pieces. Place rolls in prepared muffin cups (below). Brush with butter; sprinkle with Parmesan cheese.

**4** Bake in the preheated oven for 18 to 20 minutes or until golden brown. Let stand in muffin cups for 2 minutes. Carefully remove from cups; serve warm. Makes 12 rolls.

Per roll: 165 cal., 9 g total fat (4 g sat. fat), 13 mg chol., 443 mg sodium, 14 g carbo., 1 g fiber, 7 g pro.

**1** In a large skillet cook and stir the spinach mixture over medium heat just until the spinach wilts.

**2** After draining off all the liquid, spread the spinach mixture over the dough; leave a 1-inch border along one of the long sides.

**3** Roll up tightly and evenly, rolling toward the long side with the 1-inch border.

**4** Place each cut roll in a greased muffin cup.

**Ask Mom** How do I crumble cheese? p. 195 / How do I drain spinach? p. 195, 285 / How do I measure butter? p. 55 / How do I mince garlic? p. 21 / How do I snip fresh herbs? p. 49 / How do I toast nuts? p. 34 / What's that nut? p. 34–35 / Why remove bread from the pan to cool? p. 350

# Wasabi Shrimp-Stuffed Buns

1 16-ounce package hot roll mix
⅔ cup tub-style cream cheese spread with chive and onion
½ cup chopped fresh pea pods
⅓ cup coarsely shredded carrot
1 to 1½ teaspoons wasabi powder*
8 ounces peeled and deveined cooked shrimp, chopped
1 egg, lightly beaten
1 tablespoon water
4 teaspoons white and/or black sesame seeds

**1** Prepare hot roll mix according to package directions through the kneading step. Cover; let dough rest for 10 minutes. Divide dough into 16 portions; shape each portion into a ball (photos 1–3, page 349). Cover; let dough rest for 10 minutes.

**2** Meanwhile, for filling, in a medium bowl combine cream cheese spread, pea pods, carrot, and wasabi powder; mix well. Fold in shrimp.

**3** Preheat oven to 375°F. Grease a large baking sheet; set aside. On a lightly floured surface, roll each dough ball into a 4½-inch circle. Place about 2 tablespoons of the filling in the center of each dough circle. Shape the dough into a round ball by pulling the edges of dough up around filling; pinch to seal. Place buns, seam sides down, on prepared baking sheet. Cover; let buns rise for 15 minutes.

**4** In a small bowl lightly beat egg and water with a fork; brush over buns. Sprinkle with sesame seeds. Bake in the preheated oven for 20 to 25 minutes or until golden brown. Immediately remove buns from baking sheet. Cool slightly on wire racks; serve warm. Makes 16 buns.

*Note: Wasabi powder, sometimes called Japanese horseradish, is a pale lime green condiment with a sharp, pungent, fiery flavor. If you can't find it in the Asian section of your supermarket, look for it at Asian markets.

Make-ahead directions: Prepare and bake buns as directed, except cool completely. Return buns to baking sheet; freeze about 1 hour or until firm. Transfer buns to a covered freezer container. Freeze for up to 1 month. To reheat, preheat oven to 350°F. Wrap frozen buns in foil; heat in the preheated oven about 30 minutes or until warm.

Per bun: 182 cal., 6 g total fat (3 g sat. fat), 63 mg chol., 271 mg sodium, 23 g carbo., 0 g fiber, 8 g pro.

**Ask Mom** How do I grease a baking pan/dish? p. 59 / How do I shred carrots? p. 48 / How do I work with eggs? p. 26–27 / What is a lightly floured surface? p. 60 / Why remove bread from the pan to cool? p. 350

1 Skill Level

# Pine Nut and Herb
# Twirled Breadsticks

12 10- to 12-inch bamboo skewers or wooden chopsticks

⅓ cup very finely chopped pine nuts

⅓ cup grated Parmesan cheese

¼ cup butter, melted

2 teaspoons dried Italian seasoning, crushed

¼ teaspoon garlic powder

1 11-ounce package (12) refrigerated breadsticks

**1** Grease bamboo skewers; set aside. Lightly grease a very large baking sheet; set aside. Stir together pine nuts and Parmesan cheese; spread evenly on a sheet of waxed paper. In a small bowl stir together the melted butter, Italian seasoning, garlic powder, and ¼ teaspoon *ground black pepper*.

**2** Preheat oven to 350°F. Unroll breadstick dough and separate into 12 strips. Wrap each dough strip around a greased bamboo skewer to within ½ inch of each end (below). Brush each dough strip with some of the butter mixture (below). Roll dough strips in pine nut mixture (below). Place skewers on prepared baking sheet, pressing under ends of dough to secure.

**3** Bake in the preheated oven for 13 to 15 minutes or until golden brown. Immediately remove breadsticks from baking sheet. Cool slightly on wire racks. Remove breadsticks from skewers (below); serve warm. Makes 12 breadsticks.

**Make-ahead directions:** Prepare as directed through Step 2. Cover and chill for up to 2 hours. Continue as directed in Step 3.

**Per breadstick:** 137 cal., 8 g total fat (4 g sat. fat), 12 mg chol., 246 mg sodium, 13 g carbo., 0 g fiber, 4 g pro.

**1** Stretch and twist each dough strip around a skewer. Leave about ½ inch at each end of the skewer.

**2** Use a pastry brush to generously brush some of the butter mixture over each twirled dough strip.

**3** Roll each buttered dough strip in the pine nut mixture until well coated.

**4** When cool enough to handle, gently pull the breadsticks off the skewers.

**Ask Mom** How do I grease a baking pan/dish? p. 59 / How do I measure butter? p. 55 / How do I store baked goods? p. 68 / What are chopped nuts? p. 34 / What is garlic powder? p. 36 / What's that nut? p. 34–35

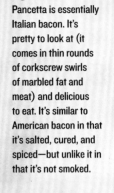

**Ingredient Info**
Pancetta is essentially Italian bacon. It's pretty to look at (it comes in thin rounds of corkscrew swirls of marbled fat and meat) and delicious to eat. It's similar to American bacon in that it's salted, cured, and spiced—but unlike it in that it's not smoked.

# Potato Pancetta **Galette**

    4  ounces pancetta, bacon, or ham, chopped
       Cornmeal
    1  13.8-ounce package refrigerated pizza dough
    4  ounces tiny new red potatoes
    2  tablespoons olive oil
    1  tablespoon fresh thyme leaves
  ¼  teaspoon freshly ground black pepper
  ⅓  cup finely shredded Asiago cheese

**1** In a large skillet cook pancetta or bacon over medium heat until crisp and brown. (If using ham, you don't need to cook it.) Drain on paper towels; set aside.

**2** Preheat oven to 400°F. Grease a large baking sheet; sprinkle with cornmeal. Unroll pizza dough onto prepared baking sheet.

**3** With a very sharp knife, slice potatoes into 1/16-inch-thick slices. Arrange potato slices over pizza dough. Brush potato slices generously with olive oil; sprinkle with thyme leaves and pepper. Top with pancetta; sprinkle with cheese.

**4** Bake in the preheated oven for 12 to 15 minutes or until crust is golden brown and potatoes are tender. To serve, cut in half lengthwise and into thirds crosswise to make 6 pieces. Makes 6 servings.

Per serving: 284 cal., 16 g total fat (4 g sat. fat), 20 mg chol., 624 mg sodium, 28 g carbo., 2 g fiber, 8 g pro.

# Spiced Maple Pull-Aparts

- 1 cup packed brown sugar
- 2 teaspoons pumpkin pie spice
- 1 teaspoon instant espresso powder (optional)
- ½ cup butter, melted
- 1 teaspoon vanilla
- 3 11-ounce packages (12 each) refrigerated breadsticks
- 2 tablespoons maple syrup

**1** Preheat oven to 350°F. Meanwhile, generously grease two 9×5×3-inch loaf pans; set aside.

**2** In a medium bowl stir together brown sugar, pumpkin pie spice, and, if desired, espresso powder. Sprinkle 1 tablespoon of the brown sugar mixture into each prepared loaf pan; tilt pans to distribute sugar across the bottoms and along sides (below). Shake any excess brown sugar mixture back into the remaining brown sugar mixture. Set loaf pans and remaining brown sugar mixture aside. In a small bowl stir together melted butter and vanilla.

**3** Unroll breadstick dough and separate into 36 strips. Roll each strip into a spiral, starting from a short side (below). Dip each dough spiral into the butter mixture; roll in the brown sugar mixture to coat (below). Place 18 of the dough spirals in each loaf pan, arranging the spirals in 2 layers in each pan (below). Sprinkle any remaining brown sugar mixture over the tops. Stir maple syrup into the remaining butter mixture; drizzle over spirals.

**4** Bake in the preheated oven about 40 minutes or until puffed and brown. To prevent overbrowning, cover loosely with foil during the last 10 minutes of baking. Cool in pans for 10 minutes; remove from pans. Cool slightly on wire racks; serve warm. Makes 36 pull-aparts.

Per 2 pull-aparts: 239 cal., 8 g total fat (5 g sat. fat), 14 mg chol., 410 mg sodium, 39 g carbo., 1 g fiber, 4 g pro.

**1** Tilt and tap the greased loaf pans to distribute the brown sugar mixture evenly.

**2** Roll each dough strip into a tight spiral.

**3** After dipping in the butter mixture, roll the spirals in the brown sugar mixture until well coated.

**4** Make 2 layers of dough spirals in each pan.

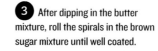

**Ask Mom** How do I grease a baking pan/dish? p. 59 / How do I measure butter? p. 55 / How do I measure sugar? p. 55 / What does drizzle mean? p. 69, 85 / What is pumpkin pie spice? p. 36, 37 / What is pure maple syrup? p. 300 / What is vanilla? p. 128

# A BUNCH FOR BRUNCH. This generous recipe makes two pans of these fun, ooey-gooey, hands-on sweet rolls, making them a perfect pick for a hungry crowd.

These sticky buns are stacked in the pan, as monkey bread and a bubble loaf are. It's best to invert them onto a platter for easy serving (and they look prettier that way too).

# Easy Cinnamon Spirals

Nonstick cooking spray
2 11-ounce packages (12 each) refrigerated breadsticks
⅓ cup butter, softened
¼ cup sugar
2 teaspoons ground cinnamon
½ cup caramel-flavor ice cream topping

**1** Preheat oven to 375°F. Lightly coat twelve 2½-inch muffin cups with cooking spray; set aside.

**2** Unroll breadstick dough and separate into 24 strips. Press each strip to flatten slightly. Press ends of 2 strips together to make 1 long strip. Repeat with remaining strips, making 12 long strips. Spread some of the butter over each long strip. In a small bowl stir together sugar and cinnamon; sprinkle over each strip. Roll each strip into a spiral, starting from a short side (photo 2, page 360). Place dough spirals in prepared muffin cups.

**3** Bake in the preheated oven for 12 to 15 minutes or until golden brown. Immediately remove from muffin cups; cool slightly. Drizzle with ice cream topping. Makes 12 spirals.

Per spiral: 245 cal., 8 g total fat (5 g sat. fat), 13 mg chol., 443 mg sodium, 40 g carbo., 1 g fiber, 4 g pro.

NO-RISE, LOTS OF SHINE. These quick caramel rolls start with refrigerated breadsticks and end with a drizzle of prepared caramel sauce. You get to bask in the happiness that homemade cinnamon rolls say to inspire—with very little effort.

**Ask Mom** How do I measure butter? p. 55 / How do I measure liquids? p. 55 / How do I measure sugar? p. 55 / How do I soften butter? p. 28, 76 / What does drizzle mean? p. 69, 85 / What is cinnamon? p. 36 / Why remove bread from the pan to cool? p. 350

③ Skill Level

# Cinnamon **Rolls**

4 to 4½ cups all-purpose flour

I package active dry yeast

I cup milk

⅓ cup granulated sugar

⅓ cup butter, cut up

½ teaspoon salt

2 eggs

¾ cup packed brown sugar

¼ cup all-purpose flour

I tablespoon ground cinnamon

⅓ cup butter, softened

½ cup golden raisins (optional)

½ cup chopped pecans, toasted (optional)

I recipe Vanilla Icing or Cream Cheese Icing (page 361)

**1** In a large mixing bowl combine 2 cups of the flour and the yeast (photo 1, page 342); set aside. In a small saucepan heat and stir milk, granulated sugar, ⅓ cup butter, and salt just until warm (120°F to 130°F) and butter almost melts. Add milk mixture to flour mixture along with eggs. Beat with an electric mixer on low to medium speed for 30 seconds, scraping sides of bowl constantly (photo 4, page 343). Beat on high speed for 3 minutes. Using a wooden spoon, stir in as much of the remaining 2 to 2½ cups flour as you can (photo 5, page 343).

**2** Turn dough out onto a lightly floured surface. Knead in enough of the remaining flour to make a moderately soft dough that is smooth and elastic (3 to 5 minutes total). Shape dough into a ball. Place dough in a lightly greased bowl, turning once to grease surface. Cover; let dough rise in a warm place until double in size (1 to 1½ hours) (photos 6–9, page 343).

**3** Punch dough down (photo 10, page 343). Turn dough out onto a lightly floured surface; divide dough in half. Cover and let rest for 10 minutes.

**4** Meanwhile, lightly grease two 8×8×2- or 9×9×2-inch baking pans or two 9×1½-inch round baking pans; set aside. For filling, stir together brown sugar, the ¼ cup flour, and the cinnamon. Using a pastry blender, cut in ⅓ cup butter until the mixture resembles coarse crumbs. If desired, stir in raisins and pecans.

*continued on page 361*

**1** Sprinkle half the filling over each dough rectangle, leaving a I-inch border along one of the long sides.

**2** Use a pastry brush to brush water over the I-inch border on each dough rectangle.

**3** Roll up dough tightly and evenly, rolling toward the I-inch border.

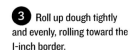

**4** Place a piece of dental floss under the dough where you want to make the cut. Crisscross floss over dough, pulling quickly.

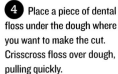

**Ask Mom** How do I grease a baking pan/dish? p. 59 / How do I measure butter? p. 55 / How do I measure flour? p. 54 / How do I measure liquids? p. 55 / How do I measure sugar? p. 55 / How do I store baked goods? p. 68 / How do I work with bread dough? p. 62, 63 / What are chopped nuts? p. 34 / What is a lightly floured surface? p. 60 / What is cinnamon? p. 36 / What is yeast? p. 63 / What's that dried fruit? p. 4I / What's that flour? p. 3I / What's that nut? p. 34–35

**SO MANY ROLLS ROLLED UP IN ONE.** With just a few tweaks and changes to one basic recipe, you have a bakery's-worth of sweet rolls at your fingertips: cinnamon, with cream cheese or vanilla icing; cinnamon and chocolate; and caramel-pecan.

1

2

Cinnamon and Chocolate Rolls

Caramel-Pecan Rolls

**5** Roll each dough half into a 12×8-inch rectangle. Sprinkle filling over dough, leaving a 1-inch border on one of the long sides (photo 1, page 359). Press filling lightly into dough with your fingers. Moisten the 1-inch border with water (photo 2, page 359). Roll up each rectangle, starting from the filled long side (photo 3, page 359). Pinch dough to seal seam. Slice each rolled rectangle into 12 equal pieces (photo 4, page 359). Arrange in prepared pans. Cover; let rolls rise in a warm place until nearly double in size (about 30 minutes).

**6** Preheat oven to 375°F. Bake in the preheated oven for 20 to 25 minutes or until golden. Cool in pans about 5 minutes; remove from pans. Drizzle with Vanilla Icing or spread with Cream Cheese Icing. If desired, serve warm. Makes 24 rolls.

**Easy Cinnamon Rolls:** Omit preparing the dough. Thaw two 16-ounce loaves frozen sweet roll dough. Roll each loaf into a 12×8-inch rectangle. Sprinkle filling over dough and continue with Step 5, letting rolls rise about 40 minutes. Bake as above.

**Vanilla Icing:** In a small bowl stir together 1¼ cups powdered sugar, 1 teaspoon light-color corn syrup, and ½ teaspoon vanilla. Add enough half-and-half or light cream (1 to 2 tablespoons) until drizzling consistency.

**Cream Cheese Icing:** In a small mixing bowl beat one 3-ounce package softened cream cheese with 2 tablespoons softened butter and 1 teaspoon vanilla. Gradually beat in 2½ cups powdered sugar until smooth. Beat in milk, 1 teaspoon at a time, until spreading consistency.

**Make-ahead directions:** Prepare as directed through Step 5, except do not let rise after shaping. Cover shaped rolls loosely with oiled waxed paper and plastic wrap, leaving room for rolls to rise. Chill for 2 to 24 hours. Uncover and let stand at room temperature for 30 minutes. Bake as directed above.

Per roll for plain or easy variation with **Vanilla Icing:** 233 cal., 8 g total fat (4 g sat. fat), 39 mg chol., 118 mg sodium, 36 g carbo., 1 g fiber, 3 g pro.

**Cinnamon and Chocolate Rolls:** Prepare as directed, except do not add raisins to the filling. Stir ¾ cup miniature semisweet chocolate pieces into the filling after cutting in the butter.

**Caramel-Pecan Rolls:** Prepare as directed through Step 4. In a small saucepan combine ⅔ cup packed brown sugar, ¼ cup butter, and 2 tablespoons light-color corn syrup. Stir over medium heat until combined. Divide butter mixture evenly between the prepared baking pans. Sprinkle ⅔ cup toasted chopped pecans over butter mixture, dividing evenly between the two pans; set pans aside. Continue as directed in Step 5, placing rolls on top of pecans in pans. After baking, immediately invert rolls onto a serving plate. Omit Vanilla Icing or Cream Cheese Icing.

**Nice to Know** Getting the rolls out of your pan depends on which kind of roll you make. The Caramel-Pecan Rolls are simply inverted onto a platter and served bottoms up so that the pecans and caramel that was created on the bottom of the pan is now on the top of the rolls. The Cinnamon Rolls need to be inverted onto a rimless baking sheet and then flipped over again onto a serving board or platter so that the top side is up before they're iced.

**Ask Mom** How do I measure butter? p. 55 / How do I soften butter? p. 28, 76 / How do I soften cream cheese? p. 57 / How do I toast nuts? p. 34 / How do I work with bread dough? p. 62, 63 / What are chopped nuts? p. 34 / What does drizzle mean? p. 69, 85 / What is half-and-half? p. 24 / What is powdered sugar? p. 29 / What is semisweet/bittersweet chocolate? p. 32 / What is vanilla? p. 128 / What's that nut? p. 34–35 / Why remove bread from the pan to cool? p. 350

# Cranberry-Orange Tea Ring

¾ cup snipped dried cranberries

1 teaspoon finely shredded orange peel

2 tablespoons orange juice

1 16-ounce loaf frozen sweet roll dough, thawed

3 teaspoons butter, melted

¼ cup packed brown sugar

2 tablespoons finely chopped pecans

1 tablespoon all-purpose flour

¼ teaspoon ground cinnamon

¼ teaspoon ground nutmeg

⅛ teaspoon ground cloves

1 recipe Orange Icing

**1** Line a large baking sheet with foil. Grease foil; set baking sheet aside. In a medium bowl stir together cranberries and orange juice; set aside. On a lightly floured surface, roll dough into a 15×9-inch rectangle (if dough is difficult to roll, let it rest for a few minutes and try again). Brush with 2 teaspoons of the melted butter.

**2** Drain cranberries; return cranberries to bowl. Stir in brown sugar, pecans, flour, orange peel, cinnamon, nutmeg, and cloves. Sprinkle cranberry mixture evenly over dough. Roll up rectangle, starting from a long side. Pinch dough to seal seam. Place roll, seam side down, on prepared baking sheet. Bring ends together to form a circle. Moisten ends with water; pinch together to seal circle (below). Cut slits at 1-inch intervals around the circle (below). Turn each slice slightly so the same sides of all slices face upward (below). Cover; let ring rise in a warm place until nearly double in size (1¼ to 1½ hours). Brush ring with the remaining teaspoon melted butter (below).

**3** Preheat oven to 350°F. Bake in the preheated oven about 20 minutes or until golden brown. Immediately remove ring from foil. Cool completely on a wire rack. Drizzle with Orange Icing. Makes 1 ring (16 servings).

**Orange Icing:** In a small bowl stir together ½ cup powdered sugar, ¼ teaspoon finely shredded orange peel, and enough orange juice (1 to 3 teaspoons) until drizzling consistency.

Per serving: 143 cal., 3 g total fat (1 g sat. fat), 8 mg chol., 154 mg sodium, 26 g carbo., 1 g fiber, 3 g pro.

**1** Pinch dough together to seal. Moistening the ends of the dough with water makes it easier to seal firmly.

**2** Using kitchen scissors, cut slits from outside edge of dough ring to center, leaving about 1 inch attached at center.

**3** Gently grasp a slice and turn it to one side. Repeat with remaining slices, being careful not to tear the dough or spill the filling.

**4** Just before baking, brush the tea ring with melted butter.

**Ask Mom** How do I grease a baking pan? p. 59 / How do I juice an orange? p. 45 / How do I line a pan with foil? p. 58 / How do I measure butter/sugar? p. 55 / How do I shred orange peel? p. 45, 105 / How do I snip dried fruit? p. 41, 102 / How do I soften butter? p. 28, 76 / How do I use a sieve? p. 65 / What are chopped nuts? p. 34 / What does drizzle mean? p. 69, 85 / What is powdered sugar? p. 29 / Why remove bread from the pan to cool? p. 350

# Index

# A

Allspice, about, 36
**Almonds**
about, 35
Almond Biscotti, 89
Almond Butter Frosting, 145
Almond-Cherry Muffins, 295
Almond Cupcakes, 179
almond paste, about, 69, 288
Almond Pastry, 261
Almond-Pear Muffins, 295
Almond-Spice Scones, 330
Brie en Croûte with Apricots
  and Almonds, 276
Chocolate-Cherry Pockets, 102, **103**
Easy Chocolate-Almond
  Croissants, 288
Lemon Curd Bars, **118**, 119
Macaroon Brownies, 127
Peach-Almond Tart, 261
Raspberry and White Chocolate Brownies,
  132, **132**
Toffee-Almond Banana Bread, 304
Triple-Nut Zucchini Cake, 167
White Dipped Almonds, 212
Amaretto Crème Brûlée, 218
Angel Cake, Tinted, 150
Apple pie spice, about, 36, 71
**Apples**
Apple-Cheddar Scones, 330
Apple-Cinnamon Scones, 330
Apple-Cranberry Dessert, 205, **205**
Apple Dumpling Roll-Ups, 286, **287**
Apple or Pear Cobbler, 209, **209**
Apple Pie Bread, 308, **309**
best, for baking, 39, 287
Caramel Apple Muffins, 295
Caramel Apple Pie, 235
Caramel Apples and Cranberry Pecan
  Shortcakes, 197, **197**
chopping, 39
Cinnamon-Apple Cookies, 80, **80**
PB and Apple Rolls, **346**, 347
peeling and slicing, 38
removing core, 39
selecting and storing, 39
Upside-Down One-Bowl
  Apple Cake, 156
Applesauce Cake, 165, **165**
**Apricots**
Apricot Scones, 330
Brie en Croûte with Apricots
  and Almonds, 276
Malibu Rum Baby Cakes, 152, **153**
Pistachio-Apricot Cups, 279
Artichoke-Spinach Mini Puffs, 268, **268**

# B

**Bacon**
Bacon-Onion Scones, 330
Green Onion-Bacon
  Corn Bread, 310, **310**
Herbed Cheese and
  Bacon Biscuits, 323
pancetta, about, 355
Potato Pancetta Galette, 355, **355**
Winter Vegetable Tarts with
  Bacon and Goat Cheese, 256
Baked Pastry Shell, 227
Baked Pastry Tart Shell, 227
**Bakeware.** *See also* specific pieces
aluminum, washing, 16
buying, 18
essential pieces, 16–17
materials, 16, 18
silicone, about, 18
**Baking dishes**
glass, 19, 117
gratin dish, 19
ramekins, 19
rectangular, 19
soufflé dishes, 19
square, 19
Baking mats, 21
**Baking pans**
cake pans, 16–17, 18
cookie sheets, 17, 18
fluted tube pan, 17
greasing and flouring, 59
jelly-roll pans, 17, 18
lining with foil, 58
lining with waxed paper, 58
loaf pans, 16, 18
muffin tins, 17, 18, 293
pie plates, 17, 18
pizza pan, 17
removing baked goods from, 60
springform pan, 17
tart pan, 16
Baking powder, about, 30, 71, 319
Baking powder, measuring, 54
Baking soda, 30, 319
**Bananas**
Banana Bread, 304
Banana Caramel Custard, 222, **223**
Banana-Chocolate Bread, 304
Banana-Chocolate Chip Bars, 109
Banana-Coconut Bread, 304
Banana-Coconut Muffins, 295
Banana Cream Pie, 232
Banana Crunch Muffins, 298, **298**
Banana Split Cake, 170
mashing, 40
selecting and storing, 40
Strawberry-Banana Brownies, 126
Toffee-Almond Banana Bread, 304

**Bars**
Banana-Chocolate Chip Bars, 109
Candy Bar Brownies, 129
Cappuccino Brownies, 130
checking for doneness, 118
Cherry Cheesecake Bars, 185
Chocolate Chip Cookie Bars, 75
Chunky Path Brownies, 128
Coconut-Date Bars, 122, **122**
Cranberry Pear Bars, 116
Cream Cheese Brownies, 131
cutting into diamonds, 113
cutting into triangles, 113
Fudgy Brownies, 124
fudgy brownies,
  stir-in ideas, 126–127
Holiday Layer Bars, 114
Key Lime Cheesecake Bars, 186, **188**
Lemon Curd Bars, **118**, 119
Northwest Pecan Treats, 115
Oatmeal-Caramel Bars, 120
Peanut Butter Blondie Bars, 110
Peppermint-Fudge Brownie Bites, 123
Pumpkin Bars, 121
Raspberry and White Chocolate Brownies,
  132, **132**
Rhubarb Bars, 117
saucepan brownies, preparing, 125
Sugar Cookie Squares, 99
Toffee Fingers, 111
Ultimate Bar Cookies, 112, **112**
Beat, defined, 69
**Berries.** *See also* specific berries
Berry Pie, 233
Brown Butter Tart, 260
Fresh Berry Napoleons, 280, **281**
Mixed Berry Cream Pie, 239
Mixed Berry Shortcake
  Croutons, 198, **198**
Triple-Berry Pudding Cake, 210
washing and storing, 42
White Chocolate and Berries
  Dessert Pastries, **274**, 275
Best Pumpkin Pie, 240, **241**
Big Chocolate Chip Cookies, 75
Big Oatmeal Cookies, 79
**Biscotti**
Almond Biscotti, 89
Cashew-Chocolate Biscotti, 89
Hazelnut Biscotti, 89
Pistachio Biscotti, 89
**Biscuits**
Biscuits Supreme, 319
Buttermilk Biscuits, 319
cutting out dough for, 321
Drop Biscuits Supreme, 319
Herbed Cheese and
  Bacon Biscuits, 323
Lemon-Blueberry Biscuits, 326, **327**
preparing, 320–321

**Boldfaced** page references indicate photographs of finished recipes.

Prosciutto Biscuits, **324**, 325
Savory Biscuit Sticks, 322
Blend, defined, 69
Blender, 20
**Blueberries**
Berry Pie, 233
Blueberry Cheesecake, 191, **191**
Blueberry Crisp, 206
Blueberry-Lemon Muffins, 295
Blueberry or Peach Cobbler, 209, **209**
Blueberry Streusel Coffee
    Cake, 314, **315**
Fool-Your-Family Peach Pie, 234
Lemon-Blueberry Biscuits, 326, **327**
Triple-Berry Pudding Cake, 210
Blue Cheese & Pears Mini Puffs, 268
Bowls, mixing, 12
Box grater, 21
**Bran**
Maple Bran Muffins, 300, **301**
Three-Grain Cloverleaf Rolls, **350**, 351
whole bran cereal, about, 300
**Brazil nuts**
about, 104
Lime Zingers, 104, **105**
**Bread pudding**
Bread Pudding with
    Whiskey Sauce, **214**, 215
Chocolate Bread Pudding, 216
**Breads.** *See also* Biscuits; Coffee cakes;
    Muffins; Scones; Yeast breads
Apple Pie Bread, 308, **309**
Banana Bread, 304
Banana-Chocolate Bread, 304
Banana-Coconut Bread, 304
Chocolate-Cashew Bread, 303, **303**
Cinnamon-Nut Bread, 306
Corn Bread, 311
cracks in tops of, 305
Double Corn Bread, 310
Flax Soda Bread, 336
Green Chile Corn Bread, 310
Green Onion-Bacon
    Corn Bread, 310, **310**
Quick Seed Bread, 307
removing from pan, 60
slicing, tip for, 309
storing, 68
Sweet Pepper Corn Bread, 310
Toffee-Almond Banana Bread, 304
Brie en Croûte with Apricots
    and Almonds, 276
Brie en Croûte with Cherries
    and Pecans, 276, **277**
Brittle, Caramelized Hazelnut, 181
Brown Butter Tart, 260
**Brownies**
Candy Bar Brownies, 129
Cappuccino Brownies, 130
Chunky Path Brownies, 128

Cream Cheese Brownies, 131
Fudgy Brownies, 124
fudgy brownies, stir-in ideas, 126–127
Peppermint-Fudge Brownie Bites, 123
Raspberry and White Chocolate Brownies,
    132, **132**
saucepan brownies, preparing, 125
Brown Sugar Icebox Cookies, 84, **85**
Buns, Wasabi Shrimp-Stuffed, 353
**Butter**
Butter Frosting, 83
buying, 28
cutting in with flour, 56
dotting with, 69
measuring, 55
softening, 28
storing, 28
**Buttermilk**
about, 24
Buttermilk Biscuits, 319
substitute for, 24, 71
Buttery Mint Slices, 88

**C**
Café au Lait Cheesecake, 194
**Cake pans**
fluted tube, 17
greasing and flouring, 59
jelly-roll pans, 17, 18
lining with foil, 58
lining with waxed paper, 58, 67
materials for, 16, 18
rectangular, 16, 18
removing baked goods from, 60
round, 16
square, 17
**Cakes.** *See also* Cheesecake; Cupcakes
Applesauce Cake, 165, **165**
baking basics, 136–137
Banana Split Cake, 170
Chocolate Cake, 139, **139**
Chocolate Candy-Graham Cake, 163
Chocolate Chip-Oatmeal Cake, 164
Chocolate-Peppermint
    Fantasy Cake, 140, **141**
Citrus Yellow Cake, 135
Coconut White Cake, 138, **138**
Cranberry Pound Cake, 174
dry, moistening, 66
frosted, storing, 137
German Chocolate Cake, 142
Gooey Butter Cake, 175
Lemon-Berry Ribbon Torte, 146, **147**
Lemon-Poppy Seed Pound Cake, 172
Lime-Infused Coconut Cake, 154
Malibu Rum Baby Cakes, 152, **153**
Molten Chocolate Cakes with
    Cherry Compote, **158**, 159
Orange-Rosemary

Pound Cake, 172, **173**
Pineapple-Carrot Loaves, 168, **169**
Polenta and Plum Cake, 157
Pumpkin Cake Roll, 148
removing from pan, 60
Rhubarb and Spice
    Snacking Cake, 166
Sour Cream-Walnut Date Cake with
    Tangerine Glaze, 151
storing, 68, 137
Strawberry Cake Roll, 149, **149**
Tinted Angel Cake, 150
Triple-Berry Pudding Cake, 210
Triple-Nut Zucchini Cake, 167
Upside-Down One-Bowl
    Apple Cake, 156
Upside-Down Peach Caramel
    Crunch Cake, 155
Walnut-Cappuccino Torte, 160
White Cake, 138
White Chocolate Snowdrift Cake, 143
Yellow Cake, 135, **135**
Candy Bar Brownies, 129
Candy Bar Cookies, 80
Candy Cupcakes, 179
Cappuccino Brownies, 130
**Caramel**
Banana Caramel Custard, 222, **223**
Caramel Apple Muffins, 295
Caramel Apple Pie, 235
Caramel Apples and Cranberry Pecan
    Shortcakes, 197, **197**
Caramel-Pecan French Silk
    Pie, 246, **246**
Caramel-Pecan Rolls, **360**, 361
caramel sauce, preparing, 64
Caramel-Peanut Cheesecake, 192
Chocolaty Caramel
    Thumbprints, 96, **96**
Cranberry-Pecan Caramel Pie Topper, 240
Dried Pear and Chocolate-Caramel Tart,
    262
Oatmeal-Caramel Bars, 120
Turtle Brownies, 127
Upside-Down Peach Caramel Crunch
    Cake, 155
Caramelize, defined, 69
Caramelized Hazelnut Brittle, 181
Cardamom, about, 36
**Carrots**
Carrot Cookies, 80
Carrot-Ginger Muffins, 295
Carrot-Pineapple Muffins, 296
choosing and storing, 48
Pineapple-Carrot Loaves, 168, **169**
shredding and slicing, 48
washing, 48
**Cashews**
about, 35
Cashew-Chocolate Biscotti, 89
Chocolate-Cashew Bread, 303, **303**

Toffee Cupcakes, 179, **179**
Cheddar Honey-Nut Rolls, **346**, 347
**Cheese.** *See also* Cream cheese
  Apple-Cheddar Scones, 330
  Blue Cheese & Pears Mini Puffs, 268
  Brie en Croûte with Apricots and Almonds, 276
  Brie en Croûte with Cherries and Pecans, 276, **277**
  Cheddar Honey-Nut Rolls, **346**, 347
  Chocolate-Mascarpone Raspberry Pie, 244, **245**
  Cross-Culture Focaccia, **340**, 341
  Florentine-Feta Rolls, 352
  goat cheese, texture of, 256
  Gorgonzola Cheese and Green Onion Scones, 335
  Green Chile Corn Bread, 310
  Ham and Cheese Quiche, **252**, 253
  Herbed Cheese and Bacon Biscuits, 323
  Italian cheese blends, about, 253
  Manchego, about, 270
  Manchego Cheese Appetizer Puffs, 270
  mascarpone, about, 69, 244
  Mushroom-Cheese Appetizers Bundles, 284
  Prosciutto Biscuits, **324**, 325
  Savory Biscuit Sticks, 322
  Spinach and Feta Phyllo Triangles, 285
  Spinach-Blue Cheese Cheesecake, 195
  Triple Onion Appetizer Tart, 255
  Two-Cheese Vegetable Quiche, 254
  Winter Vegetable Tarts with Bacon and Goat Cheese, 256
  Zucchini Scones, 330
**Cheesecake**
  baking basics, 188–189
  Café au Lait Cheesecake, 194
  Cheesecake Supreme, 187
  Cherry Cheesecake Bars, 185
  Chocolate Marble Cheesecake, 187
  Key Lime Cheesecake Bars, 186, **186**
  Orange-Ginger Baby Cheesecakes, 196
  removing from pan, 189
  slicing, tip for, 193
  Sour Cream-Pumpkin Cheesecake, 192, **193**
  Spinach-Blue Cheese Cheesecake, 195
  stir-in ideas, 190–191
  storing, 68, 193
**Cherries, dried**
  Almond-Cherry Muffins, 295
  Brie en Croûte with Cherries and Pecans, 276, **277**
  Cherry Scones, 330

Chocolate-Cherry Brownies, 126
Chocolate-Cherry Pockets, 102, **103**
Coconut-Cherry Cookies, 80, **80**
Northwest Pecan Treats, 115
**Cherries, fresh**
  Cherry Cheesecake Bars, 185
  Cherry Cobbler, 208
  Cherry Crisp, 206
  Cherry-Walnut Balls, 92
  Lattice Cherry Pie, 236, **237**
  maraschino, about, 185
  Molten Chocolate Cakes with Cherry Compote, **158**, 159
Chicken Salad Mini Puffs, 269, **269**
**Chile peppers**
  Green Chile Corn Bread, 310
  handling, note about, 52
  selecting and storing, 52
**Chocolate.** *See also* White baking pieces
  Banana-Chocolate Bread, 304
  Banana-Chocolate Chip Bars, 109
  Banana Split Cake, 170
  Big Chocolate Chip Cookies, 75
  bittersweet, about, 32
  Café au Lait Cheesecake, 194
  Candy Bar Brownies, 129
  Candy Bar Cookies, 80
  candy coating, about, 32
  Cappuccino Brownies, 130
  Caramel-Pecan French Silk Pie, 246, **246**
  Cashew-Chocolate Biscotti, 89
  Chocolate Bread Pudding, 216
  Chocolate Butter Frosting, 145
  Chocolate Cake, 139, **139**
  Chocolate Candy-Graham Cake, 163
  Chocolate-Cashew Bread, 303, **303**
  Chocolate-Cherry Pockets, 102, **103**
  Chocolate Chip Cheesecake, 190, **190**
  Chocolate Chip Cookie Bars, 75
  Chocolate Chip Cookie Pizzas, 75
  Chocolate Chip Cookies, 75
  Chocolate Chip Cupcakes, 178, **178**
  Chocolate Chip-Oatmeal Cake, 164
  Chocolate-Coconut Scones, 330
  Chocolate-Cream Cheese Frosting, 124
  Chocolate Cream Puffs, 265
  Chocolate Crumb Crust, 250
  chocolate curls, creating, 33, 141
  Chocolate Flan, 224, **224**
  Chocolate Frosting, 130
  Chocolate Ganache, 82
  Chocolate Glaze, 131
  Chocolate Marble Cheesecake, 187
  Chocolate-Mascarpone Raspberry Pie, 244, **245**
  Chocolate-Orange Shortbread, 100, **100**

Chocolate-Peanut Cookies, 81
Chocolate-Peanut Topper, 128
Chocolate Pecan Pie, 238
Chocolate-Peppermint Fantasy Cake, 140, **141**
Chocolate-Raisin Cookies, 81
Chocolate-Raspberry Shortcakes, 200
Chocolate Sour Cream Frosting, 144
Chocolate-Strawberry Mini Puffs, 269, **269**
Chocolate Topper, 128
Chocolaty Caramel Thumbprints, 96, **96**
chopping, 33
Cinnamon and Chocolate Rolls, **360**, 361
Cookie Cheesecake, 190, **190**
Cream Cheese Brownies, 131
Dark Chocolate Cream Pie, 232
Double Chocolate Scones, 334, **334**
Dried Pear and Chocolate-Caramel Tart, 262
Easy Chocolate-Almond Croissants, 288
Fresh Cranberry-Chocolate Scones, 333, **333**
Fudgy Brownies, 124
fudgy brownies, stir-in ideas, 126–127

**Chocolate** *(continued)*
German Chocolate Cake, 142
grating, 33
melting, 32–33
milk chocolate, about, 32
Milk Chocolate Chunk Peanut Butter Cookies, 93
Mocha Muffins, 295
Molten Chocolate Cakes with Cherry Compote, **158**, 159
No-Cook Fudge Frosting, 144
Oatmeal-Caramel Bars, 120
Oatmeal Chippers, 81, **81**
Peanut Butter Blondie Bars, 110
Peanut Butter Blossoms, 93
Peppermint-Fudge Brownie Bites, 123
Peppermint-Fudge Pie, 250, **251**
semisweet, about, 32
storing, 32
substitutions, 71
Toffee Fingers, 111
Two-Tone Peanut Butter Slices, 86
Ultimate Bar Cookies, 112, **112**
Ultimate Chocolate-Dipped Cookies, 82
unsweetened, about, 32
Walnut-Cappuccino Torte, 160
White Chocolate Snowdrift Cake, 143
Chunky Path Brownies, 128
**Cinnamon**
  about, 36

Boldfaced page references indicate photographs of finished recipes.

Cinnamon and Chocolate
Rolls, **360**, 361
Cinnamon-Apple Cookies, 80, **80**
Cinnamon-Nut Bread, 306
Cinnamon-Orange Cupcakes, 179
Cinnamon Rolls, 359–361
Easy Cinnamon Rolls, **360**, 361
Easy Cinnamon Spirals, 358, **358**
Snickerdoodles, 91
**Citrus.** *See also* Lemons; Limes; Oranges
Citrus Butter Frosting, 145
Citrus Yellow Cake, 135
juicing, 15, 45
selecting, 44
storing, 44
zesting, 45
zest of, about, 69
Citrus juicer, 15
Cloves, about, 36
**Cobblers**
Apple or Pear Cobbler, 209, **209**
Blueberry or Peach
Cobbler, 209, **209**
Cherry Cobbler, 208
Rhubarb Cobbler, 209, **209**
**Coconut**
Banana-Coconut Bread, 304
Banana-Coconut Muffins, 295
Bread Pudding with
Whiskey Sauce, **214**, 215
Chocolate-Coconut Scones, 330
Coconut Cherry Cookies, 80, **80**
Coconut Cream Pie, 232
Coconut Cupcakes, 178
Coconut-Date Bars, 122, **122**
Coconut Frosting, 122
Coconut-Macadamia
Nut Pastry, 258
coconut milk, about, 40
Coconut-Pecan Coffee Cake, 312
Coconut-Pecan Frosting, 142
Coconut White Cake, 138, **138**
cream of coconut, about, 40
Holiday Layer Bars, 114
Lemon Curd Bars, **118**, 119
Lime-Infused Coconut Cake, 154
storing, 40
toasting, 40
**Coffee.** *See also* Espresso
Café au Lait Cheesecake, 194
Cappuccino Brownies, 130
Coffee Butter Frosting, 145
Espresso Cheesecake, 191, **191**
Mocha Cream, 160
Sugar-and-Spice
Coffee Slices, 87, **87**
Walnut-Cappuccino Torte, 160
**Coffee cakes**
Blueberry Streusel
Coffee Cake, 314, **315**

Coconut-Pecan Coffee Cake, 312
Cranberry-Orange Tea Ring, 362
Cream Cheese-Berry
Coffee Cake, 313
Walnut-Pear Sour Cream
Coffee Cake, 316
Colanders, 15
Convection ovens, 70
Cookie Cheesecake, 190, **190**
Cookie cutters, 21
**Cookies.** *See also* Bars
Almond Biscotti, 89
baking basics, 76–77
Big Chocolate Chip Cookies, 75
Big Oatmeal Cookies, 79
Brown Sugar Icebox Cookies, 84, **85**
Buttery Mint Slices, 88
Cashew-Chocolate Biscotti, 89
Cherry-Walnut Balls, 92
Chocolate-Cherry Pockets, 102, **103**
Chocolate Chip Cookie Pizzas, 75
Chocolate Chip Cookies, 75
Chocolate-Orange
Shortbread, 100, **100**
Chocolaty Caramel
Thumbprints, 96, **96**
Cranberry-Fig Tassies, 98
dough, freezing, 67
drizzling icing over, 85
dropping dough from rounded teaspoon,
65
Eggnog Nut Thumbprints, 94, **95**
Everything Good Cookies, 78
freezing, 67, 87
Frosted Walnut Cookies, 83, **83**
Gingerbread Cutouts, 106
Gingerbread People
Cutouts, 106, **106**
Hazelnut Biscotti, 89
Lemon-Poppy Seed
Shortbread, 100, **100**
Lime Zingers, 104, **105**
Macadamia Nut and White Chocolate Chip
Cookies, 75
Milk Chocolate Chunk Peanut Butter
Cookies, 93
Oatmeal Cookies, 79, **79**
oatmeal cookie stir-in ideas, 80–81
packaging, for shipping, 68, 91
Peanut Butter Blossoms, 93
Pecan Shortbread Logs, 97
piping filling into, 95
Pistachio Biscotti, 89
Praline Snickerdoodles, **90**, 91
Shortbread, 101
shortbread, about, 100
Shortbread Rounds, 101
Shortbread Strips, 101
Snickerdoodles, 91
Spiced Shortbread, 100, **100**

storing, 68, 87
Sugar-and-Spice
Coffee Slices, 87, **87**
Sugar Cookie Cutouts, 99
Two-Tone Peanut Butter Slices, 86
Ultimate Chocolate-Dipped
Cookies, 82
Cookie sheets, 17, 18
Cooking terms, defined, 69
Cookware, 21
Cooling rack, 17
Corn, Double, Bread, 310
**Corn bread**
best cornmeal for, 310
Corn Bread, 311
Double Corn Bread, 310
Green Chile Corn Bread, 310
Green Onion-Bacon
Corn Bread, 310, **310**
Sweet Pepper Corn Bread, 310
**Cornmeal.** *See also* Corn bread
Corn Muffins, 311
Polenta and Plum Cake, 157
Country-Style Semolina Bread, 344
Crab Salad Mini Puffs, 268, **268**
**Cranberries, dried**
Caramel Apples and Cranberry Pecan
Shortcakes, 197, **197**
Cranberry-Hazelnut Cookies, 81, **81**
Cranberry-Orange Tea Ring, 362
Cranberry-Pecan Caramel Pie Topper, 240
Cranberry-Pistachio Cupcakes, 178
Cranberry-Pistachio Scones, 330
Cranberry Pound Cake, 174
Holiday Layer Bars, 114
**Cranberries, fresh**
Apple-Cranberry Dessert, 205, **205**
chopping, 43, 332
Cranberry-Fig Tassies, 98
Cranberry-Gingersnap
Cheesecake, 191
Cranberry Muffins, 295
Cranberry Pear Bars, 116
Fresh Cranberry-Chocolate
Scones, 333, **333**
Fresh Cranberry-
Orange Scones, 333, **333**
Fresh Cranberry-Pecan Scones, 333, **333**
Fresh Cranberry Scones, 332
selecting and storing, 43
Triple-Berry Pudding Cake, 210
**Cream.** *See also* Whipped cream
light, about, 24, 71
**Cream cheese**
Café au Lait Cheesecake, 194
Cheesecake Supreme, 187
Cherry Cheesecake Bars, 185
Chocolate-Cream
Cheese Frosting, 124
Chocolate Marble Cheesecake, 187

**Boldfaced** page references indicate photographs of finished recipes.

Coconut Frosting, 122
Cream Cheese-Berry
    Coffee Cake, 313
Cream Cheese Brownies, 131
Cream Cheese Filling, 148
Cream Cheese Frosting, 121, 144
Cream Cheese Icing, 361
Creamy Frosting, 176
Key Lime Cheesecake Bars, 186, **186**
Lime Zingers, 104, **105**
Orange-Ginger Baby
    Cheesecakes, 196
softening, 57
Sour Cream-Pumpkin
    Cheesecake, 192, **193**
Spinach-Blue Cheese
    Cheesecake, 195
White Chocolate Snowdrift Cake, 143
**Cream Puffs**, 265, **267**
Chocolate Cream Puffs, 265
Manchego Cheese
    Appetizer Puffs, 270
mini, fillings for, 268-269
Mini Puffs, 265
preparing, 266
Creamy Frosting, 176
Creamy Pumpkin Strudels, **282**, 283
Creamy White Frosting, 144
**Crème Brûlée**, 218
Amaretto Crème Brûlée, 218
Maple Crème Brûlée, 218
Raspberry Crème Brûlée, **220**, 221
Crème fraîche, about, 69, 271
Crimp, defined, 69
**Crisps**
Blueberry Crisp, 206
checking for doneness, 207
Cherry Crisp, 206
Fruit Crisp, 206, **207**
Rhubarb Crisp, 206
toppings for, 207
Croissants, Easy
    Chocolate-Almond, 288
Cross-Culture Focaccia, **340**, 341
Crumb Tart Topping, 262
Cumin, about, 322
**Cupcakes**
Little Pumpkin Cakes, 180, **180**
Peanut Butter Cupcakes, 182
simple white, stir-in ideas, 178-179
Simple White Cupcakes with
    Creamy Frosting, 176, **177**
**Currants**
Scones, 328, **329**
Custard cups, 13
**Custards**
Amaretto Crème Brûlée, 218
baking, in water bath, 219
Banana Caramel Custard, 222, **223**
Chocolate Flan, 224, **224**

Crème Brûlée, 218
Maple Crème Brûlée, 218
Raspberry Crème Brûlée, **220**, 221
Cut in, defined, 69

**D**
Dairy products, 24-25
Dark Chocolate Cream Pie, 232
Dash, defined, 69
**Dates**
Coconut-Date Bars, 122, **122**
Orange-Date Cookies, 80
Pecan-Date Muffins, 295
Pecan-Date Scones, 330
Sour Cream-Walnut Date Cake with
    Tangerine Glaze, 151
Dessert Oven Pancake, 211, **211**
**Desserts**
Amaretto Crème Brûlée, 218
Apple-Cranberry Dessert, 205, **205**
Apple or Pear Cobbler, 209, **209**
Banana Caramel Custard, 222, **223**
Blueberry Crisp, 206
Blueberry or Peach
    Cobbler, 209, **209**
Bread Pudding with
    Whiskey Sauce, **214**, 215
Cherry Cobbler, 208
Cherry Crisp, 206
Chocolate Bread Pudding, 216
Chocolate Flan, 224, **224**
cobblers, about, 209
Crème Brûlée, 218
crisps, about, 209
crisps, checking for doneness, 207
crisps, toppings for, 207
dessert croutons, preparing, 67
Dessert Oven Pancake, 211, **211**
dessert plates, decorating, 67
faux trifle, preparing, 67
Fruit Crisp, 206, **207**
Heavenly White-in-White
    Meringues, 212, **213**
Maple Crème Brûlée, 218
Raspberry Crème Brûlée, **220**, 221
Rhubarb Cobbler, 209, **209**
Rhubarb Crisp, 206
Strawberry Soufflé, 217, **217**
Triple-Berry Pudding Cake, 210
Double Chocolate Scones, 334, **334**
Double Corn Bread, 310
Dough scraper, 15
Dried Pear and Chocolate-Caramel Tart, 262
Drop Biscuits Supreme, 319

**E**
Easy Chocolate-Almond
    Croissants, 288
Easy Cinnamon Rolls, 361
Easy Cinnamon Spirals, 358, **358**

Eggnog Nut Thumbprints, 94, **95**
**Eggs**
egg substitutes, about, 27
egg whites, beating, 26
egg yolks, beating, 27
raw, note about, 26
room-temperature, 26
Scrambled Egg Mini Puffs, 269, **269**
selecting and storing, 26
separating yolks from whites, 15, 26
substitutions, 71
Egg separators, 15
**Equipment**, 10-21
bakeware, 16-18
baking dishes, 19
cookware, 21
kitchen tools, 10-15
knives, 14
measuring cups and spoons, 12
mixers and blenders, 20
**Espresso**
Café au Lait Cheesecake, 194
Espresso Brownies, 127
Espresso Cheesecake, 191, **191**
Espresso Cupcakes, 178, **178**
Mocha Muffins, 295
Sugar-and-Spice
    Coffee Slices, 87, **87**
Everything Good Cookies, 78
Extra-Chocolate Brownies, 126
Extracts and oils, about, 69

**F**
Fats and oils, about, 28
Fennel seeds, about, 36, 325
Fig-Cranberry Tassies, 98
Fire extinguishers, 72
Flan, Chocolate, 224, **224**
Flavoring, about, 69
**Flaxseeds**
Flax Soda Bread, 336
health benefits, 307
Quick Seed Bread, 307
Seeded Pull-Aparts, **346**, 347
Florentine-Feta Rolls, 352
**Flour**
adding to cookie dough, 77
all-purpose, about, 31
bread, about, 31
cake, about, 31
cutting butter into, 56
measuring, 54
self-rising, about, 31
semolina, about, 31, 345
sifting, 31
specialty grain, types of, 31
storing, 30
whole wheat, about, 31
Flute, defined, 69
Fluted tube pan, 17

Focaccia, Cross-Culture, **340**, 341
Focaccia, Onion-Sage, 348
Food chopper, 21
Food processor, 20
Fool-Your-Family Peach Pie, 234
Fresh Berry Napoleons, 280, **281**
Fresh Cranberry–Chocolate
    Scones, 333, **333**
Fresh Cranberry-
    Orange Scones, 333, **333**
Fresh Cranberry-
    Pecan Scones, 333, **333**
Fresh Cranberry Scones, 332
Frosted Walnut Cookies, 83, **83**
**Frostings.** *See also* Icings and glazes
    Almond Butter Frosting, 145
    Butter Frosting, 83, 145
    Chocolate Butter Frosting, 145
    Chocolate-Cream
        Cheese Frosting, 124
    Chocolate Frosting, 130
    Chocolate Sour Cream Frosting, 144
    Citrus Butter Frosting, 145
    Coconut Frosting, 122
    Coconut-Pecan Frosting, 142
    Coffee Butter Frosting, 145
    Cream Cheese Frosting, 121, 144
    Creamy Frosting, 176
    Creamy White Frosting, 144
    Lemon Frosting, 106
    No-Cook Fudge Frosting, 144
    Peanut Butter Frosting, 110, 129
    Penuche Frosting, 145
    Peppermint Butter Frosting, 145
    Sour Cream Frosting, 146
Frozen Whole Wheat Bread Dough Fix-Ups,
    347
**Fruit.** *See also* Berries; Citrus; specific fruits
    Brown Butter Tart, 260
    dried, cutting up, 41
    dried, rehydrating, 41
    dried, storing, 41
    Fruit Crisp, 206, **207**
    Fruit Sorbet Mini Puffs, 268, **268**
    Mixed Fruit Shortcakes, 198, **198**
Fudgy Brownies, 124

**G**
Galette, Potato Pancetta, 355, **355**
Ganache, Chocolate, 82
Garlic, fresh, about, 48
Garlic powder, about, 36
Garlic press, 21
German Chocolate Cake, 142
**Ginger**
    about, 36
    Carrot-Ginger Muffins, 295
    crystallized, about, 36
    Gingerbread Cutouts, 106
    Gingerbread People
        Cutouts, 106, **106**

Gingerbread-Sour Cream
    Muffins, 297
Ginger-Pear Scones, 330
Lemon-Ginger Cheesecake, 191
Orange-Ginger
    Baby Cheesecakes, 196
peeling, 48
selecting and storing, 48
substitutions, 71
Glazes. See Icings and glazes
Gooey Butter Cake, 175
Gorgonzola Cheese and Green Onion
    Scones, 335
**Graham crackers/crumbs**
    Candy Bar Brownies, 129
    Cheesecake Supreme, 187
    Chocolate Candy-Graham Cake, 163
    Chocolate Marble Cheesecake, 187
    Peanut Butter Blondie Bars, 110
    Peanut Butter Cupcakes, 182
    Sour Cream-Pumpkin
        Cheesecake, 192, **193**
Grater, box, 21
Grater, rasp, 10, 95
Gratin dishes, 19
Green Chile Corn Bread, 310
Green Onion-Bacon
    Corn Bread, 310, **310**

**H**
Half-and-half, about, 24, 71
**Ham**
    Ham and Cheese Quiche, **252**, 253
    prosciutto, about, 324
    Prosciutto Biscuits, **324**, 325
    Spinach-Prosciutto Palmiers, 278
Hand mixer, 20
Hawaiian Cupcakes, 178
**Hazelnuts**
    about, 35
    Brown Sugar Icebox Cookies, 84, **85**
    Caramelized Hazelnut Brittle, 181
    Cranberry-Hazelnut Cookies, 81, **81**
    Hazelnut Biscotti, 89
    Orange-Hazelnut Cheesecake, 191, **191**
    Orange-Nut Brownies, 126
    toasting, 34
Heavenly White-in-White
    Meringues, 212, **213**
Herbed Cheese and
    Bacon Biscuits, 323
Herbs, about, 49
Holiday Layer Bars, 114
Honey, measuring, 55
Honey-Mango Cheesecake, 190

**I**
**Ice cream**
    Ice Cream Mini Puffs, 268, **268**
    Peanutty Ice Cream Shortcakes, 202
    Peppermint-Fudge Pie, 250, **251**

Strawberry Cake Roll, 149, **149**
**Icings and glazes**
    Chocolate Ganache, 82
    Chocolate Glaze, 131
    Chocolate-Peanut Topper, 128
    Chocolate Topper, 128
    Cream Cheese Icing, 361
    drizzling over cookies, 85
    glaze, defined, 69
    Lemon Glaze, 326
    Maple Icing, 300
    Orange Icing, 362
    Powdered Sugar Icing, 99, 314
    Tangerine Glaze, 151
    Vanilla Icing, 361
**Ingredients, 23–52**
    apples, 38–39
    bananas, 40
    berries, 42
    carrots, 48
    chocolate, 32–33
    citrus fruits, 44–45
    coconut, 40
    cranberries, 43
    dairy products, 24–25
    dried fruit, 41
    eggs, 26–27
    emergency substitutions, 71
    fats and oils, 28
    flour, 30–31
    folding in, 65
    garlic, 48
    ginger, 48
    herbs, 49
    leeks, 50
    measuring, 54–55
    nuts, 34–35
    onions, 51
    peaches and nectarines, 43
    pears, 46–47
    peppers, 52
    rhubarb, 49
    spices, 36–37
    squash and zucchini, 50
    sugar, 29
    wet and dry, combining, 56

**J–K**
Jelly-roll pans, 17, 18
Key Lime Cheesecake Bars, 186, **186**
Key limes, about, 258
Key Lime Tart, 258
Kitchen safety, 72
Kitchen scale, 13
Kitchen scissors, 10
Knives, 14

**L**
Lattice Cherry Pie, 236, **237**

Leavening agents, 30, 63, 69, 71,
Leeks, working with, 50
**Lemons**
  Citrus Yellow Cake, 135
  juicing, 45
  Lemon-Berry Ribbon Torte, 146, **147**
  Lemon-Blueberry Biscuits, 326, **327**
  Lemon Cupcakes, 179, **179**
  lemon curd, about, 119
  Lemon Curd Bars, **118**, 119
  Lemon Frosting, 106
  Lemon-Ginger Cheesecake, 191
  Lemon Glaze, 326
  Lemon Meringue Pie, 248, **249**
  Lemon-Pistachio Bites, 271
  Lemon Curd-Oat Muffins, 299
  Lemon-Poppy Seed Muffins, 295
  Lemon-Poppy Seed Pound Cake, 172
  Lemon-Poppy Seed
    Shortbread, 100, **100**
  selecting, 44
  zesting, 45
**Limes**
  grating peel of, 105
  juicing, 45
  key, about, 258
  Key Lime Cheesecake Bars, 186, **186**
  Key Lime Tart, 258
  Lime-Infused Coconut Cake, 154
  Lime Zingers, 104, **105**
  selecting, 44
  zesting, 45
Liquids, measuring, 55
Little Pumpkin Cakes, 180, **180**
Loaf pans, 17, 18

**M**

**Macadamias**
  about, 35
  Banana-Coconut Bread, 304
  Coconut-Macadamia
    Nut Pastry, 258
  Cream Cheese Brownies, 131
  Hawaiian Cupcakes, 178
  Macadamia Nut and White Chocolate Chip
    Cookies, 75
  Ultimate Bar Cookies, 112, **112**
Macaroon Brownies, 127
Malibu Rum Baby Cakes, 152, **153**
Malted Milk Brownies, 127
Manchego Cheese Appetizer
    Puffs, 270
Mango-Honey Cheesecake, 190
**Maple syrup**
  Maple Bran Muffins, 300, **301**
  Maple Crème Brûlée, 218
  Maple-Dried Fruit Cheesecake, 190
  Maple Icing, 300
  Maple-Oat Scones, 330
  pure maple syrup, about, 300

  Spiced Maple Pull-Aparts, 356, **357**
Margarine, about, 28
**Marshmallows**
  Chunky Path Brownies, 128
  Peppermint-Fudge Brownie Bites, 123
  S'more Brownies, 127
Measuring cups and spoons, 12
Meringue, baking, tip for, 249
Meringue for Pie, 248
Meringues, Heavenly
    White-in-White, 212, **213**
Metal turner/spatula, 10
**Milk**
  evaporated, 24
  sour, preparing, 24
  sweetened condensed, 24
  whole and reduced-fat, 24
Milk Chocolate Chunk Peanut Butter
    Cookies, 93
Mini puff fillings, 268–269
Mini Puffs, 265
**Mint**
  Buttery Mint Slices, 88
  Chocolate-Peppermint
    Fantasy Cake, 140, **141**
  Mint Brownies, 126
  Peppermint Butter Frosting, 145
  peppermint candy, crushing, 123
  Peppermint Cookies, 81, **81**
  Peppermint Cupcakes, 179, **179**
  Peppermint-Fudge Brownie Bites, 123
  Peppermint-Fudge Pie, 250, **251**
  Peppermint Whipped Cream, 251, **251**
Mixed Berry Cream Pie, 239
Mixed Berry Shortcake
    Croutons, 198, **198**
Mixed Fruit Shortcakes, 198, **198**
Mixers and blenders, 20
Mixing bowls, 12
Mocha Cream, 160
Mocha Muffins, 295
Molten Chocolate Cakes with
    Cherry Compote, **158**, 159
**Muffins, 291**
  Banana Crunch Muffins, 298, **298**
  Carrot-Pineapple Muffins, 296
  cooling, 293
  Corn Muffins, 311
  Gingerbread-Sour
    Cream Muffins, 297
  jumbo, preparing, 297
  Lemon Curd-Oat Muffins, 299
  mini, preparing, 297
  preparing, 292–293
  Pumpkin-Praline Muffins, 302
  removing from tins, 293
  stir-in ideas, 295
Muffin tins, 17, 18, 293
Mushroom-Cheese Appetizers Bundles, 284

**N**

Napoleons, Fresh Berry, 280, **281**
Nectarines, about, 43
No-Cook Fudge Frosting, 144
Northwest Pecan Treats, 115
Nutmeg, about, 37, 95
**Nuts.** *See also* Almonds; Cashews;
    Hazelnuts; Macadamias; Peanuts;
    Pecans; Pistachios; Walnuts
  Blueberry Streusel
    Coffee Cake, 314, **315**
  Brazil nuts, about, 104
  chopping, 34
  Eggnog Nut Thumbprints, 94, **95**
  Everything Good Cookies, 78
  grinding, 34
  Lime Zingers, 104, **105**
  Orange-Nut Brownies, 126
  Pine Nut and Herb Twirled Breadsticks,
    354
  pine nuts, about, 35
  selecting and storing, 34
  toasting, 34
  Triple-Nut Zucchini Cake, 167

**O**

Oatmeal Batter Bread, 339, **339**
Oatmeal-Caramel Bars, 120
Oatmeal Chippers, 81, **81**
Oatmeal Cookies, 79, **79**
Oatmeal Muffins, 295
**Oats**
  Banana Chocolate Chip Bars, 109
  Big Oatmeal Cookies, 79
  Chocolate Chip-Oatmeal Cake, 164
  Cranberry Pear Bars, 116
  Everything Good Cookies, 78
  Lemon Curd-Oat Muffins, 299
  Maple-Oat Scones, 330
  Oatmeal Batter Bread, 339, **339**
  Oatmeal-Caramel Bars, 120
  Oatmeal Cookies, 79, **79**
  oatmeal cookie stir-in ideas, 80–81
  Oatmeal Muffins, 295
  quick-cooking, 351
  Rhubarb Bars, 117
  rolled or old-fashioned, 351
  steel-cut, 351
  Three-Grain Cloverleaf
    Rolls, **350**, 351
Offset spatula/spreader, 10, 246
Oils, for cooking, 28
**Onions**
  Bacon-Onion Scones, 330
  chopping, 51
  Gorgonzola Cheese and
    Green Onion Scones, 335
  Green Onion-Bacon
    Corn Bread, 310, **310**
  Onion-Sage Focaccia, 348

selecting and storing, 51
slicing and chopping, 51
Triple Onion Appetizer Tart, 255

**Oranges**
Chocolate-Orange
  Shortbread, 100, **100**
Cinnamon-Orange Cupcakes, 179
Citrus Yellow Cake, 135
Fresh Cranberry-Orange
  Scones, 333, **333**
juicing, 45
Orange-Date Cookies, 80
Orange-Ginger
  Baby Cheesecakes, 196
Orange-Hazelnut
  Cheesecake, 191, **191**
Orange Icing, 362
Orange-Nut Brownies, 126
Orange-Rosemary
  Pound Cake, 172, **173**
Tangerine Glaze, 151
zesting, 45

**P**
Palmiers, Spinach-Prosciutto, 278
Pancake, Dessert Oven, 211, **211**
**Pancetta**
about, 355
Potato Pancetta Galette, 355, **355**
**Parchment paper**
about, 21, 69
cutting into circles, 67
**Pastries.** *See also* Cream Puffs; Phyllo; Puff
  pastry
Apple Dumpling Roll-Ups, 286, **287**
decorative shapes, preparing, 276
Easy Chocolate-Almond
  Croissants, 288
splitting, for filling, 274
**Pastry, pie**
Baked Pastry Shell, 227
broken, patching, 67
decorative edges for, 229, 242–243
Pastry for Double-Crust Pie, 230
Pastry for Lattice-Top Pie, 230
Pastry for Single-Crust Pie, 227
prebaking, 229
preparing, 228–229
Quick Lattice-Top Pie, 230
**Pastry, tart**
Almond Pastry, 261
Baked Pastry Tart Shell, 227
Coconut-Macadamia Nut
  Pastry, 258
prebaking, 229
preparing, 228–229
Rich Tart Pastry, 260
Pastry bag, 21, 66
Pastry blender, 10
Pastry brush, 10

Pastry cloth, 21
Pastry wheel, 10
PB and Apple Rolls, **346**, 347
**Peaches**
Blueberry or Peach
  Cobbler, 209, **209**
Fool-Your-Family Peach Pie, 234
Peach-Almond Tart, 261
Peach Pie, 233
removing skin from, 43
selecting, 43
Upside-Down Peach Caramel
  Crunch Cake, 155
**Peanut butter**
Banana-Chocolate Chip Bars, 109
Candy Cupcakes, 179
Chocolate-Peanut Topper, 128
measuring, 55
Milk Chocolate Chunk Peanut Butter
  Cookies, 93
PB and Apple Rolls, **346**, 347
Peanut Butter Blondie Bars, 110
Peanut Butter Blossoms, 93
Peanut Butter Brownies, 126
Peanut Butter Cupcakes, 182
Peanut Butter Frosting, 110, 129
Peanut Butter Muffins, 295
Peanutty Ice Cream Shortcakes, 202
Two-Tone Peanut Butter Slices, 86
**Peanut butter chips**
Oatmeal Chippers, 81, **81**
Peanut Butter Blondie Bars, 110
**Peanuts**
about, 35
Banana Chocolate Chip Bars, 109
Candy Bar Brownies, 129
Caramel-Peanut Cheesecake, 190
Chocolate-Peanut Cookies, 81
Chocolate-Peanut Topper, 128
Peanut Butter Blondie Bars, 110
Peanutty Ice Cream Shortcakes, 202
**Pears**
Almond-Pear Muffins, 295
Apple or Pear Cobbler, 209, **209**
Blue Cheese & Pears Mini Puffs, 268
Dried Pear and Chocolate-Caramel Tart,
  262
Ginger-Pear Scones, 330
peeling, 46
removing core from, 46
selecting and storing, 47
slicing, 46
testing for ripeness, 47
types of, 47
Walnut-Pear Sour Cream
  Coffee Cake, 316
**Pecans**
about, 35
Banana Crunch Muffins, 298, **298**
Bread Pudding with

Whiskey Sauce, **214**, 215
Brie en Croûte with Cherries and Pecans,
  276, **277**
Caramel Apples and Cranberry Pecan
  Shortcakes, 197, **197**
Caramel-Pecan French Silk
  Pie, 246, **246**
Caramel-Pecan Rolls, **360**, 361
Cheddar Honey-Nut Rolls, **346**, 347
Chocolate Pecan Pie, 238
Chocolaty Caramel
  Thumbprints, 96, **96**
Cinnamon-Nut Bread, 306
Coconut-Pecan Coffee Cake, 312
Coconut-Pecan Frosting, 142
Cranberry-Pecan Caramel Pie Topper, 240
Creamy Pumpkin Strudels, **282**, 283
Fresh Cranberry-Pecan
  Scones, 333, **333**
Northwest Pecan Treats, 115
Peanutty Ice Cream Shortcakes, 202
Pecan-Date Muffins, 295
Pecan-Date Scones, 330
Pecan Pie, 238
Pecan Shortbread Logs, 97
Pineapple-Carrot Loaves, 168, **169**
Praline Snickerdoodles, **90**, 91
Pumpkin-Praline Muffins, 302
Rhubarb Bars, 117
Strawberry Cake Roll, 149, **149**
Toffee-Pecan Cookies, 81
Triple-Nut Zucchini Cake, 167
Turtle Brownies, 127
Upside-Down Peach Caramel
  Crunch Cake, 155
Penuche Frosting, 145
Pepper, black, about, 36
**Peppermint**
Chocolate-Peppermint
  Fantasy Cake, **140**, 141
Mint Brownies, 126
Peppermint Butter Frosting, 145
peppermint candy, crushing, 123
Peppermint Cookies, 81, **81**
Peppermint Cupcakes, 179, **179**
Peppermint-Fudge Brownie Bites, 123
Peppermint-Fudge Pie, 250, **251**
Peppermint Whipped Cream, 251, **251**
**Peppers.** *See also* Chile peppers
chopping, 52
removing stem and seeds, 52
selecting and storing, 52
**Pesto**
Pesto Roll-Ups, **346**, 347
Seasoned Bread, **340**, 341
**Phyllo**
buying and storing, 281
Creamy Pumpkin Strudels, **282**, 283
Fresh Berry Napoleons, 280, **281**
frozen, thawing, 282

Boldfaced page references indicate photographs of finished recipes.

Mushroom-Cheese Appetizer Bundles, 284
Pistachio-Apricot Cups, 279
Spinach and Feta
  Phyllo Triangles, 285
working with, 280
Pie Crust, Chocolate Crumb, 250
Pie plates, 17, 18
**Pies.** *See also* Pastry, pie
Banana Cream Pie, 232
Berry Pie, 233
Best Pumpkin Pie, 240, **241**
Caramel Apple Pie, 235
Caramel-Pecan French
  Silk Pie, 246, **246**
Chocolate-Mascarpone
  Raspberry Pie, 244, **245**
Chocolate Pecan Pie, 238
Coconut Cream Pie, 232
Cranberry-Pecan Caramel
  Topper for, 240
custard filling for, preparing, 232
Dark Chocolate Cream Pie, 232
decorating top crust of, 66
decorative edges for, 242–243
Chocolate-Mascarpone Raspberry Pie,
  244, **245**
Fool-Your-Family Peach Pie, 234
fruit, lattice crusts for, 237
fruit filling for, preparing, 233
Lattice Cherry Pie, 236, **237**
Lemon Meringue Pie, 248, **249**
Meringue for Pie, 248, **249**
Mixed Berry Cream Pie, 239
Peach Pie, 233
Pecan Pie, 238
Peppermint-Fudge Pie, 250, **251**
Rhubarb Pie, 233
storing, 68, 232
Vanilla Cream Pie, 232
White Chocolate Topping for, 244
**Pineapple**
Carrot-Pineapple Muffins, 296
Malibu Rum Baby Cakes, 152, **153**
Pineapple-Carrot Loaves, 168, **169**
Tropical Mini Puffs, 269
**Pine nuts**
about, 35
Pine Nut and Herb Twirled Breadsticks,
  354
**Pistachios**
about, 35
Cranberry-Pistachio Cupcakes, 178
Cranberry-Pistachio Scones, 330
Holiday Layer Bars, 114
Lemon-Pistachio Bites, 271
Pistachio-Apricot Cups, 279
Pistachio Biscotti, 89
Pizza pan, 17
Pizzas, Chocolate Chip Cookie, 75
**Plums**

Dessert Oven Pancake, 211, **211**
Polenta and Plum Cake, 157
Polenta and Plum Cake, 157
Pomegranate Sauce, 187
Pomegranates, using, 192
**Poppy seeds**
Lemon Curd-Oat Muffins, 299
Lemon-Poppy Seed Muffins, 295
Lemon-Poppy Seed Pound Cake, 172
**Poppy seeds** *(continued)*
Lemon-Poppy Seed
  Shortbread, 100, **100**
Quick Seed Bread, 307
Seeded Pull-Aparts, **346**, 347
Strawberry Lemon-Poppy Seed
  Shortcakes, 199
Potato Pancetta Galette, 355, **355**
**Powdered sugar**
about, 29
dusting with, 66, 267
Powdered Sugar Icing, 99, 314
Praline Snickerdoodles, **90**, 91
Pretzels, Salt and Pepper
  Baked, **340**, 341
**Prosciutto**
about, 324
Prosciutto Biscuits, **324**, 325
Spinach-Prosciutto Palmiers, 278
**Pudding**
Bread Pudding with
  Whiskey Sauce, **214**, 215
Chocolate Bread Pudding, 216
White Chocolate Pudding, 212
Pudding Cake, Triple-Berry, 210
**Puff pastry**
about, 273
Brie en Croûte with Apricots
  and Almonds, 276
Brie en Croûte with Cherries
  and Pecans, 276, **277**
Lemon-Pistachio Bites, 271
Raspberry Danish Rosettes, 272, **273**
Spinach-Prosciutto Palmiers, 278
White Chocolate and Berries
  Dessert Pastries, **274**, 275
**Pumpkin**
Best Pumpkin Pie, 240, **241**
Creamy Pumpkin Strudels, **282**, 283
leftover, storing, 302
Little Pumpkin Cakes, 180, **180**
Pumpkin Bars, 121
Pumpkin Cake Roll, 148
Pumpkin-Praline Muffins, 302
Sour Cream-Pumpkin
  Cheesecake, 192, **193**
Pumpkin pie spice, about, 36, 37, 71
**Pumpkin seeds**
about, 296
Carrot-Pineapple Muffins, 296

## Q-R

**Quiche**
Ham and Cheese Quiche, **252**, 253
slicing, tip for, 252
Two-Cheese Vegetable Quiche, 254
Quick Lattice-Top Pie, 230
Quick Seed Bread, 307
**Raisins**
Applesauce Cake, 165, **165**
Bread Pudding with
  Whiskey Sauce, **214**, 215
Carrot-Ginger Muffins, 295
Chocolate-Raisin Cookies, 81
Everything Good Cookies, 78
Raisin-Walnut Cookies, 80
Ramekins, 19
**Raspberries /raspberry jam**
Berry Pie, 233
Chocolate-Mascarpone
  Raspberry Pie, 244, **245**
Chocolate-Raspberry
  Shortcakes, 200
Cream Cheese-Berry
  Coffee Cake, 313
Lemon-Berry Ribbon Torte, 146, **147**
Raspberry and White Chocolate Brownies,
  132, **132**
Raspberry Brownies, 127
Raspberry Cheesecake, 190, **190**
Raspberry Crème Brûlée, **220**, 221
Raspberry Cupcakes, 178, **178**
Raspberry Danish Rosettes, 272, **273**
raspberry sauce, preparing, 60
storing and washing, 42
Triple-Berry Pudding Cake, 210
Rasp grater, 10, 13, 95
Refrigerator Dinner Rolls, 349
**Rhubarb**
about, 49
Rhubarb and Spice
  Snacking Cake, 166
Rhubarb Bars, 117
Rhubarb Cobbler, 209, **209**
Rhubarb Crisp, 206
Rhubarb Pie, 233
Rich Tart Pastry, 260
Rolling pin cover/pastry cloth, 21
Rolling pins, 10, 61
**Rolls and buns**
Caramel-Pecan Rolls, **360**, 361
Cheddar Honey-Nut Rolls, 346, 347
Cinnamon and Chocolate
  Rolls, **360**, 361
Cinnamon Rolls, 359–361
Easy Cinnamon Rolls, **360**, 361
Easy Cinnamon Spirals, 358, **358**
Florentine-Feta Rolls, 352
PB and Apple Rolls, **346**, 347
Pesto Roll-Ups, **346**, 347
Refrigerator Dinner Rolls, 349

Boldfaced page references indicate photographs of finished recipes.

reheating, 350
Seeded Pull-Aparts, **346**, 347
Spiced Maple Pull-Aparts, 356, **357**
Three-Grain Cloverleaf
Rolls, 350, 351
Wasabi Shrimp-Stuffed Buns, 353
Rubber scraper, 10
Ruler, 10
Rum, Malibu, Baby Cakes, 152, **153**

## S

Salad Mini Puffs, 269, **269**
Salmon, Smoked, Mini Puffs, 269
Salt and Pepper Baked
Pretzels, **340**, 341
Saucepans, 22
**Sauces**
caramel sauce, preparing, 64
Pomegranate Sauce, 187
raspberry sauce, preparing, 60
Whiskey Sauce, 215
Savory Biscuit Sticks, 322
Scald, defined, 69
Scissors, kitchen, 10, 14
**Scones**, 328, **329**
Double Chocolate Scones, 334, **334**
Fresh Cranberry-Chocolate
Scones, 333, **333**
Fresh Cranberry-Orange
Scones, 333, **333**
Fresh Cranberry-Pecan
Scones, 333, **333**
Fresh Cranberry Scones, 332
Gorgonzola Cheese and
Green Onion Scones, 335
leftover, storing, 334
stir-in ideas, 330
Scrambled Egg Mini Puffs, 269, **269**
Seafood. See Salmon; Shrimp
Seasoned Bread, 340, 341
Seeded Pull-Aparts, **346**, 347
Semolina Bread, Country-Style, 344
Semolina flour, about, 31, 345
**Sesame seeds**
Quick Seed Bread, 307
Seeded Pull-Aparts, **346**, 347
**Shortbread**
about, 100
Chocolate-Orange
Shortbread, 100, **100**
Lemon-Poppy Seed
Shortbread, 100, **100**
Pecan Shortbread Logs, 97
Shortbread, 101
Shortbread Rounds, 101
Shortbread Strips, 101
Spiced Shortbread, 100, **100**
**Shortcakes**
Caramel Apples and Cranberry Pecan
Shortcakes, 199, **199**
Chocolate-Raspberry
Shortcakes, 200

cutting dough, tip for, 201
cutting in half, tip for, 201
Mixed Berry Shortcake
Croutons, 198, **198**
Mixed Fruit Shortcakes, 198, **198**
Peanutty Ice Cream Shortcakes, 202
Strawberry Lemon-Poppy Seed
Shortcakes, 199
Strawberry Shortcakes, 199
Whole Shortcake, 198, **198**
Shortening, about, 28
Shortening, measuring, 55
Shrimp-Stuffed Buns, Wasabi, 353
Sieve, how to use, 65
Sift, defined, 69
Silicone bakeware, 18
Simple White Cupcakes with Creamy
Frosting, 176, **177**
Skillets, 22
Smoked Salmon Mini Puffs, 269
S'more Brownies, 127
Snickerdoodles, 91
Snickerdoodles, Praline, **90**, 91
Soufflé, Strawberry, 217, **217**
Soufflé dishes, 19
Sour cream, substitute for, 71
Sour Cream Frosting, 146
Sour Cream-Pumpkin Cheesecake, 192, **193**
Sour Cream-Walnut Date Cake with
Tangerine Glaze, 151
Southwestern Mini Puffs, 268
Spatulas, 10, 13
Spiced Maple Pull-Aparts, 356, **357**
Spiced Shortbread, 100, **100**
Spices, about, 36–37
**Spinach**
Florentine-Feta Rolls, 352
Spinach and Feta Phyllo Triangles, 285
Spinach-Artichoke Mini
Puffs, 268, **268**
Spinach-Blue Cheese
Cheesecake, 195
Spinach-Prosciutto Palmiers, 278
Spoon, slotted, 13
Spoon, wooden, 10
Spreader, 10, 13
Springform pan, 17
**Squash.** *See also* Pumpkin; Zucchini
choosing, 50
to julienne, 50
slicing, 50
storing, 50
Strainer, fine-mesh, 10
**Strawberries**
Banana Split Cake, 170
Chocolate-Strawberry Mini
Puffs, 269, **269**
slicing, 42
stemming, 42
Strawberry-Banana Brownies, 126
Strawberry Cake Roll, 149, **149**
Strawberry-Fudge Cheesecake, 191

Strawberry Lemon-Poppy Seed
Shortcakes, 199
Strawberry Shortcakes, 199
Strawberry Soufflé, 217, **217**
washing, 42
Whole Shortcake, 198, **198**
Streusel-Nut Topping, 308
Streusel Topping, 291
Strudels, Creamy Pumpkin, **282**, 283
**Sugar**
brown, about, 29
brown, measuring, 55
coarse, about, 29
granulated, about, 29
granulated, measuring, 55
powdered, about, 29
powdered, dusting with, 66, 267
Powdered Sugar Icing, 99, 314
storing, 29
sugar substitutes, note about, 29
superfine, about, 29
turbinado, about, 29
Sugar-and-Spice Coffee Slices, 87, **87**
Sugar Cookie Cutouts, 99
Sugar Cookie Squares, 99
Sweet Pepper Corn Bread, 310

## T

Tangerine Glaze, 151
Tangerines, about, 44
Tart pan, 16, 259
**Tarts.** *See also* Pastry, tart
Brown Butter Tart, 260
Crumb Topping for, 262
Dried Pear and Chocolate-Caramel Tart,
262
Ham and Cheese Quiche, **252**, 253
Key Lime Tart, 258
Peach-Almond Tart, 261
Triple Onion Appetizer Tart, 255
Two-Cheese Vegetable Quiche, 254
Winter Vegetable Tarts with Bacon and
Goat Cheese, 256
Tassies, Cranberry-Fig, 98
**Techniques, 53–71.** *See also* Tricks, kitchen
baking at high altitude, 70
baking terms, defined, 69
beating mixtures, 57
combining wet and
dry ingredients, 56
cooking terms, defined, 69
dropping dough from rounded teaspoon,
65
emergency ingredient
substitutions, 71
folding in ingredients, 65
greasing and flouring pan, 59
lightly flouring a surface, 60
lining pan with foil, 58
lining pan with waxed paper, 58
making bread dough, 62–63

**Boldfaced** page references indicate photographs of finished recipes.

making caramel sauce, 64
making raspberry sauce, 60
measuring ingredients, 54–55
packing and mailing cookies, 68
preparing to bake, 78
removing baked goods from pan, 60
softening cream cheese, 57
storing baked goods, 68
using a sieve, 65
using rolling pin, 61
Three-Grain Cloverleaf Rolls, **350**, 351
3-Way Bread Dough, 341
Tinted Angel Cake, 150
**Toffee pieces**
about, 90
Caramel Apple Muffins, 295
Caramel-Toffee Cheesecake, 192
Praline Snickerdoodles, **90**, 91
Toffee-Almond Banana Bread, 304
Toffee Cupcakes, 179, **179**
Toffee Fingers, 111
Toffee-Pecan Cookies, 81
**Tomatoes**
Cross-Culture Focaccia, **340**, 341
Southwestern Mini Puffs, 268
Tongs, 13
**Tricks, kitchen**
cutting waxed paper circles, 67
decorating dessert plate, 67
decorating top piecrusts, 66
dusting with powdered sugar, 66
filling makeshift pastry bag, 66
freezing cookie dough, 67
making dessert croutons, 67
making quick faux trifle, 67
moistening dry cake, 66
patching piecrust, 67
Triple-Berry Pudding Cake, 210
Triple-Nut Zucchini Cake, 167
Triple Onion Appetizer Tart, 255
Tropical Mini Puffs, 269
Tube pan, fluted, 17
Turtle Brownies, 127
Two-Cheese Vegetable Quiche, 254
Two-Tone Peanut Butter Slices, 86

# U–V

Ultimate Bar Cookies, 112, **112**
Ultimate Chocolate-
Dipped Cookies, 82
Upside-Down One-Bowl
Apple Cake, 156
Upside-Down Peach Caramel
Crunch Cake, 155
Vanilla beans, about, 69, 221
Vanilla beans, splitting, 220
Vanilla Cream Pie, 232
Vanilla extract, about, 128
Vanilla Icing, 361
Vegetable, Winter, Tarts with
Bacon and Goat Cheese, 256

Vegetable peeler, 13
Vegetable Quiche, Two-Cheese, 254

# W

**Walnuts**
about, 35
Apple Pie Bread, 308, **309**
Applesauce Cake, 165, **165**
Banana Bread, 304
black, about, 83
Cherry-Walnut Balls, 92
Chocolate Chip-Oatmeal Cake, 164
Eggnog Nut Thumbprints, 94, **95**
English, about, 83
Frosted Walnut Cookies, 83, **83**
Oatmeal-Caramel Bars, 120
Pumpkin Cake Roll, 148
Raisin-Walnut Cookies, 80
Sour Cream-Walnut Date Cake with
Tangerine Glaze, 151
Spinach-Blue Cheese
Cheesecake, 195
Streusel-Nut Topping, 308
Triple-Nut Zucchini Cake, 167
Ultimate Bar Cookies, 112, **112**
Walnut-Cappuccino Torte, 160
Walnut-Pear Sour Cream
Coffee Cake, 316
Wasabi Shrimp-Stuffed Buns, 353
Water bath, baking in, 219
Weeping, defined, 69
**Whipped cream**
cream for, 24
Mocha Cream, 160
Peppermint Whipped Cream, 251, **251**
preparing, 25
Whisk, 10
Whiskey Sauce, 215
**White baking pieces**
about, 32
Extra-Chocolate Brownies, 126
Holiday Layer Bars, 114
Macadamia Nut and White Chocolate Chip
Cookies, 75
Peppermint Cookies, 81, **81**
Raspberry and White Chocolate Brownies,
132, **132**
Ultimate Bar Cookies, 112, **112**
Ultimate Chocolate-
Dipped Cookies, 82
White Chocolate and Berries
Dessert Pastries, **274**, 275
White Chocolate Pie Topping, 244
White Chocolate Pudding, 212
White Chocolate Snowdrift Cake, 143
White Dipped Almonds, 212
White Cake, 138
White Cake, Coconut, 138, **138**
White chocolate. *See* White baking pieces
Whole Shortcake, 198, **198**
Winter Vegetable Tarts with

Bacon and Goat Cheese, 256

# Y–Z

Yeast, about, 63, 71
**Yeast breads**
Caramel-Pecan Rolls, **360**, 361
Cheddar Honey-Nut Rolls, **346**, 347
Cinnamon and Chocolate
Rolls, **360**, 361
Cinnamon Rolls, 359–361
cooling, 350
Country-Style Semolina Bread, 344
Cranberry-Orange Tea Ring, 362
Cross-Culture Focaccia, **340**, 341
Easy Cinnamon Rolls, **360**, 361
Easy Cinnamon Spirals, 358, **358**
Florentine-Feta Rolls, 352
frozen bread dough, thawing, 346
Frozen Whole Wheat Bread Dough Fix-
Ups, 347
making bread dough, 62–63
Oatmeal Batter Bread, 339, **339**
Onion-Sage Focaccia, 348
PB and Apple Rolls, **346**, 347
Pesto Roll-Ups, **346**, 347
Pine Nut and Herb Twirled Breadsticks,
354
Potato Pancetta Galette, 355, **355**
preparing, 342–343
Refrigerator Dinner Rolls, 349
rising, troubleshooting, 340
Salt and Pepper Baked
Pretzels, **340**, 341
Seasoned Bread, **340**, 341
Seeded Pull-Aparts, **346**, 347
Spiced Maple Pull-Aparts, 356, **357**
storing, 68
Three-Grain Cloverleaf
Rolls, **350**, 351
3-Way Bread Dough, 341
Wasabi Shrimp-Stuffed Buns, 353
Yellow Cake, 135, **135**
Yellow Cake, Citrus, 135
Zest, about, 69
**Zucchini**
choosing and storing, 50
to julienne, 50
slicing, 50
Triple-Nut Zucchini Cake, 167
Zucchini Scones, 330

# Metric Information

The charts on this page provide a guide for converting measurements from the U.S. customary system, which is used throughout this book, to the metric system.

### Product Differences

Most of the ingredients called for in the recipes in this book are available in most countries. However, some are known by different names. Here are some common American ingredients and their possible counterparts:

• Sugar (white) is granulated, fine granulated, or caster sugar.
• Powdered sugar is icing sugar.
• All-purpose flour is enriched, bleached or unbleached white household flour. When self-rising flour is used in place of all-purpose flour in a recipe that calls for leavening, omit the leavening agent (baking soda or baking powder) and salt.
• Light-colored corn syrup is golden syrup.
• Cornstarch is cornflour.
• Baking soda is bicarbonate of soda.
• Vanilla or vanilla extract is vanilla essence.
• Green, red, or yellow sweet peppers are capsicums or bell peppers.
• Golden raisins are sultanas.

### Volume and Weight

The United States traditionally uses cup measures for liquid and solid ingredients. The chart below shows the approximate imperial and metric equivalents. If you are accustomed to weighing solid ingredients, the following approximate equivalents will be helpful.

• 1 cup butter, castor sugar, or rice = 8 ounces = ½ pound = 250 grams
• 1 cup flour = 4 ounces = ¼ pound = 125 grams
• 1 cup icing sugar = 5 ounces = 150 grams
• Canadian and U.S. volume for a cup measure is 8 fluid ounces (237 ml), but the standard metric equivalent is 250 ml.
• 1 British imperial cup is 10 fluid ounces.
• In Australia, 1 tablespoon equals 20 ml, and there are 4 teaspoons in the Australian tablespoon.
• Spoon measures are used for smaller amounts of ingredients. Although the size of the tablespoon varies slightly in different countries, for practical purposes and for recipes in this book, a straight substitution is all that's necessary. Measurements made using cups or spoons always should be level unless stated otherwise.

### Common Weight Range Replacements

| Imperial / U.S. | Metric |
|---|---|
| ½ ounce | 15 g |
| 1 ounce | 25 g or 30 g |
| 4 ounces (¼ pound) | 115 g or 125 g |
| 8 ounces (½ pound) | 225 g or 250 g |
| 16 ounces (1 pound) | 450 g or 500 g |
| 1¼ pounds | 625 g |
| 1½ pounds | 750 g |
| 2 pounds or 2¼ pounds | 1,000 g or 1 Kg |

### Oven Temperature Equivalents

| Fahrenheit Setting | Celsius Setting | Gas Setting |
|---|---|---|
| 300°F | 150°C | Gas Mark 2 (very low) |
| 325°F | 160°C | Gas Mark 3 (low) |
| 346°F | 180°C | Gas Mark 4 (moderate) |
| 375°F | 190°C | Gas Mark 5 (moderate) |
| 400°F | 200°C | Gas Mark 6 (hot) |
| 425°F | 220°C | Gas Mark 7 (hot) |
| 450°F | 230°C | Gas Mark 8 (very hot) |
| 475°F | 240°C | Gas Mark 9 (very hot) |
| 500°F | 260°C | Gas Mark 10 (extremely hot) |
| Broil | Broil | Grill |

*Electric and gas ovens may be calibrated using celsius. However, for an electric oven, increase celsius setting 10 to 20 degrees when cooking above 160°C. For convection or forced air ovens (gas or electric), lower the temperature setting 25°F/10°C when cooking at all heat levels.

### Baking Pan Sizes

| Imperial / U.S. | Metric |
|---|---|
| 9×1½-inch round cake pan | 22- or 23×4-cm (1.5 L) |
| 9×1½-inch pie plate | 22- or 23×4-cm (1 L) |
| 8×8×2-inch square cake pan | 20×5-cm (2 L) |
| 9×9×2-inch square cake pan | 22- or 23×4.5-cm (2.5 L) |
| 11×7×1½-inch baking pan | 28×17×4-cm (2 L) |
| 2-quart rectangular baking pan | 30×19×4.5-cm (3 L) |
| 13×9×2-inch baking pan | 34×22×4.5-cm (3.5 L) |
| 15×10×1-inch jelly roll pan | 40×25×2-cm |
| 9×5×3-inch loaf pan | 23×13×8-cm (2 L) |
| 2-quart casserole | 2 L |

### U.S. / Standard Metric Equivalents

| | |
|---|---|
| ⅛ teaspoon = 0.5 ml | |
| ¼ teaspoon = 1 ml | |
| ½ teaspoon = 2 ml | |
| 1 teaspoon = 5 ml | |
| 1 tablespoon = 15 ml | |
| 2 tablespoons = 25 ml | |
| ¼ cup = 2 fluid ounces = 50 ml | |
| ⅓ cup = 3 fluid ounces = 75 ml | |
| ½ cup = 4 fluid ounces = 125 ml | |
| ⅔ cup = 5 fluid ounces = 150 ml | |
| ¾ cup = 6 fluid ounces = 175 ml | |
| 1 cup = 8 fluid ounces = 250 ml | |
| 2 cups = 1 pint = 500 ml | |
| 1 quart = 1 litre | |